TEACHING YOUNG LEARNERS ENGLISH

From Theory to Practice

Joan Kang Shin | JoAnn (Jodi) Crandall

NATIONAL GEOGRAPHIC LEARNING | HEINLE CENGAGE Learning

Australia • Brazil • Japan • Korea • Mexico • Singapore • Spain • United Kingdom • United States

**Teaching Young Learners English:
From Theory to Practice**
Joan Kang Shin and JoAnn (Jodi) Crandall

Publisher: Sherrise Roehr

Acquisitions Editor: Tom Jefferies

Development Editors: Nathan Gamache,
 Hadley Chatel

Director of Product Marketing: Ian Martin

Marketing Manager: Steve King

Director of Content and Media Production:
 Michael Burggren

Content Project Manager: Mark Rzeszutek

Manufacturing Planner: Mary Beth Hennebury

Cover Designer: Michael Rosenquest

Compositor: PreMediaGlobal

ISBN-13: 978-1-111-77137-9

ISBN-10: 1-111-77137-5

National Geographic Learning
20 Channel Center Street
Boston, MA 02210
USA

Cengage Learning is a leading provider of customized learning solutions with office locations around the globe, including Singapore, the United Kingdom, Australia, Mexico, Brazil, and Japan.

Cengage Learning products are represented in Canada by Nelson Education, Ltd.

Visit National Geographic Learning online at **ngl.cengage.com**

Visit our corporate website at **www.cengage.com**

Printed in the United States of America
2 3 4 5 6 7 18 17 16 15 14

Contents

Chapter 6   Storytelling   209

Chapter 7   Assessment   243

Preface

Teaching English to young learners or TEYL is an exciting and evolving field within the larger field of Teaching English to Speakers of Other Languages (TESOL). Countries around the world are lowering the age of English education to the primary school level, and students are studying English at younger and younger ages. This is a new and big challenge for many countries, especially those that have traditionally been teaching English and other foreign languages at the secondary level. As a result, there is a growing need for both pre-service and in-service teacher education programs that specifically address teaching children at the primary and pre-primary school levels. The aims of this book are to help teachers of English to young learners (EYL) understand the foundational concepts for teaching English as a foreign language in international contexts, and to prepare them to develop lessons and activities that are developmentally appropriate and that cater to children's characteristics and cognitive levels. It can be used as a basic text for prospective EYL teachers, or it can be used as a professional development tool for teachers and administrators who need to develop the special knowledge and skills to teach EYL.

Teaching Young Learners English focuses on teaching children at the primary school level (ages 5–12 years). Although most of the activities can be applied to all ages, we will make clear when certain activities are more appropriate for "very young learners" (under 7 years of age) or "young learners" (7–12 years old). We will begin by discussing the characteristics of young learners and how to create effective lessons that connect with their lives outside of class and motivate them to learn English. Other chapters will present effective activities (including storytelling) to help young learners develop oral (listening and speaking) and written (reading and writing) language skills, as well as ways to help prepare young learners to develop the kinds of skills that they will need in the interconnected world of the twenty-first century. You will also learn how to assess your young learners' progress and your own growth as an EYL teacher, with a number of suggestions for additional professional development you may want to participate in for your own success as an EYL teacher.

In addition to providing a theoretical foundation and practical applications for all the concepts outlined above, every chapter has a sample lesson plan as well as a "Teacher to Teacher" section in which you will hear the voices of practicing EYL teachers around the world. This feature will give you the opportunity to see how teachers apply the concepts and ideas from each chapter in their own classrooms, enabling you to learn from the experiences and perspectives of other teachers to improve your teaching.

About the Authors

DR. JOAN KANG SHIN

Dr. Joan Kang Shin is the Director of TESOL Professional Training Programs in the Education Department at the University of Maryland, Baltimore County, and specializes in the training and professional development of teachers of English to young learners. In her role she is responsible for administering professional development and teacher training programs that reach teachers in over 100 countries around the world.

DR. JOANN (JODI) CRANDALL

Dr. JoAnn (Jodi) Crandall is Professor Emerita and former Director of the Language, Literary and Culture Ph.D. Program, and Co-Director of the MA TESOL Program at the University of Maryland, Baltimore County. She has worked in all areas of ESL/EFL including teaching, curriculum and materials development, standards development, and teacher training.

1 Teaching English to Young Learners around the World: An Introduction

■ Getting Started

This chapter will introduce you to teaching English to young learners (TEYL). You will learn about the growth of English as a global language, the advantages of early language learning, the various kinds of program models used around the world, some of the problems associated with TEYL, and various teaching practices that have been found to be effective in teaching English to young learners. You will have the opportunity to reflect on the readings and discuss key questions related to the chapter. To help you apply new knowledge, you will respond to written journal prompts and complete hands-on activities. You will hear the voices of teachers in the field who share their experiences teaching English to young learners.

Blue Jean Images/Alamy

Think about your own experiences studying English. How old were you when you began studying English? What challenges did you face? What would have happened if you had started at an earlier age?

Now think about any experiences you have had observing young learner classes or talking with children who are learning another language. What are their experiences? Do they enjoy their language classes? If so, why?

Over the past decade, the age of compulsory English education has been lowered in many countries. Why do you think this has occurred? Has the age of English education been lowered in your country? If yes, why do you think that has happened? If not, why do you think that is?

Discovery Activity

T-Chart of Benefits and Challenges

In the T-chart below, write down what you think are the benefits and challenges facing English language programs for young learners.

PLUS +	MINUS −
Benefits of early language learning programs	Challenges of early English language programs

■ Theory, Planning and Application

Reasons for an Early Start

Although there are various points of view about the best time to begin English language instruction (see the discussion below), and minor differences in student age and program categories, the fact is that in most countries, children are learning English at younger and younger ages. In many countries, English is a compulsory subject in the early primary grades (Nikolov, 2009; Pinter, 2006). In a recent survey of EYL teachers from 55 countries around the world, Shin and Crandall (2011) found that more than 50 percent of these countries introduced compulsory English language courses by third grade. Even in countries where families may choose the foreign language for their children to study, English is "overwhelmingly the first choice" (Garton, Copland, & Burns, 2011, p. 5). The growing demand for English, plus parents' belief that English skills provide their children with a better education and better employment opportunities, have led to an increase in the number of EYL programs (Enever & Moon, 2009; Gimenez, 2009).

There are two major reasons for an early start in English:

- The value of English for education and employment
- The benefits of early language learning

The Value of English for Education and Employment Today, an estimated one billion or more people speak some English (Crystal, 2012). The number of people who are studying English increases every year, beginning at younger and younger ages.

About 400 million people have learned English as a first or native language and use English on a regular basis (Crystal, 2012). Most live in countries that Kachru (1990) calls "Inner Circle" countries, such as the United States, United Kingdom, Ireland, Canada, Australia, or New Zealand, where English is the dominant language of education, government, and other institutions.

Another 300–500 million people live in "Outer Circle" countries (Crystal, 2012). "in which English has a long history and serves a variety of functions in education, government, literature, and popular culture" (McKay, 2002, p. 133). In the 70+ countries of the Outer Circle, which include India, Pakistan, the Philippines, Kenya, Jamaica, Trinidad and Tobago, and Fiji, the populations have learned English as a second language (ESL) and have developed their own varieties of English.

But the largest number, estimated at 500 million to a billion English speakers (Crystal, 2012), live in what Kachru calls the "Expanding Circle." In these countries, such as China, Korea, Turkey, the United Arab Emirates, Germany, Sweden, Chile, Brazil, or Mexico, English has no official function and opportunities to use English are usually only with those who do not share the same mother tongue. People in these Expanding Circle countries are studying English as a foreign language (EFL) or as an international language (EIL) because of the importance of English as a "lingua franca" or link language (a common language used by people who speak different languages) for business, media and communication, air and sea travel, and science and technology. English is increasingly used as a medium of instruction in higher education, and with international sporting events like the Olympics and the World Cup, English has become a major medium for tourism.

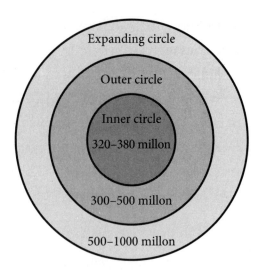

In all, according to Crystal (2012), there are three times as many nonnative speakers as there are native speakers of English. There are at least 350 million speakers of English in Asia alone—almost the combined populations of the United States, Canada, and Great Britain. At least 25 percent of the world's population can communicate to some degree in English (Crystal, 2012, p. 69). It is truly a global language.

As English becomes the world's lingua franca, countries all over the world have adopted English language instruction as part of their education system. Many countries begin at the primary level, and students are studying the language at younger and younger ages (Jenkins, 2009). New English-medium universities are being established in many countries to enable students and faculty to study the latest research and textbooks, which are often written in English. This requires students to develop academic English proficiency during their primary and secondary schooling. The global role of English differentiates the teaching of English as an international language from that of other foreign languages.

The Benefits of Early Language Learning Early studies of second or foreign language learning argued that there was a "critical period" (Lenneberg, 1967; Penfield & Roberts, 1959), or a "critical" or "sensitive period" (Oyama, 1976), prior to puberty in which children could acquire native-like proficiency in a foreign language. That perspective found ready acceptance among adults who thought children could "pick up" a language easily, often remembering their own frustration at not having mastered another language. While there is evidence for the benefits of acquiring another language naturally (for example, when two parents each speak a different language to a child), there is little evidence to support the critical period hypothesis for learning a foreign language (Garton, Copland, & Burns, 2011; Nikolov & Mihaljevic Djigunovic, 2011; Pinter, 2006; Read, 2003). A recent review of research on the critical period (Marinova-Todd, Marshall, & Snow, 2000, p. 10) concluded that adolescent learners are more efficient language learners (they have already acquired their mother tongue) and that they can learn a second language "to a very high level and that introducing foreign languages to very young learners cannot be justified on grounds of biological readiness to learn languages" (see also McLaughlin, 1984/1985).

However, a number of "language policy documents explicitly state the advantages of early language learning" (Nikolov & Mihaljevic Djigunovic, 2011, p. 98). For example, the European Commission identifies "better language skills" and "favorable attitudes to other languages, people and cultures" as benefits of early language learning, if conditions such as trained teachers and small classes are in place (Nikolov & Mihaljevic Djigunovic, 2011, p. 98).

As Rixon (1999) points out, what matters more than the optimal age are the conditions under which young learner programs are offered. These include conditions outside the classroom (for example, the social, cultural, and economic value of the language) and inside the classroom. Read (2003) suggests that younger is better when learning is:

- Natural
- Contextualized and part of a real event
- Interesting and enjoyable
- Relevant
- Social
- Belongs to the child
- Has a purpose for the child
- Builds on things the child knows but also challenges the child
- Supported appropriately
- Part of a coherent whole
- Multisensory
- Active and experiential
- Memorable
- Designed to provide for personal, divergent responses and multiple intelligences
- Offered in a relaxed and warm learning atmosphere

(Adapted from Read, 2003, p. 7)

In addition, it can create a "sense of achievement" (Read, 2003, p. 7).

With these optimal conditions in mind, then, there are a number of reasons for starting language learning early. These include:

1. The value of increased time
2. The possibility of better pronunciation and fluency

3. The possibility of greater global awareness and intercultural competence
4. The value of bilingualism

1. **The value of increased time** One reason for starting English in the primary grades is the amount of time that children will have to learn the language. As noted above, although some researchers believe that adolescents are more efficient language learners, younger learners simply have more time to learn the language, and time is an important factor in overall attainment (Carroll, 1975), as any adult who has tried to learn another language has discovered. As Curtain and Dahlberg (2010) state, "When language learning begins earlier, it can go on longer and provide more practice and experience, leading ultimately to greater fluency and effectiveness" (p. 428). However, duration is not enough. Intensity also matters. Children need the opportunity to learn English for more than two 30-minute periods a week.

2. **The possibility of better pronunciation and fluency** Moreover, some researchers have concluded that young learners are more likely to attain native-like pronunciation (Scovel, 1988), greater confidence in speaking the language, and better oral proficiency (Harley, 1998). These studies do not refute the possibility that older language learners can achieve native-like pronunciation or proficiency, but they suggest that younger learners may have an advantage. If children begin learning another language before age 11 or 12, and they are given appropriate instruction and input, they "are more likely to acquire English to native levels without an accent" (Pinter, 2006, p. 29). "Appropriate instruction" requires well-trained teachers with good English proficiency who can foster the creativity and imagination of young learners, taking advantage of children's willingness to imitate or mimic what they hear and to repeat the language, especially if the activity is fun.

3. **The possibility of greater global awareness and intercultural competence** As the world gets smaller and more interconnected through the Internet and international travel, children have the opportunity to become global citizens. Through learning another language, children can gain an appreciation for other languages and cultures. The experience can also make them more aware and reflective of their own language and culture.

Many years ago, while evaluating a bilingual program in its first year, we talked with some children in the program and we will never forget when one little boy said, "I used to think that [another child] talked funny, but now I know that he's Spanish." That kind of cultural understanding may be the most important benefit of early language learning.

4. **The value of bilingualism: mental flexibility** Being bilingual provides many cognitive advantages. Even when children are only using one of their two (or more) languages, they have access to the other language(s) and to those neural networks (Bialystok, 1999). For young learners, especially, being able to speak another language provides a number of advantages such as mental flexibility, the ability to see a problem from different perspectives. It can also increase a child's self-awareness. As Marsh (2000) explains, "What we need to realize is that the ability to use different languages, even to a modest extent, can have a positive impact on the youngster's thinking processes. Being able to see the same phenomenon from different angles, as though looking through different language 'spectacles', can have a very interesting impact on our ability to think and understand" (p. 3).

Planning for Success in EYL Programs

A number of factors can affect the success of an EYL program. As Pinter (2006) points out, these include the status of English in the country or region, the goals of English education, and the motivation for learning English. Perhaps the most important factors are:

- Effective EYL program models
- Appropriately trained EYL teachers
- Culturally appropriate materials
- Continuity of curriculum between primary and secondary English

Effective EYL Program Models Although starting a language in early grades has many advantages, we cannot rely on an early start alone to increase the levels of English language proficiency of our students, nor even the selection of an appropriate program model. As Nunan (1999, p. 3) has reminded us, programs to teach English to young learners need to be "carefully planned, adequately supported and resourced, and closely monitored and evaluated."

Young learner programs may begin in any primary grade, and the number of classes and the number of hours per week may also vary. Some programs meet for 20–30 minutes, once a week. Others may meet every day for 30 minutes. In still other EYL programs, children are taught subjects such as science or mathematics in English for as much as a full day, every day. With these different amounts of time for study and use of English, children's proficiency in English will vary. Children who have 30 minutes of English once or twice a week, even if they begin at age 6 or 7, are not likely to become bilingual by age 12. Those who use English as a medium of instruction for some of their school subjects will attain much deeper proficiency.

EYL programs can also take many forms, with different goals or objectives, depending on national and local educational policy, available resources, cultural preferences, attitudes toward English and the role of various languages in the country, and the language(s) spoken by children in the home. Consider the need for different program models in countries like India or Kenya, where English becomes the medium of instruction in later grades, and in countries like Japan or Brazil, where English is a foreign or international language.

Whatever the model, effective EYL programs are those that encourage interaction, provide engaging activities, and build positive attitudes toward English language learning. Some program models in the United States that are also adapted and used in other countries are described below. These include:

1. FLEX programs
2. FLES programs
3. Immersion programs
4. Dual-language or two-way immersion programs
5. Transitional and maintenance bilingual programs

1.   **FLEX programs** FLEX (foreign language exploratory or experience) programs introduce children to different languages and cultures. Children receive short sessions in which they learn basic words or phrases in one or more languages, sometimes in a before- or after-school program. Through music, songs, and stories, they may learn the numbers, colors, and greetings in a foreign language, but the major goal of a FLEX program is to increase children's awareness of other languages and cultures and thus of their own. The focus is on exploring or experiencing languages, rather than developing proficiency in these languages (Met, 1991). FLEX programs can also create a high level of interest and motivate children to want to study a language.

2.   **FLES programs** In FLES (foreign language in the elementary school) programs, children study one language as a regular school subject for up to 45 minutes a day, several times a week. The goal of a FLES program is to help children develop listening and speaking skills in another language, as well as some proficiency in reading and writing the language, especially in the later primary grades (4–6). Developing an appreciation of other cultures is also a typical goal of a FLES program. While there are a number of different FLES programs, all expect

children to study a language for at least two years, often throughout the primary grades. Through extended exposure to the language, children can develop some proficiency and also develop "basic language-learning skills" that will help them as they continue to study the language in secondary school (Haas, 1998, p. 44).

In content-based FLES or content-enriched FLES programs, content from other subjects from the school curriculum (mathematics, science, social studies) is taught in the foreign language. By focusing on both language and content, these programs (referred to more generally as content-based instruction, CBI, or content and language integrated learning, CLIL) offer the opportunity for learners to develop academic language and thinking skills in a meaningful context (Crandall, 2012). These programs usually also provide more time for language learning. Because of this increased time and the enriched content, learners in content-based FLES programs usually attain a higher level of language proficiency than learners in regular FLES programs (Reeves, 1989).

3. **Immersion programs** Language immersion programs, as the name suggests, immerse children in another language by using that language as the medium of instruction, at least for part of the school day. Unlike the programs discussed above, where English is a school subject, in immersion programs, English is the language of instruction for at least some courses. However, in effective (often referred to as additive) immersion programs, students retain their native language, and literacy in the native language is never abandoned or discarded.

In a total English immersion program, children study all of their subjects (except their own language) through English. In partial immersion programs, they may take half of their subjects in their own language and the other half in a foreign language. Some partial immersion programs begin with only a few subjects or hours of instruction in the foreign language and then gradually increase the number of subjects and the time in the foreign language in later grades. Some try to provide children with the opportunity to learn mathematics, science, and social studies in both the local and foreign language over the course of the six years. In some programs, children continue in an immersion program in secondary school. Additive immersion programs can begin at any age, even as late as secondary school, but most begin in the primary grades (Faulkner-Bond et al., 2011).

The goal of these immersion programs is for children to develop functional proficiency in another language (Curtain & Dahlberg, 2010) without loss of the native language. Additive immersion students, especially those who participate in "early" foreign language immersion (beginning at ages 5–7) can become very good at listening and reading in another language, and they do this without any harm to their own language. As Harley (1998, pp. 29–30) says, "Studies have shown that immersion students, without detriment to their [first language] and subject matter learning, develop excellent listening and reading comprehension skills," as well as very strong speaking and writing skills. As might be expected, the children who begin earlier generally achieve better listening and speaking skills.

4. **Dual-language or two-way immersion programs** In dual-language programs (also referred to as two-way bilingual programs), equal (or nearly equal) numbers of children who speak one language (for example, Spanish) and those who speak another language (for example, English) take some of their instruction through each language. Some programs begin with using one language 90 percent of the time in K–1, then gradually move to using each language 50 percent of the time in grades 2–6; others start using 50 percent of each and continue with that distribution throughout the program. The program may involve two teachers, each speaking one of the languages, or one teacher who carefully uses only the required language during each part of the school day. The goal of these programs is additive bilingualism, wherein children become bilingual, bicultural, and biliterate and retain their home or heritage language while they are learning another (Faulkner-Bond et al., 2011).

5. **Transitional and maintenance bilingual programs** The goal of a transitional bilingual program (also referred to as early-exit) is to help children transition from their first language into the language of schooling, usually after three years of bilingual instruction. Children begin with more instructional time in their first language, learning to read in that language, while they are also learning the new language. They also receive instruction in major subjects through both languages over time, helping to establish basic concepts in the first language, but also preparing for the switch to the language of instruction in upper grades. This program model does not support continued literacy or development of the native language after the initial years of native language use. It is subtractive in nature, in that continued development of literacy and academic learning in the native language is not a goal or expectation.

Unlike transitional bilingual programs, maintenance (also referred to as developmental or late-exit) programs continue to provide instruction through the first language for several (usually six) years of school. The goal of a maintenance bilingual program (as the name suggests) is to develop deep literacy and academic learning in the first language, while also providing increasing amounts of instruction through the second, so that by secondary school, children can make the transition to another language, though they may continue to study their first or heritage language as a subject in secondary school (Faulkner-Bond et al., 2011; Met, 1991).

Appropriately Trained EYL Teachers Educational research continually reminds us that the most important factor in any child's education is the teacher. Effective EYL programs have well-trained teachers with adequate proficiency in English to help their children learn English. Effective EYL teachers have appropriate training in teaching young learners, in teaching English, and in teaching through English (Teachers of English to Speakers of Other Languages, 2009). But with the growing number of EYL programs in the world, a major challenge is finding enough teachers or teacher training programs to prepare these teachers (Hu, 2005; Kirkgöz, 2009). Too often, EYL teachers have taught English to adolescents, but find themselves teaching young learners with no special training on how to teach children. Other times, EYL teachers are regular elementary classroom teachers and are assigned the added responsibility of teaching English, even if they do not feel comfortable using English (Curtain & Pesola, 2000; Garton, Copland, & Burns, 2011).

Most EYL programs are fortunate in having nonnative English-speaking teachers (NNESTs) who share the cultural backgrounds and educational expectations of their students and understand the contexts in which English is used in their communities and countries. Teachers who share their young learners' language and culture will understand the ways that children learn in that country and will also be able to make connections between what is learned in the EYL class and what is learned in the children's other classes. Some programs also have native English-speaking teachers (NESTs) who can complement the teaching of the NNESTs through their access to more English resources, a wider English vocabulary, and greater comfort in using the language in a range of contexts.

Culturally Appropriate Materials If English is an international language, does that affect how we should teach English to young learners? What should be our goals in teaching an international language? We will be considering this throughout the book, but first and foremost, the purpose of teaching English to young learners is not to expect them to speak American or British English. What we want is for them to be understood by other speakers of English as an international language. Nor do we want them to learn only about the cultures of countries in the Inner Circle. Because English is an international and intercultural language, we should also include materials from many cultures around the world. The children we teach will most likely use English with other EIL speakers, and what they really need is an appreciation of different cultures. We also want to include the students' home culture. This will help students to talk about their own culture in English

(McKay, 2002) and develop what Kramsch and Sullivan (1996) call a "sphere of interculturality" in the classroom, one that promotes a healthy process of learning about cultural differences through reflection on one's own culture.

Jade Albert Studio, Inc./Getty Images

Continuity of Curriculum Between Primary and Secondary English

When countries adopt early language programs, they also need to think about how those programs impact the language programs for older learners at secondary school (Curtain & Pesola, 2000; Gilzow, 2002; Read, 2003). According to Cameron (2003, p. 105), secondary school language teachers will likely have to "cope with classes of mixed levels of language skills and knowledge" and also with "the task of maintaining or restoring motivation over long periods of language learning." She continues, "English language programs in the secondary school "may look quite different from earlier models that served a system in which language learning began around 11 years of age" (p. 106). Curricula need to be aligned to promote a smooth transition for students and to help teachers meet the needs of former young learners.

Pitfalls to Avoid in EYL Programs

Curtain and Pesola (2000) identify some "common pitfalls" of early foreign language programs that need to be considered in developing effective EYL programs:

■ Scheduling language classes too infrequently or in sessions that are too short
■ Treating foreign languages differently from other subjects, rather than as "valid academic subjects"
■ Implementing a new program in all grades at the same time
■ Failing to create program cohesion from primary to secondary grades
■ Planning and scheduling foreign languages in isolation from the general curriculum

To these we could add:

- Providing insufficient professional development for EYL teachers
- Supplying inadequate or inequitable resources, especially access to technology, with urban and private schools having greater access to both print and digital materials (Butler, 2009; Enever and Moon, 2009).

Common Features of Effective EYL Programs

Nikolov and Curtain (2000), in *An Early Start: Young Learners and Modern Languages in Europe and Beyond*, identified the following characteristics of effective YL programs from 20 countries. These programs:

- Focused on meaning
- Integrated language instruction with mainstream curriculum
- Used task-based and content-based approaches
- Provided fun in the classroom
- Set up children for success
- Fostered learner autonomy
- Set realistic expectations and assessment
- Provided continuity between primary and secondary school language programs

Additionally, according to Gilzow (2002), in some contents, effective young learner programs:

- Used technology appropriately
- Had adequate funding
- Provided professional development
- Advocated for the program
- Used a standards-based curriculum

We will be discussing many of these characteristics in the following chapters.

■ Teacher to Teacher

English Education Profiles

Below are three profiles of English education written by teachers in an online professional development course from Myanmar, Madagascar, and Romania. The English education profiles were written to provide information about each country's education policy and requirements for teaching English. In addition, the writers included descriptions of the classroom environment, as well as materials and resources available. The student profile included provides information about the students' age, gender, level of proficiency, and the level of exposure they may receive outside of the EFL classroom. These examples will show how three different countries have applied the teaching of English to young learners.

As you read these profiles, consider the following:

- What factors of effective programs do you see in these profiles?
- What challenges do these teachers face?
- What are the similarities between these educational contexts and your own context?
- What did you learn from the policy or the teachers' classes that you can adopt in your own teaching?

"Every local school in Myanmar began a FLES program in 1970–1971 school year. It is designed for students in 5th standard through 10th standard and is offered as a special program at some high schools in Yangon, Myanmar. Continuity is offered at another big city like Mandalay two years after. In the 1990s, the government implemented a new education system to develop standards for foreign language education from kindergarten through grade 11. The educators and curriculum designers drew well-designed and standardized curriculum and assessment for students learning effectively. The goal of education policy for teaching foreign language in primary school is by using English, students can build up the developed nation to stand shoulder to shoulder with the other countries in the world. In the late 1990s, there were a few private schools that offered Immersion programs in their school to attract the rich families and their children starting from primary level.

In general, students in Myanmar are taught English as a regular school subject since they are in kindergarten to grade 11 (from 5 years to 16 years) in local schools. Students are taught English 4 times a week and 45 minutes in each session. There are more than 50 students in a class. The class has chairs and desks, a white board, wall posters and a computer, though some students in other schools are cramped in the room and use table and benches and blackboard in the classroom, and some classes have more than 70 students.

My Grade 3 Class

I teach in a private school called "Crane International School" located in Sanchaung Township, Yangon. My class is Grade 3 and there are 20 multinational students aged between 7–10 years. In my school, we teach in an Immersion program; all subjects are taught in English. We teach English starting at the age of 3 (in nursery) and they continue to learn it until Grade 12 (at the age of 17–18 years). Children in my school have eight English lessons per week and 50 minutes in each lesson. My class is not very spacious for students to move around to do the activities but there is enough room for teachers to walk around in the class. Each student uses a moveable chair with desk; we have a white board, a cupboard to keep classroom materials; register, dictionaries, students' homework books, a television set and a CD cassette player. We have a library that has lots of books relevant to students' level and teachers' needs. Every class has to go to the library once a week to borrow a book and write a book report. We have a computer lab where students can go once a week and have Internet access. Every student has a colorful textbook that includes vocabulary, spelling, pronunciation, comprehension check questions and grammar workbook.

There are 20 students in my class, varying in background. The majority of them are from Myanmar; I also have three Japanese students, two Indian students, two Korean students and one Australian student. The number of boys is two times more than girls. Because they are all of different ages, ranging from 7 to 10, and their cultural backgrounds, and different learning experiences, they have different learning styles and preferences, but all are motivated, curious, and active. One new learner has only studied English for two months; another uses English as his native language. Some prefer working in pairs, working individually, working in groups, playing games, copying from the board, and repeating after the teacher. Two boys prefer working by themselves, whereas, the rest enjoy playing games and working in groups. On the whole, the students' goal is to improve their use of the language as a means to communicate with other people and to move to an English speaking country for their further studies. **"**

—Sanda Than Pe, Primary English Teacher, Myanmar

"The education policy for English in this public primary school falls in line with the national education policy for English In Primary (EIP) established by the Ministry of Education of Madagascar in 2002. This school is one of the first 42 pilot schools around the country where English education was introduced in the Malagasy primary education system, beginning in the 4th grade. Before 2002, English instruction began in secondary schools only, from 6th grade on. The school is currently using the national 4th grade curriculum, which was revised and finalized by the Ministry of Education in 2006 for all the pilot programs. The Ministry of Education of Madagascar provided the following description of its national curriculum for primary school: 'This curriculum provides classroom material through 5 thematic units based on topics which are relevant to Malagasy children's lives at this age, falling in line with the Competency Approach that all other school subjects are to follow. This curriculum is based mainly on listening and speaking skills and thus features such activities as songs, dialogues and games, which are also used to promote motivation and interest in children. The objectives of introducing English at the fourth grade include the possibilities of exposing children at an early age to the language so that they can obtain better proficiency and fluency before adolescence, preparing them for entrance to the secondary school or CEG (College d'Enseignement Général), and finally preparing them for international communication, business, tourism, and travel.' At this initial familiarization stage, EFL is introduced in an enjoyable way and neither assessments nor grades are required. English is taught as a separate regular school subject and is time-tabled for two hours a week, spread out into 20 minutes of instruction a day during the 9-month school year. There is only one teacher—Marie Rose, a former primary school teacher who was one of the 42 pilot primary school teachers to be trained to use the curriculum and to teach the lessons via the Communicative Approach, with the objective of learning English for communication.

Marie Rose's 4th Grade Class

Marie Rose's 4th grade FLES class is made up of 40 nine- and ten-year-old boys and girls. These children do not have much literacy in English and do not seem to have much exposure to the language outside the EFL classroom either, as English is not widely spoken yet and such media forms as newspapers, TV and radios are mostly in Malagasy and French.

Marie Rose's fourth graders learn English in a typical concrete-floored classroom which is quite spacious though basic as it comes equipped with only a small cassette player, a large chalkboard, a teacher desk, and 20 wooden student desks. The students sit in pairs on the wooden desks arranged in 5 rows of 4 desks that can be moved easily. Unlike the students and teachers in primary schools in the US and Europe who have access to audiovisual equipment, textbooks, a library, a computer lab and to the Internet, Marie Rose and her students do not in the Analamahitsy EPP. The only resources available to her are the curriculum accompanied by supporting materials such as sample lesson plans and pictures provided by the Ministry of Education and the materials provided by the Teacher Resource Center (TRC) in the downtown area. As for her students, they do not have any textbooks or workbooks for reading and writing. They only have copybooks in which they are to keep the handouts Marie Rose gives them. These are handouts of the songs and chants they learn and perform in class as well as of pictures they can color at home and that illustrate vocabulary and grammar covered in class."

—*Laingo Ramanantoanina, English Teacher, Madagascar*

"Ever since I was a student myself, the Romanian education system has been promoting foreign language studies. Back then, students started learning the first foreign language in the 5th grade (at the age of 11) and the second one in the 6th grade (at the age of 12). Nowadays, the national curriculum introduces the first compulsory foreign language in the 3rd grade (at the age of 9) and the second in the 5th grade. All the teachers of English in state schools have to follow the common national program designed by the Ministry of Education. They are free to use any of the ministry-approved textbooks which they find suitable for their needs or their students' profile. Students are assessed according to the common criteria; therefore, at the end of each year of study they have to be assessed according to the competencies mentioned in the national program. According to the Common European Frame of Reference for Language (CEFR, 2001), by the end of high school students should have reached the B2 level.

Most Romanian schools choose English either as the first or the second compulsory foreign language. If students start learning English in primary school, they usually have the same specialist teacher from the 3rd grade until they are in the 8th grade, when they finish secondary school. During primary and secondary school years, foreign language studies are allotted 2, maximum 3 hours a week for expanding or improving linguistic competencies. In high school the number of hours per week stays the same, except for the special philology classes, which can have 4 up to 5 English lessons per week and have a special test every semester.

My Class

I teach English as a separate school subject to primary and secondary school learners at a public school located in the largest university town in eastern Romania. My school is a state school with 755 primary and secondary level pupils, built in the first decade of the 20th century, and located in the centre of the town. It is a very old, but impressive building, with 15 large, tall classrooms. Some classrooms have individual desks; others have desks for two or three children. Each of them has a chalkboard and a teacher's desk in front of it. Every classroom is shared by two classes of children, as primary school children have lessons in the morning, and secondary school learners study in the afternoon. All teachers have at their disposal a CD player, a whiteboard, a laptop and two OHPs. Nevertheless, the Internet connection is not available in all the rooms. Moreover, because of its low budget, the school cannot afford to make photocopies of written materials for students, and teachers have to make them at their own expense.

The school management team has decided to have English as the first foreign language and French as the second one. Both languages are taught as separate school subjects in a FLES program, with 2 or 3 lessons a week. There are three teachers of English (including myself) working with both primary and secondary level students, and a teacher of French. All through the school year the committee has special activities such as open lessons and presentations of new teaching materials. It also organizes language contests and celebrations (such as the Foreign Languages Day, Halloween, Christmas, or Europe's Day). Every semester we have meetings with all teachers of English in the region where matters such as effective planning or teaching methods and materials are discussed.

The children's environment is favorable to learning English. Their families encourage them to learn the language, either because they consider it useful to be proficient in a global language, or because they have older relatives who study English. They also listen to modern international and Romanian music extensively, and these days most Romanian dancing songs are in English, so children are curious about what the lyrics mean. In addition, most pupils in this class have personal computers and Internet connection at home. Thus, they are exposed to lots of information or games in English.

To conclude, I could say that I think of my work with the children as a continuous challenge, but their enthusiastic, inventive and playful nature has won me over. Therefore, I try to make their experience with English as pleasant as possible, even if I am aware of the fact there is always room for improvement.**"**

—*Simona Balan, Primary and Secondary English Teacher, Romania*

■ Chapter Summary

To Conclude

Reasons for an early start to English language learning Because of the role of English as a global language and its potential for providing education and employment advantages to English speakers, English is being introduced at earlier and earlier ages around the world. Many children now start English as early as age 6 (or first grade).

While there are many points of view about the best time to start learning another language, there are potential benefits to an early start, especially if optimal conditions occur within the language classroom. EYL programs can provide more time to learn the language and can lead to better pronunciation and fluency, enhanced intercultural competence, and mental flexibility.

Factors affecting success of an EYL program A number of factors affect the success of an EYL program. These include the choice of the EYL program model, the presence of appropriately trained teachers, the availability of culturally and linguistically appropriate materials, and the continuity of the English curriculum from primary to secondary school.

Models of effective EYL programs There are a number of models of effective EYL programs. These include FLEX, FLES (including content-based or content-enriched FLES), immersion, dual-language, and transitional and maintenance bilingual programs. Another way to look at program models is in terms of their topics and amount of time for instruction. Programs can develop their curricula around traditional topics found in student language textbooks, topics drawn from other subjects, community-based topics, or actually teaching part of the curriculum in English.

Need for appropriately trained EYL teachers Appropriately trained EYL teachers know how to develop engaging, motivating activities and have adequate English proficiency to help their young learners in learning English. Unfortunately, the growth in demand for EYL classes has outstripped the capacity of many countries to provide appropriate TEYL training. There are few specialized training programs or courses for EYL teachers.

Need for culturally and linguistically appropriate materials and curricula Materials and curricula need to be culturally and linguistically appropriate. The local and national culture and cultures of other countries, including the cultures of the traditional, Inner Circle countries, all need to be included to help children develop intercultural competence and grow in understanding of their own culture.

Need for continuity of primary and secondary school English curriculum The primary and secondary school curricula need to be aligned so that students make a smooth transition in their language learning. Children who have participated in EYL programs will need higher-level English classes in secondary school than those who begin at the secondary school level.

Additional factors affecting EYL program success There are a number of additional factors that programs need to consider if they are to be effective. These include scheduling, integrating the English class into the overall school curriculum, and gradually introducing young learner classes, when teachers and materials are available, as well as providing appropriate resources and professional development for current EYL teachers.

■ Over to You

Discussion Questions

1. What are some reasons why more people around the world are learning English? What is the main reason your program or programs in your country were developed?

2. What are some differences in studying or teaching English in countries in the Inner, Outer, and Expanding Circles? In which "Circle" are you teaching English?

3. What are some goals of teaching English as an international language? What are your program goals or the goals of programs in your country?

4. What are some benefits of learning English at a young age? Have you seen these advantages in your students?

5. What are some of the pitfalls of TEYL? Have you experienced any of these?

6. What are some program models for EYL and the differences in their goals and objectives?

7. Discuss how your views apply to the various program models. Would a FLEX or FLES program be a better fit for your context? Or would a bilingual program be better? Why?

8. What kind of program do you teach in or will you teach in? Do you see similarities in your program to the kinds of programs discussed in this chapter?

9. Do you identify with any of the teachers whose story is told? If so, how?

English Education Profile

Now that you have read about different countries and their uses and policies about English, think about your own country. Use the English Education Profile on pg. 388 to describe the English education profile of your country, region, local school system, and classroom.

Write About It

Reflection on policies toward English in your country: Write a 1–2 page reflective essay using the prompts below. Explain your views and provide examples for support based on your own teaching context:

- Has the age of compulsory English education in your country been lowered? Why or why not?
- What do you think are some benefits of starting English language instruction early? Are there any disadvantages of an early start?
- What do you think are the most important factors for improving the conditions for English language learning for children?
- What are some things that teachers, teacher supervisors, teacher trainers, and curriculum developers can do to create an optimum English language learning environment for children?

■ Resources and References

Print Publications

Enever, J., Moon, J., & Raman, U. (2009). *Young learner English Language policy and implementation: International perspectives.* Reading, UK: Garnet Education.

Garton, S., Copland, F., & Burns, A. (2011). *Investigating global practices in teaching English to young learners.* Aston University, UK: British Council.

Genesee, F., Paradis, J., & Crago, M. B. (2011). *Dual language development and disorders: A handbook on bilingualism and second language learning.* Baltimore, MD: Brooks Publishing.

Marinova-Todd, S. H., Marshall, D. B., & Snow, C. E. (2000). Three misconceptions about age and L2 learning. *TESOL Quarterly, 34*(1), 9–34.

McKay, S. L. (2002). *Teaching English as an international language: Rethinking goals and approaches.* Oxford, UK: Oxford University Press.

Useful Web Sites

American Council on the Teaching of Foreign Languages: www.actfl.org

British Council: http://www.teachingenglish.org.uk/teaching-kids

Center for Applied Linguistics: www.cal.org/resources/digest

Nandu Early Language Web site: www.cal.org/earlylang

National Network for Early Language Learning: www.nnell.org

References

Bialystok, E. (1999). Cognitive complexity and attentional control in the bilingual mind. *Child Development, 70*(3), 636–644.

Butler, Y. G. (2009). Teaching English to young learners: The influence of global and local factors. In J. Enever, J. Moon, & U. Raman (Eds.), Young learner English language policy and implementation: International perspectives (pp. 23–29). Reading, UK: Garnet Education.

Cameron, L. (2003). Challenges for ELT from the expansion in teaching children. *ELT Journal, 57*(2), 105–112.

Carroll, J. B. (1975). The teaching of French as a foreign language in eight countries. New York, NY: John Wiley.

Crandall, J. A. (2012). Content based instruction and content and language integrated learning. In J. Richards & A. Burns (Eds.), *Cambridge guide to pedagogy and practice in second language teaching,* 2nd ed. Cambridge, UK: Cambridge University Press.

Crystal, D. (2003). *English as a global language,* 2nd ed. Cambridge, UK: Cambridge University Press.

Curtain, H., & Dahlberg, C. A. (2010). *Languages and children— Making the match: New languages for young learners,* 4th ed. New York, NY: Pearson.

Curtain, H., & Pesola, C. A. (2000). *Planning for success: Common pitfalls in the planning of early foreign language programs.* ERIC Digest EDO-FL-11. Washington, DC: Center for Applied Linguistics. http://www.cal.org/resources/digest/0011planning.html

Enever, J., & Moon, J. (2009). New global contexts for teaching primary ELT: Change and challenge. In J. Enever, J. Moon, & U. Raman (Eds.), Young learner English language policy and implementation: International perspectives (pp. 5–21). Reading, UK: Garnet Education.

Faulkner-Bond, M., Waring, S., Forte, E., Crenshaw, R., & Tindle, K. (2011). *Language instruction educational programs (LIEPs): Lessons from the research and profiles of promising practices.* Washington, DC: U.S. Department of Education, Office of Planning, Evaluation, and Policy Development, Policy and Program Studies Service.

Garton, S., Copland, F., & Burns, A. (2011). *Investigating global practices in teaching English to young learners.* London, UK: British Council and Aston University.

Gilzow, D. F. (2002). *Model early foreign language programs: Key elements.* Washington, DC: Center for Applied Linguistics. Available at http://www.cal.org/resources/digest/0211gilzow.html

Gimenez, T. (2009). English at primary school in Brazil: Challenges and perspectives. In J. Enever, J. Moon, & U. Raman (Eds.), *Young learner English language policy and implementation: International perspectives* (pp. 45–51). Reading, UK: Garnet Education.

Haas, M. (1998). Early vs. late: The practitioner's perspective. In M. Met (Ed.), *Critical issues in early second language learning.* Glenview, IL: Scott Foresman, Addison-Wesley.

Harley, B. (1998). The outcomes of early and later language learning. In M. Met (Ed.) *Critical issues in early second language learning.* Glenview, IL: Scott Foresman, Addison-Wesley.

Hu, G. (2005). English language education in China: Policies, progress and problems. *Language Policy, 4,* 5–24.

Jenkins, J. (2009). *World Englishes: A resource book for students,* 2nd ed. London, UK: Routledge.

Johnstone, R. (2009). An early start: What are the key conditions for generalized success? In J. Enever, J. Moon, & U. Raman (Eds.), *Young learner English language policy and implementation: International perspectives* (pp. 31–42). Reading, UK: Garnet Education.

Kachru, B. B. (1990). *The alchemy of English: The spread, functions and models of non-native Englishes.* Chicago, IL: University of Illinois Press.

Kirkgöz, Y. (2009). English language teaching in Turkish primary education. In J. Enever, J. Moon, & U. Raman (Eds.), *Young learner English language policy and implementation: International perspectives* (pp. 189–195). Reading, UK: Garnet Education.

Kramsch, C. (2002). In search of the intercultural. *Journal of Sociolinguistics, 6*(1), 275–285.

Kramsch, C., & Sullivan, P. (1996). Appropriate pedagogy. *ELT Journal, 50,* 199–212.

Lenneberg, E. (1967). *Biological foundations of language*. New York, NY: Wiley.

Marinova-Todd, S. H., Marshall, D. M. & Snow, C. E. (2000). Three misconceptions about age and L2 learning. *TESOL Quarterly, 34*(1), 9–34.

Marsh, D. (2002). *Using languages to learn and learning to use languages: An Introduction to CLIL for parents and young people.* Available at http://clilcompendium.com/1uk.pdf

McCloskey, M. L., Orr, J., & Dolitsky, M. (2006). *Teaching English as a foreign language in primary school.* Alexandria, VA: TESOL.

McKay, S. L. (2002). Teaching English as an international language: Implications for cultural materials in the classroom. *TESOL Journal, 9*(4), 7–11.

McLaughlin, B. (1984/1985). *Second language acquisition in childhood,* Vols. 1 & 2. Hillsdale, NJ: Erlbaum.

Met, M. (1991). Elementary school foreign languages: What research can and cannot tell us. In E. S. Silber (Ed.), *Critical issues in foreign language instruction* (pp. 63–79). New York, NY: Garland Publishing.

Nikolov, M. (2009). *Early learning of modern foreign languages: Processes and outcomes.* Bristol, UK: Multilingual Matters.

Nikolov, M., & Curtain, H. (Eds.). (2000). *An early start: Young learners and modern languages* in *Europe and beyond.* Strasbourg Cedex, FR: Council of Europe.

Nikolov, M., & Mihaljevic Djigunovic, J. (2011). All shades and every color: An overview of early teaching and learning of foreign languages. *Annual Review of Applied Linguistics, 31,* 95–119.

Nunan, D. C. (1999). President's message. *TESOL Matters, 9*(3), 1–3. Available at http://davidnunan.com

Nunan, D. C. (2003). The impact of English as a global language on educational policies and practices in the Asia-Pacific region. *TESOL Quarterly, 37*(4), 589–613.

Oyama, S. (1976). A sensitive period in the acquisition of a non-native phonological system. *Journal of Psycholinguistic Research, 5,* 261–285.

Penfield, W., & Roberts, L. (1959). *Speech and brain-mechanisms.* Princeton, NJ: Princeton University Press.

Pinter, A. (2006). *Teaching young language learners.* Oxford, UK: Oxford University Press.

Read, C. (2003). Is younger better? *English Teaching Professional, 28*(5–7). Available at http://www.carolread.com/articles/ETp28_Carol_Read.pdf

Rixon, S. (1999). *Young learners of English: Some research perspectives.* Harlow, UK: Longman.

Reeves, J. (1989). *Elementary school foreign language programs.* Washington, DC: Center for Applied Linguistics. Available at http://www.cal.org/resources/archive/digest/1989elemfl.html

Scovel, T. (1988). A time to speak: A psycholinguistic inquiry into the critical period for human speech. Rowley, MA: Newbury House.

Shin, J. K., & Crandall, J. A. (2011). A survey of English young learner programs, policies, and teachers. Unpublished MS.

Singleton, D. (1995). Introduction: A critical look at the critical hypothesis in second acquisition research. In D. Singleton & Z. Lengyel (Eds.), *The age factor in second language acquisition* (pp. 1–29). Bristol, UK: Multilingual Matters.

Teachers of English to Speakers of Other Languages. (2009). *Position statement on teaching English as a foreign or additional language to young learners.* Alexandria, VA: TESOL.

2 Basic Principles of TEYL

■ Getting Started

This chapter will lay the foundation for the approaches this book supports for teaching young learners English as an international language. It will explore the characteristics and learning styles of primary school students and encourage teachers to make their classrooms an enjoyable place where children can learn through fun, creative, and social activities. In addition to providing a theoretical foundation for TEYL, this chapter will introduce useful activities and teaching ideas specifically designed for teaching young learners English as an international language.

Think About It

Before reading about how to teach young learners, try to get into the mind of a child by imagining yourself when you were six years old. In order to understand the content of this chapter more deeply, it will help to connect to yourself as a young learner. You might want to take a deep breath, close your eyes, and picture yourself when you were six years old.

As a six-year-old child, what was your typical day like from start to finish? Who did you interact with most often—parents, siblings, grandparents, friends? What activities did you do at home? Did you often go to the park, beach, field, forest, or other location? What was your favorite part of the day, and why? What was your least favorite part of the day, and why?

Eco Images/Getty Images

> Now think about yourself at school when you were in first grade. What kind of student were you? What subjects did you like the most? The least? What subjects were you the most or least successful in? What class activities did you most enjoy? Least enjoy? Why?

Discovery Activity

Adjective Splash and T-Chart

How would you describe young learners? Write down in the circle below or on a piece of paper all the adjectives you can think of that describe the characteristics of young learners. Just splash the words down in the circle in any order and in any direction.

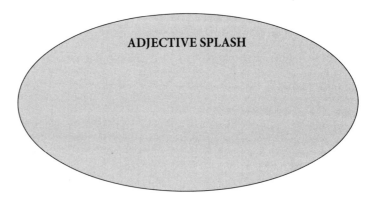

ADJECTIVE SPLASH

Now read through the adjectives you wrote down and categorize them into the T-chart below. On one side list the positive adjectives. On the other side list the negative adjectives.

POSITIVE	NEGATIVE

■ Theory, Planning and Application

Considerations for Teaching Young Learners

After reflecting on yourself as a child, as well as exploring the characteristics of young learners, you have probably thought about some of the concepts you will read about in this chapter. Remembering what it was like to be a six-year-old child reminds us of how differently we think and learn as adults. In order to teach young learners effectively, it is important to know them in depth and be able to put ourselves in their shoes. Children ages 5–12 years are growing and developing rapidly. Teaching young learners English requires an approach that is developmentally appropriate, which means that learning is dependent on the stage of a child's physical, social, emotional, and mental maturity (Coltrane, 2003; Nissani, 1990). The right approach is to work with their natural tendencies instead of against them. In order to find the right approach for teaching young learners English, it is important to explore the following:

- ■ Characteristics of young learners
- ■ How children learn
- ■ How children learn language

For each section, the main points will be explained, followed by examples showing how teachers can apply this information. Within these three main categories, there will be 12 considerations for teaching young learners English, which will be summarized at the end.

Characteristics of Young Learners How a primary school teacher describes her/his students can depend on the day. On a good day s/he might say young learners are energetic, social, spontaneous, and curious. On a bad day s/he may say they are hyperactive, too talkative, can't sit still, and are easily distracted. These two different interpretations (both positive and negative) reflect the same characteristics of young learners, which most teachers agree on. Children are:

1. Energetic and physically active
2. Spontaneous and not afraid to speak out or participate
3. Curious and receptive to new ideas
4. Imaginative and enjoy make-believe
5. Easily distracted and have short attention spans
6. Egocentric and relate new ideas to themselves
7. Social and are learning to relate to others

All of these characteristics can make teaching young learners exciting and inspiring; however, the same characteristics can present challenges for teachers who may have anywhere between 15 and 50 students in one classroom. It is important to look at these characteristics in a positive way and use them to develop an effective teaching approach.

1.   **Children are energetic and physically active** Teachers at the primary level need to consider how to harness the dynamic energy of young learners and use it toward effective learning. Therefore, teachers should utilize children's natural tendency to be physically active and not get frustrated with the fact that young children cannot sit still for long periods of time. You might incorporate kinesthetic activities that encourage young learners to get up and move around. For example, Total Physical Response (TPR) is a commonly used method with children because it connects language to movement (Asher, 1977). In TPR you would give a physical command, such as "Sit down," and sit down while saying it. Children at even the lowest level of English language proficiency can connect the oral utterance with the movement and can follow the commands through repetition. The game Simon Says is a perfect example of a fun activity that uses TPR.

Simon Says

Simon Says is a popular children's game that uses TPR. It is great way to check comprehension of vocabulary related to body parts and physical movement and bring lots of laughter to your classroom.

Instructions:
- Tell students that they have to do what Simon says, or they will be out.
- Always begin every sentence with "Simon says. . . ."
- Then give a command to do a body movement while physically doing that movement. For example:

Teacher: "Simon says . . . touch your toes!" (Teacher touches her toes)

- Students have to do what Simon says. So students should touch their toes.
- However, the game is to listen carefully. Sometimes the teacher can say one movement while physically doing another movement. Then if the student does not do what "Simon says," s/he is out and cannot keep playing. For example, Teacher: "Simon says . . . touch your head!" *(Teacher touches her toes)*
- If a student touches her/his toes, then s/he is out. The teacher can make it funny by saying, "But Simon didn't say touch your toes!"

2. Children are spontaneous and not afraid to speak out or participate

Young learners are not very inhibited. Older learners can be more self-conscious and concerned with how people judge them. Young learners are much more willing to participate in activities and speak out in English without feeling embarrassed. They are good imitators of language, in part because they are not afraid to repeat after the teacher or sing along to fun songs, even if their use of the language isn't exactly right or even if they don't understand every word. Teachers can use simple songs, rhymes, chants, and dialogs with kids because they are ready to follow along. The sample lesson Meet and Greet on pp. 49 takes advantage of young learners' spontaneous nature by asking them to dramatize a simple dialog in many different ways—by miming, mouthing the words, and doing their role using different emotions, such as angrily, happily, fearfully, etc. Because they are not afraid to speak out and participate, activities like these are very effective for improving students' oral proficiency through repetition that is not boring and that gives young learners a chance to be expressive.

3. Children are curious and receptive to new ideas

Young learners have a natural curiosity. The world is a new place for them, and they want to know more about it. Teachers should prepare activities that arouse students' curiosity. For example, the Mystery Bag game is a commonly used activity for fun at parties or in class to teach English.

Mystery Bag

Instructions:

- The teacher can put different objects in any opaque bag, like a brown lunch bag or a cloth bag.
- Students have to reach into the bag, feel the object, and describe it.
- Then students have to guess what the object is.
- The teacher could prepare a few bags for students to use in groups and put in objects that have different qualities, like hard, soft, big, small, long, short, round, square, etc. The students have fun guessing what the objects are.

In addition, teaching about new and interesting topics like exotic animals and plants that don't exist in their local environment can capture young learners' attention. Unusual animals like kangaroos or bizarre plants like venus flytraps can keep learners interested and teach them about the amazing world we live in. Introducing international cultures can also arouse their curiosity and introduce them to the world where they may be using English in the future. It is important to expose students to lots of different cultures, not just American and British cultures that are usually associated with English. Cultural topics that are particularly interesting for young learners are food, dress, music, holidays, celebrations, greeting customs, and folktales.

4. **Children are imaginative and enjoy make-believe** Young learners love activities that encourage them to use their imagination. Using role plays and drama games allows them to play "make-believe" and pretend they are someone or something else. For example, children can learn new vocabulary about animals and have fun pretending to be an elephant, lion, or giraffe, making the movements with their bodies and sounds with their voices. This can be the basis for a fun game of charades in which the children take turns picking the name of an animal from a bag and acting it out until their classmates can guess what animal they are imitating. Teachers can also use stories or plays to create an imaginary world for students while learning new language. Many popular children's stories and TV shows take place in a fantasy world with fairy godmothers, wizards, superheroes, monsters, or animals that talk. Students can use their imagination and creativity to make and use their own pictures or puppets to retell a story. They can also play make-believe by dressing up in costumes and pretending to be characters to reenact a story using English.

5. **Children are easily distracted and have short attention spans** Young learners are known for being easily distracted. Although children have short attention spans, they can concentrate on longer activities if they are fun and interesting to them. Teachers should try to engage children with fun activities that arouse their curiosity and imagination, as the previous sections suggested. Teachers can also capture their attention with brightly colored pictures, photos, and posters. Incorporating different kinds of audio-visual aids such as playing songs, TV or movie clips, or YouTube videos can help keep children's attention and interest. In addition, it is a good idea to plan lessons as a series of short activities. Shin (2006) points out that, "As children get older, their ability to concentrate for longer periods of time increases. So for students ages 5–7, you should try to keep activities between 5 and 10 minutes long. Students ages 8–10 can handle activities that are 10 to 15 minutes long. It is always possible to revisit an activity later in class or in the next class" (p. 4). However, these time limits are not written in stone. It all depends on the particular activity. Although teachers may have longer tasks they would like their young learners to accomplish, it is recommended that teachers try their best to break long activities down into smaller steps and check on progress or give students a short break. For example, if there is a story-writing activity for ten-year-old students that may take more than 15 minutes, the teacher might break the task down into parts and check on students' progress after each part in order to keep them focused and on track. In addition, teachers could have students take a break after concentrating very hard on the activity. The break could be one minute long

Bob Ebbesen/Alamy

and would require students to stand up and move their bodies around with some TPR, or even play a quick game of Simon Says to get students up, moving, and laughing.

If students have been focused on a writing activity, it is recommended for teachers to take a quick break and do the "Hand Shakes," which is a TPR activity. To do the Hand Shakes, the teacher leads the students in TPR by saying and doing the following three or four times in a row:

> Shake your right hand. One. Two. Three. (*Shake your right hand for 3 seconds*)
> Shake your left hand. One. Two. Three. (*Shake your left hand for 3 seconds*)

Young learners are still learning to write well, so they often hold their pens and pencils too tightly and can use a physical as well as mental break from the activity. Sometimes these are called "brain breaks" and are recommended for young learners with short attention spans.

Writing the Story from a Video (*25 minutes*)

In this activity, the class just watched a video (or listened to the teacher tell a story). The students are responsible for writing the story they watched. The teacher can break the task down and check progress after students do each of the following steps:

- Brainstorm ideas (3 minutes): In small groups, students brainstorm ideas for the story in a web.
- List ideas (2 minutes): In small groups, students order their ideas in a list.
- Share ideas (5 minutes): WIth the whole class, students share their ideas from their list while the teacher writes their ideas in complete sentences on the board. If students make any grammatical mistakes when expressing their ideas, the teacher can model the correct sentences as she writes on the board.
- Write sentences (5 minutes): Individually, students write a sentence for each idea using the teacher's model on the board.
- Brain break (2 minutes): The teacher leads the whole class in a TPR brain break. They do the Hand Shakes three or four times, and then stretch their hands up high and touch their toes a few times.
- Add details (3 minutes): With the whole class, students discuss what details to add to make the story more interesting.
- Write story (5 minutes): Individually, students write the story in good handwriting on a clean sheet of paper.

The teacher can check on progress after each step and tell students to move to the next step. While students are working in small groups, pairs, and individually, the teacher can walk around and help students or groups who are struggling.

6. Children are egocentric and relate new ideas to themselves Young learners are egocentric, centered on themselves and their immediate surroundings. They have difficulty perceiving things from another person's perspective. As they get older, they improve in this area, but they still have a tendency to relate new ideas to themselves while at primary school ages. Teachers need to provide opportunities for young learners to personalize what they are learning. This means to connect new information and language to themselves. For example, if you are teaching children about adjectives to describe people, they will enjoy writing an acrostic name poem about themselves. See the example below for a young learner named Minh.

> **M**usical
> **I**ntelligent
> **N**ice
> **H**appy

An activity like this is engaging for children because it is about them, and it helps them practice new vocabulary by relating it to themselves. The teacher could have students draw or bring in pictures of themselves to put on the paper with the poem and have them decorate the poem using their own creativity. Then the teacher can post students' acrostic name poems around the room and have them present their poems and pictures to the class. These activities reinforce the language and cater to children's egocentric nature. Not only is personalizing a good strategy to use with young learners; it is also good to relate cultural topics to their own native culture. If the teacher uses stories or topics from other international cultures, it helps young learners when they get a chance to relate it to their own culture or immediate context. This can help teachers see if students understand the information, help students remember the information, and build their understanding of cultural differences.

7. Children are social and are learning to relate to others Young learners are very social and like to talk to each other. They are learning how to relate to others as part of their socialization process to their culture. They love to play games with each other and can cooperate to do activities. Teachers should have a balance of activities that allow students to have various types of interaction, such as student–student in pairs, students–students in groups, teacher–student one-on-one, and teacher–students as a whole class. First, varying the kinds of interaction from activity to activity, including ones that encourage students to work alone, is important to keep the class engaging. It is also important for students to experience all types of social interaction with each other and the teacher, because communicating in different contexts is like real life. Learning how to communicate with and work with peers is an important part of personal growth and development for each child. Finally, plenty of interaction with the teacher is very important for young learners because the teacher has the role of supporting students through the process of learning English. This part of social interaction will be discussed further in the next section, "How Children Learn."

As the examples associated with each characteristic show, taking advantage of the characteristics of young learners will create a classroom environment that is exciting and dynamic. Although a class full of energetic, spontaneous, curious, imaginative, easily distracted, egocentric, and social learners can be challenging, teachers can cater to those characteristics to keep learners engaged in order to teach English effectively.

How Children Learn   This section focuses on how children learn, based on the major educational theorists who have set the foundation for current approaches for teaching young learners. It will go a step beyond the characteristics of young learners described earlier, which are easily witnessed even by an untrained observer. The previous section tried to explain how to keep children engaged based on seven of their characteristics; this section goes on to explain how children learn and process new information. Children:

8. Learn by doing and interacting with their environment
9. Need support and scaffolding by the teacher

8.   Children learn by doing and interacting with their environment
Confucius said, "I hear, and I forget. I see, and I remember. I do, and I understand." This is particularly true for young learners, who are just beginning to make sense of the world around them. Piaget (1970) emphasized that children are active learners and thinkers. Children construct knowledge from interacting with the physical environment in developmental stages. Students in primary school can be found in Piaget's Preoperational and Concrete Operational Stages. Very young learners at 5–7 years old who are in the Preoperational Stage are extremely egocentric and highly imaginative, although they are starting to distinguish between fantasy and reality compared to younger children in this stage. As young learners reach the Concrete Operational Stage (7–11 years old), they are able to think more logically but are still grounded in concrete objects and what is happening here and now. It is not until adolescents are over 12 years old that children start to exhibit intelligence through their understanding of abstract concepts.

Brief Review of Piaget's Stages of Cognitive Development

Sensorimotor Stage: Children . . .

- are 0–2 years old
- show intelligence through physical interactions and experience
- have limited use of symbols and language

Preoperational Stage: Children . . .

- are 2–7 years old
- show intelligence through strides they make in language development
- are extremely egocentric and have difficulty seeing things from another's perspective
- develop memory and imagination
- do not think logically

Concrete Operational Stage: Children . . .

- are 7–11 years old
- show intelligence through logical and organized thought related to concrete objects
- are less egocentric but still have a tendency to relate new ideas to themselves and their immediate surroundings
- can reverse their thinking through reasoning

Formal Operational Stage: Children . . .

- are 11 years old and older
- show intelligence through logical use of symbols related to abstract concepts
- can hypothesize and use deductive reasoning

According to Piaget (1970), children learn through their own individual actions and exploration. For example, a young child does not learn the meaning of a door by listening to a definition of a door and having someone explain the function of a door. Children learn what a door is by opening and closing the door repeatedly. They may slam the door and laugh or cry as they learn that the door separates two rooms. Creating opportunities for children to learn by doing and to learn by interacting with their environment is extremely important in the young learner classroom. Teachers can bring in realia for students to interact with. For example, if the lesson is about different fruits and vegetables, the teachers can bring in those fruits and vegetables for students to taste. If the lesson is about animals, the teacher can have students bring in their stuffed animal toys or even take a trip to the zoo. Or if students are learning about nature, the teacher could take the students outside to a local park or a nearby beach or forest, depending on what is available in the local environment, in order to allow students to interact with real-life objects connected to the language they are learning.

9. **Children need support and scaffolding by the teacher** Equally important is an understanding of how children learn through social interaction. Vygotsky (1962) found that children construct knowledge through other people, more specifically through interaction with adults or more competent peers. Adults work actively with children in the Zone of Proximal Development (ZPD), which by definition is the difference between the child's capacity to solve problems on her/his own and her/his capacity to solve them with assistance or "scaffolding." The adult's role is very important in a child's learning process (Bruner, 1983; Vygotsky, 1962). In the classroom, the younger the learner, the more important the teacher's role is in scaffolding the learning process. Like Vygotsky, Bruner focused on the importance of language in a child's cognitive development. Bruner carefully studied how parents provided effective scaffolding. Cameron (2001, p. 8) outlines in a concise manner what Bruner's studies found as effective scaffolding techniques used by parents to support a child's learning:

- They made the child interested in the task.
- They simplified the task, often breaking it down into smaller steps.
- They kept the child on track toward completing the task by reminding the child what the goal was.
- They pointed out what was important to do or showed the child other ways of doing parts of the tasks.
- They demonstrated an idealized version of the task.
- They controlled the child's frustration during the task.

Working with a child individually is different from being a teacher with a class full of young learners; however, we can apply these scaffolding principles to devise an effective approach for teaching young learners. Below are suggestions for EYL teachers using the scaffolding techniques listed above. Note that there are five suggestions rather than six because the fourth and fifth points have been combined into one.

Create interest in the task First, before a teacher creates interest in the task, s/he should choose tasks for young learners that cater to their sense of fun, curiosity, and imagination. It is an uphill battle for teachers to try to create interest in a task that is not relevant or enjoyable for their learners. Therefore, teachers should know their learners in depth and should first consider learners' preferred topics or activities. As we discovered in the section on "Characteristics of Young Learners," the following activities can engage learners and keep them interested: TPR, songs, rhymes, chants, stories, videos, games, dramas, and role plays. In addition, tasks that encourage creativity and imagination or those that allow students to express themselves in relation to their lives, families, and friends usually work well. Also, tasks that entail talking or cooperating with their peers can create interest since they love socializing. As mentioned earlier, teachers can spark students' attention through the use of brightly colored visuals and use of audio-visual aids. Most of all, the teacher's own attitude and demeanor can create interest in the task for children. If you are enthusiastic and passionate about the topic and activities, your students will be, too.

Simplify the task Teachers must prepare their lessons by examining every task they will give to students very carefully and consider their level of English language proficiency and cognitive development. Then the teacher needs to break the task down into smaller steps in order to simplify it for children. Sometimes the steps that work for most learners may not work for every learner; therefore, teachers should be ready to break down the task into yet smaller or different steps. Depending on the skill emphasized or the specific activity, the process can take different forms. Refer back to Writing the Story from a Video on p. 30, which showed how a teacher could break down a writing task into smaller steps to help students succeed with the task.

Singing a New Song

Here is another example of simplifying a task for children. If a teacher wants to teach students to sing a song, s/he could use the following steps:

- Introduce the topic of the song and see if the students know anything about it or have likes or dislikes related to it.
- Review the vocabulary words students already know, using visuals or realia.
- Pre-teach the new vocabulary words using visuals or realia.
- Sing the refrain of the song in chunks and have students repeat it. (The refrain is the set of lines in the song that is repeated after each verse. Most songs have a refrain that is repeated multiple times.)

(*Continued*)

- Ask questions about the meaning of the refrain.
- Then teach the tune of the verse using "la la la" instead of the lyrics, but sing the refrain with the lyrics.
- Then teach the verses one by one, always singing the refrain after.
- Ask questions about the meaning of each verse.
- If there are words that rhyme at the end of each line, point them out and practice repeating them when teaching each verse.

Notice that the teacher is breaking down the song in different ways: from topic to isolated words to whole meaning; refrain and verses; tune and lyrics; syllables that rhyme to words to sentences to song. This is how to simplify the task of singing a song by breaking it down into smaller parts.

Keep children on task Part of a teacher's challenge when teaching young learners is to keep them "on task" by reminding them of the purpose or goal. The phrase "on task" is often used by teachers in the United States to indicate that a learner is engaged in a particular activity and working productively toward accomplishing a particular task. Teachers all over the world struggle to find solutions to this common challenge. Inherent in the statement is that each task or activity has a real purpose or goal. If there is no real purpose to the activity, then you will have a difficult time keeping students engaged. Therefore, creating tasks that are not just interesting but also have a purpose or goal is very important when teaching children. Having a reason to use English to accomplish a task will make students focus less on learning and more on using the language to communicate something real. For example, if the goal of the activity is to make a valentine for a classmate using an acrostic poem about her/him, which needs to be ready tomorrow, the activity has a real purpose for the students. The goal is to finish the activity by the next day, which is February 14th or Valentine's Day. This is a fun way to introduce a holiday from a foreign culture while encouraging a real communicative act, which is expressing something nice to a friend.

Sometimes children can get distracted from the activity and get "off task," so it might be necessary to remind them about the purpose or goal and point out important parts of the task. The teacher can do this by first praising and encouraging the student, then reminding her/him of the goal and giving suggestions to help the student accomplish the task. If the child is distracted, then the teacher could say, "Looks great so far! Don't forget! You have to finish it today. Tomorrow is Valentine's Day." Maybe the student has a blank line and is struggling to finish. The teacher could point out how to think of a word for a particular letter

by saying, "I like your poem so far! One line needs a nice word. What are nice words that start with P? Let's think together: pretty, pal, peaceful. Let's look up other P words in our dictionary." Here the teacher is making suggestions and offering a strategy for finding a good word. Keeping children on task is an important part of the scaffolding process, especially since children need reminders for what they are doing and why.

Model the task, including different ways to do the task Always remember to model the task and show students what your expectations are. Particularly with language learning, if students are not given proper models to follow, it is not reasonable to expect them to perform at the desired level. For example, when students are first learning to write, teachers can model the product they expect. In Writing the Story from a Video on p. 30, the teacher models how to write students' ideas into sentences correctly. The students use this as a model to write their own sentences. They have to add more detail and add their own sentences, but they are given guidance directly by the teacher to put the sentences together accurately. In addition to giving clear models, it is important to consider that students learn in different ways; therefore, your modeling should reflect what you know about your learners and the various ways they can accomplish a particular task. This means considering and incorporating different learning styles and multiple intelligences (Gardner, 1983, 1999) into instruction to help students who learn differently to learn to successfully. The sample lesson Meet and Greet on p. 49 shows how to incorporate different learning styles and intelligences and how to accomplish the task of greeting a friend and meeting someone new in different ways. For instance, there is a chant to appeal to musical learners; the activities encourage interpersonal intelligence through interaction and emotional expression; there is a focus on gestures, which appeals to kinesthetic learners; and the activities are introduced with visuals and a video to appeal to visual learners. This approach makes learning more effective for different types of learners, helps develop different kinds of intelligences, and creates an exciting and dynamic classroom environment for young learners of English.

Gardner's Multiple Intelligences

There are eight widely accepted intelligences that were defined by Howard Gardner (1999).

- **Spatial-visual (picture smart):** Children may think in pictures and images and show special abilities in drawing. They may learn through visuals and organize ideas spatially through graphic organizers.

- **Bodily-kinesthetic (body smart):** Children may learn through gestures and manipulatives and enjoy activities that involve movement, dancing, running, jumping, and touching.

- **Musical (music smart):** Children may learn through auditory rhythms and melodies and enjoy singing, chanting, tapping rhythms, and listening activities.

- **Linguistic (word smart):** Children tend to think in words and enjoy reading, writing, discussions, and dialogs. They also have the ability to figure out grammatical patterns.

- **Logical-mathematical (number smart):** Children do not just show a propensity toward math but also tend to be more analytical. They learn through reasoning and enjoy puzzles and experiments.

- **Interpersonal (people smart):** Children like interacting with people and show ability to relate to others. They enjoy discussing and socializing with their peers and cooperative activities.

- **Intrapersonal (self smart):** Children have a tendency to be self-reflective and like to work alone. They may be more in touch with their emotions, feelings, and abilities.

- **Naturalistic (nature smart):** Children have an affinity toward nature, including the environment, plants, and animals. They may enjoy activities that take place outdoors in nature.

Control children's frustration during the task Sometimes young learners can get frustrated with a task. The first step is to take a closer look at what is upsetting the child. Don't automatically assume that the child has a problem. Your first thought should be that the task might be too difficult. See if other students are having the same issue. Then review your planning and see where your scaffolding may need to be altered. This probably means you did not break down the tasks into small enough steps. Or maybe you didn't cater to enough learning styles or intelligences. However, it may not be possible to change the activity at that moment, so the teacher needs to know how to alleviate frustration on the spot. Young learners usually respond well to attention, encouragement, and praise. If the student or students need some help, then the teacher should give them the hints they need to succeed without giving them all the answers. For example, if students are doing a fill-in-the-blank activity, but they can't remember the correct vocabulary word and are getting frustrated or distracted, the teacher can give them two or three choices to select from or give the first letter of the word and make it into a game. If you have established a comfortable environment that is lively and fun, then you can more easily move students from frustration to good feelings. Chapter 8 will discuss classroom management in more detail and focus on how to build a comfortable and controlled classroom that encourages student participation and leads them to success.

How Children Learn Language

This section is an extension of the previous section describing how children learn; it looks specifically at the ways children handle learning language. It describes the important aspects of how children learn their first language (L1) in order to show how to approach teaching children another language. Children:

10. Need a learning environment similar to first language acquisition
11. Learn language through lots of meaningful exposure and practice
12. Do not learn language through explicit grammatical explanations

10. Children need a learning environment similar to first language acquisition As discussed in Chapter 1, there is a popular assumption that starting English classes at younger ages, before the "critical period," will produce better speakers of English because of the ease in which children seem to acquire their first or native language. However, this is not necessarily true. Success in second or foreign language learning also depends on the characteristics of the classroom environment. Children may use similar processes to acquire a first or native language (L1) and a second or foreign language (L2); however, the environment for L1 and L2 acquisition can be quite different (Brewster, Ellis, & Girard, 2004). Krashen (1987) first described the difference between L1 acquisition and L2 learning. Typically, we think of the L1 environment as situated in the real world; therefore, the language used is always authentic and contextualized. Children are highly motivated to learn and use the language because it enables them to meet immediate needs and respond to their surroundings. For example, when a child is hungry and wants milk, s/he will learn the word for milk in order to ask for it. In contrast, the L2 classroom environment tends to have the opposite characteristics—that is, the language used and presented is artificial because it is not based in real life. Traditional L2 classes tend to focus heavily on form and isolated structures rather than a meaningful context in which the message is more important than form. If the language used is not in context and not meaningful to young learners, then it will be difficult to motivate them to participate and learn. Children will be motivated if there is a real purpose or reason to use the language, just like the child learning to use the word "milk" because s/he is hungry. Therefore, teachers should engage learners in purposeful activities that are appropriate for them and that mirror first language acquisition, like storytelling, singing, chanting, talking with each other socially, letter writing, e-mailing, reading recipes, and watching plays, TV shows, and movies.

11. Children learn language through lots of meaningful exposure and practice In the L1 environment, children are surrounded by their native language. It is being spoken and used in various contexts all around the child. This constant source of meaningful exposure to language in authentic contexts helps children acquire language naturally and quickly. However, when learning English as a foreign language, usually the only place and time learners can hear or use English is the classroom. Most EYL classes meet approximately 2–4 hours per week for 30–45 minutes per class (Shin, 2014). Because this is not much time per week of exposure to English, the challenge of the EYL teacher is to create an English-speaking classroom environment and use English as much as possible during the 30–45 minutes s/he has the students. To create an optimal environment for learning English, the input in the classroom needs to be comprehensible and just above the students' current level of English (Krashen, 1981). Teachers can support comprehension of input by using lots of visuals, realia, gestures, and caregiver speech. Caregiver speech refers to the adjustment of language done by a child's caregiver, which for first language acquisition is the parent or grandparent. Teachers can also use caregiver speech to help make language input in the classroom more comprehensible, such as a slower rate of speech, using shorter and simpler sentences, and repeating or rephrasing utterances.

In addition to giving lots of meaningful, comprehensible input, it is important to give students plenty of chances to practice using English in class. This means giving them the opportunity to produce meaningful and comprehensible output (Swain, 1985). Without enough opportunities to produce output, students will not be able to test their hypotheses about how English works. Furthermore, language learners need to have the opportunity to interact with each other and negotiate meaning (Long, 1987). In addition to using lots of purposeful, authentic activities to expose young learners to real English, teachers have to prepare students for the language needed to negotiate meaning (Curtain & Dahlberg, 2010). In other words, teachers should train students to use classroom language in English, such as:

> Why?
> What is this?
> What does _____ mean?
> How do you spell _____?
> I need help.
> Can you help me?
> Could you repeat that?
> What is the answer for number _____?
> The answer is _____.
> How do you say _____ in English?

This can increase the amount of meaningful classroom interaction in English because students will know how to use English for classroom purposes. This will also help EYL teachers create an English-speaking environment in the classroom. Young learners may use their L1 in class, especially when they are engaged in an activity and don't have the language to express themselves. When students use L1, teachers should always recast those utterances in English and encourage students to reformulate their thoughts in English.

12.   Children do not learn language through explicit grammatical explanations Grammatical structures are the building blocks of language, but the approach to teaching grammar should match the way students learn. The approach to teaching grammar should be "learning-centered," which Cameron (2003) describes as ". . . meaningful and interesting, require active participation from learners, and will work with how children learn and what they are capable of learning" (p. 110). As we explored in the previous section, children learn by doing. With language this means that learners need to experience the language through lots of exposure. They will not learn through grammatical explanations; rather, they will gain an understanding of the grammar implicitly through repetition and recycling of the language in different contexts. As Pinter (2006) and Cameron (2001) emphasize, this approach to teaching young learners encourages them to "notice" the grammar rather than being taught the structures explicitly. Pinter explains that teachers should give plenty of meaning-focused input that will help young learners notice grammar. For example, in the sample lesson Meet and Greet on p. 49, the teacher is focusing on greeting someone using the question, "How are you?" and answering, "I'm _____" using "fine," "good," or other words to describe how one feels. S/he is not teaching the grammar explicitly—that questions are formed by reversing the subject and verb. When the teacher focuses students on different ways to express how they are and feel, s/he is getting students to notice the grammatical constructions and use them correctly.

As Cameron (2003) wrote, "children see the foreign language 'from the inside' and try to find meaning in how the language is used in action, in interaction, and with intention, rather than 'from the outside' as a system and form" (p. 107). "In action" means learning by doing; "in interaction" means through social activities; and "with intention" means the activities have a real purpose to use language. Therefore, teachers should expose children to language in authentic and meaningful contexts and use repetition and recycling in order to improve young learners' ability to understand the new language structures and use them correctly.

Summary of 12 Considerations for Teaching Young Learners

CHARACTERISTICS OF YOUNG LEARNERS

CHILDREN ARE . . .	SO TEACHERS SHOULD . . .
1. ENERGETIC AND PHYSICALLY ACTIVE	• Use kinesthetic activities, like Total Physical Response (TPR), Simon Says game
2. SPONTANEOUS AND NOT AFRAID TO SPEAK OUT AND PARTICIPATE	• Use songs, rhymes, chants, and dialogs • Use drama activities that encourage students to be expressive, like the Meet and Greet lesson on pg. 49
3. CURIOUS AND RECEPTIVE TO NEW IDEAS	• Arouse students' curiosity with games, like Mystery Bag • Use topics like exotic animals and plants and international cultures, e.g., food, dress, music, holidays.
4. IMAGINATIVE AND ENJOY MAKE-BELIEVE	• Use role plays and pretend games, like Animal Charades • Use stories that involve fantasy and imagination • Have students use their creativity to make their own pictures or puppets to retell stories • Let students play make-believe by dressing in costumes and role playing characters

5. EASILY DISTRACTED AND HAVE SHORT ATTENTION SPANS	• Make learning fun • Capture students' attention with brightly colored pictures, photos, and posters • Use audio-visuals like songs, TV shows, movie clips, YouTube videos • Move quickly from activity to activity, spending about 5–10 minutes per activity • Use brain breaks
6. EGOCENTRIC AND RELATE NEW IDEAS TO THEMSELVES	• Encourage students to personalize new information and language, like the acrostic name poem • Relate new information and language to students' native culture and local surroundings
7. SOCIAL AND ARE LEARNING TO RELATE TO OTHERS	• Make learning interactive • Incorporate group games and cooperative activities • Use a variety of different kinds of interactions, i.e., S–S in pairs, Sts–Sts in groups, T–S one-on-one, T–Sts with whole class

HOW CHILDREN LEARN

CHILDREN . . .	SO TEACHERS SHOULD . . .
8. LEARN BY DOING AND INTERACTING WITH ENVIRONMENT	• Make learning active • Use realia like food, toys, and other real objects • Organize field trips in the local environment like the zoo, park, beach, or forest
9. NEED OF SUPPORT AND SCAFFOLDING BY THE TEACHER	*Create interest in the task* • Use engaging activities; see nos. 1–8 • Be enthusiastic and passionate about tasks *Simplify the task* • Break tasks down into smaller tasks, like Writing the Story from a Video on p. 30 and Singing a New Song on p. 35–36 *Keep children on task* • Have a real purpose and goal like creating a valentine for a friend which must be completed by Valentine's Day • Focus them on the task by praising, encouraging, reminding, and giving suggestions to students *Model the task, including different ways to do it* • Clearly show your expectations and the ideal end product • Cater to different learning styles, i.e., visual, audio, kinesthetic, and multiple intelligences: spatial-visual, linguistic, logical-mathematical, bodily-kinesthetic, musical, interpersonal, intrapersonal, naturalistic

Control children's frustration
• Assess if the task is too hard
• Break task down into smaller steps
• Give students hints or make a game out of figuring out the right answer
• Create a comfortable classroom atmosphere in which students can succeed

HOW CHILDREN LEARN LANGUAGE	
CHILDREN . . .	*SO TEACHERS SHOULD . . .*
10. NEED A LEARNING ENVIRONMENT SIMILAR TO L1 ACQUISITION	• Use authentic contexts and situations that mirror real life • Use activities with a real purpose and reason to use English, like storytelling, singing, chanting, dialogs, plays, TV shows, movies, letter writing, e-mailing, recipes, etc., that present language in a real context
11. LEARN LANGUAGE THROUGH LOTS OF MEANINGFUL EXPOSURE AND PRACTICE	• Create an English-speaking classroom environment by using English as much as possible • Give plenty of comprehensible input (just above students' current level) • Make input comprehensible by using visuals, realia, gestures, and caregiver speech • Train students to use classroom language in English • Recast any use of L1 in English
12. DO NOT LEARN LANGUAGE THROUGH EXPLICIT GRAMMAR EXPLANATIONS	• Avoid using grammatical terms and rules that young learners will not understand • Help learners "notice" the grammar by repeating and recycling new language, i.e., Meet and Greet lesson

Effective Language Teaching Practices for Young Learners

In this chapter we have outlined the main considerations for teaching young learners English and have given examples of how teachers might apply those considerations to the classroom. Effective teaching practices have been explained through those examples; they can be organized into six main recommendations for teaching young learners English.

Recommendations

Recommendation #1: Use fun and engaging activities Teachers should make sure that their delivery of language instruction connects to the characteristics of young learners and the way children learn. First, activities should be fun for young learners. In addition, students should be engaged and active in the learning process.

Recommendation #2: Students are engaged in a variety of interactions
Teachers should connect learners with a variety of different interactions in the classroom. Students need to have plenty of chances to interact with each other and the teacher. In addition, students should also have a balance of activities that they accomplish individually.

Recommendation #3: Cater to different learning styles and intelligences
Teachers need to also be aware of how they are connecting learners to the language content using different learning styles and multiple intelligences. The examples given combine the three main learning styles, i.e., visual, auditory, and kinesthetic, with multiple intelligences, i.e., spatial, musical, bodily-kinesthetic, logical-mathematical, linguistic, interpersonal, intrapersonal, and naturalistic.

Recommendation #4: Make language learning meaningful and relevant
Teachers need to connect the language they are teaching to real-life contexts that are meaningful and relevant to young learners and related to their local context. Realia as well as authentic situations that have a real purpose should be incorporated into instruction. If possible, students should be able to connect what they are learning to themselves and get a chance to personalize the new content and language.

Recommendation #5: Introduce learners to different cultures It is important to connect learners with different cultures. Teachers should use materials that reflect both home and international cultures. Since young learners will grow up using English as an international language to speak to people from all over the world, it is important to learn about all international cultures, not just English-speaking cultures.

Recommendation #6: Use various teaching strategies that set up learners for success Connecting learners to success is very important when teaching young learners. We want them to build a positive attitude toward English and set them up for success in the English classroom. Some of these strategies can be used in the planning process, such as preparing plenty of comprehensible input, breaking the tasks down into achievable tasks, and modeling expectations. Some of them are general strategies that should be used in class, such as training students to use classroom language in English, building a positive attitude toward learning English, and supporting learners through praise and encouragement.

TEYL Instruction Chart

When developing a teaching approach and planning a lesson, it is important to make the right connections for young learners. Based on the six recommendations earlier, it is helpful to create a checklist for your lesson plans to make sure you are making these connections while planning your lessons. Whether you have a prescribed curriculum or have to create your own lessons from scratch, it can be helpful to analyze your lessons based on these recommendations.

The TEYL Instruction Chart below can help you make sure you are giving effective instruction to your young learners. (Note that in the TEYL Instruction Chart, the last section, based on Recommendation #6, "Connect learners to success," includes only the strategies listed for lesson planning.) The chart can also be used to observe a teacher to assess effectiveness of instruction, in which case you can include the strategies to use while teaching listed in Recommendation #6. Teachers should try to have all six of the recommendations in their lessons. You should be able to check off as many as possible in every lesson or unit plan. If you can check off all of the items, then you are definitely providing effective and dynamic instruction to your young learners.

TEYL INSTRUCTION CHART
Use this chart to analyze your EYL lesson plans.

1. Write YES or NO for each item.
2. If you marked YES, briefly describe which part of your lesson reflects that item.
3. If you marked NO, try to incorporate that item into your lesson plan to make your instruction more effective and dynamic for young learners.

Connect	Yes/No	Describe Your Lesson
1. Connect delivery with characteristics of YLs *(should have both in every lesson)*		
a. Fun b. Active (learn by doing)		
2. Connect learners with a variety of interactions *(should have at least 3 different interactions per lesson)*		
a. Individual work b. Student to student in pairs c. Students to students in groups d. Student to teacher one-on-one e. Teacher to students whole class		

3. Connect learners to different learning styles
(should incorporate at least 5 different learning styles per lesson)

a. Spatial-visual

b. Audio-visual

c. Musical

d. Bodily-kinesthetic

e. Logical-mathematical

f. Linguistic

g. Interpersonal

h. Intrapersonal

i. Naturalistic

4. Connect language with meaningful/relevant contexts
(should have at least 2 per lesson)

a. Use authentic contexts/situations b. Use realia c. Encourage personalization		

5. Connect learners with culture
(should have all 3 per lesson or unit)

a. Learners to own culture b. Learners to target language culture (English-speaking) c. Learners to international cultures		

6. Connect learners to success
(should have all 5 per lesson)

a. Give plenty of comprehensible input b. Use techniques to make input comprehensible (i.e., visuals, realia, gestures, repetition, rephrasing.) c. Break down long or difficult tasks into achievable tasks d. Model tasks and clarify expectations e. No explicit grammar teaching		

Note: This TEYL Instruction Chart can also be used to observe an EYL class to give feedback on effectiveness of instruction.

Designing a Lesson for Young Learners

When designing activities for young learners, it is important to apply all the recommendations within a lesson. Lesson planning will be explained in more detail in Chapter 3; however, it will be helpful to see a lesson as an example of effective instruction for young learners. The basic steps of an effective English language lesson are: warm-up, presentation, practice, application, assessment, and follow-up. The steps are briefly described below:

Title of lesson	Title that indicates the topic/subject/context of the lesson.
Student profile	Your students' age, grade, and proficiency level.
Skills to be emphasized	Indicate which language skills this lesson will focus on building: listening, speaking, reading, or writing.
Language	List the target language structures (i.e., target grammar structures and vocabulary), including classroom language.
Objectives	List the objectives that students should meet by the end of the lesson. Start with "By the end of the lesson, students will be able to. . . ."
Materials	List everything the teacher needs to implement the lesson.
Warm-up	In this step, the teacher prepares students for the listening or reading input. S/he should create interest and connect students to the topic of the lesson by accessing their prior knowledge and experiences. In addition, the teacher should review known vocabulary and teach new language found in the listening or reading input.
Presentation	In this step, the teacher presents the target language structures within a meaningful/communicative context. S/he should give listening or reading input, check comprehension of input, build listening or reading skills, and "teach" target language structures.
Practice	In this step, the teacher prepares post-listening or post-reading activities, which can integrate speaking and writing activities. These activities should be focused on practicing the target language structures in context. They should start with guided exercises and then progress to more independent opportunities for practicing language communicatively.
Application	In this step, the teacher provides opportunities for students to apply new language to real-life contexts. The activities should be authentic and encourage students to use the language communicatively.
Assessment	In this step, the teacher assesses whether students have met the stated objectives for the lesson. It could be another activity, or it could be a description of how the teacher should assess whether the objectives are met during the presentation, practice, and application steps.
Follow-up	In this step, the teacher prepares a follow-up activity, such as homework. It should practice the target language structures in this lesson and/or connect to the next lesson in the unit.

Sample Lesson

Meet and Greet The following is an example of a fun and effective lesson for young learners. The activities and the process for planning the lesson can be applied to any level. The source of input for the lesson is the following dialog:

Dialog:
Lisa and Rosa run into John on the street.
Lisa: Hi, John! How are you? *(Wave hand.)*
John: Hi, Lisa! *(Wave hand.)* I'm fine. How are you?
Lisa: I'm good. This is my friend Rosa.
Rosa: Hi! I'm Rosa. *(Shake hands with John.)*
John: Nice to meet you. *(Shake hands with Rosa.)*
Rosa: Nice to meet you, too!

Meet and Greet	
Student profile	Grades 3–4, beginner level of English language proficiency
Skills to be emphasized	Listening and speaking
Language	Hi, ____! How are you? I'm ____. (fine, good) This is my friend ____. Nice to meet you (too).
Objectives	By the end of this lesson, students will be able to: • Greet a friend • Introduce a new friend • Meet new friends
Materials	Name tags, beret, megaphone (or paper megaphone)

Warm-up step When giving listening or reading input, it is important to warm up students and get them ready for the input. In this example, there is listening input in the form of a dialog. In this warm-up, the teacher creates interest in the dialog by showing different ways to greet people in different countries. Then the teacher breaks the dialog down linguistically by reviewing the known structures and previewing the new expressions. See how the teacher prepares a warm-up activity for the dialog.

Warm-up

Capture their attention	Ask students to show how they greet a friend. Ask them if they know how other cultures greet each other. If children are unfamiliar, demonstrate by shaking hands, bowing, or kissing on the cheek, depending on what is appropriate for your culture. Ask students to pretend to greet each other with a partner. Ask a few pairs to demonstrate in front of the class.
Create interest in topic	Introduce topic: Tell students they will learn how to greet a friend in English and how to meet a new friend.
Review known structures	Ask students to review the expression learned last class for greeting a friend. Write the words on the board as students say them out loud. Students practice in pairs using the different expressions. Hi, how are you? I'm _____. How are you? (fine, good, OK, so-so, great, etc.)

Pre-teach key expressions	**Round the Circle**
	a. Turns to the person on her left saying
	    This is my friend _____. *(fill in name of student on left)*
	    Check comprehension of the phrase, allow students to use L1.
	b. If you meet someone new, you can say "Nice to meet you." (Let students translate the meaning in L1 to check comprehension.) Then have students practice this expression in a chant with claps on a beat. Repeat it until students can say it fluently.
	    Nice to meet you. Nice to meet you, too!
	    (clap) (clap) *(clap)* _____ *(clap)*
	c. Now go around the circle and start again "This is my friend Linda." Cue students to chant, "Nice to meet you!" Then Linda chants, "Nice to meet you, too!" Go around the circle student by student.

In this warm-up, the teacher did all six recommendations:

Recommendation #1: Use fun and engaging activities

- The teacher made learning new language fun by using a chant and clapping.
- Students were actively involved in showing how to greet each other with a partner.

Recommendation #2: Engage students in a variety of interactions

- Student to student in pairs: Students demonstrated how to greet one another in pairs, using body language and reviewing the material from last class.

- Teacher to students, whole class: The teacher introduced the topic and pre-taught the key expression with students as a whole class.

Recommendation #3: Cater to different learning styles and intelligences

- Spatial-visual: When reviewing known structures, the teacher wrote the words on the board.
- Musical: Students chanted the key expressions with clapping.
- Bodily-kinesthetic: Students showed through body language and gestures how to greet someone. They were moving their bodies to clap with the chant.
- Linguistic: When reviewing known structures, the teacher wrote the expressions on the board. Students could see the grammatical structure with the blank, which can be helpful for noticing the pattern.
- Interpersonal: Students demonstrated greeting each other in pairs.

Recommendation #4: Make language learning meaningful and relevant

- The teacher used an authentic situation with a real purpose: meet and greet.
- The teacher encouraged personalization of the content by asking students to show how they greet a friend.

Recommendation #5: Introduce learners to different cultures

- Students showed how they greet in their own culture.
- Students showed what they know about greeting in other cultures. If the students do not know, then the teacher demonstrates how to greet in other cultures.

Recommendation #6: Use various teaching strategies that set up learners for success

- The teacher used body gestures to aid in comprehension.
- The teacher broke the task down into manageable steps by reviewing the known vocabulary and expressions and teaching the new expressions.
- When the teacher was pre-teaching the new expressions, she modeled them and had students repeat them after her.
- The teacher avoided the use of grammatical terms and rules that learners would not understand.

As seen in this example of a warm-up step, the teacher was able to apply all six recommendations in different ways. When planning a lesson, even in the warm-up or introduction, it is important to apply as many of the recommendations as possible.

Presentation step   The next step in an effective young learner lesson is to present the new language input. The presentation step usually gives some listening or reading input to learners. In the example here, there is a dialog being presented as listening input. The dialog is in a meaningful and communicative context that will expose learners to real language. In the following activities, the teacher will do a series of fun activities to check comprehension of the input and "teach" the new language.

Presentation	
Presentation of new language in context	Play a video of the dialog or demonstrate the dialog with two volunteers (prepare volunteers in advance). If you have two volunteers, have name tags for all three characters, so students can follow the dialog easily.
Prepare for group work	Break students into groups of three. Hand out name tags with John, Lisa, and Rosa to stick on students. Tell students to choose one role and put that name tag on.
Comprehension check	**Miming Activity** a. Tell students to act out the dialog using only gestures, without speaking out loud. Point out instructions on a handout or PPT slide (see p. 53). b. Model the first line of Lisa before students begin. Wave hand, smiling, and gesture "How are you?" shrugging your shoulders and hands. Then tell students to begin. c. Ask one group to demonstrate their mime of the dialog. d. Ask students to show their gestures for each line of the dialog.
Demonstrate correct use of language	**Silent Movie Activity** a. Show students an example of a silent movie from an actual silent movie, a clip of a YouTube video, or by demonstration with the picture on p. 53 of the silent movie text screen. b. Tell students to copy their lines on paper like the silent movie text screen on the handout or PPT. Each student should have two lines on two pieces of paper. Check to see if each student has the right lines on two pieces of paper.

c. Tell students to practice the dialog with no speaking, mouthing the words using an exaggerated movement with the lips. Hold up the paper with the line.

    i. Model the part of Lisa, mouthing "Hi, John! How are you?" with your lips and no sound. Hold up the sign that says "Hi, John! How are you?"

    ii. Tell students to begin their silent movie.

    iii. Have one group demonstrate their silent movie.

    iv. Tell students to change roles. Take off name tag and give it to the person on your left. Model it. Then give that person your two lines. Now do the silent movie again. Tell students to change roles again. Take off name tag and give it to the person on their left.

MIMING ACTIVITY

ACT OUT DIALOG.
NO SPEAKING.
USE ONLY FACE AND BODY.

SILENT MOVIE ACTIVITY

WRITE YOUR LINES ON PAPER

ACT OUT DIALOG.

1. SHOW YOUR LINE.
2. ONLY MOVE YOUR LIPS.
3. NO SPEAKING.

Photo Researchers/Getty Images

In the presentation step, all six recommendations were applied:

Recommendation #1: Use fun and engaging activities

- The Miming and Silent Movie Activities were fun, engaging, and kept the students active. These are examples of activities that incorporate drama into teaching English to young learners.

Recommendation #2: Engage students in a variety of interactions

- Student to student in groups: Students did the miming and silent movie activities in groups of three.
- Teacher to students, whole class: The teacher presented the dialog to the whole class and gave demonstrations of the activities to the whole class.

Recommendation #3: Cater to different learning styles and intelligences

- Spatial-visual: The teacher used the name tags as visual cues for students to know their roles. In addition, she gave a sample of a silent movie on a video to aid in comprehension of the activity and engage visual learners.
- Bodily-kinesthetic: The Miming Activity was completely based on movement and gestures to show comprehension of the main idea of the dialogue. Then the Silent Movie Activity focused students on the movement of their mouths to pronounce the words correctly.
- Linguistic: The focus on the Silent Movie Activity was to practice pronunciation without actually speaking out loud. This focused students on how they use their mouth to form words in English.
- Interpersonal: All of the activities in the presentation encouraged students to communicate in groups, so students were practicing their interpersonal communication skills.

Recommendation #4: Make language learning meaningful and relevant

- The whole context of greeting a friend, introducing a new friend, and meeting a new friend was presented through the dialog. It is an authentic situation with a real purpose.

Recommendation #5: Introduce learners to different cultures

- Students practiced how to meet and greet friends using body language and gestures from an English speaking culture. The Miming Activity emphasized the body language and focused students on that aspect of the communication that is based on culture.

- The teacher broke the task down into manageable steps by first checking comprehension of the main idea using the Miming Activity.
- The Silent Movie Activity encouraged students to copy down just two sentences from their role in the dialog and mouth those words. Then they got a chance to read the lines of the other two roles when they switched name tags.

Practice and application steps

In the practice and application steps, students have a chance to practice using the target structures in context. Young learners need lots of repetition, but too much repetition can be boring for them. The Movie Stars activity is a fun way to encourage students to practice the language without getting bored. In addition, the teacher incorporates different cultures into the lesson to create interest and build intercultural competence.

Practice	
Controlled practice	**Movie Stars Activity** Tell students that they are movie stars and will speak out now. Tell students to switch to their original roles. Have students play the characters in different ways: nervously fearfully angrily happily laughing naturally Point out the handout or PPT slide and tell students that you will be the movie director and give the actors directions. Tell them to do the scene nervously. Then interrupt them by saying, "Cut! Cut! No, that's not right. I want to see more emotion. Do it with anger this time! ACTION!" You can wear a beret and roll a piece of paper into a pretend megaphone. Walk around the room to listen to the students complete the activity and assess whether they are speaking correctly.
Independent practice	**Performance Without Script** Have each group demonstrate some of their movie scenes without looking at the dialog. Usually angrily, happily, and laughing are fun to watch.

Application

Cross-cultural application	Have students demonstrate the dialog naturally by memory. Ask students to show the different ways to meet and greet people in different cultures using their bodies. Write the words on the board to reinforce the language. Then ask students to do the dialog with the correct gestures in their country's culture and at least two other countries' cultures:
	
	    waving hands
	    shaking hands
	    hugs
	    kiss on one or two cheeks
	    bowing

MOVIE STARS ACTIVITY

YOU ARE ACTORS IN A MOVIE.
LISTEN TO THE MOVIE DIRECTOR.

ACT OUT DIALOG.
SAY YOUR LINES.
DO IT WITH EMOTION.

NERVOUSLY
FEARFULLY
ANGRILY
HAPPILY
LAUGHING
NATURALLY

In the practice and application steps, all six recommendations were applied:

Recommendation #1: Use fun and engaging activities

■ The Movie Stars Activity was very funny, and students enjoyed speaking out using different expressions. Although the activity was repetitive, it was not boring due to the use of drama.

Recommendation #2: Engage students in a variety of interactions

- Student to student in groups: Students did the Movie Stars Activity and dialog practice in groups of three.

Recommendation #3: Cater to different learning styles and intelligences

- Interpersonal: These activities promoted interpersonal communication that also included emotional expression.

Recommendation #4: Make language learning meaningful and relevant

- These activities used an authentic situation with a real purpose: meet and greet.
- In addition, it prompted students to use different gestures for meeting and greeting people to make the use of English as an international language more authentic.

Recommendation #5: Introduce learners to different cultures

- Students practiced how to meet and greet friends using body language and gestures from an English speaking culture as well as other cultures.

Recommendation #6: Use various teaching strategies that set up learners for success

- The teacher used an activity that got students to practice a dialog repeatedly, which will help learners remember the language outside of class.

Assessment and follow-up steps During the presentation, practice, and application steps, the assessment of the students is included.

Assessment	
Monitoring small group work	**Silent Movie Monitoring** The teacher goes around the room to check whether students wrote their lines correctly. **Movie Stars Monitoring** The teacher walks around listening to the students do the dialog in groups to evaluate whether they are able to say the dialog correctly.
Group assessment	Having groups demonstrate their movie scenes is another informal way of assessing the success of the students in the activity.
Follow-up	
Homework	Tell students to write down the full dialog in their notebook. They can use any culture and write instructions for the characters in parentheses.

Hopefully, by the end of the lesson you have set your learners up for success. After showing comprehension of and practicing the dialog multiple times, students should be able to complete the homework assignment easily and even have fun writing the dialog using gestures from any country of their choice.

■ Teacher to Teacher

Effective Approaches for Teaching Young Learners

This chapter described effective approaches for teaching young learners. Of course, different teachers from around the world may apply these approaches in their own unique way. Below are excerpts from an online course discussion in which teachers from around the world describe the most important principles for TEYL according to their experience and local context. Think about how their perspectives compare to your teaching context.

First, many teachers addressed the topic of creating an English-speaking environment in the classroom. Read about one teacher describing her selective use of L1.

> **"**In some countries, students are exposed to English and have the opportunity to use it **only** in the classroom, sometimes this being just 3-4 hours a week; therefore I think the teacher must make an effort to use English all the time. The teacher is the principal source of useful comprehensible input, so we should make the most of it; the more time we spend speaking in English in the classroom, the better. However, we should consider that in some cases using L1 can be useful, specially when we want to make sure students understood instructions or explanations, or to compare certain features of the native language and target language in order to discuss some common errors or to review how well students understood certain grammar structures. Of course before resorting to L1 we can always try using visual aids, mime, gestures and expressions to convey meaning. Personally, as my partners have mentioned, I use L1 when my students are too anxious or blocked, or when I look at their faces and I see they are at a complete loss and they are not following me.**"**
>
> —*Alina Gil, Primary English Teacher, Uruguay*

Another teacher describes exactly how she builds communication in English with her young learners from the first day of class.

"One of the most important principles of teaching young learners is using English from the first day of studying. Why is it so important? First, it's building an English speaking environment in the class. I remember the children's reaction when I said for the first time, "Good morning, children. Sit down, please." They were shocked and surprised that I didn't speak Russian as they were used to doing with their other teachers. I expected that. In my country when the lesson starts, the children usually stand up and say "hello" to their teacher nodding their heads. So, after "Good morning, children," I nodded my head and showed with my hands that they might sit down. They understood my gestures. YLs are very receptive and my students accepted the silent rule to use only English in the lesson. In order to help them I use gestures. I started my first lesson with presenting classroom language, the words that are often used in the class and very helpful for the students. For example, "Can I ask you?" "What does _____ mean?" "How can I translate the word _____?" After drilling I put paper with classroom language on the walls and my YLs can refer to them any time because children will forget language unless it is repeated."

—*Tatiana Pak, Primary English Teacher, Kyrgyzstan*

Some teachers may feel that it is impossible to avoid using L1 in their English class.

"I agree with the majority of you when you talk about using L1 in the English class. Often we cannot avoid the translation of the words and their meanings into our native language especially with the beginners. The greeting, farewell and simple instructions should be in English only, it goes without saying. Gestures and mime is a usual thing in the classes with young learners, and the kids like them very much. As for grammar, it should be only in L1, because pupils are not very good at grammar in their own language. In Kazakhstan all the pupils study Kazakh and Russian from the first grade, which are completely different languages. One of the main reason of using L1 is to make the understanding clearly and accessible."

—*Sholpan Alimova, Primary English Teacher, Kazakhstan*

However, in response to teachers who do not believe they can create a completely English-speaking environment in class, a teacher in Peru described her experience teaching Quechua-speaking children in her local context.

"Once I had the experience of teaching in a small community in the country side of my city (Cusco in Peru). It was very challenging getting into a class where the kids spoke just Quechua which is the native language in the Andes of South America. Unfortunately I don't speak any Quechua, so the first day of class was frustrating for me. I thought I couldn't deal with this!!! But luckily we are teachers, so what I did was first drawing kids on the board giving them names. So I started teaching them greetings, and some other expressions and let me tell you that every single class was so challenging because I had to create games and chants just using English. I did not speak Quechua and the kid did not speak Spanish. At the end I could see that it is possible to create an English environment in any circumstances."

—*Cecilia Ponce de Leon, Primary English Teacher, Peru*

This chapter also described the characteristics of young learners and how they learn; for example, children are social learners who are quite dependent on the teacher for scaffolding and assistance. A teacher from Oman describes these characteristics of young learners while also illustrating how central the teacher is to young children and how much students try to get the attention of the teacher.

"First of all I can say that my YLs in Oman are very sociable. They are really willing to talk to new colleagues and even teachers without feeling shy. So I think this helps them develop their personality and be confident. They are also physically active that they would help a teacher carrying her/his materials, books or even fetching anything a teacher needs. In addition, I can say that they are so curious, spontaneous and willing to participate that they would raise their voices saying "Teacher!" just to answer. They also come to me as I enter the class to show me their homework or their achievement. I can see all these characteristics in my previous students and my current students as well. So I can say that these are the common characteristics of YLs in Oman."

—*Asma Al Dhahab, Primary English Teacher, Oman*

Building a good relationship between a teacher and young learners can be based on the local context. Read how one teacher in Korea found a way to build a better rapport with her young learners.

"I have been teaching in an elementary school for years and I have found that to engage my students (9–12 years) in elementary school, one important thing is to establish a close rapport with each student in my classes. I realize the more students like me, the more they like English. When the students were 11 or 12 years old and the number of them was over 30, I often felt irritated by some mischievous boys and I yelled at them to be quiet and pay attention to me, but they were always the same after some seconds. The first year of the elementary school was a catastrophe to both the students and me. However, I started trying to have a close relationship and calling their names instead of by their student number. I could make them engaged in the activities more and listen to me in the respectful way, though all of the students were not changed suddenly. Reflecting on the last two years in the elementary school, I found that I should make them like me to make them like English"

—*Eun Young Kim, Primary English Teacher, South Korea*

It is clear from the voices of primary school teachers around the world that a teacher needs to be confident, versatile, and creative to keep children engaged in learning English. Teachers need to be as active as their young learners in this process. This teacher from Mauritius expresses the importance of the teacher's effort and attitude in engage young learners.

> **"**. . . a lively class of YLs depends much on the liveliness of the teacher. It is up to us to deliver the goods by providing all relevant materials, using appropriate language and different ways to keep the students active and participating. What is more important is the teacher's own attitude towards speaking English at all times with the students, be it in or out of class.**"**

> —*Anitah Aujayeb, Primary English Teacher, Mauritius*

Finally, it seems appropriate to end this chapter with words from a teacher in Tunisia who wrote a poem that is a letter to teachers of young learners everywhere. It summarizes the main points from this chapter in a creative and inspiring way.

You Are the Kids' Best Companion

Dear teacher,
Young learners eagerly tend to thrive
Into a foreign language they need to dive
They are naturally zealous, curious, energetic, and alive
And sometimes are hyper and loud as if in a beehive
You should scaffold them all along the drive,
Provide them with adequate tools to survive
And consider the appropriate ways you should contrive

Dear teacher,
Young learners are fragile and vulnerable
With affection and care you should handle
With them into language learning you will travel
To stroll around their world that is not ample
But cozy, overwhelming and still humble
Use your magic to make them twinkle
And make their learning setting real and meaningful

Dear Teacher,
Young learners are individuals with different smarts
Some use their brains, others prefer to see their targets
Some favor auditory styles, others fancy kinesthetic arts
Consider these differences when designing lesson parts
And make your objectives clear as if playing darts
Engage them in activities and assign purposeful projects
Make of their performance a shiny surface that reflects
Your successful mission to embrace those sweet hearts

Chaouki M'kaddem , Tunisia

■ Chapter Summary

To Conclude

Characteristics of young learners It is important to consider the characteristics of young learners to give effective English instruction at the primary level. Harness their energy, spontaneity, imagination, curiosity, and social tendencies to make your classroom an exciting and dynamic place to learn English.

Learning by doing Children learn by interacting with their physical environment. They learn by doing.

Teacher scaffolding Children learn through scaffolding by adults. Teachers can support young learners and apply effective scaffolding techniques to their classroom instruction.

Meaningful input The EFL classroom environment for young learners should resemble characteristics of first language acquisition, such as language that is highly contextualized and used for real communication. Teachers should give meaningful and comprehensible input and provide lots of opportunities for meaningful practice and interaction.

Effective instruction Effective instruction in the EFL classroom should include activities that are meaningful and relevant to young learners, engage them in a variety of interactions, cater to different learning styles and intelligences, and introduce them to different cultures.

■ Over to You

Discussion Questions

1. What are the characteristics of young learners that can make teaching them fun and exciting as well as challenging?
2. How do children learn? How does that affect how teachers should approach teaching English?
3. What are the key elements to successful English teaching in the young learner classroom?
4. Scenario: You are an English teacher in a primary school. Your supervisor comes to visit your classroom and is surprised to see your students out of their seats playing games and having fun.

In addition, some parents have complained that their children's English homework looks like an art project and they aren't really learning English. The supervisor thinks that you are not doing your job and wants to see more grammar and vocabulary exercises. Given this situation, how would you explain why you are teaching this way?

5. In your opinion, are there cultural differences in the approaches to teaching English to young learners? Are the characteristics of young learners different from your experience? Are the approaches suggested in this chapter different from the approaches used to teach primary students in your country? How would you incorporate the principles and approaches described in this chapter into your classroom situation?

Lesson Planning

Use the TEYL Instruction Chart on pg. 46–47 to analyze a lesson plan and see if it is providing effective instruction for young learners. Choose a lesson for young learners from your curriculum that you designed or that you were given. You could even find a lesson for YLs online that you are interested in using. Then, using the chart, label YES or NO for each item. For all the items you labeled NO, try to revise your lesson to be more effective for young learners.

Write About It

Philosophy for TEYL: Now that you have read about all the characteristics of young learners, how children learn, how children learn a foreign language, and the application of all these considerations to the EYL classroom, think about what is most important when developing an approach for TEYL. Next, think about how you can apply all of these concepts to your local context and country. Incorporate aspects of what you have learned in this chapter with your own experience, knowledge, and local context, and write your own 1–2 page philosophy for teaching English as an international language to young learners. You can revisit your philosophy for TEYL at the end of the book and compare your thoughts.

■ Resources and References

Print Publications

Curtain, H., & Dahlberg, C. A. (2010). *Languages and children— Making the match: New languages for young learners,* 4th ed. Boston, MA: Pearson.

Linse, C. (2005). *Practical English language teaching: Young learners.* New York, NY: McGraw-Hill International.

Nunan, D. (2011). *Teaching English to young learners.* Anaheim, CA: Anaheim University Press.

Pinter, A. (2006). *Teaching young language learners.* Oxford, UK: Oxford University Press.

Shin, J. K. (2014). Teaching young learners in ESL and EFL settings. In M. Celce-Murcia, D. Brinton, & M. A. Snow (Eds.), *Teaching English as a second or foreign language,* 4th ed. Boston, MA: National Geographic Learning/Cengage Learning.

Useful Web Sites

British Council, Teaching English: www.teachingenglish.org.uk /try/teaching-kids

British Council, LearnEnglish Kids: http://learnenglishkids .britishcouncil.org/en/

International Reading Association (IRA), ReadWriteThink: www .readwritethink.org

U.S. Department of State's Office of English Language Programs, Resource page: http://americanenglish.state.gov /materials-teaching-english

Young Learners & Teenagers Special Interest Group of the International Association of Teachers of English as a Foreign Language: http://www.yltsig.org/

References

Asher, J. J. (1977). *Learning another language through actions: The complete teacher's guide book.* Los Gatos, CA: Sky Oaks Productions.

Brewster, J., Ellis, G., & Girard, D. (2004). *The primary English teacher's guide.* London: Penguin.

Bruner, J. (1983). *Child's talk: Learning to use language.* Oxford, UK: Oxford University Press.

Cameron, L. (2001). *Teaching languages to young learners.* Cambridge, UK: Cambridge University Press.

Cameron, L. (2003). Challenges for ELT from the expansion in teaching children. *ELT Journal, 57*(2), 105–112.

Coltrane, B. (2003). Working with young English language learners: Some considerations. Washington, DC: Center for Applied Linguistics. (ERIC Document Reproduction Service No. EDO-FL-03-01)

Curtain, H., & Dahlberg, C. A. (2010). *Languages and children— Making the match: New languages for young learners,* 4th ed. Boston, MA: Pearson.

Gardner, H. (1983). *Frames of mind: The theory of multiple intelligences.* New York, NY: Basic Books.

Gardner, H. (1999). Are there additional intelligences? The case for naturalist, spiritual, and existential intelligences. In J. Kane (Ed.), *Education, information and transformation* (pp. 111–131). Englewood Cliffs, NJ: Prentice Hall.

Haas, M. (2000). Thematic, communicative language teaching in the K-8 classroom. *ERIC Digest.* EDO-FL-00-04. Retrieved August 29, 2004, from http://www.cal.org/resources/ digest/0004thematic.html

Krashen, S. D. (1981). *Second language acquisition and second language learning.* New York, NY: Pergamon Press.

Krashen, S. D. (1987). *Principles and practice in second language acquisition.* Upper Saddle River: NJ: Prentice-Hall International.

Long, M. H. (1987). Native speaker/non-native speaker conversation in the second language classroom. In M. H. Long & J. C. Richards (Eds.), *Methodology in TESOL: A Book of Readings* (pp. 339–354). New York, NY: Newbury House/Harper and Row.

Nissani, H. (1990). Early childhood programs for language minority students. Washington, DC: National Clearinghouse for Bilingual Education. (ERIC Document Reproduction Service No. ED337033)

Piaget, J. (1970). *The science of education and the psychology of the child.* New York, NY: Oxford.

Pinter, A. (2006). *Teaching young language learners.* Oxford, UK: Oxford University Press.

Read, C. (1998, April). The challenge of teaching children. *English Teaching Professional, 7,* 8–10.

Read, C. (2003, July). Is younger better? *English Teaching Professional, 28:* 5-7.

Scott, W., & Ytreberg, L. H. (1990). *Teaching English to children.* London, UK: Longman.

Shin, J. K. (2006). Ten helpful ideas for teaching English to young learners. *English Teaching Forum, 44*(2), 2–7, 13.

Shin, J. K. (2014). Teaching young learners in ESL and EFL settings. In M. Celce-Murcia, D. Brinton, & M. A. Snow (Eds.), *Teaching English as a second or foreign language,* 4th ed. Boston, MA: National Geographic Learning/Cengage Learning.

Slatterly, M., & Willis, J. (2001). *English for primary teachers.* Oxford, UK: Oxford University Press.

Swain, M. (1985). Communicative competence: Some roles of comprehensible input and comprehensible output in its development. In Gass, S. M. & Madden, C. G. (Eds.), *Input in second language acquisition* (pp. 235–253). Rowley, MA: Newbury House.

Vygotsky, L. (1962). *Thought and language.* Cambridge, MA: MIT Press.

3 Contextualizing Instruction: Creating Thematic Units and Lesson Plans

■ Getting Started

This chapter will help you contextualize and organize your instruction. It will focus on how to contextualize and organize instruction and create meaningful activities that help link the classroom with the students' worlds at home and in school. It will consider long-term and short-term planning and identify ways that you, working with or without an assigned textbook, can organize instruction for the school year, for several class periods (into units), and for daily lesson plans. You will learn ideas for selecting interesting themes and organizing them into thematic units that will help children to extend their knowledge of both language and content. In addition, you will also learn how to plan for daily lessons within that unit and considerations for adapting, creating, and evaluating activities for your lessons.

Think About It

Think about a successful class for young learners that you have observed or taught. What do you think made it so successful? Consider the theme or topic (in the story, song, poem, or other text), the kinds of activities, the order in which the activities were presented, and the ways in which the children were involved. Were there any opportunities for children to be creative? Was a textbook used? If so, were the activities interesting and relevant to YLs?

KidStock/Getty Images

Now think of a class where you saw bored or confused children. What do you think went wrong? Was it the theme? Was it the activities? Was it the way the lesson was organized?

What are some considerations in choosing themes for young learner lessons and units?

What are some things to consider in planning which activities to include? (Think back to the characteristics of effective lessons for YLs discussed in Ch. 2.)

Discovery Activity

Textbook Analysis

Look at any EYL student textbook. It can be a textbook published by a major publisher or one developed by your ministry of education. A good textbook should have interesting themes that connect several hours of lessons into units. While you may need to adapt the units and create individual lesson plans for use with the textbook, some of the organization should be provided. Fill in the sheet below and then consider how well the instruction has been planned in the textbook.

TEXTBOOK ANALYSIS SHEET

Title of Text:
Author(s):
Publisher:
Date of Publication:

Overall Plan of the Book

Look at the Scope and Sequence to provide the following information. (The Scope and Sequence is usually in the beginning of the textbook. It lists all the themes or titles of all the units, the grammar and vocabulary in each unit, etc.) The Scope and Sequence should give you an idea of what **the long-term plan** for the school year is. If there is no Scope and Sequence, look at the Table of Contents or through the pages of the text to identify the major themes of the units.

Unit Themes for the Book (animals, sports, foods, friends, etc.):

Sample Unit

Now look at any unit in the Scope and Sequence or look through pages of a sample unit and identify the language and other objectives.

Language Objectives
    Language Functions (identifying animals and where they live, describing what sports children like to play, etc.):

    Grammar Patterns:

    Vocabulary:

    Language Skills (listening, speaking, reading, writing):

Other Objectives
    (academic/creative-thinking skills, learning strategies, content knowledge, etc.):

Comparing Two Sample Units

Now look through two sample chapters to see what kinds of activities (**the short-term plan**) are included and the order in which the activities are planned for the following:

Activities Presented (in order) in Unit X
    (list them here in the order of the unit):

Activities Presented (in order) in Unit XX
    (list them here in order):

Overall Evaluation of the Student Textbook:

Based on your review of the textbook, answer these questions:
    Do you think it is well planned? Why?

    Are the themes ones that children will find interesting? Why or why not?

    Are there a number of different activities focusing on different language skills (listening, speaking, reading, writing), different grouping strategies (pairs, small groups, whole class), and appealing to different learning styles or multiple intelligences? Give some examples of the variety of activities.

    Are they well organized?

    What changes might you recommend?

As you read through this chapter, think back to the textbook you reviewed and how you would adapt it or add to it for children you may be teaching.

■ Theory, Planning and Application

Contextualized Instruction

Although the processes of learning a first and second language are quite similar, the contexts in which these occur are very different (Brewster, Ellis, & Girard, 2004). Children learn their first language (their mother tongue) in an environment in which they have authentic or real reasons to use the language; they are surrounded by its use and they are highly motivated to use it. In the classroom with the second language, however, there is much less reason to use the language or to be motivated to do so.

The classroom should encourage learners to use the language to express their feelings and ideas and to have the opportunity to communicate and interact, using the language with you and the other learners. We want our learners to use their knowledge of the world, to bring what they know into the class, and to build our instruction around that (Curtain & Dahlberg, 2010). We need to provide reasons for children to use English, to motivate them and engage them, and to connect the classroom with their home, neighborhood, and community. Genesee (2000) points out that "instruction for beginning language learners, in particular, should take into account their need for context-rich, meaningful environments" (p. 2), providing settings that foster communication, settings in which new language is understandable and familiar language becomes more memorable and useful. Very young learners who are at Piaget's stage of concrete operations may not be able to understand abstract concepts even in their own language, unless the teacher provides a concrete, meaningful context.

An effective, contextualized EYL class involves:

- Creating opportunities to use English with a meaningful purpose
- Building on the knowledge and skills learned through the first language
- Linking the EYL class with home, community, and local environments
- Organizing instruction around themes that relate to children's experiences at home and in other classes
- Providing a variety of ways to make English comprehensible; for example, through actions, gestures, games, pictures, and objects
- Keeping the language level of the activity at a comprehensible level, just above their current proficiency level
- Focusing children's attention on the game, song, story, or other activity, rather than directly on the language
- Organizing the classroom to facilitate communication among the children
- Developing classroom routines to keep communication in English (for example, at key points in the lesson, such as beginning the class, moving from one activity to another, giving directions, ending the class)

The use of an engaging theme to organize instruction around a meaningful context can also help make the language understandable or comprehensible. As discussed in Chapter 2, children can understand something slightly above their current language level or level of comprehension—what Krashen (1982; Krashen & Terrell, 1995) refers to as comprehensible input—because of the context, the organization around themes, and the various supports that link language with actions, such as pictures, gestures, role plays, games, or finger plays. As Krashen and Terrell (1995) state, "Language is best taught when it is being used to transmit messages, not when it is explicitly taught for conscious learning" (p. 55). While they were primarily referring to older learners, this is especially true for young learners, who have few opportunities to use the language to communicate meaningfully outside of class.

There are a lot of ways in which a classroom can contextualize instruction: bright and lively posters or pictures related to the theme of the lesson; displays of children's drawings, stories, or other work; realia (objects related to the theme or story); a storytelling corner where children can sit on the floor close to the teacher while s/he reads or tells a story; maybe even special centers to which children can move for a new activity.

The most important support is to have carefully planned and organized instruction, with clear directions and classroom management strategies. It is very helpful to develop routines for starting the class, moving to new activities, and ending the class.

You can also support them during the activities by providing them with models before doing an activity and assist them when they are having difficulty expressing themselves. As discussed in Chapter 2, training students to use classroom language in English also helps to keep the class in English.

You may have noticed when you reviewed the EYL textbook that the authors had tried to find meaningful themes around which to organize the units in the textbook. They didn't just provide a series of activities that were unrelated. But were the themes likely to be engaging to young learners? What makes an effective theme?

Thematic Instruction

The Importance of Content In his analysis of the key elements in model early foreign language programs in the United States, Gilzow (2002) found that "a focus on content" was a major feature, with programs using content to link language learning "to the immediate context or to specific lessons in the regular curriculum [classes other than the language class]" (p. 1).

Content-centered, content-related, content-enriched, or content-based instruction (CBI), also referred to as content and language integrated learning (CLIL), is a way to contextualize language instruction by integrating it with other learning, especially what is being taught and learned in other classes. It provides opportunities to reinforce the academic skills and knowledge learned in other classes, and draws on topics and activities to bring the experiences of learning another language to those academic content areas (Crandall, 1994, 1998; Curtain & Dahlberg, 2010). It connects the English curriculum with other parts of the students' academic lives. It can also make the EYL class much more interesting. If we are teaching about wild animals, learning about where they live (geography) and what they eat (science) will connect the English class to what they have been learning in other classes. We can grow beans in a pot when reading *Jack and the Beanstalk* or create experiments with magnets in our EYL classes (science). Students can even plan a simple budget for a class party and calculate the money needed to buy cake and juice (math). There is so much content that can be used as the basis for motivating children to learn English and to support what they are learning in their other classes.

While integrating academic content with English is important for all learners, it becomes increasingly important as children get older, especially if at some point they will need to study a subject through the medium of English. Students cannot develop academic knowledge and skills without access to the language in which that knowledge is embedded, discussed, constructed, or evaluated. Nor can they acquire academic language skills in a context devoid of content (Crandall, 1994). Besides, as Mohan (1986) has reminded us, in the real world, people learn language and content simultaneously, as can young learners in EYL classes.

The Value of Local and National Culture
But not all content has to be drawn from other classes or subjects. Some of it can relate to children's daily lives or the lives of their families: the jobs their parents have, the ways their families spend leisure time or live a typical day, the kinds of food they eat.

Rahma Abdul Rahman, Primary English Teacher, Maldives

"Themes selected based on our folk stories, tourism, and fisheries create a variety of opportunities for the teachers to take students for field trips, carry out interviews with people, write reports, or draw and name what they saw and also do presentations. They can create leaflets or booklets based on their findings. Students can explore and create knowledge and present it to the class. Such learning becomes important because it creates meaning, interest, and also they are learning by doing."

We can draw on local and national culture for content in the EYL class. It can be a place where local traditions, stories, folktales, games, customs, and holidays are included and children's experiences in their own language are linked to their new one: English. They can learn to talk about their culture in English and share these experiences with other English speakers. By showing pictures or videos of people or including stories about holidays or traditions in other parts of the world, the EYL class can also broaden children's cultural knowledge and experiences.

Billy Hustace/Getty Images

The Importance of Themes

A theme is a "big idea" that connects language with content and culture (Curtain & Dahlberg, 2010). We usually refer to a theme as the focus of a unit that integrates several lessons, and a topic as the focus of an individual lesson, but the terms are sometimes used interchangeably. Well-chosen themes are the basis of effective contextualization, because they help to create a meaningful context, where the focus is on something of interest, rather than the language itself. They can help to make language learning relevant and provide a purpose for learning and communicating. They can also create a rich context that motivates language learning and links the EYL class with the children's other classes and their world outside school. They can create a context for bringing a variety of activities into the language class, including stories, games, projects, and tasks, and provide real reasons for children to use English to communicate their thoughts, feelings, and experiences. They also provide a context for creative thinking and the use of English for academic learning, something that is often missing in language classes where the focus is only on language, not on the use of that language to express ideas through the language. Themes can help children to keep using the English that they know and to build on it. They naturally result in recycling of the most important (content-related or content-obligatory) vocabulary and allow review or indirect introduction of other (content-compatible) vocabulary (Snow, Met, & Genesee, 1989).

Planning Thematic Units

A unit that you develop around a theme can be used for several classes or periods of instruction or for longer periods of time in what is referred to as sustained content instruction. For young learners, with short attention spans, it may be best to limit units to two weeks of instruction, but it is always appropriate to return to these themes and to link later units and themes to ones that you have previously taught.

Six Steps Toward Thematic Units Here are six steps to follow in developing a thematic unit consisting of several class periods and lessons:

1. Select a theme **OR** Select an appropriate text and identify the theme(s) in the text.
2. Identify the language focus (vocabulary and grammar).
3. Identify content objectives (links to other content areas).
4. Identify learning strategies or critical thinking skills.
5. Develop activities.
6. Sequence the activities.

   1. **Select a theme OR Select an appropriate text and identify the theme(s) in the text**   There are two major ways of selecting themes for your classes; they are equally effective:

■ **Theme first:** Identifying a theme that is either in the textbook or that you want to use, based on your knowledge of your learners' interests
■ **Text first:** Choosing a story, poem, song, video, or other text that will be engaging to your children and then identifying the themes that emerge from that text

A theme should be an umbrella under which you can integrate a number of coordinated activities—for example, stories, games, and projects—linking language, content, culture, and thinking skills. Any topic that connects with children's learning and experiences can become a theme.

Linse (2005) says that one way to identify potential topics for thematic units is to see what children carry around or have in their bookbags. Moon (2000) has developed a simple survey for children to use in identifying what they are most interested in, either in their first language or by responding to or drawing pictures. This could be done as a whole class activity, with simple questions such as "Who likes pets?" "Who likes sports?" and asking children to raise their hands. An especially productive source of topics involves those related to what the children are learning in their other subjects or classes. This can also lead to meaningful interaction and communication, as children transfer some of what they may be learning in their own language to English. Over time, you will get a sense of what themes are most interesting to young children. You can also ask your learners what they like or don't like about English class, maybe using smiley faces or sad faces as you ask the whole class or small groups about the things you have been doing (Moon, 2000).

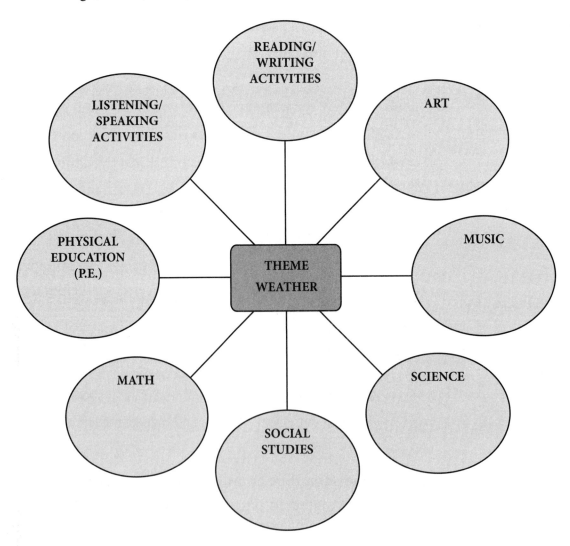

Theme first If you identify a theme or want to add to a theme from the textbook you are using, you can use a number of ways to brainstorm connections you could make and the kinds of activities you might use. On the next page is a brainstorming web for planning a thematic unit. Note that the theme is in the center; around it are the kinds of content areas or activities you might use. We will be looking at a unit plan around the theme of weather later in this chapter.

Text first In the other approach you can identify stories, poems, songs, video segments, or other print or visual texts as the basis of a thematic unit. Later in this chapter, we will look at a unit plan and a lesson plan using popular children's literature written in English as the basis for a unit on healthy eating and life cycles *(The Very Hungry Caterpillar)* and the value of trees to animals and people *(The Great Kapok Tree)*.

2. **Identify the language focus (vocabulary and grammar)** As you consider the theme, note the following:

- New vocabulary
- Vocabulary to review
- Grammar patterns
- Language functions

Keep the language at the level of the children. This may mean that you will need to simplify the grammar in some of the texts you plan to use. It will certainly mean that you will need to pre-teach some vocabulary and also the target grammatical structure, as well as review grammar and vocabulary needed to understand the activities or the text.

3. **Identify content objectives (links to other content areas)** The more you can link what the children are learning in English to what they are learning in their other subjects, the deeper their learning will be, both in English and in their other subjects. Those links might be to mathematics, science, social studies, art, music, or physical education (gym). Some will come to you naturally as you consider the theme or analyze the text that is the basis for the theme.

4. **Identify learning strategies or critical thinking skills** A major criticism of many language classes is that they focus so much on repetition of language that they ignore the possibility of building in learning strategies needed in any

academic class—strategies such as previewing or predicting what something is going to be about (perhaps from a picture or title), listening or reading for a main idea, classifying information, guessing the meaning of a word from context, sounding out a word to pronounce it and figure out its meaning, taking notes, even visualizing a situation. The same is true for developing critical thinking skills, skills that encourage questioning and developing opinions. Some of these will not be appropriate for very young learners, but children over 7 should be provided with opportunities to apply these skills in their language learning. Even very young learners should be invited to predict what a story will be about, to visualize a scene, and to ask questions or offer their opinions, especially about what they like or don't like.

5. **Develop activities** We will be spending more time on this later in this chapter, but at this point we need to remember that a unit should have activities that provide lots of practice. The unit should also provide opportunities for children to apply what they have learned, perhaps in developing a project such as a poster or a collage, giving a brief oral summary with the help of pictures or sentence starters, or writing a brief e-mail about what they have done. At least one of these activities, at the end of the unit, should allow you to evaluate students' progress in meeting the unit objectives.

Ideally, a unit should have activities that:

Andrés Guadalupe Muñoz Del Rio, Primary, Secondary, and University English Teacher, Zacatecas, Mexico

"I believe a high percentage of success in the classroom is undoubtedly the teacher's attitude. When a teacher is tired or bored, his students perceive this, and they will respond to this and act in the same way. In contrast, when a teacher feels a deep emotion, it will be transmitted to the young learners, and they will be invited to learn through the work in the classroom."

- Foster authentic language use
- Involve the use of all four skills (listening, speaking, reading, and writing)
- Draw upon students' prior knowledge
- Lead to higher levels of understanding
- Encourage a variety of learning styles (multiple intelligences)
- Use a variety of grouping strategies
- Use a variety of media to make things understandable
- Motivate learners to use English in a variety of situations and tasks
- Engage learners in critical thinking
- Interest the teacher

6. **Sequence the activities** In sequencing the activities, you will want to consider the following:

- Engaging learners in receptive tasks before productive tasks
- Presenting language (vocabulary and grammar) before asking students to practice

- Using controlled practice activities before more independent activities
- Connecting one activity to the next
- Sequencing the content to recycle language
- Ordering the tasks to mirror the real-life application of the tasks

After going through these six steps, you are ready to develop your thematic unit.

Theme-First Unit Planning
Here is an example of using the brainstorming web to plan a thematic unit on weather.

After brainstorming different topics and activities around the theme of weather, here is a possible unit plan for several days of instruction.

Unit Plan for Weather

Theme: Weather

Student Profile: Young learners, ages 7–8, in their second year of English

Language Objectives:

    Grammar: What's the weather like today?

                        It's _____ (sunny, cloudy, rainy, snowy, windy) today.

                        Is it _____?

                        Our favorite weather is _____.

                        _____ is wearing _____.

                        Take off, put on

    Vocabulary: Weather: sunny, cloudy, rainy, snowy, windy, cold, hot

                        Clothes: hat, jacket, gloves, coat, scarf, umbrella, jeans, shorts, t-shirt, shoes, boots, socks, sneakers, bathing suit, raincoat

                        Review names and characteristics of animals

Content Objectives: **Review animals**

                        Identify where different types of animals live

                        Identify differences in the way people dress in different weather (in different countries)

                        Do a bar graph of class favorite weather

Sample Activities for Language Skills:

    Listening: Listen to a story *The North Wind and the Sun*

                        Listen to "The Weather Song"

                        Listen to a simple news weather report

    Speaking: Ask and answer "What's the weather like today?"

                        Talk about clothes they wear in different weather

                        Talk about clothes they wear for different sports

                        Talk about their favorite weather

    Reading: Read story *Polar Bear, Polar Bear, What Do You Hear?*

                        Read about animals that live in the Arctic

                        Answer true/false questions

                        Read about what children wear who live in different climates

    Writing: Using a picture or drawing of themselves, write about what the weather is like and what they are wearing.

Learning Strategy Activities: Make predictions and confirm or disconfirm them (where animals live, what children wear in different countries)

                                        Use a graphic organizer (bar graph)

Text-First Unit Planning Now let's look a unit plan for 6- to 8-year-olds that begins with a popular children's story book, *The Very Hungry Caterpillar* by Eric Carle. The story is about a caterpillar who "pops out" of his egg on a Sunday, becomes very hungry and gets hungrier every day. On Monday he eats one apple. He eats two pears on Tuesday, three plums on Wednesday, four strawberries on Thursday, and five oranges on Friday, but he is still hungry. Then, on Saturday, he eats everything he can: cake, ice cream, and all the other things that young children love to eat (but are not necessarily good for them) until he falls asleep—and then wakes up as a beautiful butterfly. As you can see, this story would be a fun way to introduce favorite foods—those that are good for children and those that are not so good for them. It would also be a meaningful way to review numbers and the days of the week. And it would link nicely to basic science (the life cycle of a butterfly and even of other creatures), though most caterpillars would not be eating much of what this caterpillar eats! It also offers a great way to do some basic mathematics.

Some of the activities you might use with this story include:

- Teaching the names of food using the pictures in the story
- Matching the names of food with pictures
- Asking children about their favorite foods
- Creating a class graph of "Our Favorite Foods"
- Listening to the story being read
- Listening again and chanting the repeated lines
- Talking about the life cycle of a butterfly
- Acting out the life cycle of a butterfly
- Relating the life cycle of a butterfly to other life cycles (humans, pets)
- Answering Yes/No questions about what a caterpillar eats
- Observing the life cycle of a butterfly from the Internet

Select from among these activities and sequence them, from activities to present the content and language, to practice language in controlled activities, and finally to engage students in independent activities. For an example, see the sample unit plan below.

Unit Plan Using *The Very Hungry Caterpillar*

Theme:	Food and nutrition, life cycles
Student Profile:	Young learners, ages 6–7, with beginner level English

Language Objectives:

    Grammar: On + days of the week

                        Past tense

                        Like/don't like (Review)

    Vocabulary: Fruits: apples, plums, pears, strawberries, oranges, watermelon

                        Other foods: cake, ice cream, cheese

                        Caterpillar, cocoon, butterfly

                        Adjectives: little, tiny, big, beautiful, hungry (Some review)

                        Days of the week (Review)

                        Numbers 1–7 (Review)

Content Objectives: Identify the value of different foods

                        Review days of the week

                        Create a bar graph for fruit

                        Identify the life cycle of a butterfly; compare with other animals

Sample Activities for Language Skills:

    Listening: Listen to the story *The Very Hungry Caterpillar* (Storytelling by author Eric Carle is available on YouTube)

                        Act out the stages of a butterfly's life

    Speaking: Talk about foods (favorite foods; good for you/not so good)

                        Choral read repetitive parts of the story

                        Develop dialog for the caterpillar and act out the story

                        Play caterpillar board game

                        Sing a caterpillar song

                        Color a butterfly and tell the class the colors you used

                        Answer true/false questions about a caterpillar and butterfly

    Reading: Dictate a language experience story (a story that the teacher will write)

                        Read and sequence pictures from the story

                        Match names of fruits with pictures

    Writing: Fill out a calendar/graph of caterpillar's foods

                        Fill out a chart of foods liked/not liked (drawing/pictures)

                        Make a caterpillar book and label

Learning Strategy Activities: Sequence information

                        Make predictions and confirm or disconfirm them

                        (Do caterpillars eat ice cream?)

                        (Do caterpillars become butterflies?)

Long-Term Planning

We have discussed the importance of contextualizing instruction and developing unit plans that integrate activities for several classes, but it is also important to do long-term planning. It may seem obvious that a good EYL class is carefully planned, not only for daily lessons and weekly or longer units, but also for the entire year. Even if you have a textbook, where much of the planning has been done for you, you will need to adapt the textbook based on your children's experiences and your teaching context.

Planning for the Term or Year

Your textbook can provide a basic plan for your school term or year, but you may want to look at a calendar and think about what would be most appropriate at various times of the year, such as special holidays or festivals or local, national, or international sports events such as the World Cup or the Olympics that would be good to align your units with. Take out a calendar and then look closely at the themes in the textbook listed in the Scope and Sequence or the Table of Contents.

upstudio/Shutterstock.com

You may want to move a unit on sports to a time when an important sports event is occurring in your region or a unit on weather during a time of the year when everyone is talking about the weather. As you look through the textbook, note the places where local stories, customs, or events might be integrated into the unit, and then, based on that, you may want to adapt some of these units or insert an additional thematic unit based on your local context. You may also want to talk with other teachers in the school to find out what the children will be doing in their other subjects (working with magnets, studying dinosaurs, learning to make graphs or tables) and build units or add lessons to the textbook that reflect these other subjects. If there are standards related to English teaching that must be addressed, you will also want to review these and make sure the students are being helped to meet the standards for students at their language level and age.

Daily Lesson Planning

**Awena A. Muhsin,
Primary English Teacher,
Kenya**

"There is a wise saying that goes, 'If you fail to plan, you plan to fail.' So if you don't want to fail, you need to plan, and plan to the best of your ability. I plan because there is no job that can be done without a tool. A teacher's tool is the lesson plan."

We have already talked about thematic units as one way of organizing the EYL curriculum, but after developing units, you will need to develop daily lesson plans for the classes in which you will be teaching the units. Most administrators will require you to prepare a lesson plan. It is something that they can show parents to help them understand what is being taught in the language class and to reassure them that their child's teacher is well prepared. It is also something that a substitute teacher can use if you are sick or not available to teach your class. But a lesson plan also has other benefits:

- It builds confidence. You know where you are going and how you are going to get there. It also assures your students that you know what they will be doing. It gives them confidence in you and in the structure of the class.
- It helps you prepare for the class. You know what materials you need and how long you will need for each activity.
- It provides you with a guide during the class as you move from one activity to another, from controlled to freer activities.
- It requires you to have specific objectives for the class and guides you in ensuring that these objectives are met.
- It helps you to see if you have provided different activities for different learning styles (auditory, visual, kinesthetic) and provides you with options if you find that your initial plan is not working.
- It gives something to reflect on for future planning. You can make notes of changes you would make the next time you teach the lesson (Harmer, 2007; Moon, 2000).

Planning a Lesson You may be given a lesson planning form that you will need to complete for each class. Lesson plans may vary a bit, but each will have the same basic categories and sequence of activities. Here is a sample of a lesson plan for a thematic unit on food and nutrition using *The Very Hungry Caterpillar* as the core text, rather than a textbook.

The Very Hungry Caterpillar by Eric Carle	
Student profile	Grades 1–2, beginner level of English proficiency
Skills to be emphasized	Listening and speaking

Language	• Grammar: like/don't like • New vocabulary: fruits (apples, pears, plums, strawberries, oranges, watermelon); cake, ice cream, cheese, egg, caterpillar, cocoon, butterfly • Review vocabulary: days of the week, numbers 1–5
Objectives	By the end of this lesson, students will be able to: • Talk about what the hungry caterpillar ate • Talk about some of their favorite foods • Fill out a food calendar
Materials	Fruit that is available; picture cards of fruit and food that children will probably like or not like; *The Very Hungry Caterpillar* book (or a video version in which the story is being read/told to a class); a small stuffed caterpillar, if possible; a towel to use as a cocoon

Warm-up **Before-storytelling Activities**	
Capture their attention	Talk to students while rubbing your stomach and acting hungry. Say, "Oh! I am very hungry! Are you hungry? Who is hungry? What can we do? Let's eat food! What should we eat? Let's see!"
Connect to prior knowledge and experiences Review language students have learned	Show pictures of food or actual food items. Ask the students if they like/don't like these. When you hold up each item, ask students to give "thumbs up" if they like it or "thumbs down" if they don't. Record the results next to a picture of that food on the board. Like: 10 Don't Like: 11 Like: 21 Don't Like: 0
Pre-teach new vocabulary or expressions	Show students a small stuffed caterpillar or a brightly colored picture of a caterpillar. Say, "What is this? This is a . . . caterpillar. Repeat after me 'caterpillar!' Have you seen this before? Where?"

	Caterpillar Toss
	Tell students, "I will call your name and throw the caterpillar. If you catch it, say 'caterpillar,' then throw this to a friend. Ready? Adriana, catch!" Toss the stuffed caterpillar to Adriana. When she says "caterpillar," cue her to say a friend's name and throw it. Continue until all students get a turn.
Preview the cover of the storybook	Show the cover of *The Very Hungry Caterpillar*. Say, "What do you see here? Right! A caterpillar! Today we're going to read about this very hungry caterpillar." (*rub your stomach when you say "hungry" and point to the caterpillar*)
Predict what will happen	Encourage students to predict. Ask them, "Is this caterpillar hungry? Very hungry? Very, very hungry? What do you think?" Give children a chance to guess and answer. Ask, "What do caterpillars like to eat?" Write down students' answers on the board to check after the storytelling. Then say, "OK, let's see!"

Presentation
During-storytelling Activities

Storytelling with a big book	Begin the story, stopping to talk about the foods, the caterpillar, etc., and asking students if they like/don't like the foods the caterpillar eats. Encourage students to chime in on the repeated parts such as "But he was still hungry."
Comprehension check using their bodies	**Science Mini-Lesson** Review the life cycle of a caterpillar. Encourage students to show it with their bodies. Show the picture of the egg in the storybook and tell students to show you the egg with their bodies (curled up in a ball). "What are you now? Right! An egg!" Then tell them to show you what a caterpillar looks like with their bodies (slithering around). "What are you now? Right! A caterpillar!" Then show a cocoon by taking a towel and wrapping it around yourself. Ask a few students to come up as a caterpillar, wrap them in the towel, and ask "What are you now? Right! A cocoon!" Finally, ask students to imitate you as you make your arms flutter like the wings of a butterfly. "What are you now? Right! A butterfly!"

Check predictions	Look at the list of food on the board that students predicted. Ask them, "Did we guess right? What did the caterpillar eat? Did he eat ____?" (say the first word on the list) If the guess was right, circle it. If the guess was wrong, cross the word out. If some food from the story is missing, ask them which ones. "What else did he eat?" Write their answers on the board.

<table>
<tr><td colspan="2" align="center">Practice
After-storytelling Activities</td></tr>
<tr>
<td>Review and retell part of the story</td>
<td>

Put or draw a one-week calendar on the board.

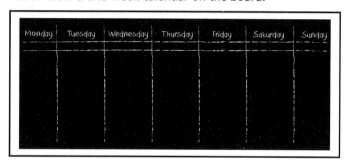

Ask students to help you fill in what the caterpillar ate each day. Have volunteers take the picture cards of the food and put them on the right day. Repeat the story with them while filling in the calendar.

"On Monday . . . he ate through one. . . . But he was still hungry.

On Tuesday . . . he ate through two. . . . But he was still hungry.

On Wednesday . . . he ate through three . . . ," etc.

</td>
</tr>
</table>

<table>
<tr><td colspan="2" align="center">Application
After-storytelling Activities</td></tr>
<tr>
<td>Paired Interview Activity</td>
<td>

Food for Two

Have students work in pairs, filling out the chart called "Food for Two" on a handout. First, they fill out "My Favorite Food" with their favorite food. They can draw a picture and/or write the word. Then they will interview a partner using "Do you like ___?" asking about their favorite food. Their partner can answer.

Yes, I do.

No, I don't. I like _____.

In either case, students draw and/or write the food their partner likes.

</td>
</tr>
</table>

Survey Activity	Our Favorite Food
	As a whole class, the teacher leads a survey of Our Favorite Food as a class. Students take turns saying "I like _____." Then the teacher asks the whole class, "Do you like _____?" and counts how many students like that food. The teacher continues until all the different food in students' lists are represented.
Assessment	
Monitor progress	While the students are working in pairs in the Food for Two activity, circulate around the room listening to the children talking about the foods they like. Make a note of what they are having trouble with and be sure to recast corrections as you collect answers during the Our Favorite Food activity.
Assessment	As students leave class, have each one tell you one thing they liked/learned today.
Follow-up	
Homework	Ask the students to tell their parents about the story they heard in class and to find out one food that their parents like. If they don't know the name of it, they can draw it or bring a picture of it to class. They will report the food their parents like in the next class.

Paired Interview Activity: Food for Two

Food for Two

MY FAVORITE FOOD			MY FRIEND'S FAVORITE FOOD		
Name: _____			Name: _____		
Picture	Word		Picture	Word	

Survey Activity: Our Favorite Food (can be drawn on board or put on a flip chart)

Our Favorite Food		
Food we like		**How many like it?**
Picture	Word *Watermelon*	IIII

At the next class, you can begin by asking the students about their parents' favorite foods. You can review the caterpillar's favorite foods and use that as a warm-up for the class.

The lesson format you will be expected to use in your school or program may vary somewhat from the one presented earlier but almost all lesson plans include objectives and the following stages of a lesson: warm-up, presentation, practice, and application. Let's look at each of these.

Writing Objectives Objectives are the most important part of the lesson plan, since they state the purpose for the lesson and what students are expected to learn from the lesson. It is important to have objectives that address both content and language learning. It is also a good idea to include objectives that relate to academic skills or what are often referred to as learning strategies: the kinds of skills that help students to achieve academically, such as predicting, sequencing information, or listening or reading for specific information. Objectives should be measurable—that is, you should be able to determine if the students have met an objective or are in the process of meeting it—and refer to what the students should be able to do by the end of the lesson. They should be as specific as you can make them (avoid using "understand," since it is difficult to measure). They might also include a specific language function, such as describing, asking for, expressing likes or dislikes, stating opinions, etc. related to the topic or theme.

A typical format for objectives is what has come to be known as SWBAT: *Students will be able to* + the objective. In the previous example the objectives were:

Students will be able to:

- Talk about what the hungry caterpillar ate
- Talk about some of their favorite foods
- Fill out a food calendar

If this were a unit plan, we would have more objectives, some of which might ask students to:

- Create a simple chart with the number of apples, plums, etc. that the caterpillar ate
- Create a chart of favorite fruits
- Draw the life cycle of the caterpillar
- Relate the life cycle of a caterpillar to the life cycle of people
- Bring a caterpillar to school and keep a class journal of the caterpillar's growth

Choosing Activities   After setting objectives, you will need to plan activities to help children achieve them. Sometimes you will think of activities before setting objectives, but the activities then need to be tailored to your specific objectives. Brainstorm as many activities as you can, beginning with those that are included in your student textbooks, workbooks, or teacher's manual. Also look for other materials you have access to, and think about others that your students might find engaging. You will be using the same theme for several classes, so activities that may not fit one lesson may be perfect for another.

As explored in Chapter 2, you will want to find activities that:

- Provide opportunities for active learning, since children make sense of the world by interacting with their environment (Piaget)
- Provide opportunities for children to interact with each other (in pairs or small groups) and with the teacher (as a whole class or when engaged in individual tasks)
- Provide opportunities for comprehensible input (through listening and reading) and output (through speaking and writing)
- Are interesting, fun, and relevant to children's lives (to their interests outside class, their families and homes, etc.)
- Are varied (songs, chants, games, stories, poems, role plays, projects, etc.)
- Appeal to different learning styles (auditory, visual, kinesthetic) or multiple intelligences (logical-mathematical, spatial, intrapersonal, interpersonal, natural, etc.)
- Connect to the larger school curriculum (to what is being learned in science, mathematics, social studies, etc.)
- Appeal both to children who are very outgoing and to those who are more shy or silent (Moon, 2000; Scott & Ytreberg, 1990)

In some textbooks, the activities will primarily focus on presenting and practicing grammar and vocabulary with limited context or opportunities to use the language to communicate meaningfully. You may need to provide a theme that provides a larger context in which to add a variety of activities that meet the criteria above.

Organizing Activities

After brainstorming activities to help children achieve the objectives, you will need to organize these into a sequence. In general, for children, you will want to begin with listening and speaking activities, and then move to reading and writing. The activities should be organized to fit the following stages in your lesson plan:

1. Warm-up activities
2. Presentation activities
3. Practice activities
4. Application activities

1.   Warm-up activities   At the beginning of any unit, and of any lesson, you will want to provide activities that help build learner engagement, set the direction for the unit or lesson, and link the day's lesson with previous lessons: activities that "warm up" the class. Warm-up activities help to:

- Activate background (or prior) knowledge about both the content and the language (grammar and vocabulary) so that you know what the children already know about the topic and the language and what you will need to teach or re-teach (because the children have forgotten it)
- Create interest and excitement about the unit or lesson
- Get students thinking in English
- Create transition from what the students were learning or doing in a previous unit or lesson to what they will be learning and doing this day
- Review known (and needed) vocabulary and introduce new vocabulary and language that will be needed to understand the listening or reading input that will be presented in the presentation stage. The review can also include homework from the previous class.

There are a number of activities that can be used in a warm-up. You can do any of these that relate to the theme of the new lesson:

- Ask a question to get children excited, such as "How many of you like ice cream?"
- Show pictures or bring in real objects that they know. Ask, "Who knows what this is?"

- Refer to a known song or retell a short story. For example, "Remember our story about a beautiful, blue fish? Well, today we're going to hear a story about a green caterpillar."
- Play a game, such as a calendar game, with students coming to the front of the class and pointing to the correct day of the week for that day, for yesterday, and for tomorrow, or reviewing what they do on special days such as Mondays and Fridays.

2. Presentation activities In the presentation stage of the lesson, the teacher presents the relevant vocabulary and language structures in a meaningful context, usually by having the students listen to (or for older children, read) a story or a song and determining if the students have understood that input. The focus in this stage is on providing the students with a lot of repeated input, and then teaching the target language structures and vocabulary they will need to use that language in speaking and writing, as well as additional practice in listening and reading in the practice stage. Presentation activities include:

- Talking about a picture
- Teaching vocabulary with pictures or objects
- Teaching the language structure to understand and talk about the story
- "Reading" (or telling) the story to the children (perhaps in adapted form)

3. Practice activities During this stage in the lesson, students need opportunities to practice using the topic and the new language in predictable ways, beginning with being provided with a great deal of support (controlled activities or guided practice) to those in which they take on more of the responsibility of providing the appropriate responses and using the language more meaningfully (independent activities). The activities can be post-listening or post-reading activities that include speaking and writing. You will find lots of suggested activities in the student workbook or a teacher's edition (also referred to as a lesson planner). You can also find lots of ideas online (see the suggested Web sites at the end of this chapter) or in activity books for young learners.

In the earlier example, since the presentation was the story of a hungry caterpillar, the following are the kinds of activities you might include (in order of most to least support):

- Matching (of vocabulary and pictures, characters in the story and activities they were involved in, etc.)
- Circling something (a picture, or for older children, a word)

- Sorting pictures or names of foods by category (food that is good for you and food that is not)
- Talking with a partner about favorite foods
- Playing a game (Bingo, Old Maid, Hangman, or Concentration) with the names of foods
- Acting out a story (role play of the stages of a caterpillar's life)
- Completing sentences (from the story or a summary of the story)

Some of these activities can be done in a large group; others in small groups or in pairs. Some can be done in class; others might be assigned as homework. The time you have in class will help determine how you group students and what will need to be completed at home (and then become the review in the warm-up stage of the next lesson).

The following is an example of a controlled practice activity that gives students a chance to use the vocabulary and pattern you have presented in very predictable ways, with a lot of repetition and few chances of making an error after they have done the activity a number of times. The teacher, with the whole class, models the grammar and engages in a simple dialog that practices "like" and "don't like" + the names of fruits:

> T: *I like apples. [Student Name], Do you like apples?*
>
> S1: *Yes, I do.*
>
> T: *_____, Do you like pears?*
>
> S2: *No, I don't.*

After a few times with this pattern, the students can work in pairs and expand the structure:

> S1: *I like apples. _____, Do you like apples?*
>
> S2: *Yes, I like apples. _____, Do you like apples?*
>
> *OR No, I don't like apples. I like pears.*

A guided practice activity, with less support, might be to have the children draw a picture of their favorite fruit and keep it turned toward them. Their partner has to guess what fruit the other one has, asking, "Do you like _____?" until the partner guesses the right fruit. After both have answered correctly, they wait until the teacher blows a whistle and then find other partners and repeat the activity.

S1: *The first student asks her partner*
Do you like apples?

S2: *The second student has a picture of a banana, so he answers:*
No, I don't.

S1: *The first student asks her partner again.*
Do you like bananas?

S2: *The second student answers and then asks his partner:*
Yes, I do.
Do you like watermelon?

You might have pairs of pictures and when two children each pick up the same picture, they can turn to the teacher and say:

Ss: *We like _____.*

An independent (or freer) practice activity might have the students in small groups pick their favorite fruits from the ones that have been presented (or add ones that they have learned the words for from their teacher or each other) and then present these in ranked order to their classmates. From this a class favorite fruit graph can be developed.

Group 1: We like grapes, apples, and bananas.
Group 2: We like apples, pears, and plums.
Group 3: We like grapes, pears, and apples.
Group 4: We like bananas, apples, and grapes.

Together, the class would decide that their favorite fruit is apples, and that the second is grapes. The teacher could do a bar chart with 4 apples in the first bar, 3 grapes in the second, and 2 pears and 2 bananas in the last two bars, labeling the graph: "We Like Fruit" or "Our Favorite Fruit."

4. Application activities In the application stage of the lesson, students are acting more independently, using the new language they have learned to

OUR FAVORITE FRUIT

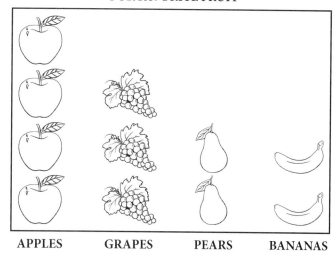

APPLES   GRAPES   PEARS   BANANAS

communicate something that is meaningful to them. Application activities almost always involve speaking or writing. Sometimes (such as in Reader's Theater) they involve both. The goal of the application stage is to encourage students to use the language authentically or in authentic contexts. Often application activities involve a project. For example, students might be asked to create a poster collage of foods that are "good for you" and those that are "not as good for you."

They might be invited to work in small groups and then role play the stages of a butterfly's life. Or each child could be given a picture from *The Very Hungry Caterpillar* which only they can see and they then describe to the class; on the basis of the description, they will line up in the sequence of the activities in the story. Older students with more advanced English proficiency could create dialog for the pictures or episodes of a story and then read these lines in the sequence of the story (Reader's Theater), or they might write a letter to the author.

What about Assessment? Assessment should be integrated into the lesson, not necessarily a separate activity. While we want children eventually to speak and write English accurately, as well as fluently, our major emphasis with young learners (especially those in the first years of English classes) is on fluency, motivating them to use English, to enjoy doing it, and to feel confident that they can learn and are learning the language. We want to provide them with an environment in which they can take risks, in which they can communicate using whatever resources they have (gestures, actions, drawings, or anything else) while they are using English. We don't want to make them afraid of making mistakes or to lose their natural sense of enjoyment and confidence (Vale & Feunteun, 1998). Moreover, few of us, adults included, can pay attention to both fluency and accuracy at the same time. When we ask children to talk or write freely to each other or us, we are asking them to be as fluent as possible, to use all their language resources, which will usually result in making some errors. But that is not the time for corrective feedback. We might note, however, a common error and then add an activity in the next class that helps develop the accurate vocabulary or grammar pattern.

When students are in the practice stage, especially in the beginning with very controlled activities where they only have to repeat a target structure (such as "I like ___" or "I don't like ___"), we can praise their effort and model the correct form, keeping the conversation moving. For example, if a student says, "I like swim," the teacher can say, "That's great. Devon likes to swim," inserting the "to." "What do you like to do, Miko?" Then at the end of the activity, you can ask all the students to repeat the correct form.

Indirect assessment can be built in throughout the lesson, especially in the practice and application stages. You can determine how well the students are learning the language and content as they respond in class, or you can circulate and listen to them when they are engaged in pair work or independent activities. You can do a quick review that focuses on a structure or word that is giving several students trouble or plan on addressing that in the next class. You might also have a checklist of new structures and vocabulary and a list of students, where you can jot down notes about those who seem to be having the most difficulty and may need additional help. You can also note those who have seemed to grasp the content and language well and could be paired with a student who is having difficulty in a kind of peer-tutoring arrangement or plan the next class to have enrichment activities for these students to do while you are spending more time on the problem areas with the students who are having difficulty. Some teachers have an "exit strategy," asking children (individually or in small groups) to provide a brief answer as they leave class—maybe one of several new words they learned that day, the name of a character in a story, or what they liked best about the story. You will want to have a formal assessment at the end of a unit, but informal assessment throughout the lesson. Chapter 7 will provide more discussion of appropriate assessment activities.

What about Grammar?
Although you will be focusing on a specific grammar pattern during a unit or series of lessons, for young children, it should not involve the direct teaching of grammatical rules (Cameron, 2001; Pinter, 2006; Shin, 2014). Instead, by careful repetition in a number of activities, and occasionally

pointing something out, children will "notice" the grammar and slowly acquire it by using it. That's why it is so important to provide a number of opportunities for children to recycle the grammar (and vocabulary) in meaningful and relevant activities that involve all four language skills. In a successful EYL class, children are using the language to learn how it works.

As stated above, it is also important not to overtly correct children's grammatical mistakes when they are trying to communicate in class, especially when you are trying to keep the communication in the class in English. Make a note of problems that individual or many students are having and provide more activities to practice that grammar in another class. You can also praise their contributions and rephrase what they have said using the correct forms.

Sample Lesson

The Value of Trees Following is a sample lesson from a unit on The Value of Trees for 9–10-year-olds with intermediate English language proficiency. The centerpiece of the unit is *The Great Kapok Tree* by Lynne Cherry, but there are many children's books focused on trees that could be substituted, such as *The Giving Tree* by Shel Silverstein or *The Woman Who Hugged a Tree*, an East Indian classic folktale. (If you do not have access to any of these books, you can find a number of versions of *The Great Kapok Tree* on You Tube and continue with an original or adapted version of *The Woman Who Hugged a Tree* at http://sunnysidestories. wordpress.com/the-woman-who-hugged-a-tree/.)

In *The Great Kapok Tree,* a man walks into a rainforest with an ax and begins trying to cut down a huge tree. Soon, he grows tired and falls asleep. The sounds of his ax have been heard by many creatures in the forest, and one by one, they come and tell the man in a dream why the kapok tree is valuable to them and why he should not cut it down. Each animal comes in a characteristic way: the boa constrictor "slithers"; the monkeys "scamper"; the tree frog "crawls." They also talk in characteristic ways: the jaguar "growls"; the porcupines "whisper"; and the toucan, macaw, and cock-of-the-rock "squawk." Finally, a young child from the Yanomamo tribe murmurs, "Senhor, when you awake, please look upon us all with new eyes." We don't know what the man with the ax will do, but after hearing from all the animals and the young child, we are hopeful that he will leave, and after waking and looking at the animals and the child, he does.

The Great Kapok Tree makes a wonderful centerpiece for a unit on the value of trees. (There is also a Spanish-language edition.) It has beautiful illustrations of each animal, of the vegetation in the rainforest, and even a map of the world, with areas of rainforest marked, and an illustration of the various layers of a rainforest. The following lesson plan is only for one class, but it could be the basis for a long and fascinating unit for children.

In previous lessons, the learners have taken a walk around the school grounds, pointing to different trees and talking about the leaves, trunk, bark, flowers, and seeds. They have also collected various leaves and reviewed vocabulary to talk about them: colors, shapes, sizes, etc. (Note: If it is not possible to take this walk, then pictures of various forests, trees, and leaves can be substituted). They have also completed an in-class activity using a K-W-L graphic organizer, discussing what they KNOW about trees, what they WANT TO FIND OUT about trees, and later, they will fill in what they have LEARNED about them.

Title: *The Great Kapok Tree by* Lynne Cherry	
Student profile	Grades 4–5, intermediate level of English proficiency
Skills to be emphasized	Listening and speaking
Language	Grammar: Need + tree for _____ Vocabulary: kapok tree; names of the animals in the story; rainforest; kapok tree; parts of the tree; Amazon River
Objectives	By the end of this lesson, students will be able to: Talk about the value of the tree in relation to several of the animals in the story
Materials	Beautiful pictures of different kinds of trees from their context and other countries (printed from the Internet on paper or put in a PowerPoint slide show) A graphic organizer of a tree with lines pointing to the roots, trunk, branches, and leaves of the tree—2 copies for each student Pictures of animals from the book *The Great Kapok Tree* by Lynne Cherry
Warm-up	
Capture their attention	Show students many beautiful pictures of different kinds of trees from their country and other countries. Some of the trees may look very strange and wondrous to them. Ask them, "What are these? Where can you find these trees?" Take a globe or a map and point out where there are rainforests where these trees are found.

Connect to prior knowledge and experiences	**Think-Pair-Share (T-P-S)** Ask the students to **think** individually about all the ways in which we use trees—their value to us. Then share their ideas in a pair with one partner, filling out one of the tree graphic organizers. Then as a class, **share** their ideas and fill out a large tree organizer on the board.
Preview the cover of the storybook	Tell the class that you are going to read *The Great Kapok Tree* to them. Show them the cover picture and ask them if anyone has seen a kapok tree. Let them describe it and what they see on the cover. Point to the animals, the man with the ax, and all the flowers. Ask them where they think the story takes place and what they think the book is going to be about.
Pre-teach new vocabulary or expressions	Using picture cards of the individual animals, with their name on the card, teach the names of the animals. Introduce the rainforest, show them a map of the world where there are rainforests, and then point to the Amazon River and Brazil, where the story takes place. Have them name the animals.
Give students a purpose for listening	Tell the students that as you read, you want them to listen specifically for the names of the animals and the value of the tree to that animal. They can take notes as you read.
Presentation	
Storytelling using the book	Break students into 10 pairs or groups, so each pair/group has one graphic organizer with WHO? WHAT? WHY? to use together. (Make sure that the students note the ways that animals communicate; for example, the boa constrictor hisses as he tells the man with the ax not to cut down the tree.) Assign each group an animal and tell them to write the name of the animal in the WHO box.

	WHO?	WHAT?	WHY?
	Boa constrictor	Hissed don't chop down the tree	Ancestors lived there, tree of miracles

Pause with each page and review what happened with students. Cue each pair/group to take notes on their graphic organizer as you read. But also tell the students to listen to the information about other animals because they will need it later.

Practice

Retell part of the story	**Draw and Retell**
	Pairs or groups draw the scene about their animal and prepare to present "who," "what," and "why" based on the story. They take their notes from the graphic organizer and write the sentences they will present. Be sure each member of the group or pair presents an equal amount. Put all of the pictures on the board in the order of the story, then begin to retell the story, having each group present what they prepared.
Controlled practice	Put up a large picture of the kapok tree. As you name an animal, ask students to explain the value of the kapok tree and point to the part of the tree that is valuable to that animal and say, "_____ needs the tree for _____."

Application

Independent activity: Personalize content	**Our Tree**
	Ask students to name the trees in their local context. "What trees do we have here?" Make a list. Then have students choose one, draw it, and write their own page modeled after what their animal said, using their own reasons for needing the tree.

Assessment

Assessment: Exit Ticket	As each student leaves class, ask them to name one of the animals and something that animal needs from the kapok tree. Or they can explain their own personal reason for needing trees.

Follow-up	
Homework	Ask the students to search for rainforests on the Internet and to see what other trees and animals live there. The next class will be about rainforests.

In subsequent classes, the story will be read again, and this time the class will listen for how each animal moves and communicates and complete a chart on the board. Each child will then have a chance to act out one of the animals, moving as the animal does and imitating the way the animal speaks, as you read the animal's lines (or if the students are able to read at this level, they can read the parts). Later you could have them play a game of Who Am I? with the class asking questions as a student moves the way the animal moves or makes the sounds of the animals. They will also be given several short texts about what is happening to the rainforests and the endangered animals that live there, and from that, as a class they will write a letter to a forestry official, asking what the company or agency is doing to protect the rainforest and the animals that live there.

**Ernest Kalotoueu
Gbeada, Cote d'Ivoire
(Ivory Coast)**

When I was presenting this lesson on "endangered species" 5 years ago, I conducted a role play between a rare wild animal species and a hunter. The animal asked the hunter "Why always him and not another animal?" The hunter answered that his skin was of greater value for humans than other animals' skin; and the animal answered back that this skin was of more value for himself than to human beings; the discussion went on till the hunter decided to stop hunting this species from that day on. The students really appreciated and learnt the dialog by heart.

Evaluating Thematic Units and Lessons

After teaching a lesson, you may want to make notes on its success or any problems that you encountered. About each activity, you might want to note:

■ Did the children enjoy it?
■ Did they have any problems with it?
■ How might you change the activity to reduce the problems?
■ Was the time allotted appropriate?
■ Was the activity in the right place in the lesson, or should it be moved?

You might also want to make a note of anything that was confusing to the class that you should review with them the next time that you meet. If you have your lessons on a computer, it should be relatively easy to revise your lesson the next time, and over time, as you build up a number of units and lesson plans, your planning will take much less time.

You will also want to reflect on the relative interest that students have shown in a unit—in the story, video, song, or other text—to decide if you want to adapt the theme or even change it the next term or year.

■ Teacher to Teacher

Contextualizing Instruction

There are many ways of contextualizing instruction through interesting themes. Sometimes teachers develop their own thematic units and lessons. Other times they are present in the required textbooks. This teacher from Belarus describes the themes in her EYL textbooks.

"The textbooks in our country have thematic building. During the first year, our children learn such thematic units as:

- *Good morning*
- *My family*
- *Appearance*
- *Our pets*
- *Food*
- *My room*
- *At the lesson*
- *Seasons*
- *I like animals*

The units for the second year are the following:

- *My friend*
- *Family*
- *Daily routine*
- *My day off*
- *Clothes*
- *School*
- *My birthday*

You see the topics are different and close to young learners. They are interrelated. Studying the topic 'My friend,' children remember the words learnt in ' Appearance,' 'Food,' and 'Our pets.' I want to offer some themes for the topic 'My friends': Things which my friend likes and dislikes:

- *My friend's breakfast*
- *My friend's pet*

- *My friend's hobbies*
- *We both like. . . .* **"**

—Irina Melikhava, Primary and Secondary English Teacher, Belarus

The following teacher explains that thematic instruction is also popular in Sri Lanka, where English textbooks use interesting content as the basis for language instruction.

"Content related language instruction is very popular in the EFL context at present. In Sri Lanka, textbooks have been designed to teach English through content. Rather than learning decontextualized and isolated sentences, content related instruction aims in providing language that helps the learner to comprehend the content while acquiring language skills. It is important to include several useful and related lessons threaded under a single theme so that students gain both meaning and language forcefully. For example, a lesson with the topic, 'Let's Play Basketball' under the theme of 'Sports' will help learners acquire language skills while playing a game of basketball and will teach children the basic rules and techniques of the game. The lessons can be organized with a formal discussion inside the classroom on the game, its history, present status of the game in the world, international heroes of the game, etc., supported by videos, poster presentations, etc. Students will speak of their favorite players and teams. One lesson may consist of a brief training session on the court with an experienced coach.**"**

*—Sanath Jayalath, MA TESOL Student and Assistant Director of Education
at the Ministry of Education, Sri Lanka*

Teachers can also contextualize instruction by taking the content and turning it into songs that relate to young learners' lives, as this teacher from Uzbekistan describes.

"In my young learner class, I like to use songs with actions. For example to read: "With the song, 'This is the way," I sing and act out the words:"

*This is the way we wash our hands,
wash our hands, wash our hands,
This is the way we wash our hands,
Every day in the morning.*

*The same with 'wash our face,' '
clean our teeth,' '
brush our hair,' '
drink our milk'*

and other daily routine actions, with students miming with the teacher. Then I check comprehension by playing the game, 'Show me.' I say, for example, 'Drink your milk' and students should mime the action. Then we sing this song again moving in the classroom—using visual, auditory, and kinesthetic learning. Another example is 'Morning exercises':

Hands up!
Hands down!
Hands on hips!
Sit down!
Stand up!
Hands to the sides!
Bend left!
Bend right!
Hands on hips!
One, two, three – hop!
One, two, three – stop!
Stand still!"

—*Natalya Yusupova, Primary & Secondary English Teacher, Uzbekistan*

■ Chapter Summary

To Conclude

The importance of contextualizing instruction Contextualizing instruction is critically important to make language learning meaningful for young learners and to motivate them to learn and use English.

Thematic instruction Choosing a central theme that unites the language and content learning is an important way of providing context. The themes should be relevant to children's lives as students, family members, and community members. They can be drawn from other content areas, from local and national culture, or from important ideas that emerge from good children's literature, especially stories.

Planning thematic units In developing thematic units, it is possible to choose a theme and then develop the unit (identifying engaging written and oral texts to include) or to choose a text (usually a story) and identify the thematic focus. After choosing the theme and the major text(s) for children to listen to, watch, or (if older) read, the next steps are to identify links to other content areas and learning strategies that can be included, and to develop and sequence activities to use in teaching the theme. Classroom observations are helpful in identifying themes and activities to use or adapt for other learners.

Long-term and daily lesson planning Planning should occur before the term or year, in order to identify important holidays or events that can serve as unit themes or be incorporated into units from the curriculum or textbook.

Daily lesson planning is important for a number of reasons: for the sense of confidence it provides to both the teacher and the student, for the guidance it offers in managing the lesson, and for reflecting upon the success of the lesson and how to adapt it for the future.

A lesson plan needs to have clear and measurable language and other (content-related or learning strategy) objectives, as well as a progression of activities that help learners move from the warm-up to presentation, practice, and application stages. These activities should be interesting, varied, and provide for active learning, interaction, and different learning styles.

■ Over to You

Discussion Questions

1. Now that you have read about thematic units and lesson planning, return to the textbook analysis that you did at the beginning of this chapter. Look over what you found in the textbook you reviewed and decide how well it meets the criteria established in this chapter. What would you change? What activities would you add?

2. Choose a theme that you think would be of interest to a group of young learners. Decide on their age and English language level. Then, using the web from p. 74, brainstorm ideas for a unit. Can you think of a traditional story, folktale, or custom that you could include in the unit?

3. Look at the unit and lesson plans in this chapter. How interesting do you think these units or lessons would be for your learners? Are there ways that you could adapt them to make them more meaningful for them? What other activities could you suggest for each stage of the unit or lesson: warm-up, presentation, practice, and application?

4. What are some effective themes you might use with your young learners? Make a list of these. Look again at the textbook you analyzed to see what kinds of themes were included. Also think about your experiences with young learners. What themes interest them?

5. Look at the list you made for question 4. What activities might you use in lessons with these themes? List some of them under each theme. Keep adding to this list for use in future unit or lesson planning.

Classroom Observation

Now that you have read and thought about how to contextualize and organize instruction, choose themes, and then plan daily lessons that move from presentation to practice, to application and evaluation, observe a young learner classroom and complete this form.

1. Find a young learner class to observe and ask permission from the teacher.

2. Meet with the teacher before the class. Share your instructions for the assignment, and ask the teacher for a lesson plan (if s/he has one).

3. Observe the class and fill out the Class Observation worksheet on pg. 389.

4. Reflect on the experience and write your Class Observation Report.

Write About It

Reflection on classroom observation: Write a two-page report on the following topics:

1. What did you learn from the observation experience?

2. How did the teacher address the following aspects of language teaching?
   - Classroom environment
   - Sequencing of lesson
   - Student participation
   - Motivation and interest
   - Teaching language in context
   - Assessement

3. What could be improved? What would you like to incorporate?

Resources and References

Print Publications

Crandall, J. A. (1998). Collaborate and cooperate: Teacher education for integrating language and content instruction. *English Teaching Forum, 36*(1), 2–9. Available at: http://exchanges.state.gov/englishteaching/forum/archives/1998.html

Crandall, J. A. (2001). Rethinking classroom management: Creating an effective learning community. *ESL Magazine, 4*(3), 10–13. Reprinted in I. A. Heath & C. J. Serrano (Eds.), *Perspectives on teaching English language learners.* Newbery, FL: Glanzer Press.

Curtain, H., & Dahlberg, C. A. (2010). *Languages and children: Making the match,* 4th ed. New York: Pearson.

Kaufman, D., & Crandall, J. A. (Eds.). (2005). *Content-based instruction in elementary and secondary school settings.* Alexandria, VA: TESOL.

Moon, J. (2000). *Children learning English.* Oxford, UK: MacMillan Heinemann.

Schinke-Llano, L., & Rauff, R. (Eds.). (1996). *New ways in teaching young learners.* Alexandria, VA: TESOL.

Shin, J. K. (2007). Developing dynamic units for EFL. *English Teaching Forum, 45*(2), 2–9.

Useful Web Sites

English Club: http://www.englishclub.com/

English for Kids: http://www.englishclub.com/kids/

English for Young Learners: http://englishforyounglearners.org/

International Association of Teachers of English as a Foreign Language, Young Learners & Teenagers Special Interest Group: http://www.yltsig.org

MES-English: http://www.mes-english.com/games.php

References

Brewster, J., Ellis, G., & Girard, D. (2004). *The primary English teacher's guide,* 2nd ed. Essex, UK: Penguin/Pearson Education.

Cameron, L. (2001). *Teaching languages to young learners.* New York, NY: Cambridge University Press.

Crandall, J. A. (1994). *Content-centered language learning.* Washington, DC: ERIC Clearinghouse on Languages and Linguistics, Center for Applied Linguistics.

Crandall, J. A. (1998). Collaborate and cooperate: Teacher education for integrating language and content instruction. *English Teaching Forum, 36*(1), 2–9. Available at http://exchanges.state.gov/englishteaching/forum/archives/1998.html

Crandall, J. A. (2001). Rethinking classroom management: Creating an effective learning community. *ESL Magazine, 4*(3), 10–13. Reprinted in I. A. Heath & C. J. Serrano (Eds.), *Perspectives on teaching English language learners.* Newbery, FL: Glanzer Press.

Crandall, J. A., & Tucker, G. R. (1990). Content-based instruction in teaching second and foreign languages. In A. M. Padilla, H. H. Fairchild, & C. M. Valadez (Eds.), *Foreign language education: Issues and strategies* (pp. 187–200). Newbury Park, CA: Sage.

Curtain, H., & Dahlberg, C. A. (2010). *Languages and children: Making the match,* 4th ed. New York, NY: Pearson.

Genesee, F. (2000). *Brain research: Implications for second language learning.* ERIC Digest. Washington, DC: ERIC Clearinghouse on Languages and Linguistics, Center for Applied Linguistics.

Available at http://www.cal.org/resources/digest/digest_pdfs/0012-genesee-brain.pdf

Gilzow, D. F. (2002). *Model early foreign language programs: Key elements.* Washington, DC. Available at http://www.cal.org/resources/digest/0211gilzow.html

Haas, M. (2000). *Thematic communicative language teaching in the K–8 classroom.* ERIC Digest. Available at http://www.cal.org/resources/digest/0004thematic.html

Harmer, J. (2007). *The practice of English language teaching,* 4th ed. Essex, UK: Pearson Longman.

Jackup, R. (1996). Matching pictures. In L. Schinke-Llano & R. Rauff (Eds.), *New ways in teaching young children* (p. 3). Alexandria, VA: TESOL.

Kaufman, D., & Crandall, J. A. (Eds.). (2005). *Content-based instruction in elementary and secondary school settings.* Alexandria, VA: TESOL.

Krashen, S. D. (1982). *Principles and practice in second language acquisition.* New York, NY: Pergamon. A 2009 Internet edition with slight revisions is also available at http://www.sdkrashen.com/Principles_and_Practice/Principles_and_Practice.pdf

Krashen, S. D., & Terrell, T. (1995). *The natural approach: Language acquisition in the classroom,* rev. ed. Englewood Cliffs, NJ: Prentice-Hall.

Linse, C. (2005). *Practical English language teaching: Young learners.* New York, NY: McGraw Hill.

Mohan, B. (1986). *Language and content.* Reading, MA: Addison-Wesley.

Moon, J. (2000). *Children learning English.* Oxford, UK: Macmillan Heinemann ELT.

Pinter, A. (2006). *Teaching young language learners.* Oxford, UK: Oxford University Press.

Scott, W. A., & Ytreberg, L. H. (1990). *Teaching English to children.* London, UK: Longman.

Shin, J. K. (2014). Teaching young learners in ESL and EFL settings. In M. Celce-Murcia, D. Brinton, & M. A. Snow (Eds.), *Teaching English as a second or foreign language,* 4th ed. Boston, MA: National Geographic Learning/Cengage Learning.

Snow, M. A., Met, M., and Genesee, F. (1989). A conceptual framework for the integration of language and content in second/foreign language programs. *TESOL Quarterly, 23*(2), 201–217.

Vale, D., & Feunteun, A. (1998). *Teaching children English: A training course for teachers of English to children.* Cambridge, UK: Cambridge University Press.

4 Teaching Listening and Speaking

■ Getting Started

The purpose of this chapter is to look at some basic principles behind the teaching of listening and speaking for young learners. It will explore ways to make listening input comprehensible and check comprehension. In addition, it will look into aspects of vocabulary building and pronunciation work while building communicative abilities of students. This chapter will give examples of specific techniques and activities that are appropriate and effective for primary classrooms. This includes fun activities for teaching aural and oral skills including Total Physical Response, songs, rhymes, chants, games, and more.

Think About It | Think about everyday life for a child. What are some real-life examples of listening that a school-aged child might hear? Imagine what they are listening to inside the classroom, outside the classroom, and at home.

Michele Burgess/ Alamy

Marmaduke St. John/Alamy

Think about real-life communication that children engage in on a day-to-day basis. What types of conversations are primary school–aged children engaged in? What are the kinds of speaking that children do every day inside the classroom, outside the classroom, and at home.

Discovery Activity

Brainstorming Table

Now that you have thought about the kinds of authentic or real-life listening and speaking the young learners are engaged in on a daily basis, write down your ideas in the table below. Also consider the kinds of listening and speaking activities that very young learners versus young learners do every day.

	Listening	Speaking	Both
VYLs	*Example: TV cartoons*	*Example: Singing songs*	*Example: Buying candy at the store*
YLs			

■ Theory, Planning and Application

Considerations for Teaching Listening and Speaking

Now that you have thought about authentic listening and speaking that children do in their real lives, it is important to think about how to incorporate these types of tasks in the classroom. As Chapter 2 and Chapter 3 both emphasize, we should use activities related to children's interests and real lives including their lives in other classes in school. Children may be listening to language while they watch a cartoon on TV or when they hear an announcement by their teacher at school.

They might listen to their grandmother sing a traditional song or hear a pop song over the radio while in a restaurant. Teachers should try to bring real-life listening like these examples that children can relate to into the classroom. Although there could be some one-way listening, like hearing a song or watching TV, children are also engaged in different kinds of two-way conversations. It is important to teach students to communicate orally in real conversations, recognizing that with real communicative acts it is impossible to separate the skills of listening and speaking. Children might interact with the cashier in a candy store or have a conversation about the school day with their mother during dinner. They often have conversations with their peers about what they like and don't like. The foundation of an effective approach for teaching listening and speaking in the EYL classroom is the use of meaningful text types and a focus on building oral communication skills.

In this part of the chapter, we look at important considerations for teaching listening and speaking in the EYL classroom by defining each skill and establishing some basic principles for teaching each skill. Of course, it is impossible to completely separate the two skills, so in each case there is reference to the other skill.

Considerations for Teaching Listening

First, we will explore how to approach teaching listening. This skill might be overlooked because it seems passive. When people listen they do not move their lips or take any outward action that can be perceived. However, as this chapter will show, it is an active process that requires different kinds of skills and strategies. It is important for EYL teachers not to overlook this skill even though is not visible to the eye or audible to the ears. Morley (2001) points out that listening is actually used more than any other skill. "On average, we can expect to listen twice as much as we speak, four times more than we read, and five times more than we write" (p. 70). As the most used of the four language skills, it is essential to make sure our young learners are able to listen well and gain meaning from listening input. To find the best way to teach listening, it is important to gain an understanding of what listening is. This section will address the following aspects of listening:

- What is listening?
- Bottom-up and top-down listening
- Principles for teaching listening to YLs

Jupiterimages/Getty Images

What Is Listening?

It is important to remember that the process of listening is active. The listener must interact with what is heard and interpret the message accurately in order to make sense of it. This is a complex process that happens so quickly in our native language that we can easily forget all the steps that must occur for a message to be understood through listening. Peterson (2001) describes listening as "a multilevel, interactive process of meaning creation" (p. 88). From a cognitive psychology point of view, Anderson (2009) defines listening comprehension in three stages: perceptual processing, parsing, and utilization. In the first stage, there is a sound encoded with language that is perceived and recognized as language; then the language is decoded and stored in short-term memory; finally, comprehension occurs in the utilization stage as the listener matches the language heard with ideas stored in long-term memory. Of course this process can be quite difficult for a second language learner, who is still learning the language, and especially for a young learner, who does not have much information or schemata stored in long-term memory.

Bottom-Up and Top-Down Listening

Listening is an interpretive skill, like reading. Interpreting language is often broken down into two psycholinguistic processes: bottom-up and top-down. Bottom-up processing starts with interpreting the sounds linguistically and gaining meaning by decoding parts of the language, whereas top-down processing refers to interpreting the message through the context in which the message in being delivered. Think about the popular Berlitz television commercial that shows a young German Coast Guard radio dispatcher on duty who has an ill-timed misunderstanding caused by his faulty bottom-up listening skills.

Sailor on sinking boat:	*Mayday mayday. . . . Hello, can you hear us? Over.*
	We are sinking.
German Coast Guard:	*Um . . . hello? Zis is zee German Coast Guard.*
Sailor on sinking boat:	*We are sinking! We are sinking!*
German Coast Guard:	*What are you zinking about?*

The commercial ends with "Improve your English" after this sketch that makes fun of the Coast Guard dispatcher who cannot hear the difference between "th" and "s" and responds to "We are sinking!" with "What are you thinking about?" Of course, in reality this would be an impossible scenario because within the context of the Coast Guard and communication with boats, there is no way to confuse the communication. In other words, top-down processing skills would prevent this scenario from ever happening! However, it does illustrate the difference between bottom-up and top-down listening skills and shows the importance of developing both in our learners.

Bottom-up processing means that listeners are using linguistic knowledge to make sense of an utterance, starting with the smallest parts of language and putting them together to construct meaning. Listening from the bottom up means a learner may proceed from sounds to words to sentences to literal meaning. This means putting the smaller parts of language together to figure out what someone is saying. This is what the Coast Guard radio dispatcher was doing; he was putting together the sounds he heard into an utterance he thought was "We are thinking." Thus, bottom-up techniques for teaching listening usually focus on sounds, words, intonation, grammatical structures, and other discrete components of spoken language.

Some examples of listening activities for young learners that focus on bottom-up processing skills are:

- Students listen to a pair of words and circle if the words are the same or different.
- Students match a word they hear with its picture.
- Students listen to a series of sentences and distinguish the subjects from the verbs.
- Students listen to a short dialog and fill in the blanks of a transcript.

However, top-down processing starts with schemata or background knowledge based on the context of the communication. It also includes the listeners' knowledge of the text type within the context. Instead of focusing on linguistic parts of the utterance, learners learn how to gain meaning from the context and might be able to predict what will be said. Like the Berlitz commercial, the context of the Coast Guard and the predictability of boats calling in to the radio dispatcher when there is a problem makes it impossible to believe that the young dispatcher could have interpreted the utterance "We are sinking" as the opener for a casual friendly conversation. The text type would be a distress communication with "Mayday, mayday!" and would already be known to the listener.

In order to work on top-down techniques that focus on the activation of background knowledge and the meaning of the text, teachers can do the following with their young learners:

- Before students listen to an announcement, they are shown the context of an airport and predict what they might hear.
- Students listen to some utterances and describe the emotional reaction they hear: happy, sad, etc.
- Students listen to a conversation between a doctor and a patient and choose a picture showing the correct location of the dialog with the correct people having the conversation.

It is important to use both bottom-up and top-down techniques when teaching listening. With young learners who are at the beginning stages, it could be easy to focus more on bottom-up techniques that focus on isolated language structures, because they are learning the building blocks of language from letter to word to sentence. However, as Pinter (2006) explains, "In comparison with adults, children have less developed schematic knowledge about many topics; they know less about the world in general and therefore guess and infer meaning with more difficulty. The younger the children, the more this applies" (p. 46). Therefore, for young learners, teachers need to also focus the listening activities on meaning and help them develop strategies for top-down processing in the foreign language. Teachers of young learners should be sure to strike a good balance between the two.

Principles for Teaching Listening to YLs
In EYL classes there is an enormous amount of listening. It is the main source of communication for instruction between teacher and YL students. They are not only learning to listen but also listening to learn. For VYLs in particular, there is minimal reading since they are just beginning to gain literacy skills in both the native and foreign

language, so the majority of language input for students is through listening. Curtain and Dahlberg (2010) state that "Listening is considered by many teachers and researchers to be the cornerstone of language development. In beginning classrooms, listening is the main channel by which the student makes initial contact with the target language and its culture" (p. 71). In fact, the main source of listening input is the teacher giving instructions and demonstrations. Therefore, teachers of YLs have to be very conscious about their approach to giving students listening input.

When designing listening activities for young learners, it is important to remember the following seven principles.

1. Prepare teacher talk carefully.

2. Use listening activities that reflect real-life listening.

3. Use listening activities that are developmentally appropriate.

4. Use a variety of techniques to make listening input comprehensible.

5. Check comprehension using a variety of response types.

6. Keep listening active—always give learners a listening task.

7. Equip your students with intelligent guesswork strategies.

1. **Prepare teacher talk carefully** Children will spend most of their time listening to the teacher giving instructions, modeling language, singing songs, doing chants, dramatizing dialogs, and telling stories (Brewster, Ellis, & Girard, 2004; Pinter, 2006). Therefore, teachers need to carefully plan how they use language in the classroom. In fact, Brewster, Ellis, and Girard (2004) comment specifically about the use of L1: "The teacher will have to decide how much of the general 'classroom language' such as instructions, questions or praise will be in the pupils' L1 and how much in English" (p. 98). The decision to use L1 to give more complicated instructions for an activity or for classroom management purposes should be very deliberate and absolutely necessary to give optimum time for YLs to listen to and use English that is at an appropriate level for them.

However, when preparing teacher talk in English, think about both the level and the amount as you prepare for your lessons. It can be overwhelming to have long stretches of explanations when students have low levels of proficiency. In addition, YLs have short attention spans, so long stretches of input that is not comprehensible will likely be the cause of students zoning out or acting up.

Teachers can start by teaching YLs to understand and respond to some basic classroom language:

- Come in.
- Sit down.
- Be quiet.
- Listen carefully.
- Let's begin!
- Look here.
- This is . . .
- That is . . .
- Are you ready?

- Great!
- Come to the board.
- Open your books.
- Turn to page . . .
- What is the answer?
- What is . . . ?
- Where is . . . ?
- Who is . . . ?
- When is . . . ?

Try to prepare short segments or comprehensible listening input when giving instructions, doing demonstrations, or explaining language.

2. **Use listening activities that reflect real-life listening** Activities should involve authentic language and real-world contexts as much as possible to make the learning more meaningful, motivating, and useful for students. As Chapters 2 and 3 established, using real-life text types helps YLs use English to mirror and contextualize language instruction. The following are some often-used examples of text types that reflect real-life listening and are motivating for YLs:

- Songs (traditional songs, children's songs, pop songs)
- Chants and raps
- Stories
- Plays
- TV shows (game shows, comedy shows, soap operas)
- TV commercials
- Radio ads
- News reports
- Weather reports
- Announcements (school, airport, train station)
- Cartoons
- Movies

- Documentaries
- Jokes and riddles
- Tongue twisters
- Dialogs (conversations)

3. Use listening activities that are developmentally appropriate If the activities are developmentally appropriate (see Chapter 2), they will be more intrinsically motivating and comprehensible. All activities should take into consideration learners' age, background knowledge, and interests. For example, for VYLs you can use children's songs like "Itsy Bitsy Spider," or nursery rhymes like "Hickory Dickory Dock." However, with older YLs in grades 4–6, you may start to use pop songs or rap instead of traditional songs and chants. It helps to find out what cartoons, TV shows, and movies interest children at different ages and try to incorporate them or similarly themed activities into instruction. A good place to find appropriate materials that are grouped by age is the Web site of Common Sense Media (www.commonsensemedia.org). This is an American organization whose mission is to provide trustworthy information about the media to help families make good decisions about the media children are exposed to. They suggest good cartoons, TV shows, movies, books, and so on for children by age, and it could be a good place to see what kinds of media are attractive as well as appropriate in terms of content and delivery by age group.

4. Use a variety of techniques to make listening input comprehensible Preparation for a listening activity: Because young children are still new to our world and do not have a lot of background knowledge, it is important for teachers to help make input comprehensible by preparing students for the context. In other words, the teacher needs to consider how to tap into students' background knowledge and build schemata that may not be there in order to understand the listening context in an activity. In addition, young learners of English do not have a high proficiency in English and their English vocabulary is limited. Therefore, teachers should prepare students with vocabulary needed to understand the listening activity. Preparing context clues like pictures and realia are helpful, too. Marley and Szabo (2010) did a comparison with kindergarteners and first graders to see if there was a difference in listening comprehension during storytelling when pictures were shown versus when students were given objects that they could manipulate. They found that physical manipulation of objects that are described in the story enhanced listening comprehension and increased recall of information more than the use of pictures that depicted the story. This supports the use of realia and hands-on activities with young learners to support listening comprehension. As Chapter 2 explained, children are active learners and will gain more comprehension and remember more when hands-on activities are used.

Interactional modifications In addition to preparing ways to help students understand the listening input in a lesson, teachers should be ready to make interactional modifications during the activity—for example, repetition, comprehension checks, and gestures. These interactional modifications have been studied in young learner EFL classrooms, and research found them to be highly effective in promoting comprehension of listening input (Cabrera & Martínez, 2001; Peñate & Bazo, 1998). Peñate and Bazo found in their study of primary EFL teachers that repetition, comprehension checks, and gestures were the main interactional modifications used. Cabrera and Martínez found that teachers who used these three interactions in a primary EFL class increased young learners' understanding of oral discourse, specifically storytelling. They found statistically significant differences in levels of comprehension between groups of 10-year-olds when the teacher used repetition, comprehension checks, and gestures as interactional modifications during storytelling and when the teacher did not.

5. **Check comprehension using a variety of response types** Often we ask students, "Do you understand?" Of course, the response is always, "Yes, Teacher!" But how can you know if students truly understand without something concrete or observable? Teachers can check comprehension using a variety of response types that should be both verbal and nonverbal. For young learners who have a beginning level of proficiency, it can be very stressful to show comprehension by having to produce language and respond verbally using new language. There are many ways that a learner can respond.

Lund (1990, p. 259) provided a comprehensive list of ways to check students' comprehension:

- **Doing:** Listener responds physically (i.e., TPR, making a recipe)
- **Choosing:** Listener selects from alternatives such as pictures, objects, texts, or actions (i.e., matching, placing pictures in right order, picking up objects according to description)
- **Transferring:** Listener transfers information into another form (i.e., drawing, tracing a route on a map, constructing a table or chart)

- **Answering:** Listener answers questions about the message
- **Condensing:** Listener reduces the message (i.e., outlines, notetaking, oral or written summaries)
- **Extending:** Listener provides text that goes beyond what is given (i.e., giving the end of a story, solving a problem, filling in missing lines)
- **Duplicating:** Listener repeats exact message (i.e., dictation, translation, oral repetition)
- **Modeling:** Listener uses text as a model for imitation (i.e., ordering a meal after listening to a model)
- **Conversing:** Listener is active in face-to-face conversations

This is a useful taxonomy for conceptualizing the ways teachers can check comprehension of a listening activity. Detailing Lund's (1990) taxonomy more specifically can give lots of practical ideas to teachers for planning appropriate ways to check comprehension for young learners. For teaching young learners, many sources express the activities using a "Listen and . . ." format (Brewster, Ellis, & Girard, 2004; Cameron, 2001; Scott & Ytreberg, 1990; Slatterly & Willis, 2001). In this chapter, we will suggest "Listen and . . ." activities that are commonly used in EYL classrooms. They are classified into three main categories that take into account level of difficulty:

- **Nonverbal demonstration of comprehension**, such as listen and do, point, move, mime, choose, etc.
- **Nonverbal demonstration of comprehension but require some reading**, such as listen and choose, transfer, sequence, match, classify, etc.
- **Demonstration of comprehension with production**, either oral or written, such as listen and transfer, answer, condense, extend, duplicate, model, converse, etc.

6. **Keep listening active—always give learners a listening task** Every listening activity should give YLs a purpose for listening and, better yet, a task to complete. All too often teachers will say "Listen to this," and then sing a song or play a tape without giving learners a task or a reason to listen. YLs have short attention spans and can't always focus themselves on a learning activity. Instead, teachers should say "Listen and . . . ," filling in the blank with an appropriate task. For example, a teacher could ask students to listen and then point to the correct picture, with three pictures of different contexts to choose from. If the students know they must point to the correct picture after listening, then they will pay attention to the listening in order to figure out which picture is right. It will focus them on the listening and make them more active in the listening process.

7. **Equip your students with intelligent guesswork strategies** In order to develop students' ability to listen more effectively, it is important to incorporate various listening strategies in your instruction. Peterson (2001) wrote, "When things are going well, the listener is not conscious of using skills at all. At the point when the comprehension breaks down for some reason, the listener becomes aware of the need for repair and seeks an appropriate strategy for comprehension" (p. 90). Equipping our YLs with a whole range of strategies can actually help them improve their listening comprehension beyond the classroom, which is one of our goals.

In terms of listening strategies for YLs, Brewster, Ellis and Girard (2004) wrote that developing "intelligent guesswork" is a very important skill for young learners (p. 99). They suggest the following strategies: predicting, working out the meaning from context, and recognizing discourse patterns and markers (p. 100). Within these important listening strategies, we can put together a list of the most helpful ones for YLs to develop in order to gain meaning from the listening.

Using prediction strategies will help learners make intelligent guesses and then check whether their predictions are correct. Even if the students do not know all the vocabulary or language structures presented, they can still make sense of the listening text using these strategies and guess meaning based on the context. The more you can connect these strategies with real-life listening, the better it will be for listening that happens outside the classroom.

- **Predict what a listening text will be about:** Any real-life listening will be embedded in a context. For example, in a candy store, the clerk will probably ask if you need help finding something, if you are ready to pay, and tell you how much the candy costs. If students are presented with a context, they can probably predict what they will hear.

- **Predict what will happen next (or the ending):** In most contexts, it is possible to predict what someone will say next. In a conversation between a student and a school nurse, after the school nurse asks the student a series of questions, students can probably predict the school nurse will make a prognosis or give some advice.

- **Use discourse markers or signal words to guess what happens next:** Real discourse makes use of signal words such as first, then, finally, but, so, etc. to guide the listener. For example, when students are given instructions on how to make a peanut butter and jelly sandwich, they can follow along each step, which is introduced by a marker: "First you take the peanut butter, and you spread it on the bread. Then you take the jelly, and you. . . ." Helping students automatically recognize these signal words is a strategy they can use to improve their listening.

- **Use background knowledge of the context:** Students' own background knowledge of the context can help them make sense of the story. For example, in a story like *The Very Hungry Caterpillar,* the students can understand the meaning of the new words, like caterpillar, cocoon, and butterfly, based on their background knowledge of the life cycle of a butterfly. If not, then the teacher has to build the background knowledge before the story or through the story.

- **Listen for the main idea:** We listen for the main idea of a listening text to help gain comprehension. For example, if you are telling your YLs the story *The Tortoise and the Hare,* even if students do not understand all the vocabulary, they can still understand the gist of the story, which is that the tortoise wins the race even though the hare is a faster animal. Then the teacher can help build comprehension of the language starting with students' understanding of the main idea.

- **Listen for specific details:** If the activity is to listen to a description of a person and figure out in a picture who is being described, then students can listen for specific descriptions that match the different people in the picture, i.e., gender, height, hair color, clothes, etc.

- **Listen for key words:** In real-life listening, we can pick out key words that we understand which can help us comprehend the message. For example, if the listening text is a weather report, then you can get your YLs to listen for certain key words, like sunny, rainy, cold, warm, hot, etc.

- **Look for nonverbal cues to gain meaning:** In real life, there are usually nonverbal cues from the speaker, such as facial expressions, hand gestures, and body language, that can help interpret meaning of the language input. For example, when people learn simple greetings, students can understand from body language cues, like shaking hands or waving hello.

- **Guess the meaning of unknown words:** Using a variety of strategies in combination, YLs can guess the meaning of unknown words. For example, if YLs are listening to a commercial for a department store, which might be a familiar context, they can catch the gist of the commercial, which is to make you want to buy toys at the store. Then they may notice there are higher and lower prices for each toy. From these different strategies working together, they may be able to guess the meaning of difficult unknown words used repeatedly, like sale or clearance.

These are some intelligent guesswork strategies that teachers should help young learners develop through listening tasks. If learners can develop the use of these strategies independent of the teacher, then they will be improving their ability to listen effectively on their own.

Considerations for Teaching Speaking

Next let's explore how to approach teaching speaking. Although we have divided this chapter into teaching two skills, listening and speaking, it is impossible to separate the two. Much of the listening we do in real life occurs as part of a two-way conversation that requires speaking in response. Even many of the so-called one-way listening text types, such as TV shows, movies, and cartoons, actually depict two-way conversations. For many reasons, speaking is often considered a very difficult language skill to learn to do well. As Pinter (2006) points out, "This is because to be able to speak fluently, we have to speak and think at the same time. As we speak, we have to monitor our output and correct any mistakes, as well as planning for what we are going to say next" (p. 55). In addition, for many people, speaking out in a classroom or interacting in everyday conversations, even in the native language, is not easy. There are affective factors that can create anxiety in students that will prevent them from speaking out. In addition, in some cultures around the world speaking out in class is not customary or valued. For example, a Japanese proverb reflects the value of not speaking out: "He who speaks has no knowledge and he who has knowledge does not speak."

We will look at considerations for teaching speaking as an integral skill working in tandem with listening for oral communication. In addition, the activities we will explore will include oral presentation skills:

- What is speaking?
- Fluency vs. accuracy
- Principles for teaching speaking to YLs

What Is Speaking?

> **"**A mouse saved her young from a ferocious cat by barking "bow-wow." After the cat ran away, the mouse said to her offspring "See, children, it pays to know a second language.**"**
>
> — *Efstathiadis*

This story illustrates the power of being able to speak another language, even if it is only one word. If you understand the context, know the appropriate use of the word,

Ryan McVay/Rise/Getty Images

and can pronounce it well, then you can communicate effectively and achieve your objective!

For most people, speaking is the language skill that represents the main mode of communication. In the native language, the first skill parents work on teaching their babies is speaking. It is the skill that helps children become an interactive part of a family and a community. In most cases the point of speaking is two-way oral communication. Young learners are still learning how to communicate effectively in their native language, and when they are VYLs, they are still working on their ability to respond appropriately to questions and explain their ideas. Therefore, EYL teachers have to consider what kinds of oral communication are appropriate activities for learners at certain ages, in addition to helping them communicate orally in English. Teachers should check with YLs' regular classes to see what kinds of speaking skills are expected at different age levels (Pinter, 2006).

First language listening and speaking skills It is important to check what kinds of listening and speaking skills are expected at different ages. In the United States, teachers have a set of standards they can refer to known as the Common Core Standards. They show the knowledge and skills school-age students should be able to master at each grade level in the U.S. Similar standards in your country could be helpful to figure out what children are capable of. With respect to oral communication (listening and speaking), here are the standards for a kindergartener versus a fifth grader:

Common Core Standards—Listening and Speaking

Kindergarten	5th Grade
Comprehension and Collaboration	**Comprehension and Collaboration**

Comprehension and Collaboration

SL.K.1. Participate in collaborative conversations with diverse partners about *kindergarten topics and texts* with peers and adults in small and larger groups.

– Follow agreed-upon rules for discussions (e.g., listening to others and taking turns speaking about the topics and texts under discussion).

– Continue a conversation through multiple exchanges.

SL.K.2. Confirm understanding of a text read aloud or information presented orally or through other media by asking and answering questions about key details and requesting clarification if something is not understood.

SL.K.3. Ask and answer questions in order to seek help, get information, or clarify something that is not understood.

Presentation of Knowledge and Ideas

SL.K.4. Describe familiar people, places, things, and events and, with prompting and support, provide additional detail.

SL.K.5. Add drawings or other visual displays to descriptions as desired to provide additional detail.

SL.K.6. Speak audibly and express thoughts, feelings, and ideas clearly.

Comprehension and Collaboration

SL.5.1. Engage effectively in a range of collaborative discussions (one-on-one, in groups, and teacher-led) with diverse partners on *grade 5 topics and texts,* building on others' ideas and expressing their own clearly.

– Come to discussions prepared, having read or studied required material; explicitly draw on that preparation and other information known about the topic to explore ideas under discussion.

– Follow agreed-upon rules for discussions and carry out assigned roles.

– Pose and respond to specific questions by making comments that contribute to the discussion and elaborate on the remarks of others.

– Review the key ideas expressed and draw conclusions in light of information and knowledge gained from the discussions.

SL.5.2. Summarize a written text read aloud or information presented in diverse media and formats, including visually, quantitatively, and orally.

SL.5.3. Summarize the points a speaker makes and explain how each claim is supported by reasons and evidence.

Presentation of Knowledge and Ideas

SL.5.4. Report on a topic or text or present an opinion, sequencing ideas logically and using appropriate facts and relevant, descriptive details to support main ideas or themes; speak clearly at an understandable pace.

SL.5.5. Include multimedia components (e.g., graphics, sound) and visual displays in presentations when appropriate to enhance the development of main ideas or themes.

SL.5.6. Adapt speech to a variety of contexts and tasks, using formal English when appropriate to task and situation.

Clearly these standards for English language arts cannot be used as standards for the English as a foreign language class. However, they can show a teacher what students at a certain age or grade level are capable of in terms of communication. These Common Core Standards could be useful to gauge what kind of oral communication students at each grade level should be able to do at their cognitive level. To find out more about the Common Core Standards as an example, see http://www.corestandards.org.

When teaching oral communication skills, teachers should not forget how complex the process of communication can be. As Cameron (2001) notes, "Listening can be seen as the active use of language to access other people's meanings, whereas speaking is the active use of language to express meanings so that other people can make sense of them" (p. 40). When using English as an international language to communicate across cultures, it increases the difficulty in understanding one another. Read the passage below written by French writer Bernard Werber (in both French and English).

> *Entre ce que je pense, ce que je veux dire, ce que je crois dire, ce que je dis, ce que vous voulez entendre, ce que vous entendez, ce que vous croyez en comprendre, ce que vous voulez comprendre, et ce que vous comprenez, il y a au moins neuf possibilités de ne pas se comprendre.*

> *Between what I think, what I want to say, what I think I am saying, what I say, what you want to hear, what you hear, what you think you understand, what you want to understand, and what you understand, there are at least nine chances that we will not understand each other.*

Mixed into this message are the different steps of communication, including what you think and want to say, how to encode the thoughts into language, how the listener decodes what you have said, and all the mishaps that can happen based on the intentions and expectations of both sides. Even when there are two people who are native speakers of the same language, there can be many opportunities for misunderstanding. In addition to teaching how to listen and speak, to improve oral communication skills, teachers also have to give students skills to negotiate meaning and clarify any misunderstandings.

Fluency vs. Accuracy With speaking as a productive skill, the main concerns are issues of fluency versus accuracy. Teachers are always concerned with both, and with young learners there is no exception. We want our students to speak accurately with respect to grammar and pronunciation and to speak fluently with respect to speed and natural flow of the language. Brown (2007) states that "The fluency/accuracy issue often boils down to the extent to which our techniques should be message oriented (or, as some call it, teaching language use) as opposed to language oriented (also known as teaching language usage)" (p. 324). With young learners, our approach is not focused on grammatical explanations, so the approach should be more message-oriented or based on meaningful activities within a realistic context. At the beginning levels, the language being taught is in small chunks, so the possibility of repetition and drilling for accuracy is just as possible while doing activities to build vocabulary and practice meaningful expressions. It is possible and necessary to teach YLs short, fixed chunks of language. As Pinter (2006) explains, "The first building blocks that allow children to move from listening to speaking and to begin to participate in interactions with others are so-called 'unanalysed chunks'" (p. 56). This is also known as "formulaic language" (Brewster, Ellis, & Girard, 2004, p. 105) or "formulaic sequences" (Cameron, 2001, p. 50). For example, "How are you?" is a fixed chunk that can be taught as a greeting and repeated at the beginning of class. Students don't have to analyze this fixed chunk of meaning and understand it when the teacher uses it every day to greet the class. The teacher can get students to respond with another chunk, "Fine, thank you."

In terms of pronunciation, we have established that young learners have an advantage because they are excellent imitators. Their ability to repeat after a model accurately is one aspect of speaking that should be easy to develop with YLs. So providing them with plenty of models and chances to imitate is important. Repetition is very important for YLs, but teachers have to make it fun, engaging, and as meaningful as possible through activities like songs, chants, rhymes, and games to help them start to memorize new chunks and use them correctly.

Principles for Teaching Speaking to YLs

In EYL classes teachers find it challenging to build a nurturing and comfortable environment for YLs that is motivating and encourages maximum participation from students. The teacher needs to find every opportunity to build real communication into the classroom since EFL contexts have a shortage of opportunities for communication in English outside the classroom. Teachers of our youngest learners have to create fun activities that keep learners active; even if they use repetition, it has to be meaningful. Remember that our goal is to build a classroom that is English speaking, provides plenty of opportunities for practice, and is engaging for YLs.

When designing speaking activities for young learners, it is important to remember the following seven principles:

1. Build classroom routines in English.
2. Use speaking activities that reflect real-life communication.

3. Use speaking activities that are developmentally appropriate.

4. Use a variety of activities to improve both accuracy and fluency.

5. Build classroom interaction by giving students plenty of opportunities to participate.

6. Keep the speaking environment active—do not correct errors explicitly.

7. Equip your YLs with negotiation strategies.

1. Build classroom routines in English Young learners need to speak out in order to build their oral proficiency in English. It is important to give time every class for all students to practice speaking. Building classroom routines in English will ensure that every day you have students using the language communicatively, such as greeting you and each other, saying the day's date, sharing what they did yesterday, and saying farewell to everyone. If the classroom is a warm, inviting place to learn, and the teacher sets up routines to communicate in every class, then students will feel more comfortable and confident about speaking out and trying to communicate in English. YLs will remember these routines in English better than some course content because of all the repetition in a meaningful context. Here are some examples of classroom language for what Winn-Smith (2001) refers to as "social rituals" (p. 22).

Hello!
Hi!
How are you?
I'm fine. And you?
Who is missing?
Where is Adam?
Good-bye!
See you tomorrow!

2. Use speaking activities that reflect real-life communication Appropriate text types for YLs will be the same as the list given in the listening section. That list included songs, chants, rap, storytelling, plays, TV shows and commercials, news and weather reports, announcements, cartoons, movies, documentaries, jokes, riddles, and dialogues. These are all oral text types that teachers can use to encourage students to practice speaking. In most EFL classrooms, teachers use lots of dialogs to practice speaking, particularly ones found in the textbook. These dialogs usually reflect real-life tasks, like greetings, buying something at a store, visiting a doctor, asking for directions, asking for the time, etc. In addition, the different modes of one-way input, like TV shows and commercials, news and weather reports, and movies, are actually models of communication among two or more people. For YLs, who like to be active and move around, it is very helpful to use role play and drama to practice the language. These scenarios can be brought to life and practiced in a way that mirrors real life.

3. **Use speaking activities that are developmentally appropriate** As stated before, if activities are developmentally appropriate they will be more intrinsically motivating to students. All activities, both listening and speaking, should take into consideration learners' age, background knowledge, and interests. As Cameron (2001) explains, "Discourse in young learner classrooms should follow patterns children find familiar, from their home and family, or from their school experience, and should not demand more of children than they can do, in terms of imagining someone else's state of mind or expressing causes and beliefs" (p. 53). Checking out the standards and expectations for communication at each grade level in the native language can be helpful in defining realistic expectations for what kinds of interaction YLs are capable of. It is also important to consider the types of conversations and discussions young learners would be having at their age or would find interesting:

- Conversation with friend about favorite things: "What is your favorite . . . ?" (color, animal, season, etc.)
- Asking someone for directions: "Where is the . . . ?" (school, grocery story, library, etc.)
- Games like Telephone, 21 Questions, or Jeopardy
- Discussion about a shopping list for a classmate's birthday party

There are also one-way speaking presentations that young learners like that can give them plenty of practice with the language. Activities like songs, chants, and plays provide good practice based on clear models. In terms of extended discourse, narrative and description are the discourse types considered most appropriate for YLs based on their cognitive level (Cameron, 2001). In addition, presentational activities that are about YLs' personal lives are very appropriate because they are still at a very egocentric stage. The following are some good activities for one-way speaking practice:

- Sing a fun song (as a whole class, small group, or individual)
- Retell a story (narrative)
- Show and tell presentation (description)
- Make a presentation to class about the members of your family, your favorite celebrity, etc., with a picture or poster (personalization)

These are just some examples of different speaking activities, both interactive and presentational, that are appropriate for YLs.

4. **Use a variety of activities to improve both accuracy and fluency** In order to give YLs plenty of practice that also builds both accuracy and fluency, teachers should use a variety of activities. These activities can be classified as controlled practice, guided practice, and independent activities (see Chapter 3). Speaking activities that focus on accuracy can be quite mechanical or controlled, which means students are practicing structure, but it is not necessarily meaningful. For example, repetition is considered very mechanical. When a teacher says "Repeat after me. It's a horse." and then students repeat "It's a horse," it is possible for students to practice pronunciation of "It's a horse" without knowing the meaning. Even with flashcards showing the meaning of the word horse, this would be considered a very mechanical drill. This is the most controlled type of activity, practicing accuracy of sentence structure (It's a . . .) and pronunciation (horse). The responses are completely predictable, with very little chance of making a mistake, and the use of target language structures is completely controlled by the teacher. Activities that are still structured but give students some choice are considered guided. See the Sample Lesson Plan later in this chapter for an example of guided practice.

At the opposite end are independent or free activities that are open-ended and do not have predictable responses. These are message oriented and more focused on meaning and communication than correctness. Free activities help build fluency and give students a chance to be creative with the language on their own. This is the most challenging because there are more chances for error. For example, the teacher might have students do a short presentation role playing a farm animal. The model would be: "I am Dorothy Duck. Quack quack. I live on a farm. Quack quack. I am in the pond. Quack quack!" In this example, learners get a chance to choose their own animals and create with the language based on what they have learned. These activities usually come after students have had a chance for more controlled and guided practice; they encourage real-life communication. Once students can use the language independently, it is important to give them opportunities for speaking activities that are applied to real-life, authentic situations or to personalize.

5. **Build classroom interaction by giving students plenty of opportunities to participate** In EFL settings, usually the only place where students can use and practice English is in the classroom. If this is just once or twice a week, then teachers need to make sure that they provide as much opportunity as possible for students to practice using English in the classroom. The teacher should have as a goal that

every student has a chance to speak out and practice during every class. There are a number of teacher-directed, whole-class techniques and student-centered, cooperative learning activities that can be used.

The teacher-directed, whole-class techniques are more controlled and can be used to check comprehension and for controlled practice in speaking. The following techniques are based on a content-based proficiency-oriented approach by Ron Schwartz (book in preparation). Look at the following examples based on a map of a town:

- **Repetition:** The example below shows a controlled interaction with students repeating after the teacher. The teacher is providing a model of the Q&A interaction.

  > T: *Repeat after me. Where is the school?*
  > Ss: *Where is the school?*
  > T: *It's on Main Street.*
  > Ss: *It's on Main Street.*

- **Question and answer (Q&A):** Below are three examples of the different types of Q&A teachers can encourage students to do: teacher to student(s), student to student, and students to teacher.

Teacher–Student(s)
The teacher is getting everyone involved by asking them to repeat the student's answer.

> T: *Marwa, where is the library?*
> M: *It's on Center Street.*
> T: *Everyone, where is the library?*
> Ss: *It's on Center Street.*

Student–Student
In order to encourage paired interaction that is controlled, the teacher can break students into pairs at the beginning of class: Partner A and Partner B. Then you can encourage quick paired Q&A any time during the class.

> T: *Class, where is the museum?*
> Ss: *It's on Pratt Street.*
> T: *Partner A, ask Partner B "Where is the museum?" Partner B, answer.*

Students–Teacher
The student-to-teacher interaction can help the teacher give a new model. See the example below, where the teacher cues students to ask a question.

> T: Class, ask me, "Where is the mall?"
>
> Ss: Where is the mall?
>
> T: It's on the corner of Pratt and Charles.

- **Paraphrasing:** Students can practice multiple ways of answering the same question. The teacher can give multiple examples and models, so students can try using their own words instead of exact repetition.

> T: See the mall? It is on Pratt Street [point to Pratt Street on map], and It's on Charles Street [point to Charles Street]. Where is the mall?
>
> S: It's on Pratt and Charles.

- **Giving examples:** The teacher can elicit examples from students based on their lives. This is a way that they can participate with new information.

> T: What streets are in our neighborhood?
>
> Ss: Al Khan Street! Al Arouba Street! Corniche Street! Jumeirah Street!
>
> T: Where is our school?
>
> Ss: It's on Al Khan Street.

- **Personalizing:** The teacher can elicit examples based on students' personal lives. This is a way to check comprehension and give them a chance to express something about themselves.

> T: Where is your house?
>
> S: It's on Jumeirah Road.

In addition to teacher-directed techniques to increase classroom interaction, student-centered, cooperative learning activities can be used to increase the amount of time students speak English. These are best utilized for less controlled, more independent activities. First, it is important to realize that YLs do not have long attention spans and cannot focus their own learning. The younger they are, the less independent they can be. Therefore, cooperative learning activities need to be short in length and monitored carefully. In addition, students need to have clear instructions and a model to follow. Teachers may have to explain instructions for a cooperative activity in the native language in order for students to spend their time in class practicing the target language instead of wasting time trying to figure out what to do. See the box for tips for teachers to meet with success when using cooperative activities.

TEYL Tips—Success with Cooperative Learning

■ Choose a short activity with a clear goal and end product.

■ Avoid complicated activities with multiple steps.

■ Plan groups in advance and select groups rather than letting students select them.

■ Give each group a fun name, e.g., name them after words from a previous lesson, like Sun Group, Moon Group, Star Group, Sky Group.

■ Give clear instructions, written and verbal if possible.

■ Give instructions with pictures and examples.

■ Give clear models that show the end product.

■ Give a time limit.

■ Use a signal to indicate the start and end of the activity (e.g., alarm, whistle, lights off, bell, etc.).

■ Assign roles when necessary (e.g., reader, recorder, time keeper, presenter, etc.).

■ Monitor the groups; walk around the classroom and check progress.

■ Always share end products after the activity, e.g., for assessment purposes and to hold students accountable for quality of product.

6. **Keep the speaking environment active—do not correct errors explicitly** Because the language output should be message oriented or meaning focused, it is not a good idea to correct errors of individual YLs explicitly. First, if the activities are focused on meaning more than form, as is customary for an EYL classroom, then making frequent grammar or pronunciation corrections can interrupt the flow of class. In addition, although children can be less inhibited compared to adults and will speak out in class more readily, they also have fragile egos and can close up if you embarrass them in front of their peers. Since YLs learn a foreign language best by mirroring first language acquisition and building an English-speaking environment, teachers should create a classroom atmosphere that makes YLs comfortable speaking out and working with the language. If correction is necessary for a common error or a difficult word, then a teacher can use choral repetition instead of individual repetition, so everyone gets practice and no one is singled out.

7. **Equip your YLs with negotiation strategies** For speaking, students need strategies for negotiation of meaning. For the EFL classroom, this includes use

of classroom language and knowing how to ask questions and make clarification requests. Young learners can learn these chunks of language to help them clarify meaning with the teacher in the whole class or when working with peers in cooperative groups for less controlled activities. Here are some ideas:

I don't understand.
I don't know.
I'm sorry, could you repeat that?
Can you help me, please?
Can/could you repeat that?
Can/could you say it again?
I have a question.
What does _____ mean?
What does it mean?
How do you say _____ in English?
How do you spell _____?
What do you think?
What do you mean?
Really? Why?
Really? Then what?

These are typical classroom expressions that help promote the learning process and are good strategies for real conversations when students use English outside the classroom. Of course, teachers can encourage students to use "Excuse me . . ." before each expression to be more polite.

TEYL Tips—Real Language for Responding

Teachers often forget to teach YLs to give responses to conversations. Usually they follow a strict Q&A routine, such as:

- Student A: What's your favorite food?"
- Student B: It's pizza!

Teachers can liven up the classroom and teach real language to give a response. These are fun and mirror real-life conversations:

- Really? Me, too!
- Really? That's interesting!
- Really? That's terrible!

(Continued)

- That's great!
- That's funny!
- Wow, that's cool!
- Wow, that's too bad!
- Oh, I see!
- Oh no, really?
- No way!
- Great!
- Super!
- Excellent!

So the Q&A above would become:
- Student A: What's your favorite food?"
- Student B: It's pizza!
- Student A: Really? Me, too!

Effective Listening and Speaking Activities

When developing listening and speaking activities, teachers can conceptualize them in three distinct stages: before, during, and after listening. Activities before listening prepare students for the listening input in the presentation step of the lesson. The activities for during listening consist first of ways to make listening input comprehensible as the listening input is being presented. Then there are a number of "Listen and . . ." activities that give the teacher different ways to check comprehension both verbally and nonverbally. Finally, after-listening activities will be suggested, which are speaking activities that move from more controlled to more independent.

Here are some activities that can be incorporated into a listening and speaking lesson for young learners, which will be shown in the following section.

Activities before Listening (Warm-Up Stage) Before the listening activity, prepare students for the activity by activating schemata, connecting the activity to their background knowledge, getting them to predict what they will be listening to, and introducing useful words and concepts.

Examples of activities:

- Prepare students for listening by contextualizing and/or personalizing to make it more accessible and more realistic.
- Activate prior knowledge by showing pictures or realia (e.g., menu, movie schedule).
- Involve students in the specific topic by brainstorming what students know about it with a graphic organizer (e.g., word map, T-chart, listing).
- Review known vocabulary.
- Pre-teach unknown vocabulary.

To review and pre-teach vocabulary, teachers can use any of the following techniques to make the vocabulary items comprehensible:

- Use realia
- Use pictures
- Use flashcards
- Use facial expressions
- Mime/act out the item
- Draw on the board
- Define
- Translate
- Give examples of the item
- Personalize the item
- Give synonyms
- Give antonyms
- Use item in a sentence
- Help students examine morphemes to figure out the meaning and use of the item (e.g., review can be broken into "view" = to see and "re" = again)
- Tell what an item is not (e.g., a moose is not a person)

Activities during Listening (Presentation Stage)

While students are listening, be sure that they are actively listening by using visuals, such as pictures, facial expressions, body movement, asking them questions and eliciting answers, having them respond to the listening by doing, choosing, etc. Give them chances to understand the text through multiple exposures. Teachers should try to sequence the multiple exposures from easier to more challenging.

First is a list of ways a teacher can make listening input more comprehensible.

Techniques for making input comprehensible:

- Use visual cues, like pictures and flashcards
- Use gestures and body movement
- Use realia
- Use graphic organizers (e.g., T-charts, Venn diagrams, mind maps, timelines)
- Translate difficult words (only when necessary)
- Give a definition, synonym, antonym
- Explain the word or expression
- Demonstrate
- Give an example
- Use item in a sentence
- Pronounce words clearly
- Speak slower (without distorting the natural flow)
- Repeat
- Rephrase
- Use shorter and simpler sentences and phrases
- Connect students to background knowledge

Below is a comprehensive list of listening activities. They are listed based on difficulty for students in terms of the following categories:

1. Students listen and show comprehension through action
2. Students listen and read and show comprehension through action
3. Students listen and show comprehension through production (speaking or writing)

1. **Students listen and show comprehension through action:** This is the least demanding on young learners because it does not require production, either oral or written.

- **Listen and point:** Students point to correct picture or object.
- **Listen and move:** Students respond by moving their body, i.e., Total Physical Response.
- **Listen and do:** Students complete a simple task, like putting a sticker or placing an object in the correct place.
- **Listen and raise your hand:** Teachers can cue students to raise their hand if they agree, then raise it if they disagree; or if a particular sound is heard, "Raise your hand when you hear th."

- **Listen and show your fingers:** Students can show the number of fingers to answer a question. For example, the teacher could ask, "How many animals are in the story?"
- **Listen and perform actions:** Students can perform or mime what they hear, such as animal movements, how to play sports, the steps for making a sandwich, etc.
- **Listen and follow directions:** The teacher may give instructions to close the door, turn lights off, turn the page, etc.
- **Listen and color:** The teacher gives students a picture of a boy. S/he gives instructions, such as "Color the hair brown. Color the shirt red. Color the pants blue."
- **Listen and draw:** Students listen to the teacher describe a picture of a house and have to draw it correctly. For example, the teacher might say, "There are two windows. One is on the left side. The other is on the right side. The door is in the middle."
- **Listen and make:** Students listen to the teacher explain how to make a paper plate mask with holes for the eyes and mouth.

Renee Keith/Vetta Collection/iStockphoto.com

- **Listen and follow a map:** Students are given a map and draw a line on the map showing they can follow directions from point A to point B.
- **Listen and circle the correct picture:** Students are given pictures of the context of a dialog or story. They listen and circle the correct picture.
- **Listen and match:** Students can listen to a description and match it to the correct picture, person, place, object, etc.
- **Listen and sequence pictures in the correct order:** Students are given a series of pictures. The teacher could have large pictures on the board or a series of pictures on a handout. Students have to put the pictures in the correct order.
- **Listen and pick the next picture:** Students are given a choice of various pictures that show different endings of a story. They can choose the picture showing what they think happens next.

■ **Listen and detect mistakes in a picture:** Students listen and pick out the mistakes in the picture that was described. For example, if the description is of a person, the teacher could say "The girl has brown hair" when the picture is of a girl with red hair.

2. **Students listen and read and show comprehension through action:** This is a bit more demanding for young learners because it requires some reading in addition to listening.

■ **Listen and discriminate:** Students circle the correct word with minimal pairs presented, such as pin and pen.

Students can also listen for a word and use a fly swatter to hit the correct word on the board. This makes the listening exercise more fun and active for YLs.

■ **Listen and circle:** Students can circle the key words on a page of text or the correct word with a multiple choice.

■ **Listen and sequence words or sentences:** The teacher can provide word cards or strips of sentences for students to put in the correct order on their desks.

■ **Listen and detect mistakes in sentences:** Students can listen and detect mistakes in sentences provided on a handout or on the board.

■ **Listen and mark multiple choice:** Students can answer a set of comprehension questions by choosing the correct answer in a set of multiple choice questions.

■ **Listen and mark true or false:** Students can read (or listen to) a series of sentences and decide if they are true or false.

■ **Listen and mark stress or intonation:** On a handout, students can mark the stressed words or syllables as they listen to the teacher or recording. For example, in a simple dialogue "Hello! How are you?" The stressed syllables can be marked like this:

[Stressed syllables]

       /   /

Hello! How are you?

3.   **Students listen and show comprehension through production (oral or written):** This is the most demanding because it requires YLs to produce language in order to show their comprehension of the listening input.

- **Listen and repeat (orally):** This is a mechanical exercise in which the teacher says, "Repeat after me!" It can be used to practice pronunciation and is a good tool to correct errors through choral repetition

- **Listen and write (dictation):** This is a mechanical exercise in which the student has to write every word the teacher says on a piece of paper

- **Listen and translate information:** This is used to check comprehension and should not be used often in an EYL classroom.

- **Listen and label:** The teacher can give students a picture, and students have to label it correctly. For example, students could have a picture of a house and they have to listen and label the rooms correctly.

- **Listen and fill in the blanks:** The teacher could give the listening text with blanks in the text. If the text is a song, the students can listen to the song and write the missing words in the blanks.

- **Listen and complete a graphic organizer:** The teacher can give students a map, diagram, table, chart, etc. and have students fill it out to show comprehension. For example, the diagram could be of the life cycle of a frog.

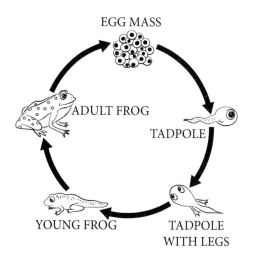

- **Listen and fill out a form:** Students can listen to instructions and fill out a form with their personal information, such as registering for a library card or filling out the form at the doctor's office.

- **Listen and write true or false:** Students can listen to or read statements and write whether they are true or false. The teacher can also prompt students to take the false statements and change them to make them correct.
- **Listen and correct text with mistakes:** Students can correct a dialog with mistakes to show they understand what they listened to. In the example below, the mistakes are in italics.

Doctor:	Hi, John. What's wrong?
John:	I'm *great*! My throat feels *good*.
Doctor:	Are you coughing a lot?
John:	Yes, I am *laughing* a lot!
Doctor:	You have a cold. Drink a lot of water, and take one *pillow* every day.
John:	Thank you, doctor!
Doctor:	You're welcome. Take care!

- **Listen and say/write responses:** Students say or write a response to the listening to show their comprehension, from a few words to extended discourse, depending on their level. The teacher can elicit the following kinds of responses orally or in writing:

  - **Key words:** Show recognition of the main vocabulary words.
  - **Specific information:** Pick out the most important information.
  - **Predict what happens next:** Express what will happen next or what the ending of the dialog or story will be.
  - **Main idea:** Express the main idea of the listening activity.
  - **Answer questions:** Answer comprehension questions with one word, phrases, or full sentences.
  - **Paraphrase:** Say it again in your own words.
  - **Summarize:** Say it again in your own words expressing, only the main idea.
  - **Converse:** Engage in a two-sided conversation.

Teachers can use these lists of different types of responses to plan a variety of listening activities that will check comprehension in multiple ways. There are different kinds of responses that can be used for learners with different learning styles and intelligences—for example, pictures for visual learners, graphic organizers for spatial learners, translating for linguistic learners, realia and miming for kinesthetic learners, and marking stress and intonation for auditory learners.

Activities after Listening (Practice and Application Stages)

After the listening activity, be sure to follow up with some comprehension checking activities, which can include the same types of activities mentioned above. In addition, the post-listening activities can flow smoothly into a speaking activity that practices the language learned in the listening activity. They can integrate listening with other skills as well. These activities will reinforce students' understanding of the text and new vocabulary and grammar by getting them to apply the new language through controlled, guided, and independent activities. Students can personalize the topic as well as apply the language to a real-life situation.

Examples of more controlled practice:

- **Listen and repeat.**
- **Read aloud** to practice pronunciation (see Chapter 5).
- **Sing a fun song, say rhymes, chant or rap** as a whole class, small group, or individual to practice pronunciation, stress, and intonation.
- **Practice and/or dramatize a dialog with substitution:** Students practice and/ or dramatize a dialog with blanks that require them to recreate parts of the dialog.
- **Use jokes:** Teachers can use jokes to liven up the classroom. Teachers can find different kinds of jokes for children at www.ahajokes.com/kids_jokes.html. One category of jokes that is fun for young language students is Knock Knock jokes.

Example #1:

A: Knock knock
B: Who's there?
A: Abe!
B: Abe who?
A: Abe C D E F G H . . . !

Example #2:

A: Knock knock
B: Who's there?
A: Banana
B: Banana who?
A: Knock knock
B: Who's there?
A: Banana
B: Banana who?
A: Knock knock
B: Who's there?
A: Orange

B: Orange who?

A: Orange you glad I didn't say banana?

- **Use riddles:** Teachers can use riddles to connect to content and have students make up their own. These are fun ways to practice questioning and answering. Wherever possible, teachers should find funny riddles that match the content for the day's lesson. More riddles can be found at http://iteslj.org/c/jokes.html.

  Examples:

  What has four legs but can't stand? **Answer:** A table or chair

  What has two hands but can't clap? **Answer:** A clock

  Which month has 28 days? **Answer:** All of them, of course!

  What begins with T, ends with T and has T in it? **Answer:** A teapot

  What word is spelled wrong in every dictionary in the world?

  Answer: The word WRONG

- **Use tongue twisters:** Sentences that have words that begin with the same letter are great for practicing pronunciation. The following are some famous ones in English, but students can make up their own, too. More tongue twisters can be found at www.funenglishgames.com.

  Examples:

  Peter Piper picked a peck of pickled peppers.

  She sells seashells by the seashore.

  How much wood could a woodchuck chuck, if a woodchuck could chuck wood?

- **Use language games:** Teachers can use different games to make practicing listening and speaking more fun and active. More games can be found at http://iteslj.org/games.

  Examples:

  Running Dictation: Students work in groups. One student runs to the teacher at the front of the classroom, listens to the teacher whisper the sentence, runs back to team, and dictates the sentence. The group has to work together to write the sentence. After every student has had a chance to dictate a sentence, the teacher goes over the sentences to see which group has the most sentences correct.

  Telephone: Students work in groups. They can be grouped by the rows that they are sitting in or groups can stand in a line. The first student in the row or line goes to the front of the classroom, listens to the teacher whisper the sentence, runs back to the next person in line, and whispers the sentence. Each student in

the row whispers the sentence to the next person until the last person hears the sentence. The last person writes the sentence or whispers the sentence to the teacher. The teacher reveals the original sentence and sees which team has communicated the correct sentence all the way down the row.

Hot Seat: Choose a student to be in the hot seat. That student sits on a chair with her/his back to the board. The teacher writes a word on the board (or prepares flashcards and sticks the word or picture on the board). Students have to describe the word without saying the word until the person in the hot seat says the word out loud. For example, if the word is "dog," they can say "It is an animal" or "It is like Snoopy" or "You have it." They can use the word in a sentence but substitute the word with a "blank." For example, if the word is "dog" they can say, "The (blank) barks."

Examples of more independent activities:

- **Perform a role play or dialog:** Students can prepare and use realia or props to dramatize the dialog (e.g., doctor and patient, store clerk and customer, mother and child).

- **Perform real-life tasks:** Students can complete tasks that mirror real life (e.g., buying a movie or theater ticket ordering at a restaurant).

- **Interview a native speaker or someone from another country in English:** Students practice using English as an international language (e.g., the teacher can set up Skype pals with a class from another country).

- **Perform a play:** Students can perform a play or create a dramatization of a story they have read, i.e., Reader's Theater (see Chapter 5).

- **Retell story after a storytelling:** Students can retell a story after they engage in a storytelling led by the teacher (see Chapter 6).

- **Show and tell:** Students bring in an object from home that is meaningful to them and present it to the group (e.g., the teacher prepares for a unit on toys, and asks students to bring in their favorite toy and describe it).

- **Presentation to the class that personalizes the lesson content:** Students prepare a presentation related to their real lives based on the lesson content. This can be done with pictures or a poster, such as a family tree poster to show the members of their family; a collage with pictures from magazines to tell about their favorite celebrity; a poster with a drawing of their home and neighborhood to tell about their home.
- **Pretend to be a TV presenter:** Students pretend to be a TV presenter to show how to play their favorite sport or game, demonstrate how to make their favorite food, do a weather forecast, etc.
- **Make a poster presentation:** Students create a poster for a movie advertisement, public service information, research about a country, etc. and present it to the class.
- **Discuss or do task in groups:** Students work together in small groups to discuss a topic or complete a task (e.g., planning a class party, recipe for making favorite food in home culture, favorite animal)
- **Do an information gap activity:** Students work in pairs to complete a task in which each student needs some information from the other student in order to complete the task.

Example:

Give students two pictures of a farm. Student A has a farm with no animals. Student B has a farm with animals in different locations. Student A has to ask Student B questions to fill his farm with animals correctly.

■ Conduct a questionnaire or survey: Students are given a survey and have to go around the classroom and ask/answer questions with various classmates. In the following example, the students will survey the favorite class sport. After students ask all their classmates, they will count the total and determine which sport is the most popular.

Example:

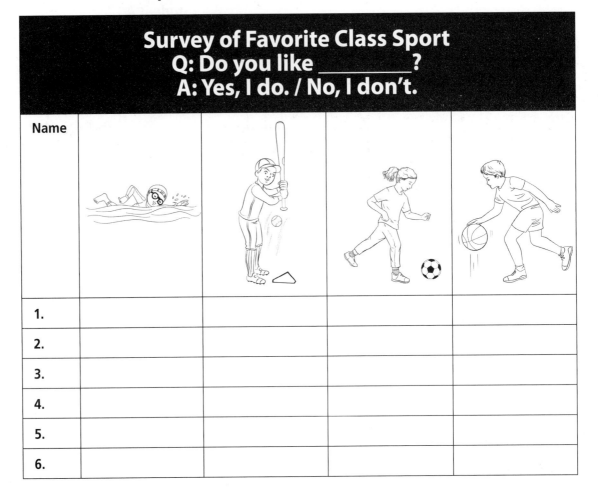

Name				
1.				
2.				
3.				
4.				
5.				
6.				

Designing a Listening and Speaking Lesson

Here is a sample lesson plan for a listening and speaking lesson.

Sample Lesson

Fun with Farm Animals

Title: Fun with Farm Animals	
Student profile	Grade 2, beginner level of English language proficiency
Skills to be emphasized	Listening and speaking

Language	What is this?
	It's a . . . horse/cow/pig/duck/chicken/dog.
	Where is it?
	In the . . . barn/field/mud/pond/coop/house.
	Animal sounds: neigh, moo, oink oink, quack quack, bawk, ruff
Objectives	By the end of this lesson, students will be able to:
	• Identify farm animals
	• Identify where animals live
Materials	Pictures of a farm
	Pictures of different farm animals
	Pictures of different locations on a farm
	Handouts with pictures of a farm and farm animals
Warm-up	
Before-listening Activities	
Review	"What did we learn last class?" Point to the calendar. Point to the pictures from the previous lesson. "Right! Pets." Review the animals: dog, cat, mouse, rabbit, parrot, house.
Capture their attention	"Look at this picture!" Show picture of a farm. "What is this? It's a farm. Today we will learn about . . . **farm** animals." Point to farm and point to animals. "Repeat after me, 'farm animals.'"
Connect to prior knowledge and experiences	"What sounds do these animals make?" Elicit the animal sounds from the native language.
Pre-teach new vocabulary	**Word Time: Five Seconds Game**
	"What time is it? It's Word Time! Let's play the Five Seconds Game. You have 5 seconds to. . . ."
	• **Look:** Show one flashcard per second. "5–4–3–2–1!" Show flashcard of horse, cow, pig, duck, chicken.
	• **Listen and look:** Show one flashcard and say the word each second. "Horse! Cow! Pig! Duck! Chicken!"
	• **Listen and point:** Put the flashcards in a row on the board or wall in the same order left to right. "Now 5 seconds to listen and point to the picture. Fingers up! Go! Horse! Cow! Pig! Duck! Chicken!"
	• **Listen and repeat:** "Now 5 seconds to repeat after me. Go! Horse! Cow! Pig! Duck! Chicken!"
	• **Listen and point:** Put the picture cards on the board or wall in a different order. "Now 5 seconds to listen and point. Ready? Go! Horse! Cow! Pig! Duck! Chicken!"
	Play the game again to teach the location words.

Presentation **During-listening Activities**	

Present text	**Chant with Lap-Clap-Point-Clap**
	 The teacher points to each animal in its correct place on the farm and teaches the chant (see below).
	 Listen and chant:
	 Ready? (Lap-Clap)
	     Go! (Point-Clap)
	     What is this? (Lap-Clap)
	     It's a . . . horse/cow/pig/duck/chicken/dog. (Point-Clap)
	     Where is it? (Lap-Clap)
	     In the . . . barn/field/mud/pond/coop/house (Point-Clap)
	
	 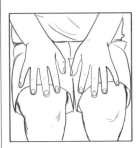   

Comprehension check	**Q & A (Listen and respond)**
	 The teacher points to an animal and asks questions with the following responses:
	     T: What's in the barn?
	     Ss: It's a . . . horse.
	     T: What does a horse say?
	     Ss: Neeeeeeigh!

Practice **After-listening Activities (Speaking activities)**	
Controlled pair work	**Picture Perfect** 

	Students work in pairs to take turns asking "What is this?" and answering "It's a. . . ." They are given a picture of a farm with the following animals on it which are numbered 1–6: (1) horse; (2) cow; (3) pig; (4) duck; (5) chicken; and (6) dog. When the teacher goes over the answers, she reviews the animal sounds, "A horse says, Neeeeigh!" So the progression will be "What is this? It's a horse. A horse says, Neeeeigh!"
Guided practice	**Silly Animals!**   Students work in pairs back to back. Student 1 puts the animals on the picture in any place (not the correct place). The horse could be in the mud, the cow in the house, the duck in the chicken coop, etc. The dialogue is: <div style="text-align:center">S1: *What's in the mud?* S2: *It's a horse!* Both: *A horse says, "Neeeeeigh!"*</div>Then Student 1 has to make her/his picture match Student 2. At the end of the activity they compare pictures.

Independent activity	**That's not right!**
	Tell students to give each animal a name that starts with the same letter, such as Harry Horse, Carol Cow, Peter Pig, Dorothy Duck, Chuck Chicken, and Donald Dog. Then students listen to the teacher dictate which animal goes in which location. The teacher will tell students to put the wrong animals in each place, like: "Put the dog in the barn. Put the duck in the mud. Put the horse in the house," etc. Then students will do a chant in pairs with their own animal names. When the animal is in the correct place, they will make the animal noise. For example,
	S1: *What's in the mud?*
	S2: *It's Dorothy Duck.*
	S1: *That's not right!*
	S2: *What's in the mud?*
	S1: *It's Peter Pig.*
	S2: *Oink oink oink*

Application

Personalization	**Role Play: I Live on a Farm**
	Choose an animal and prepare a presentation about yourself as that animal. Be sure you make the animal sounds in between each sentence.
	"I am Chuck Chicken. Bawk bawk. I live on a farm. Bawk bawk. I am in the chicken coop. Bawk bawk!"

Assessment

Monitoring activities	For each activity, the teacher will assess how well students are using the target language structures. The chant rhythm will ensure that the students build their fluency.
Assess for accuracy and give feedback	The next class, students will have their presentations prepared, and the teacher can assess both fluency and accuracy of the target language for this lesson and make any corrections through choral repetition and reviewing all the different chants.

Follow-up

Homework	Finish preparing the role play I Live on a Farm at home (see above). The next class they will have to perform in front of the class.
Next class	**Song: "Old MacDonald Had a Farm"**
	Students are ready to learn "Old MacDonald Had a Farm."

Teacher to Teacher

Teaching Listening and Speaking to Young Learners

This chapter described effective approaches for teaching listening and speaking to young learners. Below are excerpts from an online course discussion in which teachers from around the world describe the ideas and issues related to teaching listening and speaking to YLs according to their experience and local context. Think about how their perspectives compare to your teaching context.

First, a primary school teacher from Taiwan shares how she uses TPR every day in class.

> "TPR provides authentic and meaningful language. I strongly recommend it for younger learners. I always start with TPR (it would normally last for 3 minutes) in my grade 2 classes (They have only one lesson per week.). 'Point to the ceiling! Point to the floor! Point to the window! Point to the door!' I ask them to listen and point only (Teachers have to point to show them). I add two more items in each lesson. Children are so thrilled with the movement and the rhyming words. AND THEY ARE PERFECTLY QUIET! Thus knowledge of classroom items and instructions is learned by listening to the teacher. At the end of a semester we end up with the following pointing rhyme:
>
> > Point to the ceiling / Point to the floor / Point to the window / Point to the door / Point to the blackboard / Point to the lamp / Point to the television / Point to the fan / Point to the computer / Point at your desk / Point to the speaker / Point to the clock / Point to the mirror / Point to the box. . . .
>
> And the list can go on and on. It works because: 1. They don't have to talk. 2. They love rhymes. 3. They love the pointing movement."
>
> —*Huichen Chang, Primary English Teacher, Taiwan*

This application of TPR would work well with young learners of all ages who are at a beginning level, and as the teacher explains, students don't have to talk but can show their listening comprehension by pointing to the correct object. Next is an example of an activity that is interactive and requires both listening and speaking.

> "[One] listening activity which is worth mentioning is the information-gap activity, which I used in the 3rd grade (9 year olds). The activity practices the use and meaning of everyday objects, furniture and prepositions. The students worked in pairs. Each of them is given two pictures of rooms: room A and room B. First, they are to draw 5 objects (for example, a ball, a guitar,

a pen, etc.) in room A, so that their partner could not see it. Then, they have 7 minutes to tell their partner to draw the objects from their rooms in room B. The students are provided with model sentences to help them; for example: 'There is a ball under the table' or 'There are four pens on the chair.' The goal is to finish with the same pictures. This activity combines listening and speaking and is authentic, as it has a clearly defined purpose. In order to complete the activity students have to exchange information, which makes them truly involved and motivated. **"**

—*Anna Kocur, Primary English Teacher, Poland*

As discussed in this chapter, information gaps are great communicative activities that make sure students are practicing new language in a meaningful way. In addition, the activity was motivated by the pictures of rooms, and students were active in drawing the objects in the rooms. Teachers can also use puppets as a way to introduce vocabulary and give students some hands-on visuals to manipulate.

"Using puppets in presenting and practicing vocabulary. A student teacher introduced some new vocabulary related to items of clothing (children, first graders, already knew some) using paper puppets representing a girl and a boy and paper items of clothing; then groups of four got puppets and paper pieces of clothing to color and each child in the group 'dressed' either a 'boy' or a 'girl' and described what 'he' or 'she' was wearing, using new vocabulary and recycling already known (items of clothing and colors). All children were engaged in the activity and motivated to make own combinations of 'clothes' for the puppets and to describe them. The activity worked perfectly with student teacher monitoring and facilitating group work. To my mind it was so successful because the activity was enjoyable, learner-centered, involved guided practice with some sort of choice in a familiar context, children had enough language to do the task, the atmosphere of a small group was relaxed, teacher control was minimal (Scott & Ytreberg, 1990). **"**

—*Vera Savic, Teacher Educator, Serbia*

The next few comments are related to using songs in the EYL classroom. This is a very popular technique that teachers enjoy using.

"The first listening experience I got with my students was a song; after presenting a lesson on school subjects I composed a song by myself; using the melody of an old song I put the vocabulary of the new lesson as the lyrics; the students had to listen and write the names of the school subjects they heard; after listening twice they wrote the list of the subject they heard in groups; after the feedback I wrote the whole song on the board and we sang together. It was a good experience as the students kept the song and vocabulary in mind. It made the learning experience both enjoyable and educational.**"**

—*Ernest Kalotoueu Gbeada, Primary English Teacher, Cote d'Ivoire*

In the next example, a teacher describes her fear of singing in the classroom, but she found a way to overcome it and even gives advice to other teachers who may share her initial feelings of embarrassment.

"I was once one of those teachers who was embarrassed when I had to model singing or chanting in the classroom. I was afraid that my students might make fun of my 'out-of-tune' voice and my inability to follow an upbeat tempo. I am musically inclined but I had a traumatic experience with singing when I was in Grade 5, hence my 'fear'. In spite of my fear of singing and chanting aloud, I used them a lot in my classes because I really like music. And I found it useful in teaching. A teacher can always ask one of the students to sing in her/his place or use a music player to present the song. S/he can also record somebody singing the song. Bringing a musical player in the classroom can be a novelty for the students. (At least in the Philippines). Music is very popular among the young so playing a song by a popular artist can be a help in teaching language through songs. That way, s/he does not need to sing. I remind the teachers that it is just like modern rap music so they can let the students follow to the beat of a rap song or prepare their own rap materials. Students prefer upbeat tempos so chants will be popular with them. They even converse in rap style so asking them to chant will be an easy task. At first, it is difficult to break the mind set of learners when something they normally do in their daily lives is done in the classroom. What a teacher can also do is explain what the content of their dialogue should be.**"**

—*Maria Elizabeth Austria, Primary English Teacher, Philippines*

In the next example, a teacher used an audiotape of a song sung by someone else instead of singing the song herself.

"I have an interesting listening exercise to share. I played an audio tape for my students—a song sung by a native English speaker. I distributed sheets where 10 lines from the song were written in a jumbled manner. While listening to the song they had to indicate the correct sequence by putting numbers 1 to 10 one against each line. They were very enthusiastic and mid-way through the song some of them got confused and asked the song to be replayed. Once the song was over I replayed and all of them were able to complete the work. They were all giggling at the end. Later for the same song

I again distributed sheets where the song was written in correct sequence but 1 or 2 words per line were incorrect and they had to underline the incorrect word while listening to the song. This was a really interesting experience for both my students as well as me. **"**

—*Syedah Fawzia Nadeem, Teacher Education, India*

In addition to songs, many teachers like to use TV shows or movies. This teacher incorporated a movie into her thematic unit, but had an interesting way to create interest in the lesson and encourage prediction with a creative game.

"One successful listening activity I did with my fourth grade students was using movies. I chose a movie that was connected to the thematic unit I was working with at that time and I selected some scenes that I found appropriate for my lesson objectives. Before watching the scenes, I covered the TV with a blanket and I asked my students to listen and make a list of all the noises that they could hear. After that, they had to discuss in groups what the situation might be and what movie they could be listening to. I think it was successful because they were not only 'watching' a movie in a different way but also playing a game. Each group had to explain their ideas about what was happening. At the end we contrasted each group's ideas with the movie without the blanket. They loved it and it was wonderful to see how hard they tried to listen in order to win the game. **"**

—*Silvia Iglesias, Primary English Teacher, Uruguay*

Finally, many teachers have some restrictions in their classroom based on their curriculum. Some teachers are required to use a textbook, which is not always motivating for students and often does not reflect best teaching practices for TEYL. This teacher from Korea explains how she uses drama and role playing in her classroom based on the unit materials in her textbook.

"I use a textbook which is composed of 16 units and each unit has a short role-play as a speaking activity using the key expressions. The students watch the animation presented by the textbook CD-ROM and revise the expressions they learned. Then, I give each group of 4–5 students about 10 minutes to practice the role play with action. Even if the English expressions of the role-play are very limited so that the students can enjoy the activity without much pressure about language, it seems to be an effective way of teaching with respect that it gives children chances to speak English in the communicative context. Sometimes, their acting is a lot beyond my expectation, and I am amazed to find that they don't just mimic what they watch but they act out the roles in a creative way. Plus, I teach them how to respect others by good manners while other groups are performing, telling that they are being graded by their manners as well as their performance. As time goes by, role-play becomes one of the favorite activities among the students in my class."

—Eun Young Kim, Primary English Teacher, Korea

■ Chapter Summary

To Conclude

Listening is an active skill In order to interpret a message, learners must use both bottom-up decoding skills and top-down contextual skills in order to make sense of listening input. At the beginning, YLs should have plenty of chances to show their listening comprehension without needing to produce language.

Speaking is an interactive skill Most speaking is one part of a two-way conversation. It is a complicated process that requires speaking and thinking at the same time. YLs need a comfortable environment that encourages them to speak out. They can begin learning to speak in "chunks" or "formulaic language" that can be memorized and not analyzed for use in certain contexts.

There are 7 principles for teaching listening and speaking

Listening Activities	Speaking Activities
1. Prepare teacher talk carefully.	1. Build classroom routines in English.
2. Use activities that reflect real-life communication.	
3. Use activities that are developmentally appropriate.	
4. Use a variety of techniques to make listening input comprehensible.	4. Use a variety of activities to improve both accuracy and fluency.
5. Check comprehension using a variety of response types.	5. Build classroom interaction by giving plenty of opportunities to participate.
6. Keep listening active—always give learners a listening task.	6. Keep the speaking environment active—do not correct errors explicitly.
7. Equip your students with intelligent guesswork strategies.	7. Equip your YLs with negotiation strategies.

The listening and speaking activities can be integrated into a lesson plan The warm-up step of a lesson plan can consist of various before-listening activities that connect learners to the context, activate their background knowledge, and review and pre-teach vocabulary. Then the presentation step can consist of a wide range of during-listening activities that follow the "Listen and . . ." format. These

"Listen and . . ." activities can be used in both the warm-up and the presentation steps to teach new language and check comprehension. Then the practice step will include after-listening activities, which will provide plenty of practice with speaking.

Speaking activities should move from controlled to independent practice In the practice step, the speaking activities should start more controlled, meaning there is not much choice in the language used. The most controlled practice is to listen and repeat. Then the practiced language can gradually become less controlled and more guided, which allows students to have more choice in the language used. The goal is to reach a level of independence or creativity with the language. The independent activity should give learners the chance to use the new language freely, and then show they can apply the language in a new or more authentic situation.

■ Over to You

Discussion Questions

1. Watch a children's TV program that is in English, like Sesame Street or SpongeBob SquarePants. Then watch a children's program that is popular in your country. What are the characteristics of those TV programs that make YLs enjoy watching them so much? Make a list and see how many of those characteristics you can use when you present a listening activity in class.

2. Using songs and chants is a fun way to engage young learners in the EYL classroom. However, YLs can easily repeat and memorize songs they like without fully understanding the meaning. What can teachers do to avoid this common problem?

3. Listen to the interactions between your students in their native language between classes, in the cafeteria, on the playground, in the hallway, etc. What topics do they discuss? What kind of vocabulary and expressions are they using? How much of the topics and language can you incorporate into your class in English to give them authentic tasks to accomplish?

4. Why is it important to give a task before every listening activity? How does this principle for listening activities mirror real-life listening?

5. On your first day of class, you plan to prepare a poster with some basic classroom language expressions that your students will need. What would be your first ten chunks of language that will go on that poster? Choose five expressions for teacher talk and five expressions for students to negotiate meaning.

6. If you want to plan a cooperative activity for your young learners, what are the essential steps you should take to make sure they get good practice in English rather than get distracted and/or speak in the native language?

Lesson Planning

Choose any lesson for young learners from your curriculum that you designed or that you were given. Incorporate the following into this lesson using the lesson plan format:

- One vocabulary game for the warm-up
- Two "Listen and . . ." activities for the presentation
- Three practice activities that are controlled, guided, and then independent
- One application activity that encourages YLs to personalize the content or puts the language in a real-life context

Write About It

Reflection on Repetition: Young learner classes often have fun songs and chants that are repeated. Children love them, and they can be used to teach vocabulary and grammar in a fun and engaging way. These can be very useful for improving students' oral skills; however, "When children repeat set phrases it does not necessarily mean language acquisition is taking place" (Slattery & Willis, 2001). Write about how a teacher can make sure language acquisition is taking place in her/his EYL classroom, particularly with respect to oral communication. Wherever possible, connect your main points to your own teaching situation and give examples to support your point.

■ Resources and References

Print Publications

Brewster, J., Ellis, G., & Girard, D. (2004). *The primary English teacher's guide.* Essex, UK: Penguin English.

Lewis, G., & Bedson, G. (1999). *Games for children.* Oxford, UK: Oxford University Press.

Read, C. (2007). *500 activities for the primary classroom.* Oxford, UK: Macmillan.

Slatterly, M., & Willis, J. (2001). *English for primary teachers: A handbook of activities and classroom language.* Oxford, UK: Oxford University Press.

Wright, A. (2001). *Arts and crafts with children.* Oxford, UK: Oxford University Press.

Useful Web Sites

Common Core Standards: www.corestandards.org

Common Sense Media: www.commonsensemedia.org

Games & Activities for the ESL/EFL Classroom: http://iteslj.org/games/

Fun English Games: www.funenglishgames.com

Joan Kang Shin Resource Page: https://sites.google.com/site/shinjinshil/resources

Songs for Teaching: www.songsforteaching.com

Super Simple Songs: www.supersimplesongs.com

References

Anderson, J. R. (2009). *Cognitive psychology and its implications seventh edition.* New York: Worth Publishers.

Brewster, J., Ellis, G., & Girard, D. (2004). *The primary English teacher's guide.* Essex, UK: Penguin English.

Brown, D. H. (2007). *Teaching by principles: An interactive approach to language pedagogy.* White Plains, NY: Longman.

Cabrera, M. P., & Martínez, P. B. (2001). The effects of repetition, comprehension checks, and gestures, on primary school children in an EFL situation. *ELT Journal, 55*(3), 281–288.

Cameron, L. (2001). *Teaching languages to young learners.* Cambridge, UK: Cambridge University Press.

Curtain, H., & Dahlberg, C. A. (2010). *Languages and children: Making the match,* 4th ed. New York, NY: Pearson.

Lund, R. J. (1990). A taxonomy for teaching second language listening. *Foreign Language Annals, 23,* 105–115.

Marley, S. C., & Szabo, Z. (2010). Improving children's listening comprehension with a manipulation strategy. *The Journal of Education Research, 103,* 227–238.

Morley, J. (2001). Aural comprehension instruction: Principles and practices. In M. Celce-Murcia (Ed.), *Teaching English as a second or foreign language* (pp. 69–85). Boston, MA: Heinle Cengage.

Peñate, M., & Bazo, P. (1998). Ajustes en la interacción e input comprensible en el aula de inglés. *Lenguaje y Textos, 12,* 27–39.

Peterson, P. W. (2001). Skills and strategies for proficient listening. In M. Celce-Murcia (Ed.), *Teaching English as a second or foreign language* (pp. 87–100). Boston, UK: Heinle Cengage.

Pinter, A. (2006). *Teaching young language learners.* Oxford, UK: Oxford University Press.

Schwartz, R. (in preparation). Fundamentals of teaching and learning English as a foreign language using classroom interactions.

Scott, W. A., & Ytreberg, L. H. (1990). *Teaching English to children.* Harlow, UK: Longman.

Slatterly, M., & Willis, J. (2001). *English for primary teachers: A handbook of activities and classroom language.* Oxford, UK: Oxford University Press.

Winn-Smith, B. (2001). Classroom language. *English Teaching Professional, 18,* 12–14.

5 Teaching Reading and Writing

■ Getting Started

The purpose of this chapter is to discuss the teaching of reading and writing to young learners. It will present some of the challenges young learners face in learning to read and write in English and some approaches to help them to meet the challenge. It will also provide suggestions for a number of activities to motivate very young and young learners to read and write in English, to assist them while they are reading and writing, and to encourage them to do more.

Think About It

Can you recall a favorite book that you read and re-read when you were a child? Why was it your favorite? What was it about? Who were the characters? Who read it to you? Now think about what characteristics will guide your choice of books to include in your young learners classes.

Also, think about the kinds of writing you did as a child. Are there any that were memorable? Why do you think you remember them? What were you writing about? Who were you writing for? Who were you writing to? Now think about the kinds of writing that you will include for your very young learners. What will be some of the earliest opportunities?

In contrast, what kinds of writing might you ask your young learners to do?

What are some ways to motivate young learners to read and write?

Are there ways in which you can integrate reading and writing activities?

Visage/Stockbyte/
Getty Images

Discovery Activity

Reading and Writing Chart

In the chart below, list all the types of reading and writing activities that you can think of that you might use with both very young (5–7) and young (8–11) learners. You may want to look through some EYL textbooks to see the kinds of reading and writing activities they have included. After listing them, indicate which ones are most likely to motivate your learners to read and write and also, in a few words, why or why not. What makes a reading or writing activity engaging for young children?

READING AND WRITING ACTIVITIES FOR YOUNG CHILDREN

VYLs	
READING ACTIVITIES	MOTIVATING OR NOT?
WRITING ACTIVITIES	MOTIVATING OR NOT?
YLS	
READING ACTIVITIES	MOTIVATING OR NOT?
WRITING ACTIVITIES	MOTIVATING OR NOT?

If you have the opportunity to visit EYL classes, note the different reading and writing activities that are included in the lessons (and homework) for very young and young learners. What are some of the reasons for the differences?

■ Theory, Planning and Application

Considerations for Teaching Reading and Writing

You may think that when you are reading, you are simply getting meaning from the text, but actually you are also bringing meaning with you. Reading is an interactive process involving the reader, the text, and the writer. And when you are writing, you are likely to read (or even re-read) what you wrote to make sure you are communicating your intended meaning to your audience (the reader). You will notice as you read through this chapter that when we are discussing reading we also are mentioning ways in which reading can lead to writing, and when we are discussing writing, we are also mentioning ways in which these writings can serve as texts to be read, not only by the students who wrote them, but also by others in the class. Reading can be thought of as preparation for writing, and writing as producing something to be read.

But in some ways, listening and reading are similar: They are both receptive skills, processing what others have said or written, but doing so in an active way.

Pressmaster/Shutterstock.com

We bring all that we know about the world, about oral and written texts or discourse, and about language to our attempts at understanding what someone has said or written. Speaking and writing are also similar: They are both productive skills, where we take what we know about the world, about texts, and about language to express an idea or opinion, to make an observation, to provide information, to communicate our thoughts or needs, or to create a poem, a story, or a song. Many listening activities can also be reading activities, and many speaking activities can become writing activities as well.

First and Second Language Reading and Writing Most EYL programs focus on oral activities until the children have learned to read and write in their own language, or at least have enough oral English language development to build on for literacy. There will be beginning reading or writing activities such as using flashcards to match key vocabulary from the story with pictures or putting labels on pictures or drawings to support the story, but it will usually be the teacher who does the actual reading aloud (of a story or poem or other text) and also the writing of what children say on the board, though children will be encouraged to join in at predictable places.

Learning to read and write is complex and difficult enough in a language the child already knows; doing it in another language is even more difficult. But the good news is that when there is sufficient English language development, many of the child's skills and strategies used in reading and writing in the first language will transfer to another language (Cummins, 1979). One only has to become "literate" once. Very young learners are probably still learning to read and write in the home or first language. Older young learners have probably already learned to read and write in their own language, and when their English proficiency is sufficient they will be able to transfer those skills into their reading of English.

All children, whether first- or second-language readers, go through the same five initial literacy steps:

1. Awareness and exploration
2. Experimenting with reading and writing
3. Early reading and writing
4. Transitional reading and writing
5. Conventional reading and writing

    (International Reading Association & the National Association for the Education of Young Children, 1998)

When children learn literacy skills in the first language, they develop several broad areas of knowledge that they can access in English. These are:

- Visual knowledge: about print and text direction
- Phonological knowledge: about sounds represented by symbols (though children will usually think of this as the sounds that symbols make)
- Lexical knowledge: about words and collocations
- Syntactic knowledge: about meaning construction and making sense of words
- Semantic knowledge: about social use of language as discourse
  (Brewster, Ellis, & Girard, 2004)

They have learned that reading and writing can be used for different purposes, and they have likely developed a number of strategies for understanding reading and making themselves understood through writing.

That doesn't mean there won't be challenges awaiting young learners as they begin reading and writing in English. The first is the writing system. Children whose language is written in the same Roman alphabet as English (such as Spanish, French, German, or Portuguese) will have much less difficulty learning to read and write in English than those whose language is written in another alphabet (such as Arabic, Russian, or Greek) or in a language that is written in characters, such as Chinese (Cameron, 2001; Nunan, 2011).

Besides differences in writing systems, there are also differences in how text is presented on the page and whether one reads and writes from right to left (Arabic) or top to bottom and right to left (traditionally Chinese and Korean), or from left to right as in English. Children in EYL classrooms will also face the challenge of having a more limited vocabulary, different background (cultural) knowledge than may be required to interpret a text, and differences in text structure (Lenters, 2004/2005).

When we are developing literacy activities for young learners, then, we need to consider at least the following:

- Has the child learned to read and write in her/his own language?
- Is the child just beginning to learn to read in her/his own language?
- Is that language written in the Roman alphabet, another alphabet, or characters?
- How does one read and write a text in that language (from left to right, right to left, top to bottom)?
- What skills and strategies has the child developed in making meaning from and with text?

One challenge facing all children (including English-speaking children) is to learn the different ways in which English represents sounds. There are 26 letters in the Roman alphabet, but they represent the 44 sounds in English (Moats, 2001). For example, even a child who reads Spanish or German (which are much more regular and predictable languages to read, since one letter usually represents one sound) will have to learn that in English, there are many ways the same sound can be represented. According to Geva and Wang (2001) in their review of the differences in learning to read in different languages, English has a "deep" orthography, one in which it can be difficult to sound out many words from the way in which they are written or spelled, in contrast to Spanish or German, which have "shallow" orthography and more predictability in how a word sounds based on how it is written. Note the number of ways that the sound /i/ in English can be represented in letters: *be, bee, sea, ski, skied, receive.* Just as there are many ways in which a sound is represented in print (its spelling), there are many ways of pronouncing the same set of letters. Consider the following: *read, bread, break* where the "ea" is decoded as three different sounds! The following poem gives some idea of the difficulty of decoding English. (Note: You can hear this poem, with all its unusual pronunciation, being read at: http://international.ouc.bc.ca/pronunciation/poem01.html)

I take it you already know
Of tough and bough and cough and dough?
Others may stumble, but not you,
On hiccough, thorough, slough, and through.
Well done! And now you wish, perhaps,
To learn of less familiar traps?

Beware of heard, a dreadful word,
That looks like beard and sounds like bird,
And dead, it's said like bed, not bead.
For goodness sake, don't call it "deed"!
Watch out for meat and great and threat
(They rhyme with suite and straight and debt.)

A moth is not a moth in mother,
Nor both in bother, broth in brother,
And here is not a match for there,
Nor dear and fear, or bear and pear.
And then there's doze and rose and lose,

Just look them up
And goose and choose,
And cork and work, and card and ward,
And font and front, and word and sword.
And do and go, and thwart and cart.
Come, come, I've hardly made a start!

A dreadful language, man alive.
I'd learned to speak it when I was five.
And yet to write it, the more I sigh,
I'll not learn how 'til the day I die.

Author unknown

Why Include Reading and Writing in Young Learner Classes?

If you have visited EYL classes, you will likely note that the majority of time is spent on oral language activities. If there is any reading or writing, it is done by the teacher. Some of these decisions may be dictated by the amount of time that is set aside for the EYL class. If one has only 45–60 minutes a week, there is not much time for children to read and write. Another factor is class size: It is difficult to manage reading in large classes and time-consuming to read what children write. For very young learners, oral language will take precedence over written, since for reading and writing in English to be meaningful for children, they must know enough English to be able to "make intelligent guesses" (Pinter, 2006, p. 67).

Although reading and writing "are very demanding and take time and patience to learn," they "are extremely important for the child's growing awareness of language and their own growth in the language" (Scott & Ytreberg, 1990, p. 5). EYL teachers need to include reading and writing wherever and as early as possible, for a number of reasons:

- Reading and writing can reinforce what is being learned orally
- Reading expands the sources of input, and writing helps in remembering that input
- Writing provides a way to consolidate learning from the other skills, and reading helps students to see the conventions of writing
- Children enjoy reading and writing if the texts are meaningful and related to their experiences (including using the many resources of the Internet)
- Reading and writing help link the EYL class with home, as children bring home writing they have done to share with their families or do homework requiring reading and writing

- Reading and writing can also link the EYL class with other classes in school, where written language plays an important part
- Writing provides another means of self-expression and, when read by others, a sense of confidence and pride

(Pinter, 2006; Scott & Ytreberg, 1990)

As Barone and Xu (2008) state, "In all discussions about exemplary teachers, especially exemplary teachers of ELLs [English Language Learners], one central discovery is that they provide language-rich classrooms where children have opportunities to talk about and write about their learning" (p. 17). Teachers can make their classrooms especially "print-rich" by labeling objects in the classroom; posting calendars, maps, or class birthday charts; creating word walls as new vocabulary is introduced; engaging the children in drawing and labeling pictures to post in the room, and as they write more, to produce class books that can be read by children during independent reading time (Curtain & Dahlberg, 2010; Pinter, 2006; Collins, 2004). For young learners to become effective and engaged readers and writers, they must have multiple opportunities to explore, read, and write a variety of texts and to talk about what they are going to read or write or what they have read or written.

Considerations for Teaching Reading

What Is Reading? Reading is a process of relating written symbols to oral language, of constructing meaning from written text (Goodman, 2005), or "making sense and deriving meaning from the printed word" (Linse, 2005, p. 69). When we read, we interact with the text, bringing our knowledge of the world, of language, and of discourse or specific text types (a fairytale, newspaper article, poem, essay, or report) to what we read. Our understanding increases or lessens depending on our background knowledge, knowledge of the language, and our experience with discourse and text structure.

To be able to read, a child has to:

- Understand the alphabet
- Decode
- Develop sight vocabulary to read fluently (with automaticity)
- Develop strategies to help with comprehension and fluency
- Read texts that match her/his reading level and interests
- Engage in extensive reading (independent reading of a variety of texts)

  (Adapted from Lenters, 2004/2005, p. 331)

English-speaking children know that fairytales begin with "Once upon a time." Children hearing these words (and maybe even repeating them with the person saying them) have a whole set of experiences and understandings that help to guide their understanding of the text. Those experiences and that background information are known as schemata (plural of schema). They help us to make sense of the world and of what we read. It is because of more developed schemata that we are able to understand and remember much more about a cultural tradition in our own country. It is much harder to understand and remember what we are reading when the topic is a cultural tradition of another country. One of the reasons for building units around topics, where language and content are recycled (as discussed in Chapter 3) is that these help students to develop the background knowledge, the vocabulary, and the structures (the schemata) to make sense of written texts.

Approaches to Teaching Reading When we read, we activate two types of knowledge: what we know about making meaning (top-down processing) and what we know about language (bottom-up processing). With reading instruction, there is an ongoing debate about where to begin: Should we focus first on helping children see the relationship between sounds and letters, beginning with decoding letters and words, and then move to larger units to focus on meaning (the approach used in phonics instruction)? Or should we begin with context and meaning, and then move to analyzing and interpreting smaller segments of the language (the approach used in whole language)? Clearly we need to do both.

When we are reading to children, we usually begin with context and meaning, relating what we read to the children's lives and knowledge. From there, we may explain particular words, have fun with pronouncing some of them (for example, with rhymes or animal sounds), and attend to the smaller units of a text. But we don't want to neglect practice in letter and word recognition. They play an important role in comprehending a text. Children need to understand sound–letter correlations (that the initial sound of *dog* and *doll* is the same and is represented by the letter "d," and that other words that begin with that letter, such as *desk*, are pronounced with the same initial sound), so that when they encounter another word that begins with that same letter they can decode it. But this is only useful if they know what a *dog*, or a *doll*, or a *desk* is. If children do not know how to decode and have not learned the regular sound–symbol correspondences in English, when confronted with a new word, they are likely to skip over it, and doing that many times renders a text meaningless. The solution is to include phonics, discussed below, but to do it in a meaningful context (not using nonsense words nor focusing on words out of context). Ideally, in any unit, students will have opportunities to practice using both bottom-up and top-down processing skills, in a balanced approach to reading (Brewster, Ellis, & Girard, 2002).

As Cameron (2001) explains, children need to develop both top-down and bottom-up processing: "The child who picks up a set of words that she recognizes as whole words, and uses this sight vocabulary to read simple texts, needs to also develop knowledge of grapho-phonemic relationships within words to progress to more difficult texts. On the other hand, the child who has learnt the names and sounds of the letters and can read simple, regular words by 'sounding them out', needs also to recognize morphemes by sight and to draw on grammatical information at sentence level if progression is to be made." (p. 151). Asher (1998) also believes that differences in learning styles make it important to incorporate both approaches: Auditory learners will find phonics more appropriate, while visual learners will prefer the whole word or look–say approach.

In balancing an approach to reading, at least the following three approaches should be considered for young learners:

1. Phonics
2. Whole language
3. Language experience

1. Phonics Phonics is a bottom-up approach to processing a text. It focuses on the smallest unit of text: the letters. It teaches children the relationships between sounds and letters, how a particular sound is symbolized in print, and how to "sound out" a word, given those sound–symbol relationships. It usually begins with individual sounds (such as /m/ or /s/ in initial position) or short words that rhyme or share a common sound (for example, *cat, rat, hat* or *can, ran, man*). The goal is to help children decode written language, using the sound–symbol relationships they have learned, either in isolation or from other words. So, for example, when children see the word *bat,* they can recognize the letters of the alphabet and understand the way sounds are represented in writing. They can also refer back to words they have already learned that are written with similar patterns (Heilman, 2002). In this way they can be successful at decoding, since that is key to early reading success (Beck, 2006).

Recent reading research has identified instruction in phonics (as well as phonemic awareness, reading comprehension, vocabulary development, and fluency) as necessary for children to become effective readers (National Institute of Child Health and Human Development, 2000; Rose, 2006). The "Rose Report" (Rose, 2006) concluded that the best practices in teaching reading provide:

- Clear guidance on developing children's speaking and listening skills
- Direct teaching of phonics as a primary means of teaching decoding (reading) and encoding (writing/spelling)

- A "broad and language-rich curriculum" (p. 16) that takes full account of developing the four interdependent strands of language—speaking, listening, reading, and writing—and enlarging children's stock of words within which to include phonics
- Multisensory phonics instruction that engages, motivates, and excites young learners
- A focus also on word recognition (sight vocabulary) and comprehension

Both the National Reading Panel and the Rose Report conclude that children need direct teaching of phonics, embedded in a language-rich curriculum that also teaches word recognition and comprehension.

Phonemic awareness activities Before focusing on letter–sound relationships through phonics, children need practice in discriminating English sounds—what is referred to as phonemic awareness. This involves, for example, separating the spoken word *big* into three distinct phonemes, /b/,/i/, and /g/. Phonemic awareness training helps children to understand the rules of English and, over time, helps build reading fluency.

The following are some activities to help young learners to become aware of English phonemes. Learners should listen and:

- Identify the first sound in a word (/b/ in *boy*)
- Identify the last sound in a word (/t/ in *kite*)
- Identify the common sound in a series of words (/i/ in *see, me, tree*)
- Identify the word that doesn't rhyme (*dog, fog, leg*)
- Change one sound for another in the beginning (*cat to hat*), middle (*cat to cut*), and end of words (*cat to can*) to create new words
- Separate the sounds of a word (*sat* into /s/, /ae/, /t/)
- Blend separate sounds into a word (/s/, /ae/, /t/ into *sat*)
- Delete a sound (*sat to at*)
- Blend initial consonant clusters (/st/ in *stop*)
- Identify final consonant blends (/st/ in *first*)

Phonemic awareness activities can be fun. Kauffman (2007) provides a number of ways to make phonemic awareness instruction enjoyable and motivating for young learners. She suggests, for example:

- **Using traditional rhymes:** Three Little Kittens (who "lost their mittens") or Hickory, Dickory, Dock ("The mouse ran up the clock.")
- **Going on a Rhyme Hunt:** Looking for objects in the class that rhyme
- **Playing Match Mates:** Giving picture cards to each child and then having the children find a picture that begins or ends with the same sound or rhymes with the word they have

- **Developing riddles:**

  "I rhyme with sled.
  You sleep on me.
  I am a _____ (bed.)"

- **Playing Odd Man Out:** Posting pictures of objects that begin or end with the same sound or have the same medial sound, as well as some that do not. Let the children find the pictures of things that don't share a sound. This can also be done in pairs or small groups.

- **Playing Bouncing Ball:** Toss a ball to a student after saying a word such as *sit*. The student has to think of a word that begins with the same sound. When the students can think of no new words, begin another sequence with another word. This can also be done with words that end with the same sound or rhyme.

- **Playing Rhyming Words Walk-About:** Arrange students in a circle. Have them listen for rhyming words. When they hear two words that rhyme, they take one step forward. When they hear two that do not rhyme, they step back or stand still. (Adapted from Kauffman, 2007)

Phonics activities While phonemic awareness focuses on oral language, phonics focuses on written language, with the goal of learning the relationships between the sounds and letters (spelling) of English. Typically, children learn the sound–symbol relationships and then apply what they have learned in decoding words in a text.

Some phonics activities include:

- **Identifying** the number of syllables in a word
- **Pointing** to words that share a common letter-sound (As children become more familiar with English, this can include irregular spellings.)
- **Sorting** pictures or making a collage of objects that begin with the same letter-sound (*book/ball/boy*) or rhyme (*cat/hat/rat*)
- **Sorting** words that share a common letter-sound
- **Matching** words that share a common letter-sound
- **Creating** words from letters that have a common letter-sound
- **Repeating** chants with common letter-sounds that are written on the board
- **Using** predictable or patterned books

Phonics activities can also be fun. Some of the activities used for phonemic awareness can be adapted for phonics by including the written word. For example, Odd Man Out could be played with a set of picture cards with words written on them. Children find the word that does not belong because of a difference in the initial, medial, or final sound. Other engaging activities include:

- **Singing or chanting** familiar songs, chants, or rhymes while you point to the words in the song or chant displayed on chart paper, the board, or from a DVD.

Afterwards, have children come to the board and point to rhyming words or create new verses with new rhyming words.

- Creating **fill-in-the-blank** activities with clues

  The horse lives on a _____. (farm)
  arm

- **Playing Bag-It:** Matching letter or word cards with pictures displayed in the class. One way to make this fun is to write the letters for a picture on the outside of a small paper bag. Children find the picture that matches the letters and put the picture in the bag. (Note that this also keeps the activity manageable, as the pictures are then stored in their appropriate bag.)

- **Playing Hang-Up:** Hang a picture card on a clothes hanger with a clothespin. Students have to find a letter that matches the picture (such as the initial sound) and hang it on the same clothes hanger, but facing the other way. Display these in the class.

  (Adapted from Kaufmann, 2007)

Even young learners who already read a language with a similar alphabetic system will benefit from systematic, explicit instruction in sound/symbol correspondences in English (Carrell & Grabe, 2002). However, to be meaningful, phonics instruction should focus on words that children have already learned orally within a meaningful context, not in isolation (Peregoy & Boyle, 2004). Otherwise, children may get the idea that reading is "sounding out" words, even if they don't understand their meaning. The same is true of the names of the letters: Teach them as they fit into the context and content of the lesson.

2. **Whole language** A whole language approach begins with meaning and then uses language in context for further word or language study. It involves top-down processing, in which children bring their knowledge of the world, their experiences with oral language and texts, and their knowledge of the written language to constructing comprehension of written texts, using four types of clues:

- **Grapho-phonemic clues:** referring to expected sound–symbol correspondences
- **Semantic clues:** referring to what word(s) would be expected, based on the meaning thus far
- **Syntactic clues:** referring to the part of speech that would be expected in a given place in the sentence
- **Pragmatic clues:** referring to what would be expected given the purpose of the text
  (Goodman, 1976, 2005)

In early literacy, the whole language approach might begin with a focus on common words (sight words) that the children have already heard and said, perhaps in a story or song or even in popular media, in what is often referred to as a sight-word or "look-say" approach (Slatterly & Willis, 2001). Sight words are taught because they are meaningful to the children and can then be used in a variety of activities. These words and "chunks" (collocations such as *have fun, take a bath,* or *catch a ball*) can be written on individual flashcards and then matched with pictures, objects, actions, or held up and used with repeating refrains or songs. They may be posted alphabetically on a word wall, where they can be called upon to help with reading or in writing. Learning sight vocabulary helps children to see the connection between meaning and visual representation. Over time, children build up a large vocabulary of high-frequency words, including the little words that form a large portion of the 1000–2000 most frequently used words, especially in written English, as identified by the General Service List (originally compiled by Michael West and updated by James Bauman; available at http://jbauman.com/aboutgsl.html), and the Dolch sight vocabulary lists of the 200 most common written words and 95 additional common nouns, sorted by frequency and grade level (available at http://www.mrsperkins .com/dolch.htm). A large sight-word vocabulary also helps children to read with automaticity (faster and more fluently). It is ironic, but true, that the more that we read, the larger our vocabulary will be, and the larger our vocabulary, the better readers we will be (and the more likely we will want to read).

One early sight-word activity might involve helping children to recognize their own names, especially if their language is written in the Roman alphabet or if they are using English nicknames written in that alphabet. Their names provide the context for meaningful phonics activities in which children focus on the initial letter-sounds in their names. The teacher might begin by writing the children's first names as they say them, then pointing out the names that begin with the same letter and sound, and subsequently posting the names in alphabetical order. That might be followed by asking children to point to their names and to respond by standing up when the initial letter and sound of their names is made. Then the class could play a game, an adaptation of the jazz chant "Who is Sylvia?" that begins with "Who has a name that begins with S?" Children answer "I do," and then spell their names.

Teachers using a whole language approach to reading may take their learners through the following sequence of reading activities which are complemented by a similar sequence of writing activities (to be discussed).

Stage of a Lesson	Activity
Presentation	Reading aloud
Controlled practice	Shared reading
Guided practice	Guided reading
Independent activity	Independent reading

Reading aloud Beginning readers need multiple opportunities to hear stories, poems, songs, chants, and other texts read aloud, with opportunities to chime in where words or lines are repeated. With songs, where both repetition and rhyme are present, it is easy for children to learn parts and to participate after the teacher has sung the song, pointing to the words written on the board or as they are projected. Some songs provide many opportunities for children to participate. For example, when singing "Old MacDonald Had a Farm," children can make the sounds of the animals (using either the sounds as they are represented in English, or how ducks "quack" or pigs "oink" in their own language). They will be able and want to participate (even acting out the ways that the animals communicate), and the song provides a good opportunity to practice three of the long vowel sounds and letter names in English.

Old MacDonald had a farm,
E-I-E-I-O
And on this farm he had a duck,
E-I-E-I-O
With a quack-quack here, and a quack-quack there,
Here a quack, there a quack,
Everywhere a quack quack.
Old MacDonald had a farm,
E-I-E-I-O.

*(Continue with a pig, a horse,
a cow, a rooster, etc.)*

Another way for children to participate is through echo reading. In echo reading, children repeat key lines after the teacher—for example, the line "But he was still hungry" in *The Very Hungry Caterpillar* (Carle, 1994), as discussed in Chapter 3. This works best if you pause and gesture to the children, inviting them to join in.

Shared reading Shared reading (Herrell, 2000; Holdaway, 1979) is the next step after reading aloud. In shared reading, the teacher involves the students in reading together, using something as a pointer (a long stick, a laser pointer, or even the bouncing ball of a karaoke song in some EYL videos) with a big book (if the class is small), a video of a book, a PowerPoint, or a book projected on an interactive whiteboard or from a document reader. If multiple copies of a small book are available, they work well, since in shared reading, all children and the teacher need to be able to read (or follow along) together (Herrell, 2000; Gibbons, 1993). Pointing to the words while reading them helps to establish the relationship between spoken and written language. Often the text is one that has been read aloud before, so that when you read and point to the words, the children are already familiar with the story or song.

The purpose of shared reading is to involve students in enjoyable reading, to demonstrate good (or strategic) reading, and provide support while children are reading along. Another goal of shared reading, of course, is also to motivate children to pick up a book (perhaps in the reading center) and read independently. For that reason, you need to read the entire story or text before reading it to the children, to be able to read fluently and with appropriate emphasis and emotion.

It helps if the book has lots of clear pictures that help the children understand the story, even if they don't understand all of the text. (Those pictures will serve as the basis for a number of wonderful follow-up activities as well.) In shared reading, it is important to introduce the book and set the scene for the children, to show them the cover; to read the title, author, and illustrator to them; and in the beginning, to model reading from left to right, from top to bottom, and from the front to the back of the book (Herrell, 2000). Asking a few questions such as the following will activate their background knowledge:

- What do you think the book is about?
- What do you see in the picture (on the cover)?
- Have you ever seen one of these?
- Have we read any other books like this one?
- Do you think this book will be fun?

Sometimes, allowing children to discuss this in pairs before they respond to the questions will give them time to think and rehearse what they want to say. The questions about the cover, title, etc. can be followed by a picture walk (talking about the pictures in the story to familiarize the children with the story before reading it), stopping occasionally to ask children what they see and revisiting predictions about the text. The picture walk will also help in reviewing important vocabulary and identifying other vocabulary that needs to be taught for the text to be understood. During the reading, the teacher can stop occasionally and talk with the children about what has happened and ask them to predict what's coming next (this can also be done in pairs), but this should not be done so often that it spoils the story or bores the children (Scott & Ytreberg, 1990).

After finishing reading, another set of questions can be asked:

- Did you like the story?
- What was your favorite part?
- Who was your favorite character?
- Do you want to read it again?
- Do you want to see the pictures again?

At this point, it is possible to go back, page by page, through the story or text, pointing to the pictures or illustrations and asking the children to talk about what happened, and providing help with vocabulary as needed. Repeated reading of the same book, story, poem, or text will help in developing the children's vocabulary and make them more fluent readers (Samuels, 2002). Some teachers also ask children to select a new word from the story or point out a new word that becomes the "word for the day." During the next classes, you may want to follow this by asking the children to draw their favorite scenes or characters and label them and then make an illustrated "book" that they can take home and use to "read" the story to their parents (Herrell, 2000). Older young learners might want to write their version of the story, or write about their favorite character or scene to read to the class.

With more advanced readers, one approach to increase children's attention to favorite parts of a short text or poem is to use choral reading. In choral reading, children follow along while the teacher reads the text aloud, highlighting two or three places that they particularly enjoy, and on a second reading, they join in on the lines they have highlighted.

Guided reading In guided reading, the teacher works with small groups of children who are at the same reading level, providing support or scaffolding while they read. The goal is to let the children read, noting problems they have with specific words or punctuation, and providing support and modeling reading strategies for the children to practice (Herrell, 2000). This is also a time when children can have extra practice in decoding, word recognition, or grammatical structures that affect their understanding of the text. For example, children may be having some difficulties decoding a particularly difficult set of words in English (such as sounding out consonant clusters /ch/ or /th/) or ones that are pronounced differently in different words (such as the /gh/ in *tough* or *taught*), or vocabulary words that are confusing (such as homophones like *read/red* or *there/their*). Guided reading activities can also be undertaken as whole class work, engaging children in comprehension, vocabulary building, or other reading activities. Predictable books, with repeated patterns, can be very helpful in building children's decoding skills and fluency, and also help them to develop confidence in their reading. The types of activities discussed here, helping to increase "learners' knowledge of language features and their control of reading strategies," is sometimes referred to as "intensive reading" because of the focused attention to language features (Nation, 2009, p. 25).

Independent reading A major goal of any reading program for young learners is to encourage and enable them to read independently and to motivate them to want to read a variety of texts (Day & Bamford, 1998). In some schools, independent reading (also known as "extensive reading" or "sustained silent reading") is so important that time is set aside for all children and their teachers to read, in what is referred to as DEAR (Drop Everything and Read) time. Children need time to read and to choose materials from a class library or reading center that contains a variety of print and digital texts to read alone, with a partner (buddy reading), or while listening to an audio version of the text. Listening to someone read a text aloud, while they follow along silently, can be a good activity for struggling readers, but it is also engaging for good readers, who like to hear what a story sounds like when read fluently. There are lots of good stories being read aloud available on the Internet, especially through YouTube, or you may record your own reading of texts in the class reading collection.

You can encourage independent reading by giving each child a reading log to fill in when they have read something. An example is provided below:

My Reading Log　　　　My Name: _____

Rating
☺ **Great**
☺ **OK**
☹ **Not so good**

Date	Book Title & Author	Rating	Pages	Comments

Children can also be given time in class to share their reactions to books or other texts with the class, encouraging other children to read what they have enjoyed. One approach that has become popular is to divide the class into small book clubs or literature circles, with each group reading a book and then creating a poster or other product that they share with the class. It is important to help your learners select books or other materials that are at their reading level. One approach is to ask children to look at any page of the story. If there are more than a few words on that page that they don't know, the text is probably at too high a level for independent reading (though it might be appropriate for shared or guided reading).

Texts for reading The texts that children can read in shared, guided, or independent reading should be ones that encourage children to read, are enjoyable, have a variety

Provided by National Geographic Society

of purposes and text structures, and offer opportunities for a range of activities (Allen, 1994). They include:

- Songs, chants, and poems
- Comic strips or cartoons
- Folktales and fairytales
- Short stories
- Graded readers (see next page)
- Letters, e-mails, and text messages
- Greeting cards
- Maps
- Menus
- Picture books
- Plays and Reader's Theater scripts (see p.183–184)
- Recipes
- Schedules and other charts or displays of basic information

- Short informational texts (such as those included in *Explorer* magazine, published by National Geographic, and many others available online)
- Signs (international road signs, signs for hospitals, etc.)

Some of the best texts will be those written by other young learners, so be sure to keep copies of stories, poems, greeting cards, and other texts that your young learners will enjoy reading.

3. **Language experience** Language experience is an approach that uses learners' oral language as the basis of a written story. The learners (a class, small group, or individual student) dictate their "story" to someone who is a more competent writer (usually the teacher, but it may also be an older, more proficient student), who writes what the learners dictate. The language experience story can be a summary, an e-mail to the author of a story that the class has read, an invitation to parents to come to a school event, a thank-you note to someone who has visited the class, or even a message to a student who has missed an important event (Ashton-Warner, 1963; Dixon & Nessel, Nessell & Jones, 1981; Van Allen & Allen, 1976). Anything that is meaningful to the learners can be the basis for the language experience approach (LEA). With LEA, young learners follow these steps:

Jamie Grill/Iconica/Getty Images

1. Participate in a common experience (a field trip, a story, a celebration, a visitor, a picture that evokes feelings)
2. Have a discussion
3. Decide what to write, using a brainstorming web or other graphic organizer
4. Dictate the "story" to the teacher, who writes it so all can see

Graded Readers

Graded readers are small books or booklets (often based on traditional stories) that are written at different levels of language proficiency (in grammar, syntax, and vocabulary). Many publishers offer these, and some EYL textbook series have them available as well. They may even be written about the same topic as the unit in the textbook, reinforcing the unit vocabulary and grammar in the meaningful and engaging context of a story. Graded readers are especially helpful for children to acquire the most frequent vocabulary words (as in the West or Dolch lists, mentioned previously in this chapter) and can provide a systematic way of developing vocabulary through reading (Day & Bamford, 1998; Nation & Meara, 2002).

5. Read back what the teacher has written (The teacher may read it first, with students following along, and then they read it together.)

6. Decide if they want to edit anything

7. Copy what is written on the board into their notebooks

At this point, children can engage in a number of follow-up activities to develop their reading and writing skills, as well as their vocabulary (and even grammar). They can:

- Cut up the copied sentences into sentence strips and sequence them
- Add new sight words to the class word wall (an alphabetic listing of important words that the class has learned) or their vocabulary notebooks
- Find rhyming words or words that begin or end with the same sound (phonics activities)
- Complete a gap-fill, filling in important words from the story
- Play vocabulary games such as Concentration or Bingo with the vocabulary words
- Create a new ending for the story or text

The possibilities for follow-up activities are endless, now that learners have seen their own words in print. There are a number of benefits to using LEA with young learners, but perhaps the most important is the production of a meaningful text from learners' ideas expressed orally and then encoded in written language.

One question that always emerges with this approach is whether to write exactly what the children dictate or to correct what they say into "good" English:

Exact words:

- Validate the children's language
- Make a clear relationship between speech (sound) and print
- Will not likely lead to other errors or fossilization

A teacher-edited text:

- Provides a good model
- Reflects the differences between spoken and written texts
- May be viewed more positively by parents or administrators

Some EYL teachers do both. When the children are dictating the text, they write exactly what the children say. They then ask the children to "read" what they have said and ask if anyone wants to make any changes. After the children have finished suggesting changes, the teacher suggests some changes to make, editing the most serious errors, particularly if the children are going to copy the text and take it home to their parents.

Here is a partial example of how a class adapted the song "Peanut Butter and Jelly," based on a class poll of favorite foods (with substantial help from their teacher, Les Greenblatt). The children have fun with rhyme, while they are also noticing the different ways in which /i/ is spelled in common English words.

Pepperoni Pizza

Apples and bananas are really, really neat,
But
Pepperoni pizza is our favorite thing to eat.

Mario eats ice cream while standing on his feet,
But
Pepperoni pizza is our favorite thing to eat.

Silvia likes hot dogs while sitting in her seat,
But
Pepperoni pizza is our favorite thing to eat.

(The chant continues with other students' names and ends with:)

Mr. Greenblatt brought us to his room; he said he had a treat.
It was pepperoni pizza, our favorite thing to eat!

Following this, the children drew pictures of the various foods and made their own book, titled, naturally, *Pepperoni Pizza.*

■ Effective Reading Activities

A number of reading activities have been discussed in relation to various approaches to reading and stages in the lesson. In this section, activities are categorized according to:

- ■ Activities for beginning and more advanced (and generally older) readers
- ■ Pre-reading, during-reading, and post-reading activities
- ■ Reading strategies

Because reading, like listening, is a receptive skill, many of the listening activities mentioned in Chapter 4 can be adapted for use with reading. Many of the following activities also involve writing as a means of indicating understanding, as well as continued language development.

Activities for Beginning and More Advanced Readers Children go through stages in their reading and writing. In the earliest stages, before they are able to get meaning from words, they get meaning from the pictures and express meaning by drawing. At this stage, it is important to read aloud to children and engage in shared reading, using picture books and predictable stories so that they can join in.

As they begin developing literacy, young learners still need pictures and other support (from the teacher and other students), but they are able to get some meaning from words and are able to use some letters or words in copying or labeling. At this stage, language experience will be a helpful instructional approach, since children will see their words become print and will then be able to "read" what they have written, but some attention to both phonics and sight words will also be needed.

As they continue to progress, they will begin to read aloud (but not comprehend everything they are reading) and write simple texts, though they will use invented spellings (see example below) and words from their first language and will make grammatical errors. You can help them to decode (through phonics) and to use their knowledge of the world and their growing knowledge of English to comprehend (through sight words) with guided reading.

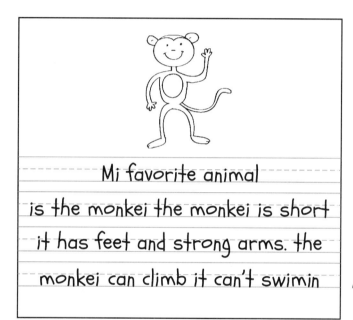

Example of invented spelling.

As their reading progresses, so will their comprehension, and they will be less reliant on pictures or visual support. Their use of reading strategies (predicting, confirming, correcting, etc.) will increase, and they can engage in some independent reading and writing, using writing workshop and focusing on revising and editing.

The following activities can be done with individual students; in small, guided reading sessions; or with the whole class.

1. **Activities for beginning readers (word level):**

   - Pointing to or circling initial or final letters in words
   - Pointing to or circling words
   - Sorting pictures of objects (or the objects) with the same initial sound
   - Sorting or matching words that rhyme
   - Labeling pictures
   - Matching words with pictures, with the same words, or with words with the same initial or final letters

- Sorting and categorizing words by type of object or similarity of sound
- Guessing a word partially completed (first and last letter, first letter)
- Completing a word or word and picture puzzle
- Playing alphabet or word games
- Noting patterns in songs or chants
- Filling in a missing letter with picture cue (e.g., ca_ with picture of a car)
- Creating words with letters
- Posting words to a word wall
- Creating letter collages

Here is an example of a sequence of activities for beginning readers that can also end with a beginning writing activity using the song "Head, Shoulders, Knees, and Toes":

Head, Shoulders, Knees, and Toes

Head, shoulders, knees, and toes, knees and toes,
Head, shoulders, knees, and toes, knees and toes,
And eyes, and ears, and mouth, and nose
Head, shoulders, knees, and toes, knees and toes.

The teacher might begin this as an oral activity, using Total Physical Response. The first time, children listen to the song and watch as the teacher uses both hands to point to the body parts. After a few times, the children follow along, doing the actions, and saying the words with the teacher. Following this, the teacher puts drawings of the body and face of a child on the board, asking children to help in labeling the various parts. This is followed by a number of activities to make sure children recognize the names of the body parts. Next, children hold up flashcards with body parts at the right time in the song. Flashcards can also be placed on the board, out of order, for children to sequence, or given to children to line up in the right order as the class sings the song. This might lead to a writing activity such as labeling the parts of the body and face on a drawing that is titled "My Head, Shoulders, Knees, and Toes," or drawing and labeling the body parts of a monster (with several heads, one eye, or three huge toes).

2. **Activities for more advanced readers (from word to sentence and text level):**

- Unscrambling words (What animal words can you find here? Cta, hifs)
- Filling in word puzzles
- Choosing among multiple choice items and pictures
- Arranging words in proper sequence in sentences and sentences in proper sequence in a text (sentence strips)

- Matching texts with similar formats (schedules, lists, e-mails)
- Following along with a text while listening to it being read (on CD or by the teacher)
- Correcting mistakes in a text (while the teacher reads the correct version)
- Sorting true and false sentences
- Skimming a text to get the major idea(s)
- Scanning a text for specific information
- Answering comprehension questions about short texts
- Looking up the meaning of unfamiliar words
- Taking notes in a graphic organizer
- Scanning a text for known word chunks (bus stop, soccer ball)
- Engaging in jigsaw reading, with each group responsible for different parts of a short text
- Writing in a reading response journal or log (see p.182)

The last items in this list illustrate that, as young learners become more proficient English readers, their activities move from a focus on learning to read to a focus on using reading to learn (Brewster, Ellis, & Girard, 2002).

Pre-Reading, During-Reading, and Post-Reading Activities
While it is possible to use a number of activities throughout the reading process, the following presents some that seem especially suited for before, during, or after reading. Note that some of them involve writing, thus integrating reading and writing activities.

1. **Pre-reading activities** There are a number of activities that help learners activate their background knowledge and prepare them to read or follow along when someone else reads. These include:

- Taking a picture walk through the story of a fictional text
- Predicting what a story or other text will be about
- Pointing to and discussing the titles, subtitles, and graphics of an informational text
- Talking about what is already known about the topic and the text (perhaps filling out a K-W-L advance organizer as a class)
- Asking a question to be answered by the text
- Engaging in a variety of vocabulary activities

2. **During-reading activities** When reading aloud to children or engaging in shared or guided reading with them, it is important to model good reading strategies for them to use when they are reading independently. These include:

- Visualizing a scene
- Drawing a picture of a scene
- Paraphrasing or summarizing at several places in the text
- Predicting what will come next
- Re-reading for better comprehension
- Filling in a graphic organizer (a chart, a table, or a web)
- Correcting a text with errors
- Comparing two texts

3.   **Post-reading activities**   Upon completion of a read-aloud or shared or guided reading, there are a number of ways of helping learners to remember or extending what they have read:

- Labeling or writing sentences with illustrations from the text
- Drawing scenes and labeling or writing sentences with them
- Putting a set of illustrations in order and then talking about each
- Answering a series of questions that lead to a summary of the text
- Arranging words in sentence strips
- Sequencing sentences (strip stories)
- Forming small groups to discuss a favorite character or animal (using cooperative learning corners)
- Talking about likes and dislikes
- Completing a graphic organizer
- Describing a character or scene
- Writing a new ending
- Creating a mini-book (see Chapter 6)
- Filling in cloze activities (see next page)
- Engaging in Reader's Theater (see next page)
- Writing in a response journal (see example below)

Reading response journals   The following response journal provides a convenient way for children to record their thoughts and feelings about texts they have read independently.

DOUBLE-ENTRY RESPONSE JOURNAL	
What is the story or article about?	Did you like it? Why did you like it? What did you like best? What is one thing you learned?

Cloze activities One way to reinforce understanding of a text or provide vocabulary practice is through the use of cloze activities. Cloze activities are a special type of gap-fill, with words omitted from a unified, coherent paragraph. Learners use context clues to help them in filling in the missing words. In a good cloze activity, the first and last lines are complete and no more than every fifth to seventh word is omitted. For beginning readers, only a few words should be omitted. Here is a sample cloze activity:

> Head, shoulders, knees, and toes, knees and toes,
> Head, shoulders, knees, and toes, _____ and toes,
> And eyes, and ears, and mouth, and _____,
> Head, shoulders, knees, and toes, knees and toes.

Students can also be provided with the words to choose from for each blank, or they may have to determine the word from context clues, as in the above example. Cloze activities can also be designed to provide grammar practice; for example, if prepositions of place (*by, in, under*) or adverbs of frequency (*never, sometimes, always*) are a focus, only those words would be omitted from the text.

Reader's Theater Unlike other dramatic productions, Reader's Theater does not require costumes, props, or scenery. All it needs are the learners, who read lines in sequence, following along in the script as others read their lines. For young learners, the teacher

will want to help with or even write simple scripts to use with picture books. Older students can work in small groups (using Writing Workshop, discussed on p. 192–193) to write their lines, deciding what a character might say in a particular scene. Reader's

Theater would work especially well with *The Great Kapok Tree*, discussed in Chapter 3, with each child reading a line in the way that the animal "spoke" to the lumberjack and moving in the way described as they read the animal's lines. Reader's Theater makes a great ending for any unit that has included a good story or informational text with possible characters. It can be a very engaging activity for parents' night at the school. (The Education World Web site, http://www.educationworld.com/a_curr/profdev/profdev082.shtml, and James Davis' Drama in ESL Web site, http://esldrama.weebly.com/index.html, have lots of ideas for Reader's Theater.)

Reading Strategies We read many different types of texts for different purposes in a day, or even in an hour, and we do so in different ways. We read for information, for enjoyment, or to keep up to date with news of our friends, family, or country. When looking for the time a TV show is on the air, we scan the schedule until we find the title of the show, and then note the time and station. When we read an e-mail, we probably look quickly to see who sent the e-mail and at the subject line, and then decide whether to read it at all. If we decide to read it, we may skim the message to get the gist (the major idea) of the e-mail and then, maybe, we will go back and read it more closely. When we read a novel, we might read parts of it fast, slowing only when there is a memorable passage. When we read an academic article or book, we might first skim the text to determine the main ideas and then read much more slowly, stopping to think about what we are reading, and maybe taking notes. When we are reading a story aloud to a child, we read with a lot of drama, hoping to engage the child.

Children differ in their reading strategies, largely based on where they are in their literacy development. Some are "code breakers," focusing on decoding each symbol; some are "meaning makers," trying to construct meaning from the text; some are "text users," who understand that different texts have different purposes and vary their reading strategies accordingly; and some are "text analysts," who understand that authors of texts have a particular perspective that needs to be critically analyzed (Luke & Freebody, 1997; Zhang, Gu, & Hu, 2008). We will need to help our learners, especially the older ones, to vary their reading strategies based on their purposes for reading and the nature of the text and become strategic users of these various approaches to reading. Some reading strategies include:

- **Predicting:** finding clues to what might come next in a text (from the cover, the title, pictures, headings, or prior knowledge of the content)
- **Monitoring:** determining whether one's reading makes sense, and if not, re-reading to understand
- **Confirming:** finding evidence of an accurate prediction

- **Connecting:** making connections to prior readings, information, or experiences
- **Questioning:** asking questions about a text while reading, which may include predicting the next parts of a text
- **Skimming:** reading to get the general topic or main points of a text
- **Scanning:** reading to find specific information such as dates or names or answers to questions
- **Distinguishing** between important and less important information
- **Using context clues:** looking at the context (the pictures, other words, the place in the sentence, punctuation) for better comprehension
- **Paraphrasing or summarizing:** while reading and after reading a text
- **Visualizing:** forming images about what has been read in order to facilitate comprehension

Considerations for Teaching Writing

What Is Writing?

Writing is the most neglected skill in EYL (and in most EFL classes). There are a number of reasons why writing is not more present in EYL classes: time, number of students, a mistaken notion that children cannot begin writing in English until they reach a significant level of proficiency in the language, or a belief that children must learn to read before they can write. Sometimes, teachers think of essays or reports when thinking about writing, and these texts take a long time to write and a long time for the teacher to evaluate. But if we consider the many purposes of writing, we will note the wide range of texts that an adult writes over a day. We write

Andrea Chu/Stone+/Getty Images

to communicate ideas, to interact socially with others (e-mails, invitations, greeting cards, thank-you notes), to remember (lists, diaries, journals), as well as to get information and learn. In a similar fashion, the range of texts that children can write is broad, but in general, writing for children should be seen primarily as a means of self-expression, with a focus on meaning, or as a means of reinforcing oral language development. In this section we will explore a variety of texts that can easily be integrated into a unit or lesson plan that will engage children and also be possible for teachers to use when they have many students and limited time to evaluate.

Some of that writing may consist of activities in which children fill in a blank or create sentences with some words provided. These can be good beginning writing activities, but children also need the opportunity to engage in creative writing and to write authentic texts for authentic purposes. When we write outside of the classroom, we write because we have something we want to communicate, a purpose for our writing, and a real audience we want to communicate with. But we sometimes forget that when we assign writing in language classes. A way to help us remember to assign authentic writing assignments is to use FAT-P in explaining those assignments.

Every writing assignment should have a specific:

Form	The type of writing text or genre—a letter, an e-mail, a journal, a list, a story, or a poem
Audience	Someone who will read the writing (other students, parents, or oneself, for example, in a diary or journal)
Topic	Something to communicate
Purpose	A reason to write—to inform, entertain, remember, express feelings

Approaches to Teaching Writing

Children learning to write go through a number of stages in their first language, and they are likely to go through these stages as well when they begin writing in English: drawing, scribbling, tracing and writing letters (not necessarily forming words), using invented spelling as they attempt to write words, and finally using more conventional writing and spelling. Throughout this process, they are creating their own meaning (even when we don't understand what they have written). Even very young children have ideas about how texts are written, and they attempt to create texts based on those ideas; over time, as their understanding of these texts changes, so does their writing.

If they have learned to write in their own language, they already know something about the purposes for writing and how to bring what they know about the world, about language, and about discourse or texts to that writing, though they may need to learn new conventions (some of what was discussed with reading: a new alphabet or a new directionality, but also conventions concerning spelling, capitalization, and punctuation). If they haven't learned to write in their first language, they will also have to learn how to hold a pencil or pen and over time to develop the fine motor skills required to form letters. Learning to make letters and use them to spell are to writing what learning to distinguish sounds and relate sounds and letters are to reading: They are the basics required to learn to write or read (Slattery & Willis, 2001).

While our goal with our young learners is to help them to construct original texts using their "intellectual and linguistic resources" (Hudelson, 1988, p. 1), we will also want to help them to revise these texts to make them as clear and understandable as possible. The question is, How do we accomplish this? Just as there are controversies about the best way to teach reading, there are controversies about how to teach writing. There are two major approaches:

1. A product-based approach—one that focuses on the final product
2. A process-based approach—one that focuses on the process of writing

A product-based approach focuses on accuracy, providing controlled or guided activities to help children learn the basics of writing, working on spelling, grammar, and mechanics, in a bottom-up fashion. A process-based approach focuses on fluency, encouraging children to write and express themselves freely, without too much worry about spelling, grammar, or punctuation until the final stage of the process, when they "publish" their work. In the end, both of these approaches are needed (Raimes, 1993).

1. **A product-based approach** A product-based approach, as the name implies, focuses on the final writing product, seeking to create as accurate a text as possible: one in which the grammar, spelling, and even punctuation and capitalization are accurate. To achieve this, students are given a series of activities (controlled and guided) that serve as small steps to complete before they move to constructing an entire text. Like phonics, a product-based approach to writing consists of a bottom-up approach, where accuracy with the various pieces of language (letters, words, sentences, paragraphs) is the focus.

Writing activities are usually referred to as controlled, guided, or free. Both controlled and guided writing activities focus on reinforcing learning of some level of language: vocabulary, grammar, or mechanics (spelling, punctuation, capitalization). The difference is in the amount of independence provided for the writer. The goal of controlled activities is to have students practice writing the language with careful control. Most of the text is provided for the student. These activities only ask the student to copy or fill in a blank with possible words provided, or for older students, to make minor choices or changes in a text (for example, changing a text about one boy to one about several boys, or changing a paragraph written in present tense to past tense). The goal of guided writing is to help learners experience success while they also learn the relationship between their ideas, words, and writing. Support is provided (for example, in the form of questions to consider, or a graphic organizer with some of the information provided). Free activities, as the name implies, encourage creativity, providing only the writing prompt (from FAT-P) or allowing the student to choose what to write. The following sections discuss controlled and guided activities; free writing will be discussed under Writing Workshop.

Controlled writing activities:

- Forming letters by tracing, creating them physically (with arms, hands, or even full bodies with other children), connecting dots
- Underlining stressed words as they are spoken
- Counting the words in a sentence or clapping with each word
- Copying words or sentences
- Completing word puzzles with the words provided
- Playing word games (Bingo, Concentration)
- Unscrambling words or sentences
- Filling in gaps with the words or sentences provided
- Creating a poem with words provided
- Building a personal word list
- Contributing words to a word wall

Guided writing activities:

- Brainstorming topics or words to include
- Completing word puzzles with clues
- Filling in blanks
- Completing sentences with picture clues or sentence starters
- Responding to questions about a picture, a scene, or a text
- Describing a picture with some vocabulary provided
- Creating a poem with model formats
- Completing language bubbles in cartoons
- Writing from dictation (including a dictogloss, a summary that students write, with the aid of a list of key words, after hearing a text read twice; Wajnryb, 1991)

- Writing from a (partially) completed graphic organizer
- Responding to a series of questions in writing
- Completing cloze activities
- Participating in the language experience approach
- Creating sentences with some of the words provided (for example, in a word grid)
- Rearranging sentences in a paragraph
- Rewriting familiar songs or stories (such as "Pepperoni Pizza")
- Writing a new ending for a familiar story
- Writing a text (invitation, poem, e-mail, etc.) from a model

Nunan (2011) reminds us that even controlled or guided activities can be fun, especially if they are turned into games or competitions, and some of these can also reinforce reading skills. Children can be asked to copy something that is relevant to the lesson or unit—for example, copying only the names of animals from a list that includes other objects, or unscrambling words that are the names of children in the class. Even lists can be made meaningful. Mary Tabaa, a primary English teacher and teacher educator, suggests the following ways to make lists meaningful: If a unit is about daily activities, students can list what they do every day (copying from a list on the board or the text that includes *brush my teeth, eat breakfast, get dressed,* or *walk to school*). If it is about food, they can cut out food items from a magazine or newspaper and make a list of what they want to buy at the store. For guided activities, children can complete a text that has been partially filled out: an invitation, a thank you, a recipe or even a song or chant, with predictable rhyme. They can use pictures and sentence starters to introduce themselves, members of their family, or workers in the school. A simple introduction of themselves could then be posted, with pictures, for children to use as reading texts and to get to know each other:

Hi, My name is _____.

I am _____ years old.

I like _____. I don't like _____.

It is also possible to include guided writing activities for children who are working on creative or free writing in small groups. Nessel and Jones (1981, pp. 85–87) describe a sample brainstorming conversation that a teacher is having with a small group of students who are preparing to write about a storm. In that conversation, she asks each child what they want to write about the storm, and in a series of scaffolding questions, helps them to put a few ideas on paper. As they begin writing, she moves from child to child, giving individual help and prompting additional words or ideas.

Poetry Poetry can be a wonderful source of guided writing activities. Children love to listen to poetry, but they can also write poetry if given models to imitate. Poetry can be written by the entire class, by children working in small groups, or by individual students.

- **Name Acrostics:** Some of the simplest poems are ones that use names. Children can find words (from the word wall or with help from others) to describe themselves:

Y oung	**H** appy
U nique	**A** thletic
K ind	**N** ice
I ntelligent	**G** irl

Acrostics can also be made for any topic or occasion. Children can send them to each other for Valentine's Day (as described in Chapter 2) or create a Happy Birthday or other acrostic poem to send to family or friends.

- **Three-Line Poems:** Some simple but clever poems can be made with single words on three lines:

Noun	**Cats**	**Children**
Verb	**Meow**	**Play**
Adverb	**Softly**	**Happily**

- **Cinquains:** These five-line poems (note *cinq*, the French word for *five*) are more appropriate for advanced young writers, but they follow a simple pattern and can be created by younger learners with considerable discussion, vocabulary practice, and clear directions, especially if they work in small groups. In the following example, children were told to write the name of an animal on the first line; to choose two colors or words to describe the animal in the second; to think of things that their animal likes to do and list these, adding -ing; to complete the fourth line with the name of the animal and "are our friends"; and then to either use the same name or another name for that animal in the last line:

Title or topic	**Panda**
2 Adjectives	**Black White**
3 Words ending in -ing	**Playing Sleeping Eating**
4-word sentence	**Pandas are our friends.**
Topic	**Bear**

- **Shape Poems:** In a shape poem, the words are written in the shape of the major topic or feeling. A famous shape poem is "r-p-o-p-h-e-s-s-a-g-r" (grasshopper) written by e. e. cummings, a poet who liked to play with language (available at http://www.poets.org/viewmedia.php /prmMID/15402). In the title and the poem, he captures the way that grasshoppers are constantly moving and hopping. There are also poems in the shape of ski slopes, roller coasters, or leaf piles. You can provide the shape or an object for the children and have them write words around the shape. Examples of shape poems can be found at http://www .readwritethink.org/classroom-resources/student-interactives/shape-poems-30044.html.

- **Poems from Prose:** A fun class activity is to divide the class into groups and make each group responsible for finding words to fit one of the senses. For example, in a tree unit, one group might look at the tree and write down what they see; another group can record what they hear; another what they smell; etc. When they come back, they can finish each of these lines:

> **We see**
> **We hear**
> **We smell**
> **We feel**
> **We taste** (if appropriate)

They will be writing strings of words, but when the sentence starters ("We see," "We hear," etc.) are removed, what will remain is poetry.

2. **A process-based approach** In a process-based approach to writing, the primary goal is for children to express their ideas, to construct meaning, and to explore their linguistic and other resources. Writing is a thinking process, and in that process, children will be learning. All process-based approaches take children through a series of steps to help them construct and communicate their ideas, focusing on expression in the early stages, and only being concerned with accurate grammar or mechanics in the final stages. The most common approach to process-based writing is Writing Workshop, but other free or independent writing may use a process-based approach as well.

Writing Workshop Writing (or Writers) Workshop is a series of activities that help children to become authors, beginning with free writing, and then moving through a series of writing steps or stages until they have produced a work that they want to share, by "publishing" it in a class book, posting it on a bulletin board, or creating their own book (Calkins, 1983; Hachem, Nabhani, & Bahous, 2008). This workshop is both interactive and individualized, with students receiving support from the teacher and other students as they work through the process of writing (Federer, 1993). Through a series of stages, Writing Workshop helps learners become both more fluent and accurate writers. Computers have made Writing Workshop much more feasible, but even without them, children can be helped to become authors with pride in their work.

The stages of Writing Workshop are:

- **Brainstorming and discussing:** identifying possible topics to write about individually, with a partner, and as a class, and talking about them with others to activate background knowledge and obtain ideas for the first draft, using a brainstorming web to capture ideas

- **Drafting:** writing a rough draft, focusing on getting ideas on paper, and not worrying about spelling, grammar, or even word choice; fluency is the goal of this stage
- **Peer reviewing and conferencing:** sharing the draft with another student with a focus on the content, helping the writer to see what his or her audience likes, understands, or needs to make the writing clearer
- **Revising:** taking the suggestions of others and also one's own thoughts and improving the content and organization of the paper
- **Reviewing and conferencing:** sharing the revised text with the teacher
- **Editing:** checking spelling, punctuation, and grammar, and improving the final version of the paper; accuracy is the focus here. Controlled and guided writing activities can help with this stage of the process.
- **Publishing:** sharing the writing with a real audience by posting it on a bulletin board or online, including it in a class book, creating an individual book, or putting it into an e-mail. It is also possible to invite children to read or share their writing with the class or groups of students in an "author's chair" while the other children listen to the text being read aloud.

Note that the language experience approach, discussed previously, can be used as a way of introducing children to Writing Workshop, where the brainstorming, drafting, revising, and editing are done as a whole-class activity. Language experience can also be used to guide children through writing their own books on a common theme or by encouraging children to create a new ending or changing the text in some other way, allowing them some independent writing that might be shared with others (Karnowski, 1989).

Sometimes, teachers only include one stage of reviewing or conferencing, with other students or with the teacher. One value of conferencing with peers or the teacher is that it provides an authentic audience and helps the learner to understand how her/his writing is being understood. Students of all ages need to be taught how to be effective peer reviewers and what kind of feedback to provide. It helps to have a form such as the following Praise-Question-Polish form. There are many versions of this form, depending on the age and English proficiency level of the student, and also on the type of writing being reviewed, but the following form (adapted from Lyons, 1981) can help beginning writers in providing appropriate comments for their partners during peer review:

PRAISE — QUESTION — POLISH

Author's Name _____

Title of Paper _____

Reviewer's Name _____

PRAISE
What do you like about my paper?

_____

QUESTION
What is one question you have? OR
What is one thing you want to know more about?

_____

POLISH
What is one thing I can do to make this better?

_____

_____

It is also helpful to provide children with simple checklists to guide their editing in preparing their final draft. (Note: Older students might be given a checklist to guide their revision—usually referred to as an editing checklist—and another one to guide their preparation of the final draft—usually referred to as a proofreading checklist. For younger learners, one checklist to use before preparation of the final draft is sufficient.) The following is one that can be adapted to reflect different levels of English proficiency and writing experience:

EDITING CHECKLIST

1. Does my story have a beginning, middle, and end?

2. Does it have a title?

3. Did I listen to what other students said?

3. Did I check my spelling?

4. Did I capitalize the first word in each sentence?

5. Did I end each sentence with a period or exclamation point mark?

6. Did I end each question with a question mark?

7. Can people read my handwriting?

Shared and interactive writing Shared writing, similar to shared reading, provides learners with a model of how to go about writing. Unlike language experience, where the teacher is a scribe recording the students' words, in shared writing, the teacher writes on the board or chart paper, asking for input from the students and explaining her decisions (thinking aloud). The shared writing lessons, with a small group or the whole class, are usually brief (a few minutes) and focused on particular challenges that face young learners and precede an opportunity for the students to write a similar text. Before writing, the teacher and the students engage in a discussion to activate background knowledge and arouse interest in the task and also establish a purpose for writing. During writing, the teacher may note words that s/he wants to look up later, make small revisions (adding or deleting a word) as they occur, re-read the emerging text several times, and discuss what needs to be written next. S/he may also note words to look up later in the dictionary. After the text is completed, the teacher reads it to the students and may ask them to orally summarize what they have learned. The text is also displayed in a place where the students can refer to it when they draft a similar text. It is important that the text be an authentic effort. The teacher should not introduce errors that s/he would not normally make, since this is an opportunity to observe and interact with an expert. As McKenzie (1985) explains, with shared writing, "Children begin to get in on the craft of writing" (p. 8). The next step after shared writing is interactive writing, in which the teacher and students collaborate on developing the text, determining together the words, phrases, organization, layout, and other considerations (McCarrier, Pinnell, & Fountas, 2000).

Dialog journals Dialog journals, another interactive writing experience, are a written conversation between a student and teacher that involve both free and guided writing. In a dialog journal, the student writes about something that interests her/him (the free or independent writing) and the teacher responds, using about the same amount and level of language (the guidance). In the beginning, children may just draw in their journals (Peyton, 1993). A teacher's response may be labeling what they have drawn and asking a simple question to encourage the student to continue responding. Sometimes a child will copy a list of words from the textbook, and the teacher's response might be to add to the list or choose some of the items and add a simple comment. There is no overt correction, though a teacher may provide a model in the next entry. For example, if a student wrote "I go zo Satirday" the teacher might respond, "How exciting! You'll go the zoo, Saturday. What animals do you want to see?" Before the student responds, s/he will read the teacher's entry and may self-correct with the next entry. With this regular and positive feedback, students become more confident of themselves as writers. They also improve their writing over time as they engage in meaningful communication at their own language level and have a private conversation with the teacher. Urzua (1987) found that through process writing and dialog journals, young learners develop a better sense of audience, voice, and the power of language. Teachers benefit by getting to know individual students and their writing strengths and needs and by being able to offer individualized support.

One concern teachers have with dialog journals is the time it takes for the students to write and for the teacher to respond. Many teachers use dialog journals only once a week (if classes meet two or three times a week) and limit writing time to the first five or ten minutes of class as a means of quieting the students and also keeping the journal response manageable. Other teachers, especially those with large classes, let the students write several entries, and then provide one response for all these entries. Some teachers collect and respond to one-half or one-third of the journals every week, rotating until all students have received feedback. The important point is to provide children with an opportunity to write freely and to receive individual feedback in authentic communication.

Texts for writing Children can be invited to write a wide range of texts. Many of these will have already been introduced as reading texts. The following list is only a beginning:

- Address labels
- Alphabet books
- Brochures
- Dialog journals
- Diaries
- Digital texts (e-mail, texts, blogs, e-pals)
- Greeting cards
- Invitations
- Lists
- Menus
- Mini-books
- Name cards
- Plays or scripts for Reader's Theater
- Poems
- Posters
- Recipes
- Response journals
- Signs
- Stories
- Thank-you notes

Reading and Writing Digital Texts The world of reading and writing has changed markedly in the last decade, with "literacy" now thought of in terms of many "literacies" (New London Group, 2000; Leu, 2000, 2002). Young learners may find that they do increasing amounts of their reading and writing online. Certainly the need for print dictionaries, encyclopedias, and other reference works will only continue to decline as these are freely and easily available on the Internet. At least some of the texts older young learners write, as well as read, should be those that communicate information to others through e-mail, blogs, texts, or paired class assignments. If actual Internet access is not available, assignments can model Internet communication with documents that resemble e-mail or other online communication. As the following example from a teacher in Greece indicates, some of our young learners are so involved in online communication that they don't know about regular (postal) mail! We need to keep up with our learners!

Some digital writing activities include:

1. E-pals and paired classes
2. Photo-autobiographies

1.   E-pals and paired classes Georgia Maneta, the teacher from Greece, described two ways in which she paired her students with others, one of them using the Internet. E-pals (or e-friends) are a modern adaptation of pen pals. Instead of writing to each other and sending the message through the postal service, pairs of English learners (in other schools or even other countries) write to each other regularly, often after discussing as a class the types of topics that would be interesting for others to read about. The topics usually begin with introductions, then move to likes and dislikes, and even to descriptions of favorite games, sports, or foods.

Some teachers decide to make this a class activity, pairing with another EYL class to exchange class e-mails (Cummins & Sayers, 1997). Children discuss what they want to know about the other class as well as what they want to communicate, and through online discussion, the

Georgia Maneta, Primary English Teacher, Greece

"Last year I was part of a project where my students had to exchange e-mails about simple topics (family, hobbies, subjects, music, etc.) with students from other European schools. It worked really well as they were excited every time they got a reply and eager to learn about their e-friends' lives! I also worked on another project where a class of mine had to write on 3 or 4 postcards (which depicted our city) things about the weather in Greece and things that students like doing! The strangest thing for me was that most of them did not know how conventional letter writing worked!!!! They didn't know that envelopes with stamps would arrive at school from different parts of the world! As soon as they realized that they checked the post box every day! So, exchanging letters was a very good way to make my students write in English."

children and teachers decide on a series of brief topics to write about. Older learners can serve as "tourist guides," introducing their communities to each other and focusing on what they think makes their community a fun place to live.

2. **Photo-autobiographies** With digital cameras in many phones or the presence of a digital camera at the school, older children can take pictures of family and friends, or of things that are important to them (pets, toys, favorite games) to develop small digital or print books. (If a child doesn't have access to a digital camera, pictures can be scanned for inclusion.) Children can create their own book, with each picture serving as a page in the book and, depending on their level of literacy, provide a brief caption (dictating it to someone who can write it for them—the teacher or an older and more proficient English speaking student, if necessary). A smaller version of this would be to have each child contribute one picture for an online class newsletter or to send to their e-pals in another class.

Designing a Reading and Writing Lesson

As discussed in this chapter, reading and writing are often integrated in a lesson. The following is a lesson plan for 7- to 8-year-olds who are in their second year of English. The children will be participating in Reader's Theater for Parents' Night. They want to invite school administrators and children from other classes in the school to come to their rehearsal.

Sample Lesson
Invitation to Our Performance

Invitation to Our Performance	
Student profile	Grades 3–4, high beginner level of English proficiency
Skills to be emphasized	Reading, writing, speaking
Language	Form: Invitation Vocabulary and expressions: You are invited (formulaic chunk); RSVP; rehearsal; Reader's Theater
Objectives	By the end of the lesson, students will be able to: • Read and analyze sample invitations • Talk about possible invitees • Write an invitation

Materials	2 sample invitations
	1 blank invitation
	Paper and markers

Warm-up	
Capture their attention	Remind children of Parents' Night and Reader's Theater. Say to them, "Class, in 2 weeks . . . what will happen at school?" (Elicit their answers.) "Right! Parents' Night! And what are we doing on Parents' Night? Reader's Theater! It's going to be so much fun!"
Connect to prior knowledge and experiences	Discuss classes and people to invite. "Class, who do we want to invite to our Reader's Theater?" (Make a list on the board.) "How will they know when it is? How will they know where to go?" (Elicit the answer.) "Right! An invitation!"

Presentation	
Reading invitations	Present two examples of simple invitations.
	Analyze the parts of an invitation:
	Please come to:
	Date:
	Time:
	Place:
	From:
	RSVP:
	Ask students, "What are the parts of an invitation? Are there differences between the two invitations?"

Practice	
Controlled practice	Give students a fun template for an invitation.
	Q&A
	Then have students ask you questions and fill in the invitation properly.

Guided practice	As a class, the students write an invitation for their Reader's Theater performance using the language experience approach. After they give their ideas, and the teacher writes them on the board, children copy the major information from the board. They address the invitation to the teacher and class that they have selected from the list. Then they design the invitation to make it look attractive.
Application	
Independent activity	**Invitation** Students individually write an invitation for their parents or relatives, using the model provided, but changing the date and time to match Parents' Night. They discuss how to present this to their parents or relatives who don't speak English.
Assessment	
Formative assessment	In the controlled practice activity, the teacher can check to see if students can make the invitation correctly given all the party details.
Feedback and correction	The teacher will collect their independent activity and correct them.
Follow-up	
Next class	After the teacher returns their invitations with corrections, students will make the corrections for the invitations to their parents or relatives. Then they make a nice design for the invitation and add the language to make the invitation complete.

■ Teacher to Teacher

Teaching Reading and Writing to Young Learners

This chapter described effective approaches and activities for teaching reading and writing to young learners. Below are excerpts from online discussions by teachers from around the world who are teaching young learners. As you read their entries, which discuss the ways in which they integrate reading and writing into their classes, think about how they might also be useful in your context.

This teacher, from Qatar, talks about how she uses both the phonics and whole word (look–say) approach in teaching beginning reading. Notice how she makes both fun.

"Teaching phonics is fun for me. I personally adapt two famous programs in teaching sounds and letters. I use the Jolly Phonics program and Letter Land. They are wonderful in teaching sound through stories such as /sh/ and /ch/ sounds through characters and stories. Children are having fun and learning. Here is an example for learning the /sh/ sound:

/S/ is a very noisy snake, while /h/ Henry is a very quiet man. He doesn't like noise, so when they are walking together /s/ snake is always making that noisy sound /sssssss/. What do you think Henry will do? Yes, Henry is looking at him saying /shshshshshsh/. So whenever you see the friends /s/ and /h/ remember this /shshshshsh/ story.

(This story was taken from Letter Land stories, but using my own words.)
If you would like to have more information please feel free to visit the websites: www.letterland.com and www.jollylearning.co.uk.
I apply the whole word approach using flashcards and word recognition activities.

- Select a group of words
- Show the flashcard and say the word
- Elicit pronunciation for class repetition
- Put all the words on the board
- Play the camera game by asking the children to imagine they have a camera to take a picture of the words
- Ask them to shut their eyes
- Take one word out
- Ask them to open their eyes and find the missing word
- Then have the children find the picture of that word in their book to connect word and its meaning."

—Najat Al-Kuwari, Primary English Teacher, Qatar

Both phonics and meaning-based approaches such as the whole word approach have a place in the very young learner's classroom. Phonics is needed to help children understand the relationship between letters and sounds and also to sound out unfamiliar words in the future.

This teacher from Haiti was skeptical of using sight words in the look–say approach, but became convinced of its usefulness.

"When I used to teach second grade my supervisor told me it was okay to use the Look and Say approach at times. I was skeptical so one day she brought a series of things to my class. Mostly it was things like different logos of various products. She held up the Coca Cola logo and asked the kids what it said. They all screamed 'Coca Cola!!!!' There were others like Sprite, Kellogg's, and even some in Creole and French but the kids knew them all. The point is even if the kids were not aware that they were reading, they recognized the words because they had seen them so many times."

—*Lorraine Taggart, Primary English Teacher, Haiti*

Beginning with words in the environment, including those in a print-rich classroom, will help children see the relationship between written words and those that they have heard or said.

The following teacher trainer, from Poland, describes her choice of texts and the many activities that she uses with her class as she moves from reading aloud, to shared reading, guided reading, and ending with a play:

"I sometimes choose longer pieces for reading, but then they are usually pieces my students know in Polish and then I read the story in English, of course with the support of pictures. Then, we read together. I read the story from the big book and students have their small books. Then, the following step is to watch the story on DVD and then listening to the CD. We end our work with a drama. It takes a month to do so, but my students like it and they do not mind working. I provide them with many exercises: searching, matching, crosswords, drawing pictures, filling the gaps and so on. Every year we work on two longer stories."

—*Urszula Kropaczewska, Teacher Trainer, Poland*

Using a story that the children already know in Polish allows the teacher to choose a longer text and also to engage students in a range of engaging activities.

Next, a teacher from Costa Rica explains how she uses a game with small groups that involves both reading and writing, as well as listening and speaking.

"The 3R technique (run, read and retell) is done in groups. The teacher pastes paper around the classroom in places where they are not easily seen. One student runs and reads the sentence or phrase and has to retell it to a writer in the group. Then, another student is the runner and another one is the writer. This is a very good activity because they read, write, speak and listen."

—*Roxanne Vargas Lopez, Primary English Teacher, Costa Rica*

This running dictation game is always fun for students. Adding competition to reading and writing makes being accurate more important and helps motivate students.

As we know, getting children to write can be a challenge. This teacher from Croatia discusses how she motivates very young learners (in grade 1) and older learners (in grade 5) to write using pictures, in an activity like photo-autobiographies.

> "On Friday I asked my first and fifth graders to report on Monday (today) what they did over the weekend. They could use pictures and words. And what did I see today? First graders brought pictures of their weekend activities (playing football, watching TV, eating, riding a bike). Some even included words that we learned like ball, bike, pizza, sandwich, dog. The focus in grade 5 is the Past Simple tense. I got amazing sentences of what they did over the weekend with correct formation of regular and irregular verbs. There were even some sentences with the verbs we didn't cover, so this means they looked for some other sources to express themselves. Of course, in both cases there were occasional L1 words, but I didn't correct one single thing. I was so happy to see their work and awarded them with stamps and stickers."

—*Darija Sostaric-Zuckermann, Primary English Teacher, Croatia*

This teacher decided not to correct the children's use of their first language since she was asking children to write freely or independently and not through the longer Writing Workshop process. The children were very responsive, which was her goal.

Here is another teacher who asked students to take photos and use them as the basis for writing about a meaningful topic that they had been reading about: pollution and deforestation.

> "I often choose reading pieces that relate to real life, like articles about global warming or marine animals that are becoming extinct. Last week I asked my second graders to walk around their home environment and take photos that prove the existence of pollution and destruction of forests and trees; at the end the students had to label the photos and present them to the class. The pupils exceeded my expectations on that project. They all put their hearts in doing it, simply because it was an interesting topic to them and because it related to their tangible reality."

—*Line Rehayem, Primary English Teacher, Lebanon*

Next, a teacher from Brazil talks about how she gets all of her children to write, by using simple and enjoyable tasks.

> "Writing certainly isn't an easy skill to teach, but maybe because we think of writing as something long and elaborate. When we start teaching writing with simple tasks like making a list, writing a recipe, an invitation, a card, a note, it may become easier. Many students are not used to writing in their native language, so they find it even harder to write in a foreign language. However, with careful planning, modeling and guidance everybody is capable of writing. Besides, making writing interactive and meaningful plays a crucial role in motivating students. A possible way to encourage our students is to do

what other teachers have suggested—ask them to write an e-mail or a text message. This is something they are used to doing in their native language. Therefore, it will probably be easier for them.**"**

—Ana Maria Scandiuzzi, EFL Instructor, Brazil

As discussed in this chapter, children can be asked to write many different texts, and Ana Maria is thinking of adding e-mail or text messages, since this is something her children "are used to doing in their native language."

Inviting children to share their entries with the class helps keep all writing, not just dialog journals, focused on communication and makes writing much more enjoyable.

Sometimes an event will stimulate children to write. This teacher used a letter addressed to the principal as a class writing assignment.

"To work out creative writing I asked my pupils to write a letter. When they were in the second form I prepared a surprise for them: during the lesson the School Principal knocked on the door and gave me a letter. And she said that she didn't understand what was written there. She said that she hadn't studied English at school. I showed the letter to the children and they could read it! It was a letter 'from an English boy who wrote about himself, his friends and his family.' The children were happy: the School Principal couldn't read the letter and they could! I offered the children to write an answer to that boy at home and promised that we should send him the best letter. This motivated the pupils to write something interesting, to be neat and tidy, to have clear handwriting. Sometimes I give the pupils a task to write about the weather or about what they did in the morning or on the weekend. They make small groups and write short letters to each other within the group.**"**

—Ella Krotova, Primary English Teacher, Russia

All of these teachers have adapted their EYL reading and writing assignments to meet the children's interests and needs and to encourage their children in continuing to develop their reading and writing skills in English.

■ Chapter Summary

To Conclude

Reading and writing are active and complementary activities We often think, mistakenly, that reading is a passive activity. But reading is an interactive process, involving the reader, the text, and the writer. Similarly, writing is an interactive process, involving the writer, the text, and the reader. When we write, we think about our reader and often re-read what we have written to ensure that our message is clear to the reader. In a young learner classroom, children can read and then write about what they have read (in a range of activities) and they can read what they or other children have written. Reading can be thought of as preparation for writing and writing as producing something for others to read.

Reading and writing activities should be meaningful, but also provide controlled and guided practice to support learners in their reading and writing development Children need to develop basic reading and writing skills that can best be addressed in a bottom-up approach. For reading, this will involve the systematic use of a variety of controlled and guided phonics activities that help children understand the relationship between print and oral language. For writing, this will involve a variety of controlled and guided product-based activities to help teach language structure (grammar), vocabulary, spelling, and writing mechanics.

They also need to do this in a meaningful context that can best be established through a top-down approach. For reading, this can be established through reading aloud or the language experience approach. For writing, this can be established through a process-based approach using Writing Workshop.

As much as possible, in each new unit or lesson plan, a meaningful context for reading and writing should be established before children focus on the smaller elements of written language.

A range of reading and writing activities and texts should be integrated into unit and lesson plans Too often, reading and writing are reduced to short, simple, controlled or guided activities in EYL classes. But children need opportunities to engage with a range of reading and writing activities, including ones that are supported by the teacher, as well as ones that encourage independent reading and writing. Time should be set aside for children to choose books or other materials appropriate to their age and English proficiency to read (extensive reading) and to create a range of writing texts, including poems, stories, and journals. Digital texts, for reading and writing, should also be included wherever possible as well as opportunities for children to read with and write to other children, both in their EYL classes and remotely, through online communication.

■ Over to You

1. Now that we have discussed approaches to teaching reading and writing and some examples of activities to use, look back at the list you made at the beginning of the chapter. Look at the activities that you thought would NOT be motivating to young learners. Are there ways that you can make them more motivating or engaging? What are some new activities that you would want to try using with your young learners?

2. What do you see as the strengths and weaknesses of both phonics and whole language approaches? How can you incorporate the best of each of these approaches in designing a reading program for young learners? Would there be differences for very young learners and young learners?

3. Look online at any one of the word frequency lists referenced in the chapter. Then compare these with what you would expect to teach to young learners. You may want to consult EYL textbooks prepared by the Ministry of Education or commercial EYL textbooks to see how the vocabulary that is included in the books or materials matches the words in the frequency lists.

4. What kinds of texts do children read and write in your community? Which of these could be used for encouraging authentic reading and writing in English?

Lesson Planning

Select any lesson you have planned or one that you have observed or reviewed and identify the reading and writing activities that are included. Are these bottom-up activities (phonics or product-based writing activities) or top-down (whole language or process-based activities focused on meaning)? Add activities to the lesson to include at least one of the four categories (controlled or guided reading and writing activities and independent reading and free writing activities).

Write About It

Reflection on Learning to Read: Think back to when you were a child learning to read in your first language. What are some ways that your parents and teachers helped you? Can you recall a favorite book that you read and re-read as a child? How might you apply this to teaching reading in English to young learners?

How did you learn to read in English? Can you recall some of the activities that your teacher and others used to help you make the transition from reading in your first language to reading in English? Could you use these in teaching EYL?

Resources and References

Print Publications

Brewster, J., Ellis, G., & Girard, D. (2002). *The primary English teacher's guide* , 2nd ed. Essex, UK: Penguin English.

Cameron, L. (2001). *Teaching languages to young learners.* Cambridge, UK: Cambridge University Press.

Peregoy, S. G., & Boyle, O. F. (2004). *Reading, writing, and learning in ESL: A resource book for K–8 teachers* , 4th ed. White Plains, NY: Longman.

Pinter, A. (2006). *Teaching young language learners.* Oxford, UK: Oxford University Press.

Slattery, M., & Willis, J. (2001). *English for primary teachers: A handbook of activities and classroom language.* Oxford, UK: Oxford University Press.

Useful Web Sites

Mother Goose nursery rhymes that can be used for phonics activities: http://www.zelo.com/family/nursery/

44 sounds of English: http://www.youtube.com/watch?v=-g35OvlNu-A

National Geographic sites: http://kids.nationalgeographic.com/kids/ or http://www.kidsgeo.com/index.php (for nonfiction or informational texts)

Short biographical texts: http://www.biography.com

Comic strips: comics.com (for strips which can be used with beginners, because they are short, several strips could be used for a lesson or a unit)

Songs, chants, rhymes: http://www.ifayed.net/Main_Folders/Resources/SPEER_02/TEAS_CH4.PDF

Reader's Theater: http://esldrama.weebly.com/index.html

Reader's Theater Editions: http://www.aaronshep.com/rt/RTE.html (for folktales and other stories by Aaron Shepard, often with wonderful illustrations that can be used with the story)

References

Allen, V. G. (1994) Selecting materials for the reading instruction of ESL children. In K. Spangenberg-Urbscat & R. Pritchard (Eds.), *Kids come in all languages: Reading instruction for ESL students* (pp. 109–128). Newark, DE: International Reading Association.

Asher, J. J. (1998). *The super school of the 21st century.* Los Gatos, CA:Sky Oak Productions.

Ashton-Warner, S. (1963). *Teacher.* New York, NY: Simon and Schuster.

Barone, D., & Xu, S. (2008). *Literacy instruction for English language learners, preK–2.* New York, NY: Guilford Press.

Bauman, J. *About the GSL.* Available at http://jbauman.com/aboutgsl.html

Beck, I. L. (2006). *Making sense of phonics: The hows and whys.* New York, NY: Guilford Press.

Brewster, J., Ellis, G., & Girard, D. (2004). *The primary English teacher's guide,* 2nd ed. Essex, UK: Pearson Education.

Calkins, L. M. (1983). *Lessons from a child: On the teaching and learning of writing.* Portsmouth, NH: Heinemann.

Cameron, L. (2001). *Teaching languages to young learners.* Cambridge, UK: Cambridge University Press.

Carle, E. (1994). *The very hungry caterpillar.* New York, NY: Penguin Philomel.

Carrell, P. L., & Grabe, W. (2002). Reading. In N. Schmitt (Ed.), *An introduction to applied linguistics* (pp. 233–250). London, UK: Edward Arnold.

Collins, K. (2004). *Growing readers.* Portland, ME: Stenhouse.

Cummins, J. (1979). Linguistic interdependence and the educational development of bilingual children. *Review of Educational Ressearch, 49,* 222–251.

Cummins, J., & Sayers, D. (1997). *Brave new schools: Challenging cultural illiteracy through global learning networks.* New York, NY: Macmillan.

Curtain, H., & Dahlberg, C. A. (2010). *Languages and children: Making the match,* 4th ed. Boston, MA: Allyn & Bacon.

Davis, J. Drama in the ESL classroom. Available at http://esldrama.weebly.com/index.html

Day, R. R., & Bamford, J. (1998). *Extensive reading activities for teaching language.* Cambridge, UK: Cambridge University Press.

Dixon, C., & Nessel, D. (1983). *Language experience approach to teaching reading (and writing): LEA for ESL.* Hayward, CA: Alemany Press.

Education World. (n.d.) Reader's theater: A reason to read aloud. Available at http://www.educationworld.com/a_curr/profdev/profdev082.shtml

Federer A. (1993). *Teaching writing: A workshop approach.* New York, NY: Scholastic Professional Books.

Geva, E., & Wang, M. (2001). The development of basic reading skills in children: A cross-linguistic perspective. *Annual Review of Applied Linguistics, 21,* 182–204.

Gibbons, P. (1993). *Learning to read in a second language.* Portsmouth, NH: Heinemann.

Goodman, K. S. (1976). Reading: A psycholinguistic guessing game. In H. Singer & R. B. Ruddell (Eds.), *Theoretical models and processes of reading,* 2nd ed. (pp. 497–508). Newark, DE: International Reading Association.

Goodman, K. S. (2005). *What's whole in whole language,* 20th anniversary ed. Berkeley, CA: RDR Books.

Hachem, A., Nabhani, M., & Bahous, R. (2008). "We can write!" The writing workshop for young learners. *Education 3–13, 26*(4), 325–337.

Heilman, A. W. (2002). *Phonics in proper perspective.* Upper Saddle, NJ: Merrill-Prentice Hall.

Herrell, A. L. (2000). *Fifty strategies for teaching English language learners.* Upper Saddle River, NJ: Merrill.

Holdaway, D. (1979). *Foundations of literacy.* Auckland, NZ: Ashton Scholastic.

Hudelson, S. (1988). Writing in a second language. *Annual Review of Applied Linguistics, 9,* 210–222.

International Reading Association & National Association for the Education of Young Children. (1998). Learning to read and write: Developmentally appropriate practices for young children. Available at http://www.reading.org/Libraries/Position-Statements-and-Resolutions/ps1027_NAEYC.pdf

Karnowski, L. (1989). Using LEA with process writing. *The Reading Teacher, 42*(7), 462–465.

Kauffman, D. (2007). *What's different about teaching reading to students learning English?* Washington, DC: Center for Applied Linguistics and Delta Publishing.

Lenters, K. (2004/2005). No half measures: Reading instruction for young second-language learners. *The Reading Teacher, 58*(4) 328–336.

Leu, D. J., Jr. (2000). Our children's future: Changing the focus of literacy and literacy instruction. *The Reading Teacher, 53,* 424–431.

Leu, D. J., Jr. (2002). The new literacies: Research on reading instruction with the Internet and other digital technologies. In A. E. Farstrup & S. J. Samuels (Eds.), *What research has to say about reading instruction,* 3rd ed. (pp. 310–337). Newark, DE: International Reading Association.

Linse, C. T. (2005). *Practical English language teaching: Young learners.* New York: McGraw-Hill.

Luke, A., & Freebody, P. (1997). Shaping the social practices of reading. In S. Muspratt, A. Luke, & P. Freebody (Eds.), *Constructing critical literacies* (pp. 185–225). Creskill, NJ: Hampton.

Lyons, B. (1981). The PQP method of responding to writing. *The English Journal, 70*(3), 42–43.

McCarrier, A., Pinnell, G. S., & Fountas, I. C. (2000). *Interactive writing: How language and literacy come together, K–2.* Portsmouth, NH: Heinemann.

McKenzie, M. G. (1985). *Shared writing: Apprenticeship in writing in language matters.* London, UK: Centre for Language in Primary Education.

Moats, L. C. (2001). *Speech to print: Language essentials for teachers.* Baltimore, MD: Paul H. Bookes.

Nation, I. S. P. (2009). *Teaching ESL/EFL reading and writing.* New York, NY: Routledge.

Nation, P., & Meara, P. (2002). Vocabulary. In N. Schmitt (Ed.), *An introduction to applied linguistics* (pp. 35–54). London, UK: Edward Arnold.

National Institute of Child Health and Human Development. (2000). *Teaching children to read: Summary report of the National Reading Panel.* Washington, DC: U.S. Government Printing Office. Available at http://www.nichd.nih.gov/publications/nrp/upload/smallbook_pdf.pdf

Nessel, D. D., & Jones, M. B. (1981). *Language experience approach to reading.* New York, NY: Teachers College Press.

New London Group, The. (2000). A pedagogy of multiliteracies: Designing social futures. In B. Cope & M. Kalantzis (Eds.), *Multiliteracies: Literacy learning and the design of social futures* (pp. 9–38). London, UK: Routledge.

Nunan, D. (2011), *Teaching English to young learners.* Anaheim, CA: Anaheim University Press.

Peregoy, S. G., & Boyle, O. F. (2004). *Reading, writing, and learning in ESL: A resource book for K–8 teachers,* 4th ed. White Plains, NY: Longman.

Peyton, J. K. (1993). *Dialogue journals: Interactive writing to develop language and literacy.* Washington, DC: Center for Applied Linguistics. Available at: http://www.cal.org/resources/digest/peyton01.html

Pinter, A. (2006). *Teaching young language learners.* Oxford, UK: Oxford University Press.

Raimes, A. (1993). Out of the woods: Emerging trends in the teaching of writing. In S. Silberstein (Ed.), *State of the art TESOL essays* (pp. 237–260). Washington, DC: TESOL.

Rose, J. (2006). *Independent review of the teaching of early reading.* Nottingham, UK: DfES Publications. Available at http://www.standards.dfes.gov.uk/rosereview/report

Samuels, S. J. (2002). Reading fluency: Its development and assessment. In A. E. Farstrup & S. J. Samuels (Eds.), *What research has to say about reading instruction* (pp. 166–183). Newark, DE: International Reading Association.

Scott, W., & Ytreberg, L. (1990). *Teaching English to children.* London, UK: Longman.

Slatterly, M., & Willis, J. (2001). *English for primary teachers: A handbook of activities and classroom language.* Oxford, UK: Oxford University Press.

Urzua, C. (1987). "You stopped too soon": Second language children composing and revising. *TESOL Quarterly, 21*(2), 279–304.

Van Allen, R., & Allen, C. (1976). *Language experience stories.* Boston, MA: Houghton Mifflin.

Wajnryb, R. (1991). *Grammar dictation.* Oxford, UK: Oxford University Press.

Wyse, D., & Styles, M. (2007). Synthetic phonics and the teaching of reading: The debate surrounding England's "Rose Report." *Literacy, 41*(1), 35–42.

Zhang, L. J., Gu, P. Y., & Hu, G. (2008). A cognitive perspective on Singaporean primary school pupils' use of reading strategies in English. *British Journal of Educational Psychology, 78,* 245–271.

6 Storytelling

■ Getting Started

Think About It

Think about your childhood. Do you remember a family member reading you stories before bedtime? Or do you remember sitting around a table listening to a family member tell stories? Close your eyes, imagine the situation, and think about how you felt while listening to these stories.

Now think about telling stories yourself. Perhaps you are a parent and you like to tell bedtime stories to your children. Maybe you are an aunt or uncle who enjoys telling your nieces and nephews funny stories about their mom and dad. Perhaps, as a teacher, you like telling fairytales to your students to light up their imaginations. What kinds of stories do you tell others? Close your eyes and think about what you do when you tell stories.

As a teacher, what are your strengths as a storyteller? What aspects of storytelling do you find challenging? Which stories do you like to tell your students? Why do you enjoy telling these stories?

Mark Gail/The Washington Post via Getty Images

In the chart below, write down what you think are the most important aspects of storytelling for a storyteller and for a listener.

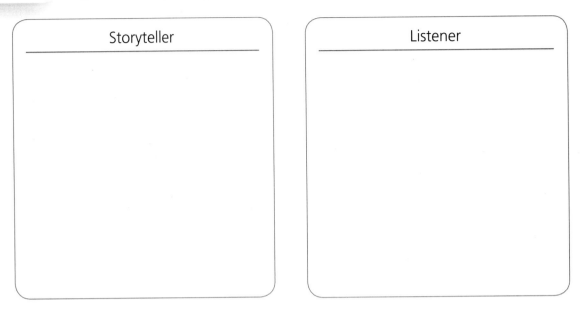

Storyteller	Listener

■ Why We Tell Stories in the Classroom

Sharing stories is an exciting and entertaining way to engage learners and present new language structures and vocabulary. It is important to provide a meaningful context in which the target language is used and taught. Stories can also be used as the basis for a thematic unit plan, as described in Chapter 3. Storytelling allows students to communicate in the language in authentic ways and introduces students to their own culture as well as to other cultures. Narrative activities develop learners' critical thinking, listening, and speaking skills, and can be integrated with follow-up activities for teaching reading and writing. Ultimately, storytelling is most beneficial for young learners of English for the following reasons:

- ■ It is an authentic form of communication.
- ■ It introduces new cultures to children.
- ■ It teaches young learners in an entertaining way.
- ■ It helps develop critical thinking skills.

Storytelling Is an Authentic Form of Communication

Storytelling is an authentic form of communication that is a part of every culture. There are many people who are famous for crafting tales, and we still read their stories today. The legendary Aesop of ancient Greece is probably one of the most famous storytellers; his fables are still told to children to teach moral lessons.

In many cultures, storytelling is also a tradition used to communicate culture from one generation to the next. For example, the elder Pueblo Indians in New Mexico pass down their culture and values to the younger generation through songs and stories (Bahti, 1996). Children are actively involved with the storyteller and genuinely enjoy this traditional form of communication between generations.

In fact, many schools often use storybooks and storytelling as part of an elementary (primary) school curriculum because stories teach valuable lessons and literacy to children while also entertaining them. As Pinter describes, "Listening to stories is the most authentic and popular activity for all children, and primary English teachers can use storytelling as additional listening practice. Children will learn new language as well as having enjoyable listening practice. Language is picked up easily because stories contain repetition which makes linguistic input more noticeable" (2006, pp. 52–53).

Storytelling Introduces New Cultures to Children

Stories are a carrier of culture. What better way to expose children to the values of various cultures than to use storytelling? As Curtain and Dalhberg state, "Story, or narrative, is a powerful vehicle for experiencing culture. Values and concepts of the culture that are embedded in myths and folktales can be shared through storytelling, story reading, and dramatization" (2010, p. 266). For example, there are many different versions of the Cinderella story that can be explored using English. In addition to the Cinderella story, which comes from German and French tradition, there is Rhodopis from Greco-Egyptian tradition, Yeh-Shen from China, Pear Blossom from Korea, Nyahsa from Zimbabwe, Domitila from Mexico, Rough-Face Girl from the Native American Algonquin tribe, and many other versions. All of these stories are about a poor girl who is good and hardworking and ends up marrying a prince or king. However, there are many variations in each story that give insight into the different cultures that these Cinderella stories come from. Teachers could use several Cinderella stories from around the world in a thematic unit to highlight cultural diversity. Comparing and contrasting Cinderella stories can highlight similar values as well as cultural differences through the plot details. This is just one example of how teachers can introduce children to people from other cultures through stories.

Storytelling Teaches Young Learners in an Entertaining Way

Well-written stories can capture the interest and imagination of children over multiple generations. For instance, many Dr. Seuss books, such as *The Cat in the Hat* and *Hop on Pop*, were written decades ago yet are still favorites among children. Children ask to hear these stories again and again because they are fun, and many teachers like them because they help children learn the rhythm and sounds of the English language. (They also provide a good basis for developing phonemic awareness leading to phonics and initial reading in English, as discussed in Chapter 5.) Stories like these ignite learners' imaginations and creativity while challenging them to learn new language or understand language in a new context. They particularly cater to young learners who have short attention spans and learn best through play and entertainment.

When done effectively, storytelling is an enjoyable activity in which the language learning process is undetectable to children. As Slatterly and Willis (2001) point out, "Young learners acquire language unconsciously. The activities you do in class should help this kind of acquisition. Stories are the most valuable resource you have. They offer children a world of supported meaning that they can relate to" (p. 98). If teachers skillfully incorporate storytelling into the curriculum, young learners will pick up new vocabulary and language structures within the context of an engaging world.

Storytelling Develops Critical Thinking Skills

Bloom's taxonomy of learning domains originally included knowledge, comprehension, application, analysis, synthesis, and evaluation. In the 1990s, a former student of Bloom's named Lorin Anderson revised Bloom's taxonomy to feature the following levels of questioning in the educational process: remembering, understanding, appearing, analyzing, evaluating, and creating.

Storytelling lends itself well to helping students of all levels develop critical thinking skills. Chance (1986) defines critical thinking as "the ability to analyze facts, generate and organize ideas, defend opinions, make comparisons, draw inferences, evaluate arguments, and solve problems" (p. 6). These are important skills for young learners to develop in a primary school curriculum because they help students gain a deeper understanding of texts, including those that provide information from a variety of cultures.

Teachers can help students develop critical thinking skills by asking questions that require students to analyze and make inferences, and by encouraging students to compare themselves and their cultures to the stories they have heard. Through this process, students can be encouraged to form their own opinions and evaluate a story for both content and delivery. When teachers encourage students to retell a story, they must also "summarize, edit, and develop" the story, not just repeat the story word for word (Spiro, 2006, p. 7).

Typical critical thinking activities, which are described in more detail in the next section of this chapter, increase the learners' level of understanding of a story while allowing them to make connections between the story and the real world, the story and their personal lives, and the story and their culture. Young learners also develop the ability to sift through new stories and cultural information through a process of critical reflective thinking. Ultimately, critical thinking activities with storytelling pose issues of cultural differences and give young learners the chance to improve their ability to communicate interculturally, using English as an international language.

How We Tell Stories in the Classroom

Storytelling is an art or a skill that can be developed. In the previous chapter, about teaching reading and writing, different ways of reading are highlighted, such as reading aloud, shared reading, and guided reading. Like reading aloud, storytelling is a listening activity. However, reading aloud is usually associated with the storybook, and teachers can point to pictures and the text while reading the story out loud. However, storytelling is not limited to the book. A teacher can tell a story without the book, using other visuals, costumes, realia, and drama in order to make the story come alive for the children.

Skilled storytellers breathe life into the characters and plot and adapt the narrative with each reading. They re-create the story so that the listener will want to hear the story again and again. In order to be a successful storyteller, it is important to consider your audience and what will capture their attention and imagination. The more engaged you are with the story and the experience of recounting it, the more connected the students will be and the more easily they will follow. As you develop your storytelling skills, consider the following points:

Choose the Right Story

Choosing the right story is the first step in successful storytelling. Curtain and Dahlberg (2010) suggest that stories that meet the following criteria can provide an effective storytelling experience for young learners, even at beginning levels of English. Stories should:

- be highly predictable
- be familiar to the home culture
- have a high percentage of known vocabulary
- include repetitive and predictable patterns
- provide opportunities to apply drama and Total Physical Response
- lend themselves well to use of visuals and realia to make input comprehensible

If stories meet these criteria, then it is possible to present an engaging storytelling experience that will keep young learners' attention and allow them to follow along in English without using their native language. If students have difficulty following the story, it is possible that the story needs to be adapted to the learners' English level, or replaced altogether. For suggestions of good stories to use with young learners, see the list of Web sites on p. 240.

Prepare to Tell a Story

Once you have chosen the right story, the next step is to prepare to tell the story effectively. As Brewster, Ellis, and Girard (2004) point out, "Simply reading a story aloud to a class without preparation could be disastrous, with a loss of pupil attention, motivation, and self-confidence. Pupils' enjoyment will increase enormously if we ensure their understanding is supported in several ways. Pupils will also need to feel involved and relate the story to aspects of their own experience" (p. 192). This section will explore how to prepare for successful storytelling.

Storyteller Alton Chung describes his style thus: "When performing, I try to connect and be fully present with the audience—to be in the here and now. At times, audience members, especially young people, seem to hunger for the connection and stories, as if they can never get enough. I believe that there is a need for true human connection and story in our society." (www .altonchung.com)

Photo courtesy of Anne Shimojima

Alton Chung is a famous Hawaiian storyteller of Korean and Japanese heritage who uses body movement, facial expressions, and voices to make stories come alive. This multicultural story-teller engages listeners with his theatrics. Chung describes his style of storytelling as being influenced by "talk story," a form of oral history found in Hawaiian culture. Talk story is the way Hawaiian people converse and share stories, a style that emphasizes collaboration and cooperation. In talk story, a person shares a story while others corroborate or add to it as it is being told (Taosaka, 2002). Chung embraces this act of collaboration in his storytelling.

Although talk story is specific to Hawaiian culture, this example of storyteller Alton Chung shows how important it is to use storytelling techniques that appeal to your audience. The human connection between storyteller and audience is key for holding the audience's attention. As such, teachers should consider the characteristics of their young learners and use storytelling techniques that are relevant to them.

Some teachers feel anxiety over storytelling because they feel that they have no natural talent for it, or they lack confidence in their own English language skills. However, with thoughtful preparation and practice, *all* teachers can create a successful storytelling experience for their students.

x

To make your storytelling engaging, prepare these four elements: theatrics, props, script, and rehearsals.

Aim to include aspects of these four elements in every storytelling session. If this is a new concept, start small and build up your skills slowly. As you gain confidence using one aspect, add another to your repertoire. The theatrics and props are particularly important as they help to generate interest and enjoyment in learners, and they make input comprehensible.

Consider the story of Goldilocks and the Three Bears. Children love to hear stories told with different character voices, so you could use a young girl's voice for Goldilocks; a squeaky voice for Baby Bear; a sweet, soothing voice for

Theatrics

- Gestures
- Body movement
- Dramatic pauses
- Character voices
- Facial expressions
- Speaking slowly and clearly

Props

- Visuals for setting and characters
- Realia
- Masks for role play
- Costumes for role play
- Hand or finger puppets
- PowerPoint slides or storyboards

STORYTELLING PREPARATION

Rehearsals

- Memorize the text, including questions for students
- Use cue cards if necessary
- Practice in front of the mirror
- Record/videotape yourself
- Rehearse using props
- Practice, practice, practice!

Script

- Use illustrations from the storybook
- Adapt the script to learners' levels
- Create roles students can play
- Integrate songs or chants
- Prepare places in the storytelling for questions and predictions

Mama Bear; and a rough, deep voice for Papa Bear. In addition, you could use hand puppets and a drawing of the Bears' house on a poster or in a PowerPoint presentation along with the character voices. The combination of voices, puppets, and the background drawing would make the storytelling fun and entertaining and would also help students understand the story better. Use a variety of theatrics and props to keep each storytelling fresh and new for learners.

Another storytelling element to consider is the script, which should be carefully prepared to be just above the learners' level of English and to incorporate both new and known vocabulary and grammatical structures. Furthermore, script preparation should also build in time for student participation and comprehension questions throughout the storytelling, which will help keep the level of student engagement high. Children can role play with the script by playing the character parts in skits or Reader's Theater activities. The script can be simplified to adjust to the learners' level to help with this.

Finally, it is vitally important to rehearse the storytelling before class. Although it is best to memorize as much of the text as possible, it can be helpful to prepare cue cards (cards with key words and plot elements from the script) to help guide your "performance." In fact, preparing cue cards that are colorful and have pictures that relate to the story can actually add more excitement to the storytelling process. Preparation for the first time you tell a particular story can take time; however, the props and activities can be reused, so you will find that the next performance of that story takes much less preparation. In the end, the smiles on the faces of your young learners will make all the effort worthwhile.

■ Effective Storytelling Activities

In order to design effective storytelling activities, it is important for teachers to think about activities before, during, and after the storytelling. In addition to the preparation for making the story come alive, the teacher needs to prepare students with the language to understand the story. Activities to keep students active and engaged in class at every stage of the storytelling should also be planned.

In the next sections, numerous activities are suggested for use before, during, and after the storytelling.

Activities before Storytelling

Before-storytelling activities are designed to aid comprehension, create interest and enjoyment, make the storytelling more meaningful, and encourage critical thinking.

Capture their attention:

Use pictures or realia to introduce the story in a fun and interesting way. You can use the cover of the storybook to capture the attention of students or create fun visuals. To make the characters come alive, the teacher could make finger or popsicle stick puppets of the characters and introduce them to the class. To draw students into the scenery of the story, the teacher could make a background on poster paper and put it up on the classroom wall, or project the scenes from a laptop onto the wall.

For example, for the story *The Rainbow Fish*, the teacher could use an underwater scene from the storybook and popsicle stick puppets of the fish. The brightly colored puppets would include different-colored fish and a multicolored Rainbow Fish with shiny silver scales. The puppets can be used with the background to excite the students for a storytelling that has a bright scene and puppets to hold and play with.

Connect to prior knowledge and experiences:

It is important to connect students' lives to the story. This includes introducing the main ideas, concepts, or characters to students. The choice of concepts the teacher introduces depends on the students' background, experience, and culture.

For example, if the story is Cinderella, the teacher may prepare students by introducing the concept of family since the story's main characters are Cinderella, her stepmother, and stepsisters. In addition, the story includes interaction between different classes of people (i.e., royalty and common people), and the teacher could explain this by introducing the characters and their backgrounds. Another way to connect to students' background knowledge could be to ask students about their own country or culture's Cinderella story since many countries have similar fairytales or folktales.

Review language students have learned:

If a story contains vocabulary and structures that students have already learned, it can help to review this language before telling the story. This is especially important when the story is a part of a larger thematic unit and recycles language previously learned. The review of language is often related to background knowledge and experiences. Since young learners don't have much experience in the world, they often learn language, both native language and English, while learning about concepts.

In Chapter 3, *The Very Hungry Caterpillar* was used as the basis of a unit on nutrition and foods. It is a commonly used storybook for young learners. It has vocabulary for food, numbers, days of the week, and the life cycle of a butterfly. The teacher may connect to students' background knowledge of food, numbers, and days of the week, which is also a review of the vocabulary associated with those concepts.

Pre-teach new vocabulary or expressions:

If there are key words or structures that are necessary to comprehend the story and cannot be inferred from the context, it is better to teach them before the storytelling. Try to do this in the context of connecting to prior knowledge.

For example, in the story Goldilocks and the Three Bears, the teacher could make a bright colorful poster or PowerPoint slide of the house with the different rooms, then review the known vocabulary and pre-teach new vocabulary. Students may already know words like *chair, bed,* and *bowl.* However, they may not know the room names, like kitchen, living room, and bedroom, and may not be familiar with porridge. In this way, the teacher can capture attention, introduce the context, review known words, and then pre-teach vocabulary.

Ask students to predict what will happen in the story:

It can be fun and helpful to encourage students to predict what will happen in the story. Prediction is a good critical thinking skill to encourage. Be sure to record the predictions to check whether they are correct later. Students could write one sentence they think will be in the story and put it in a prediction box. Then at the end of the story, the teacher can read the sentences out loud for fun. If students are at a lower level, the teacher can write three sentences on the board, then students can choose the ending by writing one of them.

For example, for Aesop's fable about the Lion and the Mouse, the teacher could give these three sentences for students to choose and write:

- The lion eats the mouse.
- The mouse saves the lion.
- The lion saves the mouse.

Making a prediction helps young learners pay attention to the story and think critically to check their predictions during the storytelling. This is not necessary for all stories, but it can add a level of interest and engagement where appropriate.

Give students a purpose for listening:

Before you begin telling a story, give students a purpose for listening (in addition to pure enjoyment). This can help them stay engaged and make them more active listeners during the storytelling. Perhaps the purpose is to check their prediction as mentioned earlier. If the story has a lesson (or moral) to learn from, tell your students to listen for it. Be sure to ask them for it at the end of the story. If there are songs, chants, or lines from the story that children can repeat, teach them before the story. Then give students a cue for participation that they can listen for.

For example, when students listen to the story of Chicken Little, the teacher can ask them to make an animal sound when they hear the name of an animal.

- Henny Penny: "Cluck cluck"
- Ducky Lucky: "Quack quack"
- Loosey Goosey: "Honk honk"
- Turkey Lurkey: "Gobble gobble"

In the storytelling, the teacher will say lines like, "Along the way she met Henny Penny," and then students can say "Cluck cluck!" Then when the teacher says "Soon they met Ducky Lucky," students can call out "Quack quack!" This keeps students listening for the animal, shows their comprehension of which animal it is, and makes the storytelling more active and fun.

Activities during Storytelling

During-storytelling activities are usually used to check comprehension. They can also be used to keep students' interest and allow students the chance to interact and practice using English.

Q & A:

Use questions during the storytelling to check comprehension of the story and keep students engaged. The teacher should keep a balance between asking questions to keep the learners engaged but not so many questions that it detracts from the storytelling. The questions should check comprehension of the characters, setting, and plot. The questions could also ask students to predict what comes next.

For example, if the teacher is telling the Aesop's fable The Hare and the Tortoise, it could progress like this:

- "Point to the hare."
- "Point to the tortoise."
- "A hare is also called a. . . ." (rabbit)
- "A tortoise is also called a. . . ." (turtle)
- "Is a hare slow or fast?"
- "Is a tortoise slow or fast?"
- "Who will win the race?"
- "What is Hare doing?" (hopping fast)
- "Is Hare hopping slowly or fast?"
- "What is Tortoise doing?" (walking slowly)
- "Is Tortoise walking slowly or fast?"
- "What is Hare doing?" (sleeping)
- "Is Tortoise sleeping, too?"
- "And the winner is . . . !" (Tortoise)

Repetition:

Repetition of key phrases or chants in a story can keep students active and give them a chance to practice set phrases or language structures. Teachers can cue students in the right places for them to join in.

For example, from the story The Gingerbread Man, it could be a call and respond, like this:

- Teacher: *Run, run, run,*
- Students: *As fast as you can.*
- Teacher: *You can't catch me,*
- Students: *I'm the Gingerbread Man!*

Alternatively, the teacher and students could chant the lines altogether and clap a beat to keep a rhythm. Since many children's stories have repeated structures, it is easy to add repetition to a storytelling.

TPR (Total Physical Response):

Movement and actions can be built into most children's stories. Some stories have movement embedded in the story. Doing TPR with students during the storytelling appeals to kinesthetic learners and makes the experience more active and fun. This also supports comprehension of the story.

For example, *Five Little Monkeys (Jumping on the Bed)* has physical actions of changing into pajamas, brushing teeth, jumping, falling, calling, and sleeping. These actions can be practiced before the storytelling and then done during the storytelling by both the teacher and the students. Whenever possible, the teacher should look for movement to accompany a storytelling.

Create your own ending:

Teachers can tell the story up to the climax and ask students to predict the ending before they finish telling the story. Students can draw a picture of their own ending or demonstrate it using the puppets from the storytelling. For lower-level students, the teacher can prepare pictures of alternate endings and have students make sentences for each, to create their own ending.

For example, the pictures below could accompany the story of the Hare and the Tortoise.

Activities after Storytelling

After a storytelling, you can do follow-up activities to check comprehension of the story. Post-storytelling activities should also give learners plenty of practice using the new language structures and vocabulary. Be sure to use all four language skills, cooperative activities, scaffolded instruction, and activities that cater to different learning styles and intelligences.

- **Check predictions:** Check the predictions that students made in the before- or during-storytelling stages. Doing this helps students explain what happened in the story as they reflect on whether their predictions were correct. If students wrote a prediction and put it in the prediction box, then the teacher can take out the predictions and read them. If the students chose a picture that predicts an ending, like the Hare and the Tortoise example in the previous section, the teacher can bring out the three pictures and have the students confirm the correct one.

- **Group retelling:** Teachers can have students work with them to retell the story. It could be as simple as retelling the story with students saying the character parts with you. Where appropriate, a retelling can include role play. Students can act out the story, or parts of the story. Or students can retell the story on their own, with the teacher filling in the gaps when they encounter difficulty.

- **Games:** Many different games can be used to check comprehension following a storytelling. In the game Start & Stop, you can retell the story with mistakes and have students stop you when they hear a mistake. You can then choose a number of errors to check comprehension: using the wrong vocabulary word or pronouncing a word incorrectly, putting pictures of major plot events out of order, or changing characters' actions to see if children truly understood the story.

- **Storyboarding:** Have students make simple drawings in boxes that show the plot of the story sequentially, like a comic book. The teacher can give a blank storyboard template like the one on the following page.

Blank Storyboard Template

Storyboard

Title:

Author:

Illustrator:

_____ _____ _____

_____ _____ _____

_____ _____ _____

_____ _____ _____

_____ _____ _____

If students need more support, the teacher can give them pictures to use in the storyboard template.

For example, for the Hare and the Tortoise, the teacher could hand out the following to the students:

In order to give students an opportunity to practice language in a different way and to be creative, the drawings can be accompanied by blank text or dialog bubbles. Students can write the characters' dialog or thoughts into the bubbles.

- **Story mapping (story analysis):** Teachers can check comprehension of the storytelling by giving students a graphic organizer to map out the plot of the story or to compare the characters of the story. Students can show deeper levels of comprehension of the story by analyzing the characters, ending, or moral of a story where appropriate. Below is an example of a story map that shows comprehension of the setting, characters, and plot.

Title:

Author:

Illustrator:

Setting (Draw and describe)

Characters (Draw and label)

Illustrate and write the story events.

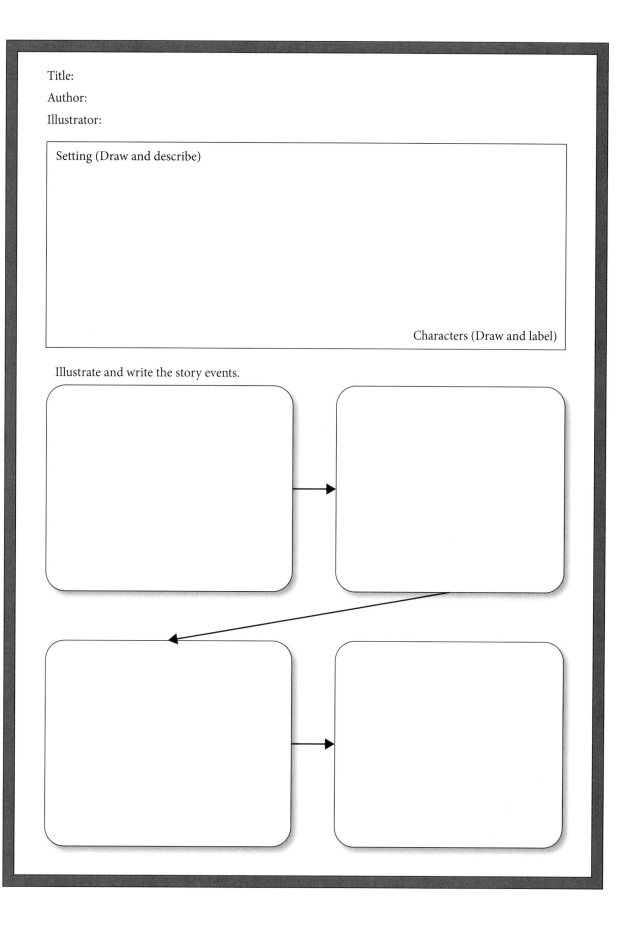

The teacher can check students' comprehension of a story by analyzing the main characters. Students can draw a character and describe him or her on a piece of paper. In addition, students can compare two characters in a story.

CHARACTER ANALYSIS

Title:
Author:
Illustrator:

CHOOSE 2 CHARACTERS.
DRAW THEM BELOW

CHARACTER #1   CHARACTER #2

NAME: _____   NAME: _____

POSSIBLE SENTENCE STARTERS:
She/He is... She/He isn't... I like... I don't like...

_____   _____

_____   _____

_____   _____

_____   _____

_____   _____

For example, students could compare the tortoise and the hare by drawing them and describing them with sentences like: *The tortoise is slow. He is hard working. I like the tortoise. He won the race.*

- **Mini-books:** Let students create their own storybooks. Teachers can show students how to make different mini-books (see Chapter 5). Then students can add their own text, pictures, or both.

  For example, the mini-book below was made by a student after her class had read , Itsy Bitsy Spider. She used the pages to illustrate the story and to write a few lines about the story.

- **Personalized or parallel story:** Have students write a story similar to the one in the storytelling but with details that draw from their own experiences, culture, and imagination. This is effective guided practice that helps students use the language learned in a creative way. For example:

  Parallel story: Instead of "The Hare and the Tortoise," the students can write a story about two new animals. They can brainstorm fast and slow animals and make a list. Then they can choose a context, like the jungle, rainforest, or the ocean and write a similar story with their new animals. For example, they might write a new story about the Cheetah and the Porcupine or the Dolphin and the Starfish.

  Cultural connection: Students can tell a similar or parallel story set in their native country or culture. As mentioned earlier, there could be a fairytale or folktale similar to the story, like Cinderella. If there is a similar story or a contrasting story, students can use the language from the storytelling and tell their own country or culture's story.

  Personalized story: If possible, have students create a new story that mirrors the story studied but relates to their lives. For example, a cute finger play story:

  Here is a turtle. (*Make fist with thumb tucked inside*)

  He lives in a shell.

He likes his home very well.

When he gets hungry, he comes out to eat. (*Pull thumb out and wiggle it*)

Then goes back to his house to sleep. (*Push thumb back into fist*)

Students could personalize this simple story by substituting the words about the turtle with their own lives:

Here is Maria.

She lives in a house.

She likes her home very well.

When she gets hungry, she goes to the kitchen.

Then goes back to her bedroom to sleep.

- **Projects:** Have students work together in small groups to complete a project that shows comprehension of a story. The project can be a part of a thematic unit requiring students to learn more about the story topic or context, author, culture, etc. You could invite students' families or other classes to see the students' work. Some examples could be:

  Creative storytelling with story maps: Groups can work together to create a poster with pictures of the characters and scenes to show the plot of the story. It could be a larger version of a story map or character file. Then the poster can be used as the starting point for creative retellings. A creative retelling of the story could have the same plot but different characters, or the same characters with different plots. In either case, the language learned would be recycled and practiced in new and creative ways.

  Explore the context: If the topic or context is related to a broader topic, then the story could be a part of a larger project.

  For example, Goldilocks and the Three Bears might be a story that is part of a larger unit on houses. Students could do a project to research the different kinds of homes of children from around the world. They could create posters or mini-books with pictures of different types of homes from various cultures and regions.

  Research the author: Students could also research information about the author with the teacher's guidance.

For example, students could do a research project about Aesop and make a collection of different fables with illustrations.

Perform a play: If there is a chance to put on a play, then students can work on making and producing a play to perform. They could role play different characters in a play or put on a puppet show. The project could include making the costumes, masks, or puppets as well as writing a play version of the story.

Eco Images/Universal Images Group/Getty Images

Designing a Lesson with Storytelling

In order to conduct a storytelling lesson, it is important to prepare activities for before, during, and after the storytelling. These can be incorporated into a lesson plan. Using the lesson plan format from previous chapters, teachers can use this form to prepare their storytelling. Preparing for storytelling is not limited to these ideas, but this is a good start for any teacher.

Stage	Type of Activities	Suggested activities
Warm-up	Before-storytelling activities	• Capture their attention • Connect to prior knowledge and experiences • Review language students have learned • Pre-teach new vocabulary or expressions • Ask students to predict what will happen after this line. • Give students a purpose for listening

Presentation	During-storytelling activities	• Q&A • Repetition • Total Physical Response • Create your own ending • Keep Ask students to predict in Warm-up
Practice	After-storytelling activities	• Check predictions • Group retelling • Games
Application		• Storyboarding • Story mapping (story analysis)
Assessment		• Mini-books • Personalized or parallel story
Follow-up		• Projects • Play performance

Here is an example storytelling lesson plan using a story called, *A Big Lesson for Little Frog* (Korey O'Sullivan, 2013).

Provided by National Geographic Learning

A BIG LESSON FOR LITTLE FROG

One day Little Frog looks up. He sees Monkey in a tree. Monkey says, "Look at me! I can swing through the trees! Can you swing, too?"

Little frog says, "No. I can't swing through the trees."

Parrot flies down to the tree. Parrot says, "Look at me! I can fly from tree to tree. Can you fly, too?"

Little Frog says, "No. I can't fly."

Giraffe walks up to the tree. Giraffe reaches up with her long neck and eats leaves at the top of the tree.

Little Frog is sad.

Giraffe sees Little Frog and asks, "Why are you sad, Little Frog?"

Little Frog says, "Monkey can swing through the trees. Parrot can fly. You can eat leaves at the top of the tree. I am sad because I can't do those things."

Giraffe says, "But Little Frog, you can do things we can't do."

"Really?" says Little Frog.

"Can Parrot hop like a frog?"

"No."

"Can I hop?"

"No."

"Can Parrot swim?"

"No."

"Can I swim?"

"No, but I can," says Little Frog.

"Can we catch flies with our tongues?"

"No, but I can," says Little Frog.

"There are many things Monkey, Parrot, and you can't do, Giraffe. I'm very sorry for you! Please don't be sad!"

Little Frog is happy now. He hops away to swim and to catch some flies.

A Big Lesson for Little Frog

Student profile	Grade 2, beginning level of English language proficiency
Skills to be emphasized	Listening and speaking
Language	Grammar: can/can't; Can you . . . ? I can . . . I can't . . . Vocabulary: • Animals: frog, giraffe, monkey, parrot • Animal actions: swing, fly, hop, swim • Expression: Look at me!
Objectives	By the end of this lesson, students will be able to: • Explain what animals can and can't do
Materials	Puppets Background scene which includes a tree Flashcards of different animals from previous lessons Word cards for all the actions

	Warm-up
	Before-storytelling Activities

Capture their attention	Make a popsicle stick puppet and introduce your new friend "Little Frog" to the class.

As the teacher:	Class, meet my friend. His name is Little Frog. Say Hello, Little Frog!
As the frog:	Hello, Kids! How are you? I'm sooooo happy to be here—ribbit ribbit! (*in a cute frog voice*)
As the teacher:	Class, say hello like Little Frog! Ribbit ribbit! We are going to read a story about Little Frog. (*Show the cover of the book*) What do you see on the cover?
As the frog:	That's right! It's me! Ribbit!

Connect to prior knowledge and experiences	Look through the pages of the storybook secretly. "I see Little Frog has some animal friends. What animals do we know?"
Review language students have learned	Make an Animal Web with pictures and/or text. The teacher can use flashcards to review the animals. When the child names an animal, the teacher can put the flashcard on the board in the web.

Pre-teach new vocabulary or expressions	"How do these animals move?" Do a TPR activity to teach different actions, including the ones in the story: swing, fly, hop, swim, etc. Use word cards for each movement and show the word card with each movement.
Ask students to predict what will happen in the story	Show the Little Frog puppet and the background with a tree. Using the puppet, ask students: **As the frog:** Can I swing through the trees? **As the teacher:** Can Little Frog swing through the trees? Then go through each action: fly, reach the top of a tree, hop, swim, etc. As you ask questions as the Little Frog and the teacher, put the word cards for *swing, fly, hop, swim*, etc., on the board in a T-chart. Then for each action, put a check if the students say, "yes," and an X if they say, "no." <div align="center">FROG</div> <div align="center">Swing X Fly X Hop ✓ Swim ✓</div>
Give students a purpose for listening	While pointing at the T-Chart, say, "Let's listen to the story and see what Little Frog can and can't do!"
Presentation **During-storytelling Activities**	
Storytelling with puppets	Do the storytelling with the puppets and the background. Use different voices for each animal and show the movements with your body.

Listen and respond/ TPR	**First storytelling:**
	"When you hear an animal, do the action."
	  • Frog: (*Fist hops on hand twice*)

	  • Monkey: (*Arm movement with hands moving toward armpits twice*)

	  • Parrot: (*Make wings with hands, flap twice*)

	  • Giraffe: (*Hold arms up, then make the head with hands.*)

Listen and respond/ TPR	**Second storytelling:** "When you hear actions, then do it!" Point to the words on the T-chart (swing, fly, hop, etc.) and practice once.

	Practice **After-storytelling Activities**

Check predictions/
Q&A
	Pairwork Q&A to check predictions
	• Put students in pairs: Partner A and Partner B. For each action on the T-chart, tell Partner A to ask Partner B "Can Little Frog ____?". Partner B has to answer:
	    "Yes, he can."
	    "No, he can't."
	    Then switch roles.
	• After the pair work, ask students to confirm each prediction on the T-chart. Check off the correct answers to confirm their predictions.

Storyboarding/ Group retelling	**Storyboard jigsaw** Prepare a large storyboard with pictures of the different scenes in the story. In the scenes the animals have speech bubbles. • First students put them in order. • Together with the students retell the story. • Works with the student to write the dialog in the speech bubbles. • Students copy the storyboard pictures and text in speech bubbles on their own paper.

Application After Storytelling Activities	
Mini-books/personalized/parallel story	Students make mini-books about themselves. They should be the main character instead of Little Frog. The other characters can be anyone the students want. Brainstorm who the other characters could be: • sibling • friend • parent • grandparent • neighbor • teacher
Assessment	
Monitor progress	Walk around the classroom and give one-on-one assistance to students who are struggling to finish their mini-books.
Collect books	Collect the mini-books when they are finished and give students feedback.
Follow-up	
Homework	Continue working on mini-books about themselves at home and at the beginning of the next class, if necessary.
Next class	Ask a few students to volunteer to share their mini-book stories by doing a short storytelling using the pictures in their mini-book to help tell their story.

■ Teacher to Teacher

Storytelling to Young Learners

Most teachers find storytelling to be a very effective way to engage learners in real language. Different teachers from around the world describe—through an online discussion board—their experience using storytelling in their classes for young learners. Reading about their experiences may help you decide how to use storytelling in your class. First, read how two different teachers from Poland and Costa Rica capture their students' attention with storytelling activities.

"Drawing and painting may be used as a way to present "students" & "feelings" in the connection with the story they have already listened to. Students may feel like real artists and offer their own pictures as ones used to present the story. It may also lead to creating their own story based on pictures students have drawn. I sometimes read part of a story and then ask students to think about the ending and present it in the form of pictures and then other students tell the ending by looking at the others' pictures. Then I sometimes read the real ending and we spend some time on comparing the endings. A lot of fun together with learning."

—*Urzula Kropaczewska, Primary School Teacher, Poland*

"Storytelling is not a part of every unit or every lesson I develop. I must include storytelling in only one unit of my program. When I do it with known stories such as fairly tales, students ask me to tell the story in Spanish, so I told them, no you know it in Spanish, let's learn it now in English. As soon as I start with the activities they are engaged, pay attention, participate, repeat, do the sounds or say some phrases.

Definitely I would like to use them more often because students really like storytelling and also because the vocabulary they learn in this activity last for a long term.

For instance, with first graders I use the Ugly Duckling tale. Students have to repeat the phrase 'ugly duckling, ugly duckling' when the duckling is rejected by different animals from the farm. So this year, they are in second grade and in a civic act about the book day, a teacher showed a book about the Ugly Duckling tale and all my second grade students started saying in English 'ugly duckling, ugly duckling!!!"

—*Roxanne Vargas Lopez, Primary School Teacher, Costa Rica*

Next, a teacher from Uzbekistan responds to the ideas expressed by Roxanne and emphasizes the importance of preparation for effective storytelling.

"I believe that many difficulties teachers face while storytelling are caused by lack of proper lesson preparation. Thorough lesson planning is really important for storytelling as young learners have short attention spans and easily get bored and de-motivated. In this case a lesson is likely to be ruined. Thus, all the stages of a lesson are to be connected logically and lead one to another. Learners need language support, otherwise they won't be able to understand the story, so words or grammar constructions you feel your students will be not able to cope with on their own are to be pre-taught. You were also right, saying that the aim and the purpose for storytelling are to be explained by a teacher in advance. While telling the story teacher and students should work together and there are a number of ways for this. Roxanne wrote about learners saying a repetitive phrase instead of a teacher, a very good example. Consequently, a teacher decides which activities to use for practicing language after storytelling. There is no universal way for preparation, as teachers are different as well as their classes. Only you can design a lesson plan ideally fitting your learners. My only advice is to think critically and creatively before the lesson and to reflect upon it after it's over."

—*Victoria Demidova, Primary School Teacher, Uzbekistan*

Every teacher has to develop his/her own approach and be creative to engage YLs in storytelling activities. Here is an approach taken by one teacher, including the use of technology to engage learners.

"Children are those open-minded little people who are always ready to do what you want them to do. As regards story telling in the classroom this is what worked for me; however, you have to bear in mind that groups differ constantly and what might work for one, might be a failure for others. I chose a story, preferably one students were not so familiar with and a short one.

I sat them in a semicircle. If there were unknown words or difficult expressions in the reader, I adapted them to already taught vocabulary. I started the reading section and every time a new character appeared in the story, I changed my voice and used a lot of mimicry so that students would immediately identify them in the story later on. Once I finished the reading, I told my students they were going to listen to it again, but this time they would join me in the story. In a matter of seconds their faces and bodies turned into whatever the character demanded them to be. You can't imagine how happy and excited they were! I think teaching reading through a story is nice, especially using technology. There are a lot of ways, for example, having a power point presentation of the story using cartoons, animation and voices. This way is attractive to children as they like to watch it and interact with it."

—*Faisal Shamali, Primary English Teacher, Jordan*

For many teachers, effective storytelling includes considering the seating arrangement in the classroom. Read how one teacher from Brazil arranges her students for storytelling using a big book.

"The seating arrangement for a storytelling is an important point. First of all, the teacher should make sure s/he can be seen by everybody, so I really like to arrange my students in a semi-circle. We sometimes go to the resource center, where there is a special corner for the children. In the classrooms for very young learners, there is also a corner for circle time and that is where most teachers sit down to tell stories. In the classrooms for older students we don't have a corner for stories, but we can open space and sit on the floor. When we stay in the classroom, I prefer to have students sitting on the floor in a semi-circle too. I think that by being closer, they feel more comfortable and

I am able to check if everybody is following the story. Then, for the follow-up activities we change the seating arrangement as appropriate for each activity. I also like signaling it's story time. We can do that by singing a song, or by putting on a hat or another accessory, or having a chant, anything that sets the mood."

—*Ana Maria Scandiuzzi, EFL Instructor, Brazil*

Finally, a teacher in South Africa describes how he uses the storytelling tradition from his native culture to engage learners in storytelling in English.

"Story telling is an important communication ingredient in my own Nguni culture. Therefore, I often draw from the Oral Tales Tradition to bring an ESL story to my learners. The arrangement is semi-circular, the narrator sits in the middle point of this sphere. I seldom use chairs. The oral-lore tradition uses mats, so to echo and emulate that scene-setting, I use the mats in the classroom. This is ideal in the summer. The desks are pushed to the back and we move forward similar to the Front-Stage of a theatre set-up. This is very different from the reading corner. Students are often excited because many can anticipate that this is 'story time!' They then take to the pre-setting bustle with all excitement. They enjoy the change of scene."

—*Zodwa Motsa, Primary School Teacher, South Africa*

■ Chapter Summary

To Conclude

Storytelling is a fun and authentic approach Storytelling is a fun, exciting way to present English in a meaningful context and to expose children to other cultures. Storytelling is an authentic form of communication for young learners in all cultures.

Storytelling promotes critical thinking Storytelling can help teachers incorporate the development of critical thinking skills while developing language skills in children. Storytelling can help children develop these critical thinking skills and deepen their understanding of how stories are connected to their lives, their culture, and other cultures.

Teachers should prepare storytelling carefully Since storytellers are performers, teachers should meticulously prepare their theatrics, props, and storytelling script beforehand, and then rehearse until ready to perform.

Good storytelling involves preparing before-, during-, and after-storytelling activities. These activities capture the attention of learners while making input comprehensible. The activities check student comprehension of the story and encourage learners to practice using the new language.

Storytelling can promote thematic learning Storytelling is a great centerpiece for a thematic unit that develops the four language skills in an integrated manner and encourages communication among students for an extended period of time.

■ Over to You

Discussion Questions

1. In what ways is storytelling an authentic form of communication?
2. Which four elements should you prepare to make your storytelling engaging?
3. What are some important steps a teacher should take before, during, and after storytelling? What are activities that you can and can't do in your classroom context?
4. How does storytelling help to increase critical thinking skills?
5. How can storytelling help students understand their culture and see similarities with other cultures?
6. Do you think there are cultural differences in the style, form, or structure of storytelling? Do a search on YouTube for videos of storytellers from different countries and regions of the world, and watch them perform. See some examples below:

   Alton Chung (Hawaiian storyteller):
   http://www.youtube.com/watch?v=5Am6Ycn6eG8

   Gregg Howard (Cherokee storyteller):
   http://www.youtube.com/watch?v=SlHtzU133NI&feature=related

   Comfort Ero (African storyteller):
   http://www.youtube.com/watch?v=WP_LTtFYt3A&feature=PlayList&p=FEE4EF61F3F06CCE&index=0

   Japanese storyteller:
   http://www.youtube.com/watch?v=7b_ON7QyLjQ

Lesson Planning	Choose a story and make a lesson plan for storytelling in your class. Prepare for the storytelling by planning out the script, props, and theatrics. Then plan your pre-, during, and post-storytelling activities and write a lesson plan using the lesson plan in this chapter as an example.
Write About It	**Effective storytelling in your context:** Think about your own use of storytelling in your English classes. Reflect on the ideas discussed in this chapter that you have already mastered in your teaching. Are there aspects of storytelling that you hadn't considered before reading this chapter? If you are currently teaching, what are your biggest challenges using storytelling? Reflect on ways to resolve these issues and improve your ability to tell stories effectively in your classroom. Write a 1–2 page essay describing your application of storytelling in your classroom context. Base your response on what you have read in this chapter.

Resources and References

Print Publications

Brewster, J., & Ellis, G. (2002). *Tell it again: The new storytelling handbook for primary teachers.* London, UK: Penguin.

Hines, M. (2005). Story theater. *English Teaching Forum, 43*(1), 24–29.

Mixon, M., & Temu, P. (2006). First road to learning: Language through stories. *English Teaching Forum, 44*(2), 14–19.

Paran, A., & Watts, E. (2003). *Storytelling in ELT.* Whitstable, UK: IATEFL.

Wright, A. (2009). Storytelling with children. Oxford, UK: Oxford University Press.

Online Resources for Storybooks

When resources are an issue and storybooks in English are hard to find, online resources can be a huge help. You will find lesson plan ideas, activities, printable handouts, and videos of the stories that can be used in class. Try doing searches for the following stories to see how easy it is to find resources online for your lessons:

- *Brown Bear, Brown Bear* by Bill Martin (For example, type "brown bear brown bear" into the search line in Google and YouTube.)
- *Five Little Monkeys (Jumping on the Bed)* by Eileen Cristelow
- *The Very Hungry Caterpillar* by Eric Carle
- *The Rainbow Fish* by Marcus Pfister

Useful Web Sites

International Children's Digital Library: http://en.childrenslibrary.org/

PBS Kids: Between the Lions: http://pbskids.org/lions/stories/

Scholastic Interactive Storybooks: Clifford: http://teacher.scholastic.com/clifford1/

Read Aloud America: http://www.readaloudamerica.org/booklist.htm

Children's Books: http://www.childrens-books.com/

Shen's Books: http://www.shens.com/

Story Arts Online: http://www.storyarts.org/

Storyline Online: http://www.storylineonline.net/

TPR Storytelling: http://www.tprstorytelling.com/index.php

Storybird: Collaborative Storytelling: http://storybird.com/

References

Bahti, M. (1996). *Pubelo stories and storytellers*. Tuscon, AZ: Rio Nuevo Publishers.

Bloom, B. S., & David, R. K. (1956). *Taxonomy of educational objectives: The classification of education goals, by a committee of college and university examiners. Handbook 1: Cognitive domain*. New York, NY: Longman, Green.

Brewster, J. (1991). Listening and the young learner. In C. Brumfit, J. Moon, & R. Tongue (Eds.), *Teaching English to children: From practice to principle*. London, UK: HarperCollins Publishers.

Brewster, J., Ellis, G., & Girard, D. (2004). *The primary English teacher's guide*. London, UK: Penguin.

Chance, K. S. (1986). *Thinking the classroom: A survey of programs*. New York, NY: Teachers College, Columbia University.

Curtain, H., & Dahlberg, C. A. (2010). *Languages and children: Making the match*. Boston, MA: Pearson.

Pinter, A. (2006). *Teaching young language learners*. Oxford, UK: Oxford University Press.

Korey O'Sullivan, J. (2013). *A Big Lesson for Little Frog*. Boston, MA: Heinle-Cengage.

Slatterly, M., & Willis, J. (2001). *English for primary teachers*. Oxford, UK: Oxford University Press.

Spiro, J. (2006). *Storybuilding*. Oxford, UK: Oxford University Press.

Taosaka, S. (2002). *Let's talk story: Professional development in the Pacific*. Honolulu, HI: Pacific Resources for Education and Learning.

7 Assessment

■ Getting Started

When you hear the word "assessment," what do you think of? For most of us, assessment is synonymous with formal testing, especially those end-of-course exams or standardized tests required by schools or educational institutions.

How did you feel about those tests when you were at school? Do you think they provided a full picture of what you could do? Did they make you feel confident with your learning?

Are there other ways in which we might assess the English development in young learners that build confidence and also serve as learning experiences?

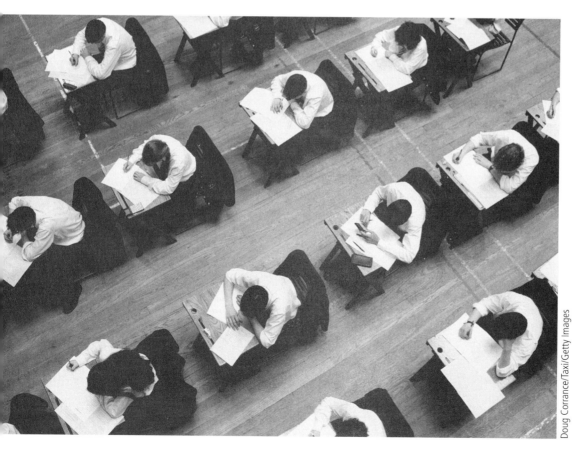

Doug Corrance/Taxi/Getty Images

Students taking traditional high stakes test.

If you have an opportunity to talk with an English for Young Learners (EYL) teacher, ask about the kinds of informal assessments that the teacher uses and the kinds of formal assessments (tests) that are required.

If you are unable to talk with a teacher, see if you can get a copy of a teacher's manual for an EYL series and analyze the types of assessment that are discussed there. They may be integrated into a unit or discussed in the front or end matter.

Here are some interview questions you might ask the EYL teacher. You might begin by saying that you think assessing young learners may be challenging and you would like to get the teacher's perspectives on the assessment strategies s/he uses. If you are analyzing a teacher's manual, see what answers are provided there.

Discovery Activity

Interview Questions

List below some of the informal ways in which we might assess children's English learning on a continuous basis.

QUESTIONS	ANSWERS
1. What tests are required for young learners?	1.
2. What are some ways you informally assess your young learners?	2.
3. Do you have any examples of assessments that you use?	3.
4. What are some of the challenges in assessing your YLs?	4.
5. Are there suggestions for assessments or tests provided by your textbook and/or by your school or the Ministry of Education? If so, can you describe these assessments?	5.

■ Theory, Planning and Application

Considerations for Assessing Young Learners

Throughout this book, we have been stressing the importance of providing young learners with engaging activities that motivate them to continue to learn English. Where does assessment fit in with this approach? Assessment can have negative consequences (Shohamy, 2001). If standardized tests are the only assessments used, then the result is likely to be a view that assessment causes anxiety.

While TEYL programs may need to use formal, standardized tests, they also need to assess their learners through alternative or informal assessments that monitor students' progress. Assessment is part of the learning process; in practice, teachers assess learners all the time. When learners participate in class or pair work, teachers note those who are successfully using new vocabulary words or grammatical structures and those who are having difficulty and need more practice or may require re-teaching. By listening to learners as they participate in class or pair work, by noting a student who is having difficulty decoding a new word, by talking informally with a student before or after class, teachers learn a great deal about their learners' progress and their own teaching.

In assessing young learners, we need to remember the characteristics of young language learners discussed in Chapter 2. Because of their age, maturity, experience, and cognitive, linguistic, and literacy development, young learners need carefully designed assessment tasks that they can perform either individually or with other students. There are a number of issues that make the assessment of young language learners complex. Among these are:

- The age of the learners and their overall motor, linguistic, social, and conceptual development
- The language focus of the EYL classroom, with more attention on oral skills in connected discourse, especially in the early years
- The types of activities used in teaching and learning such as games, songs, stories, and rhymes
- The goals of the TEYL program, which may include intercultural or social goals
- The overall approach to teaching and learning, emphasizing learning as a social activity with support from more knowledgeable teachers
  (Cameron, 2001; McKay, 2006; Pinter, 2006)

Hasselgren (2000) notes that in assessing young learners, one has to remember that "they have a particular need and capacity for play, fantasy, and fun; they have a relatively short attention span; [and] they are at a stage when daring to use their language is vital, and any sense of 'failure' could be particularly detrimental" (p. 262).

McKay (2006) notes that EYL assessment is also a relatively new field. In a collection of research articles on TEYL (Moon & Nikolov, 2000), not one article was focused on assessment; nor was there an article or even a section of an article on assessment in the collection of articles on young language learners published for the 2003–2004 "Year of the Young Learner" by Ellis and Morrow (2004).

Still, there is growing interest in young language learner assessment, not only to provide better information on young language learners' English proficiency, but also to bring the same attention to the EYL class that is given to other primary school subjects.

In this part of the chapter, we will look at important considerations for assessing young learners. We will begin by defining some of the basic assessment terms and concepts, then look at the different purposes and types of assessment that you might use in your EYL class.

Basic Assessment Terms and Concepts

Understanding the broad topic of assessment involves becoming familiar with a number of basic terms and concepts. Among these are:

- Assessment, testing, and evaluation (and their role in teaching and learning)
- Informal and formal assessment
- Formative and summative assessment
- Criterion- and norm-referenced tests
- Integrative and discrete point tests

Assessment, Testing and Evaluation Assessment, testing, and evaluation are often used synonymously, but they actually represent different practices.

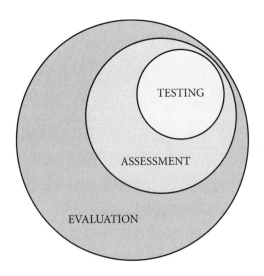

Assessment is a process of identifying learning goals and determining how well students are meeting them (Linn & Gronlund, 2000). It is something that is ongoing, a process of monitoring learning and teaching. It encompasses the multiple ways that teachers gather information about learners' knowledge, abilities, attitudes, and motivation (Ioannu-Georgiou & Pavlou, 2003) and note the progress or difficulties that students are having in learning English (Rea-Dickins & Gardner, 2000; Brown & Abeywickrama, 2010). "Whenever a student responds to a question, offers a comment, or tries out a new word or structure, the teacher subconsciously makes an appraisal of the student's performance. . . . A good teacher never ceases to assess students, whether those assessments are incidental or intended" (Brown & Abeywickrama, 2010, p. 3). Assessment is directly related to teaching and learning, but that does not mean that all learning should be assessed. Children need time to play with language and experience the joy of language learning without feeling that their every move is being judged or graded. At the same time, while children are having fun with English, teachers can also be thinking about directions for future lessons or special help that a student might need.

Testing is one type of assessment that formally measures learners' English language performance (Brown & Abeywickrama, 2010; Cameron, 2001). It is usually given at set times during the term: at the end of a unit, or the middle or the end of a term. It involves a set of clearly developed procedures for giving and scoring the learners' performance. A test can measure specific knowledge (for example, accuracy with specific vocabulary words, grammatical structures, or writing mechanics) or overall proficiency in using the language. It can be developed by a teacher or be a high-stakes, standardized test given by an educational institution or ministry. It can involve choosing among multiple-choice items, filling in blanks, completing sentences, writing texts, or giving short oral answers and yielding a score (for example, 90 percent), a grade (for example, an A or B), or, in the case of standardized tests, an overall (composite) score, scores on subtests, and often, a ranking of each student's performance compared to all who took the test.

Evaluation involves the use of test scores or assessments for some kind of decision making (Bachman, 1990; Brown & Abeywickrama, 2010). It often involves the gathering of information "to determine the extent to which a language program meets its goals" (Ioannou-Georgiou & Pavlou, 2003, p. 4). Usually, test scores or assessments are only one source of information to determine the success of a particular program, course, or approach to instruction. Other sources might include curriculum, objectives, materials, methodology, or teachers. They might also include classroom observations, interviews with students or parents, and student evaluations as evidence.

A comprehensive or ideal assessment system consists of all three. Assessment, testing, and evaluation help:

- Learners to know how they are progressing
- Teachers to know how effective the instruction is
- Administrators to know how well the program is making progress toward program goals
- Funders to see the results of their investment

Informal and Formal Assessment
As teachers, we assess our learners informally more often than we might think. We look over the shoulders of two students engaged in completing an exercise to see how they are doing; we provide brief comments like "Good job!" or "Want to try that again?" when our learners are speaking; and we write on their papers, praising their efforts and making suggestions for improvement. We actually are assessing much of the time that we are teaching, noting where students seem to be having difficulties and trying new approaches.

Formal assessments, however, are less frequent. They are systematic ways that we gauge student achievement. We use them periodically to inform both our learners and ourselves about how much students are learning. Tests are one type of formal assessment, but not all formal assessments are tests. Tests are usually short assessments, but we might ask students to keep a portfolio of their work that we then assess systematically at the end of a term; or to create a project that we can formally assess, using a rubric (defined below). While formal assessments are important (some are so important that they determine future placements or enrollments), informal assessments are more useful in daily teaching.

Formative and Summative Assessment
The primary purpose of classroom-based assessment is to provide teachers and programs with information to help in making decisions. We can do that by assessing learners during the course of instruction (formative assessment) or after the end of some portion of their course (summative assessment). Both of these are important, since they provide information about student learning. The most important for teaching may be formative, but the most critical for learners is likely to be summative.

Formative assessment Formative assessment is the (usually informal) assessment that occurs during teaching and learning (McKay, 2006). This classroom-based assessment provides an ongoing picture of students' language growth and development (Brown & Abeywickrama, 2010; Rea-Dickins & Gardner, 2000). Its primary function is to monitor students' learning and to provide teachers with information needed "to make appropriate decisions concerning modifications to teaching procedures and learning activities" (Weir, 1993, p. 167). However, it can also be used to provide students with feedback on their learning progress and to help motivate learners (Gattullo, 2000; Torrance & Pryor, 1988). Formative assessment is usually embedded in instruction; it is "assessment for learning" (Black et al., 2004). Through a range of alternative assessments such as portfolios, projects, or story retellings, formative assessment also helps learners to monitor their own learning in "assessment as learning."

Formative assessment may consist of:

- Observing students and noting strengths and difficulties in doing class work
- Maintaining a checklist of student progress in using key vocabulary or grammar structures
- Asking questions and noting students' responses
- Asking for clarification to promote self-repair
- Making suggestions or modeling correct forms orally or in writing
- Engaging in dialog journals with students (see Chapter 5)
- Creating portfolios with samples of students' work over time
- Noting student progress on written or oral performances
- Praising or rewarding good performance or effort
- Marking homework

A number of alternative assessments, used formatively, are discussed later in this chapter.

Summative assessment Summative assessment, as its name implies, "summarizes" a student's learning at the end of a year, a term, a course, or a unit of study. It involves "assessment of learning." It is formal in nature, frequently undertaken with tests that measure specific language skills or overall proficiency in the language. These tests may be chapter or end-of-term tests developed by the teacher or provided with the curriculum. They may also be high-stakes, standardized tests developed by an educational body to measure each child's English against a set of standards or expected benchmarks and to compare children's performances. These assessments are often used to report on students' language learning progress and also to help evaluate the effectiveness of a program, curriculum, materials, or student placement procedures.

The trend today is toward less focus on formal, summative assessment (which can lead to substantial anxiety and an incomplete picture of what a student knows or can do) and more attention to informal, classroom-based, formative assessment that provides a fuller picture of a student's performance and also more useful information to teachers (Black et al., 2004; Black & William, 1998; Rea-Dickins & Gardner, 2000; Ross, 2005).

Norm-Referenced and Criterion-Referenced Assessment

Norm-referenced assessment ranks each individual learner in comparison to all others who were assessed. Standardized, formal, high-stakes tests are usually norm referenced, with each test taker's score ranked in relation to the average score (the mean), the middle score (the median), and the percentile (rank) of the scores of all who took that test.

Criterion-referenced assessment compares a student's performance to a set of specific criteria, usually related to a curriculum or a course. The criteria may also be related to a set of descriptors such as benchmarks related to a set of standards or along a scale (McKay, 2006). The following is an example of criterion-referenced assessment using scaled descriptors for assessing oral fluency:

6	Speaks fluently
5	Speaks with near-native fluency; any hesitations do not interfere with communication
4	Speaks with occasional hesitation
3	Speaks hesitantly because of rephrasing and searching for words
2	Speaks in single-word utterances and short patterns
1	Repeats words and phrases

(Adapted from O'Malley & Pierce, 1996, p. 68)

If all students were to do well on a well-constructed criterion-referenced test, both the students and the teachers would be happy.

Discrete Point and Integrative Assessment

Discrete point assessment focuses on individual items, such as a particular word or grammatical structure, in isolation rather than meaningful contexts. Many paper-and-pencil (or computer-based) tests for young learners will be discrete point tests, involving multiple-choice items or filling in blanks as evidence that children have learned a particular vocabulary word or grammatical structure. These tests are relatively easy to administer and score, but they provide limited information on a student's language skills or overall proficiency.

Integrated assessment is a more holistic approach to assessing learners' knowledge and skills, involving the four language skills of listening, speaking, reading, and writing through the use of interactive activities such as chants, songs, games, role plays, writing tasks, or projects (Ioannou-Georgiou & Pavlou, 2003). Integrated assessment more closely mirrors authentic language use and classroom instruction and is more likely to create a more positive, anxiety-free classroom atmosphere that encourages children to take risks.

Principles of Assessment

Developing or identifying appropriate assessments for young learners involves (1) understanding the basic criteria that guide all assessment, as well as (2) the special guidelines for assessing young learners.

Basic Assessment Guidelines Bachman (1990) and Bachman and Palmer (1996) identify five criteria to guide the development of language assessments, especially tests. These are:

1. Reliability
2. Validity
3. Practicality
4. Authenticity
5. Washback

We will define each of these and then discuss how they apply to assessment instruments that you might use in your EYL class.

   1.   **Reliability**   For a language assessment to be reliable, the results should be accurate and consistent. According to Bachman (1990, p. 25), reliability "has to do with the consistency of measures across different times, test forms, raters, and other characteristics of the measurement context." A student should receive the same score on the assessment if it is given on the next day or if it is scored by two different raters. If students who demonstrate the same basic proficiency in listening or reading in class score very differently on an assessment, then that assessment's reliability is questionable. If two teachers score a student's writing or speaking with very different scores, then reliability is also a problem. It may be that the directions were unclear or the scoring criteria were confusing.

   2.   **Validity**   For a language assessment to be valid, the decisions made by the test must be meaningful appropriate, and useful. It also has to assess what it purports to assess (Bachman, 1990; Bachman & Palmer, 1996; Brown & Abeywickrama, 2010; McKay, 2006; Messick, 1989). If a test is assessing children's ability to talk about what they did over the weekend or to read a short text about zoo or farm animals, then we need to be sure that the task is at the appropriate level for the children and that they are not being asked to use language or content that they haven't encountered. The task should also be appropriate for assessing the desired

skill. Asking a student to read a passage aloud does not assess reading, except for decoding and pronouncing individual words. A writing test that only considers vocabulary, spelling, and mechanics is not a valid assessment of a child's writing. The uses of an assessment also need to be valid (Messick, 1989). Assessments have social and educational consequences; they must be fair, and what they are used for must match their intended purpose to be valid assessments.

3. **Practicality** An assessment task is practical if needed resources (including time and place) are available for the assessment task. Even a brief one-to-one talk with a student may not be practical if the class has 30 students and they only meet a few hours a week; but if class size is small and the time for instruction greater, it may be practical (McKay, 2006). One also has to consider the amount of time and training needed for scoring the assessment.

4. **Authenticity** A language assessment is authentic if the language being assessed is used in ways that are appropriate and relevant to young learners (McKay, 2006). For example, creating a greeting card, playing a word game, or collaboratively writing a new verse to a song or chant are basically authentic, as they are ways that children use language and ways in which they are instructed. To be authentic, an assessment should also be "child-friendly" (Saricoban & Kuntas, 2010). In general, paper-and-pencil tests do not meet the criteria of authenticity for young learners.

5. **Washback** Washback refers to the effects that tests have on teaching and learning (Wall & Alderson, 1993). Its impact can be positive or negative. Ideally, a test should promote more effective instruction: What is tested should be what is agreed upon as the most important language knowledge and use. As Cameron (2001) explains, "Teaching and learning needs should dictate the form and timing of assessment" (p. 213). However, in practice, "the scenario is quite different: assessment seems to 'drive' teaching by forcing teachers to teach what is going to be assessed" (p. 213). It can also influence the language curriculum and policy. Cameron provides several examples of how national and international tests can change the focus of instruction from communication to more grammar-based items that can be easily assessed through paper-and-pencil tests, an example of negative washback.

The above criteria apply especially to summative assessments or tests that are used to compare children's language abilities and to make educational decisions. When focusing on alternative or formative assessment (see below), their interpretation may change (Black & William, 1998; McKay, 2006; McMillan, 2003). For example, according to McKay (2006), a classroom assessment such as a project or portfolio may be valid if it "has resulted in more student engagement" or "when progress can be identified" (p. 116). Likewise, rather than determining if a particular assessment would result in the same score over time or with different raters, reliability might be determined by collecting data from a number of alternative assessment tasks. These ideas are only now being discussed, and additional research will be needed to determine the criteria for informal or alternative assessments.

Guidelines for Effective Assessment of Young Learners In addition to meeting the five fundamental criteria discussed above, assessments for young learners should:

1. Mirror learning (what is taught is what is assessed)
2. Contribute to learning (for both learners and the teacher)
3. Motivate learners and build learner confidence
4. Include a variety of techniques for learners' different intelligences and learning styles
5. Allow all learners to experience success, while providing advanced learners opportunities to demonstrate their proficiency
6. Be contextualized and reflect relevant tasks and language for young learners
7. Take place over time

1.   Assessments should mirror learning Assessment should reflect the goals and objectives of the curriculum and provide children with the opportunity to demonstrate what they know and can do with the language in tasks that are similar to the ones they have engaged with in learning. If they are principally taught English orally through songs, chants, stories, and games, then they should be assessed through similar activities, not through paper-and-pencil tests that focus on individual vocabulary and grammar items out of context, in single sentences. However, Rea-Dickins and Rixon (1999) found that the most frequent type of language assessment was a paper-and-pencil test of grammar or vocabulary items in single sentences (rather than connected discourse). This was in contrast to the way that the children had been taught: through songs, stories, games, and other connected discourse where the emphasis was on oral skills and the focus on content and communication.

It is important "that the way young learners learn best be reflected in the way they are assessed" (McKay, 2006, p. 47). If language learning involves social interaction, so should at least some assessment focus on children as they engage in communication with each other (Cameron 2001; Hasselgren, 2012;

McNamara, 2001). Cameron also notes that scaffolded support from the teacher or other students should be considered not only in teaching young learners, but also in assessing them.

2. Assessments should contribute to learning (for both learners and teachers) Effective assessment should help both teachers and learners. It should provide information to learners (and their parents) on their progress in learning English. The results of homework or class assignments can make students (especially older young learners) aware of their progress, and help them to become more independent learners (Kirsch, 2008). It should also provide teachers with information on which to base subsequent instruction, especially modifications that are needed for some or all students. As Cameron (2001, p. 115) suggests, assessment should "serve" teaching by providing feedback on pupils' learning that would make the next teaching event more effective, in a positive, upward direction.

3. Assessments should motivate learners and build learner confidence "Assessment in children's language learning, as part of their early experience, can influence whether or not pupils choose to continue learning the foreign language or whether they lose interest and motivation" (Cameron, 2001, p. 226). With formal testing, especially through standardized tests, students are understandably anxious about their performance. But much assessment takes place routinely in class instruction and on homework assignments. These assessments need to encourage learners and provide them with ways of demonstrating what they know. A word of praise for learners' performance in oral or written tasks can help learners become more confident and provide much-needed motivation. Stickers or rewards can also be used to motivate young learners and acknowledge their accomplishments. If we believe that teaching young learners should be motivating for them, then even classroom tests should have that result. If a test only measures students' performance with grammar in isolated sentences or multiple-choice vocabulary items, young learners are likely to find the assessment boring and not very motivating. Since much of the emphasis in EYL classes is on encouraging learners to develop fluency in English, too heavy an emphasis on assessing individual grammar or vocabulary items could be inappropriate.

Even high-stakes, standardized tests can be motivating. The University of Cambridge in their tests for young learners identifies the following desirable characteristics that encourage and motivate learners and build confidence:

We want our tests to be:

- fun for children to take so the tasks are varied and some look like games or puzzles
- attractive and colorful to look at so all tasks are based on colorful graphics

- interesting in content so topic areas which are relevant to children's lives are chosen; e.g. school, food, animals
- encouraging and confidence building so the tests are short and plenty of time is allowed for each task; the tests have a simple format with simple instructions for the students
- relaxed and non-threatening so all listening tasks are heard twice; speaking tasks are activity-based; oral examiners give lots of encouragement.

(cited by Brewster, Ellis, & Girard, 2004, p. 252)

4. Assessment should include a variety of techniques for learners' different intelligences and learning styles Many standardized tests focus on linguistic, logical-mathematical, and spatial intelligences, which prevent many learners with other learning styles or intelligences (Gardner, 1983, 1999) from demonstrating their language ability (Brewster, Ellis, & Girard, 2004). These tests also tend to focus on individual language skills (listening, speaking, reading, and writing), though in real life we tend to use several of these at once. We need to make sure that assessments provide all learners with the opportunity to demonstrate their diverse skills and abilities. Just as students have multiple opportunities to learn to listen, speak, read, and write English, they should also be provided with multiple opportunities to demonstrate their progress in applying the knowledge, skills, and strategies they have used in their learning (O'Malley & Pierce, 1996).

5. Assessments should allow all learners to experience success, while providing advanced learners opportunities to demonstrate their proficiency Assessment, like teaching, often focuses on the "middle" student, without providing opportunities for those who are above or below that middle to demonstrate what they know and are able to do with English (Crandall & Greenblatt, 1999). Just as teaching needs to provide differentiation of tasks for different learners, so does assessment.

6. Assessments should be contextualized and reflect relevant tasks and language for young learners Too often, quizzes and tests ask students to respond to a set of items that are not thematically related or relevant to their lives. To increase the authenticity of assessment and encourage young learners to relate both learning and assessment to their lives, assessments should provide an integrated set of items focused on a central theme (one that has been taught) that is relevant to the young learners. The language assessed should be language that children would use in their real lives. Good test items should reflect and use similar tasks and activities that are used in instruction. The topics, text types, language functions (in listening, speaking, reading, and writing), and the conditions should match what has been used in classroom instruction. They should be based on what children can do and usually do in class. Where possible, assessments should also focus on both language and content.

7. **Assessments should take place over time** In order to provide evidence of growth, assessment should not be thought of as occurring only occasionally or at times when important tests are given. Instead, it should occur over time, to provide longitudinal evidence of growth (Hurley & Blake, 2001). Portfolios, observational checklists using dates, and homework notebooks can all be used to collect that evidence.

Purposes and Types of Language Assessments

David Grossman/Alamy Limited

We assess students for many purposes:

- ■ To make decisions about where to place students
- ■ To monitor students' performance and achievement and note what else we need to focus on
- ■ To identify students who need special support
- ■ To measure and report students' progress
- ■ To monitor our own effectiveness as teachers and make appropriate instructional modifications
  (Brewster, Ellis, & Girard, 2004; Brown & Abeywickrama, 2010; Rea-Dickins & Rixon, 2000)

The types of assessments we use vary according to these purposes. They can briefly be categorized as traditional or alternative assessments.

Traditional and Alternative Assessments Traditionally, assessment has taken the form of tests or quizzes with multiple-choice items, matching, filling-in-the-blank, and true-false questions, sometimes in standardized tests that measure whether students have met specific objectives or outcomes, and other times created by the teacher (Saricoban & Kuntas, 2010). In addition to these traditional forms of assessment, there are a number of "alternative" or performance assessments that require the learner to apply the knowledge, skills, and strategies used in learning (Bailey, 1998; O'Malley & Pierce, 1996; Puckett & Black, 2000; Shabaan, 2005). Pierce and O'Malley (1992) define alternative assessment as "any method of finding out what a student knows or can do that is intended to show growth and inform instruction and is not a standardized or traditional test" (p. 2). Alternative or performance-based assessment (also known as assessment for learning) uses activities that reveal what students can do with the language, emphasizing their strengths rather than their weaknesses in using English for meaningful purposes. These performance assessments are classroom-based, involving tasks in which language is used in authentic ways or through simulations of real-life language use (McKay, 2006). Generally, performance assessments are formative and integrative in nature; they may occur over an extended period of time and involve the use of several language skills. A major goal is to link instruction and assessment, providing continuing feedback to learners and improvement of instruction. Alternative or performance assessments can be incorporated into daily classroom activities with appropriate procedures in place, though some will take time to review and mark.

Purposes and Types of Formal Tests The purposes for formal tests include:

1. **Diagnostic tests:** Diagnosing student learning difficulties or areas in need of further instruction, for example, with particular sounds or writing features

2. **Placement tests:** Initially placing students in the proper language level

3. **Achievement tests:** Measuring and reporting student progress in learning the curriculum

4. **Proficiency tests:** Providing an overall picture of a student's language development

(Brown & Abeywickrama, 2010)

   1.   **Diagnostic tests** Diagnostic tests are formative assessments used to identify features of English that are problematic for individual learners. They might consist of a brief speaking test to identify particular sounds that are difficult for the student

to pronounce or a writing sample that can be used to identify areas that need to be addressed. These tests are not commonly used with very young learners, or even young learners, unless a student demonstrates ongoing difficulties.

2. **Placement tests** Placement tests are usually repurposed achievement or proficiency tests that are used to determine the right language level for placement. The test uses portions of the content of the curriculum as the basis of the assessment, finding the appropriate place where material is neither too easy nor too difficult for the learner.

3. **Achievement tests** Achievement tests are usually what both teachers and students think of when they think of tests. They are curriculum-based: They measure learning of the specific content of a unit or course. They are also summative in nature, but can provide formative feedback to teachers and administrators on instructional changes for that unit or course.

4. **Proficiency tests** Unlike an achievement test, which tests mastery of a curriculum, a proficiency test provides an overall picture of a student's English language ability. It is almost always summative and norm-referenced. Usually, a proficiency test provides an overall score and subscores on each section of the test (often specific language skills such as listening, reading, etc.)

The results of all of these formal student assessments are used by teachers in monitoring their performance and by administrators in evaluating teachers and programs. They are also frequently used as part of an overall evaluation of an institution (Rea-Dickins & Gardner, 2000).

Purposes and Types of Alternative or Performance Assessments Alternatives to traditional assessment for young learners include:

1. Observations
2. Conferences and oral interviews
3. Story or text retellings
4. Writing samples
5. Projects
6. Portfolios
7. Other performances
8. Self- or peer-assessments

1. **Observations** "Incidental observation" of classroom learning (McKay, 2006, p. 153), also known as "kid watching" (Goodman, 1978; Gordon, 2007) occurs all the

time in a young learner classroom. According to Puckett and Black (2000), "During story time, for example, the teacher scans the listeners for facial expressions and body language and listens for verbal responses indicative of enjoyment, language development, and comprehension" (p. 217). You can observe young learners as they engage in pair work, draft an e-mail, engage in shared reading, or work individually or collaboratively on a project. Such observations are "helpful when you are interested in finding out whether your students have the know-how needed to complete a certain task or whether they can help themselves while dealing with the challenges posed by a language learning activity" or to see if they have "the strategic competence essential for completing certain tasks. By observing how your students resolve the challenges presented by the acts of speaking, reading, or writing in a second language, you can learn the extent of their students' strategic competence and ascertain what type of help would benefit language learners" (Gordon, 2007, pp. 208–209). Performance checklists can be developed to record the observations of individual students and to monitor their progress in specific listening, speaking, reading, or writing skills, or their growth in pronunciation, grammar, or vocabulary. It might be useful to develop a checklist with the objectives for each unit or for a term. It also might be helpful to identify one or two children to observe each day during times when children are interacting with each other in their learning tasks, using an observation checklist, or taking notes to record their oral language performance.

2. **Conferences and oral interviews** During writing conferences, when teachers talk with individual students about their drafts, giving guidance or revising them, it is also possible to note children's ability to communicate their ideas effectively in English. Since oral language development is usually the focus of EYL programs, especially for very young learners, it is important to provide opportunities for students to demonstrate their progress in listening and speaking. Simple questions during independent reading, such as "Why did you choose this book?" or "Can you tell me about a part that you really like?" can provide information on a child's oral language development. Although formal interviews may not be necessary, they can be an appropriate end-of-term/year oral proficiency assessment.

3. **Story or text retellings** In story or text retellings, students read or listen to the original text and then retell the major events, selected details, or the main ideas (O'Malley & Pierce, 1996). It is even possible to assess a beginning English learner whose listening skills are stronger than his/her speaking skills by telling the story in English, but allowing the learner to retell the story in L1.

4. **Writing samples** During the year, students can be asked to write a range of texts, as discussed in Chapter 5. These writing samples can be assessed and placed in

a student's portfolio. Students can also be asked to self-assess their writing (and have a peer also assess it), by using smiley faces or numbers of stars for beginners, then by checklists, and, when appropriate, through a sentence or short paragraph.

5. **Projects** Projects may include creating posters, drawings, student books, charts, or role plays, and may be undertaken individually or in groups. They are often an excellent integrated assessment, since they usually involve the use of the four language skills, especially when they are developed collaboratively. Even individual written projects usually require some type of oral presentation. Collaborative projects with carefully defined roles can also provide opportunities for learners at different levels to demonstrate their English language and other skills such as drawing or acting (Pinter, 2006). Some EYL series use projects as the summative assessment for textbook units. These projects provide an authentic way of assessing overall learning of the language and content of the unit.

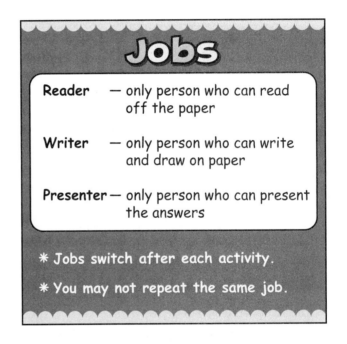

6. **Portfolios** "A portfolio is a purposeful collection of student work" that documents a student's "efforts, progress, and achievement" over time (Paulson, Paulson, & Meyer, 1991, p. 60). Portfolios may include drawings, writings, posters, journal entries, craft items, photographs (or videotapes) of projects, or participation in role plays or Reader's Theater (O'Malley & Pierce, 1996; Pierce & O'Malley, 1992). They can be used for both formative and summative assessment. For formative purposes, during the term, learners can be invited to present their portfolio to parents as a demonstration of their progress. They can also select one item they are particularly proud of to present to a small group of peers. Older young learners can also be asked to comment on work that is included in the

Darija Sostaric-Zuckermann, Primary School Teacher, Croatia

"My school is small. We have one grade per year, grades 1 to 8, so I teach all the children there. Student portfolios are passed on to me! My pupils collect all their work in one big notebook and when it is filled, they save the old one and start a new one. I teach them to always have the old one by their work area at home to find and refer to something they need. And I'm quite happy how they do it. Students who are now in secondary schools often say thank you to me for teaching them how to use their portfolios, although not many secondary teachers continue this practice. Usually, at the end of a school year, we go back to the beginning of the year and go through the portfolios to see what they have done. In the notebook I also write notes to the parents and some do read them and report back."

portfolio, as a form of self-assessment. Usually, a summative portfolio is a "showcase portfolio" (Gordon, 2007, p. 209) that includes the best work of a student, selected by the student with guidance from the teacher. Young learners develop autonomy as they decide which pieces to include. The portfolios can provide a full representation of a student's language abilities. Some programs also pass students' portfolios on to the teacher of the next level, providing valuable information to the new teacher on each student's progress.

7. **Other performances** Role plays, oral reports, and demonstrations also offer opportunities to gauge learners' speaking proficiency. Students can be asked to play the part of a character in a story, give a brief report of their or their group's project, or demonstrate something they know how to do. These can also be audiotaped or videotaped to preserve their performance. The audiotapes or videotapes can be part of the students' overall portfolios.

8. **Self- or peer-assessments** Older young learners can participate in self-assessment, or in assessing each other, if care has been taken to provide a structure for the comments (similar to the Praise-Question-Polish (PQP) approach discussed in Chapter 5). Pairing children who work well together will also help to establish appropriate cooperation (Brewster, Ellis, & Girard, 2002). Learners younger than 8 years old are not likely to be able to reflect on their performance, or if they do, they are likely to be overly optimistic about their own learning. But their ability to self-reflect and self-assess improves around age 8 (Butler & Lee, 2010; Paris & Newman, 1990).

There are a variety of ways of encouraging young learners to assess themselves. These include asking them to check off a series of "can-do" statements, such as the following, which are at different levels of English proficiency:

I can follow directions in English. (Listening)

I can name the days of the week and tell the current day. (Speaking)

I can describe the clothes I am wearing. (Speaking)

I can match pictures with words. (Reading/Listening)

I can read sentences about animals and answer questions. (Reading and Writing)

I can retell a story. (Listening/Reading and Speaking/Writing)

I can label a drawing of a classroom. (Writing)

I can write a poem with my name. (Writing)

I can describe my family. (Writing)

To provide even more information, students can be asked to indicate whether they can do this "Very well/easily," "Not very well/easily," or "Not at all." This can also be done as a class activity, with students giving examples of each of these after they have completed their can-do inventory. Students can also be asked to respond to a series of questions related to how they feel about learning English, about the class, and about specific activities in the class. (Note: Can-do statements have been developed for large-scale language testing in the United States and Europe. See the Web resources at the end of this chapter.)

"Exit tickets," where children are asked to report on something they learned in the class that day, can also promote self-assessment. Providing sentence starters, such as "One new thing I learned today is/was . . ." can provide the structure and support for children to report on their learning. Another possibility is to use sentence starters to ask children (perhaps in groups) to reflect on the day's lesson and write "3-2-1 summaries": "3 facts they have learned, 2 questions they have or wonder about, [and] 1 personal connection they can make to the information" (Dodge, 2009, pp. 22–23).

Rating Alternative Assessments

Differences in the type of assessment also result in differences in the ways in which these assessments are scored. Some ways of scoring or rating alternative assessments include:

1. Brief feedback
2. Checklists
3. Rubrics

1. Brief feedback Classroom assignments such as filling in a graphic organizer can be scored by a three-part system:

[List with symbols +, check mark, and –]

+ For excellent work

√ For acceptable work

– For work that needs improvement

Brief statements such as "Good job" or "Great, but you need work here" will individualize the assessment.

2. Checklists Checklists provide a simple way of keeping a record of students' performance in class.

Observations can be noted on a checklist that provides the names of the students on the left-hand side and the types of performances or outcomes desired at the top. For example, a student engaged in pair work using verbs such as "like to" and "don't like to," or key vocabulary such as "windy," "snowy," or "rainy" in discussion, would receive a check, indicating that this student has successfully used the grammatical structure or key vocabulary. The checklist could also use numbers 1, 2, and 3 to indicate where a learner is on any task. It could be dated and then added to or revised when a learner moves to the next level. This is a simple way of keeping a record of students' performance in class.

The following is an example of a simple "recording ladder" that could be used to monitor children's development of early spelling and handwriting:

> Copies letters neatly and correctly when watched
> Copies letters neatly and correctly independently
> Copies a small number of familiar words accurately
> Can use a simple picture dictionary or word book
> Can spell accurately most words in the coursebook units covered thus far
> (Brewster, Ellis, & Girard, 2002, p. 249)

A simple individual assessment form/checklist can be developed for each student that records the student's progress in meeting the instructional objectives. This form can be placed in the student's portfolio. Here is an example:

Student name: _____

1 = Exceeds objective
2 = Meets objective
3 = Needs improvement
4 = Does not meet objective

Objective/Skill	Date	Date	Date	Date
Responds to Y/N questions	3 10/3	2 12/4	1 2/14	
Responds to Wh-questions				
Follows oral directions				
Participates in chants and songs				
Interacts with other students in English				

The following is another example of a checklist used to rate a learner's oral language:

ORAL LANGUAGE CHECKLIST

M = Most of the time   S = Sometimes   N = Almost never

Student name: _____

Task	Date	Rating	Date	Rating	Date	Rating
Describes things	10/3	S	11/6	S	1/5	M
Answers questions						
Expresses likes/dislikes						
Follows oral directions						
Uses greetings and farewells						
Uses present tense						
Uses past tense						
Responds to Yes/No Qs						
Responds to Wh- Qs						

The following is a similar checklist for assessing writing:

WRITING CHECKLIST

M = Most of the time   S = Sometimes   N = Almost never

Student name: _____

Task	Date	Rating	Date	Rating	Date	Rating
Copies name	10/5	S	12/2	M		
Copies words from board	10/5	N	12/2	S	1/4	M
Fills gaps with words	12/2	S	1/4	S	2/14	M

Teachers can write the dates and rating in a color as a child performs the task. It can then be sent to the teacher of the next level, who can use a different color so "everyone can see at a glance how much progress has been made over the year" (Brewster, Ellis, & Girard, 2004, p. 249).

3. **Rubrics** Rubrics are scoring guides that are used in assessing students' oral or written performance on a range of criteria. Rubrics are usually provided to students before they engage in the task, enabling them to know how their speaking or writing will be assessed. As young learners become older (age 10+) and more proficient in English, they can help identify the important features to include in the rubric and how these should be evaluated. In doing so, they can become much more aware of the importance of various features.

There are two types of scoring rubrics: holistic and analytic. Holistic rubrics, which are much more common for classroom assessment, provide a single overall score indicating how well the student has used these features. Analytic rubrics provide points for each feature and then add these up for a composite score (usually on the basis of 100 points as a perfect score) (Bailey, 1998; O'Malley & Pierce, 1996). A holistic writing rubric might assess organization, communication of ideas, grammar, vocabulary, and mechanics (spelling, capitalization, punctuation). The following holistic writing rubric (adapted from Fleurquin, 2003, p. 21) is intended for use as a standardized assessment of writing. It could be simplified for classroom assessment and also adapted for assessing speaking, substituting pronunciation for mechanics.

HOLISTIC WRITING RUBRIC	
Points	**Descriptor**
9–10	Communicates all the requested information. Grammar, vocabulary, and mechanics do not interfere with the message.
7–8	Communicates the requested information. Mistakes in grammar, vocabulary, and mechanics slightly interfere with getting the message across.
5–6	Communicates most of the requested information. Mistakes make the message hard to understand.
3–4	Much of the requested information is not included. Mistakes hinder comprehension.
1–2	Attempts at expressing ideas in writing are unsuccessful.

Below is an example of an analytic rubric for narrative writing for young learners.

NARRATIVE WRITING	
Possible Points	**Score**
1. Three complete sentences	9
2. Spelling is understandable	2
3. Capitals at the beginning of sentences, "I", proper nouns	2
4. Periods, exclamation marks and question marks	2
5. Spacing between words	2
6. Descriptive language	3
Total	20

The following analytic writing rubric is adapted from one used by the Instituto Cultural Peruano Norteamericano (ICPNA) in Lima, Peru:

RUBRIC FOR WRITING SKILLS			
WRITING	**SCORES**		
	0	**1**	**2**
Accuracy	Student was unable to use target form(s).	Student was able to use target form(s) successfully some of the time.	Student was able to use target form(s) successfully most of the time.
Communication	Student demonstrates little or no focus on the topic, and ideas are not clearly connected.	Student provides some focus on the topic, and some ideas are clearly connected.	Student maintains consistent focus on the topic, and ideas are clearly connected.

ADAPTED FROM YOUNG STUDENTS PROGRAM, ICPNA, LIMA, PERU

Effective Assessment Activities

Assessing Oral Language For very young learners, the major focus of assessment will be on oral language development. Even after children have developed some literacy in English, assessment of oral language will continue to be important, since much of their learning will involve interacting with others orally. But what features of oral language should be assessed? Bachman and Palmer (1996) identify four types of knowledge that we draw on in oral interaction and that we should note in our assessment of children's developing oral communication:

1. **Grammatical knowledge:** the ability to use vocabulary, syntax, and phonology to speak clearly, with appropriate pronunciation and intonation, and to understand others' pronunciation, intonation, and word choice

2. **Textual knowledge:** the ability to speak in organized and expected ways, linking ideas together, and to listen and participate in conversations and other oral tasks

3. **Functional knowledge:** the ability to use language for different purposes and to understand other people's purposes

4. **Sociolinguistic knowledge:** the ability to use oral language appropriate to the context and the person(s) spoken to

Some specific activities for assessing listening and speaking are provided below. Note that almost any listening or speaking activity discussed in Chapter 4 can be used to assess, as well as teach, oral language.

Assessing listening Listening skills can be assessed almost from the beginning of a young learner's English development. Children can follow simple commands such as "Stand up" or "Point to the window," and their performance can be noted in a checklist. Or they can be asked to listen and identify something by circling a picture. For example, after having taught the names of wild animals or animals in the zoo, the teacher could say, "Listen. Circle the elephant."

Listen and Circle

a.)  b.)  c.)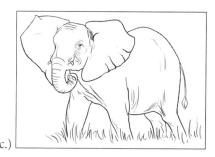

Brief listening assessments can take place during any oral discussion or when a story is being read aloud. For example, older young learners can take notes during the first few minutes of a story or discussion and then engage in a "turn and talk," discussing what is most important in what they have heard, or asking and answering questions about what happened, the main events or ideas, and important details (Dodge, 2009). This not only builds listening skills, but also helps develop active and purposeful academic listening.

Listening consists of a number of subskills to be assessed, including:

- Discriminating between individual sounds and words
- Comprehending differences in grammar (singular–plural; present–past)
- Identifying the main idea(s) in a story or oral text
- Identifying specific information

Children can demonstrate their listening ability nonverbally by:

- Circling the different sound or the same sounds
- Pointing to a picture or object
- Pointing to a word
- Responding to simple commands (as in basic TPR or a song like "Head, Shoulders, Knees, and Toes") or following oral directions
- Selecting the appropriate picture
- Drawing or coloring a picture
- Matching two pictures or a word and a picture
- Indicating Yes/No with thumbs up/down
- Numbering or putting pictures in sequence

They can also demonstrate their listening ability in speaking or writing by:

- Supplying missing words in a listening cloze
- Selecting the appropriate verbal response
- Predicting what comes next
- Retelling major episodes in a story
- Filling in a graphic organizer (as a class or in small groups or pairs)
- Identifying and correcting mistakes in a story retelling
- Providing short answers to questions
- Completing a cloze activity
- Taking dictation

In assessing listening, it is important that students know why they are listening: the purpose of the task. We should also try to make the tasks as communicative as possible, enabling us to judge how well students understand what is being said in conversation or discussion.

Assessing speaking Many assessment specialists believe that speaking is the most complex skill to assess. In assessing speaking, we are really assessing comprehensibility and communication in terms of pronunciation, grammar, vocabulary, and overall fluency.

Speaking can be assessed holistically or analytically using rubrics. Children's speaking can be assessed during class discussions, pair or small group work, conferences, or oral presentations.

Speaking assessment tasks include:

- Repeating key words or phrases (to assess pronunciation and vocabulary)
- Chanting or singing a song from memory or written text
- Engaging in information gap activities
- Using classroom language
- Retelling story episodes with pictures
- Repeating only true sentences
- Describing a picture
- Playing a guessing game
- Answering questions
- Presenting a project to the class
- Participating in role plays

Information gap activities provide an excellent opportunity to monitor children's oral language (both listening and speaking) as pairs of students work together. Some of these include:

- Describing successive items in an array or sequence (for example, clothes on a clothesline)
- Describing objects or pictures for the partner to locate its matching pair (repeated until all items have been matched).
- Following a set of directions to make something (such as making a monster's face)
- Choosing and placing objects in their right places (from a picture cue)
- Following directions to map a route
- Identifying the minor differences in pairs of pictures
  (Adapted from Education Department of Western Australia, 1997, cited in McKay, 2006, p. 205)

The time following speaking assessment can be spent on indirect error correction of grammar or vocabulary errors. Examples of common mistakes can be written on the board, read aloud by the teacher or students while students listen for mistakes, and then students can be asked to make corrections. This can also become a review for the beginning of the next class. Rather than correcting pronunciation errors, it is better to model the correct forms and have everyone repeat. With repetition, they will improve their pronunciation.

McKay (2006) gives an example of a checklist that students can use to self-assess their speaking. It asks children to check how well they think they ask or answer questions, talk about their family, introduce themselves, etc., with options of "not so well," "OK," "quite well," or "really well." She also suggests that following a self-assessment, learners can ask their peers to "check" their self-assessment, noting that engaging in peer-assessment not only increases children's "language awareness and ability to talk about language (through discussion of what makes a good performance)"; it also makes learners more responsible for their work and strengthens their "sense of being part of a classroom community" (p. 166). A way of capturing students' speaking is by audio- or videotaping them for later assessment.

Assessing Written Language
Although oral language is the foundation for written language and is more important for young learners, especially very young learners, standardized assessments ("high-stakes tests") usually involve reading and at least some basic writing, since written tests are much easier to administer and mark. Even standardized tests of listening involve some reading and writing. So assessing reading and writing, with both alternative and traditional assessment, is important. Alternative assessment (especially observation) of the beginning learner can note the incidental learning of written vocabulary or language chunks as well as initial writing tasks, such as copying or printing one's name. As children's written language proficiency increases, assessment tasks can become more comprehensive, including the use of rubrics for texts written from prompts related to unit themes and portfolios of written work.

Assessing reading Assessment of reading tasks should match the tasks used in instruction: They should also match the ways in which readers actually read. The assessment should be authentic (O'Malley & Pierce, 1996). If we want to assess how well children can skim a text for its central theme or scan it to find a specific piece of information (such as a date, the name of a character or person, or a place), then the assessment task needs to require the children to use these same processes. In designing reading assessment activities, text selection is also important. The texts should motivate the children to read, be written at the children's reading level, and be relevant. Besides stories, which are enjoyable and central to TEYL, texts can also include greeting cards, charts, poems, e-mails, or any other text that has been used in teaching.

Assessing reading, like assessing listening, is indirect, since it involves the use of actions, speaking, or writing (Pinter, 2006). Reading assessment tasks can include:

- Circling the right sound or word
- Sorting or grouping words into categories
- Matching pictures with words, phrases, or sentences
- Matching dialogs with pictures or names of characters
- Reading and coloring or labeling a diagram or picture
- Filling in words
- Rearranging letters in words or words in sentences
- Rearranging phrases or sentences of a known story or text
- Completing sentences
- Following written directions
- Answering T/F, multiple-choice, or Wh- questions
- Predicting what comes next
- Finding specific information (scanning)
- Getting the main idea (skimming)
- Using context clues to guess meaning of unknown words
- Filling in a graphic organizer (chart, table, diagram, etc.)
- Completing a cloze passage
- Retelling (parts of) a story

There are also a number of informal ways of observing children's reading: during story time, during shared reading, during oral reading, or when they are reading independently. During these times, as well, it is possible to ask children questions to determine what reading strategies they are using (and checking these off on a reading strategy checklist). For example: Are they predicting what is coming next? Do they sound out unfamiliar words? Do they re-read when they encounter a comprehension problem? Do they self-correct?

Questioning can also help determine children's vocabulary knowledge. Reading provides a meaningful context for assessing vocabulary. Children can be asked about the meaning of words in the text, and their progress can be monitored with a vocabulary checklist. During oral reading, it is also possible to keep a "running record" of children's reading, noting the "miscues" or errors that they make (Clay, 2000).

Assessing writing While the major emphasis in English classes for very young learners is on oral language, it is important to introduce writing gradually, using oral language as a basis, and to assess that writing from the beginning, when copying letters or words may be all that the learners can do. As their writing ability increases, they

Pre-K Assessment Form

1=All of the time

2=Improving on this skill (w/h=with help)

3=Needs more time

PHONICS/READING READINESS

- Interested in letters. _____
- Can recognize own name. _____
- Knows first and fast name. _____
- Sings songs and does finger plays and rhymes. _____
- Likes stories and books. _____
- Enjoys being read to. _____
- Understands that reading is done from left to right and is able to turn the pages for you in the right direction. _____
- Points to pictures in the book when asked questions about the pictures. ("Where is the dog?"... "the blue ball?" etc.) _____
- Can say the alphabet without singing it. _____
- Memorizes several short poems (nursery rhymes). _____

can be asked to write longer and more complex texts and also be expected to achieve greater fluency and accuracy. The range of texts that they write will also increase, as will the types of texts that are used in assessment. These can range from shorter and more predictable texts such as forms, greeting cards, notes, and e-mails to texts requiring more creativity and wider language (especially vocabulary) use. Eventually, children can be asked to write the following range of texts: narratives, descriptions, explanations, reports, summaries, or arguments, though in language structures and vocabulary that they have been taught and learned. We want to make writing interesting and enjoyable for children, so in evaluating children's written texts, focus first on providing feedback on the content, only correcting errors that interfere with understanding. Later, add assessment of organization, then grammar, and finally mechanics.

The following list includes writing assessments for young learners from very limited to much greater English writing ability:

- Copying letters or words
- Unscrambling letters to spell a word
- Filling in missing words (to assess vocabulary or grammar in writing)
- Labeling or describing pictures

- Doing word puzzles
- Completing sentences with sentence starters
- Writing speech bubbles for cartoon characters or characters in a story
- Rearranging sentences
- Transferring information to or from a graphic organizer
- Answering simple questions (one word, multiple choice, etc.)
- Writing a short text (such as a thank-you note, invitation, friendly e-mail, poem, or chant)
- Correcting false sentences from a story or picture
- Self-assessing using an editing or proofreading checklist
- Revising from written comments
- Responding to a writing prompt
- Describing a picture
- Writing a range of texts
- Summarizing a story or other text
- Participating in writing conferences with peers and the teacher (McKay, 2006; Weigle, 2002)

Assessing Vocabulary and Grammar

The best way to assess proficiency in vocabulary and grammar is within the context of assessing oral or written language skills, where students demonstrate their ability to understand or use English vocabulary and grammar in meaningful ways (Hughes, 2003). However, vocabulary and grammar are often tested separately in standardized tests because of the ease of administering and scoring these tests and thus, students need to be prepared for these types of assessments in their classes. Directly assessing vocabulary and grammar can also provide useful information in diagnostic or placement testing, or in achievement testing, where a set of vocabulary and grammar items are specified in the curriculum objectives.

Many of the assessment procedures discussed under "Assessing Oral Language" or "Assessing Written Language" also assess vocabulary and grammar. But the following activities can be used specifically to assess vocabulary and grammar.

Assessing vocabulary Because vocabulary comprises a large portion of what we teach young learners, it needs to be assessed using the same activities that are used to teach that vocabulary, such as the following:

- Matching pictures with words
- Labeling pictures
- Unscrambling words

- Providing missing letters in words
- Completing word puzzles
- Sorting words by content

Students can also be asked to self-assess or report their own growing English vocabulary (McKay, 2006). They can keep a vocabulary notebook, writing down new words they encounter and indicating whether they:

- Have seen the word before
- Have seen the word, but do not know what it means
- Think that the word means _____ (using synonyms or translation)
- Know that the word means _____ (using synonyms or translation)
- Can use the word in a sentence: _____ (writing a sentence)

They can be encouraged to return to their vocabulary notebooks and mark their own progress when they have learned what a word means or can use it in a sentence.

Assessing grammar Although grammar may be taught to young learners more implicitly (through repeated patterns and some discussion of these patterns, rather than through grammatical rules), we can still assess how well our students are acquiring English grammar, both in oral communication and in writing. We can also ask brief grammar-related questions when teaching a story. For example, children can be asked to describe three things a character does (verbs), the names of three animals (nouns), or three descriptive words about a character or animal (adjectives). We also can use an observational checklist of all the structures children are expected to learn during a term (such as "Can use the present tense to describe routines"), as a way of monitoring grammatical knowledge and accuracy in oral language activities. (Note that in the early stages, children will be using formulaic chunks of language, without having any knowledge of the grammar underlying their use.)

A checklist can also be used to note children's development of grammar used in speaking:

- Uses single words
- Uses chunks of language (two or more words)
- Uses phrases
- Uses simple sentences
- Uses coordinated sentences (using *and*, *but*, *or*, etc.)
- Uses complex sentences

Student Name	Uses single words	Uses chunks of language (two or more words)	Uses phrases	Uses simple sentences	Uses coordinated sentences (using *and, but, or,* etc.)	Uses complex sentences	
Mohamed Hassan	9/3/12						
Naimah Al Haiki	9/3/12	9/10/12					
Ali Al Kaissy	9/3/12						
Samir Nasri	9/3/12	9/10/12					

This can be expanded by noting how often the learner does these, using what Brewster, Ellis, and Girard (2004, p. 249) refer to as the NOFAN 5-point scale (Never, Occasionally, Frequently, Always, or Naturally), when they use a checklist that assesses how well learners perform when:

- Circling the correct verb (tense, number, etc.) or filling in blanks
- Changing a false sentence to true
- Transforming a sentence to a question
- Changing sentences from singular to plural or present to past tense
- Sequencing events with *yesterday, today,* and *tomorrow*

Designing Effective Assessment for a Lesson

In the following lesson plan (taken from Chapter 3), which is part of a thematic unit on Rainforests and the Value of Trees, there are a number of places where alternative, informal assessments can take place. These assessments provide feedback to learners; they also help the teacher make decisions about needed adjustments in instruction.

The Great Kapok Tree by Lynne Cherry

Student profile	Grades 4–5, intermediate level of English proficiency
Skills to be emphasized	Listening and speaking
Language	Grammar: Need + tree for _____ Vocabulary: kapok tree; names of the animals in the story; rainforest; kapok tree; parts of the tree; Amazon River
Objectives	By the end of this lesson, students will be able to: • Talk about the value of the tree in relation to several of the animals in the story
Materials	Beautiful pictures of different kinds of trees from their context and other countries (printed from the Internet on paper or put in a PowerPoint slide show) A graphic organizer of a tree with lines pointing to the roots, trunk, branches, and leaves of the tree—2 copies for each student Pictures of animals from the book

Warm-up

Capture their attention	Show students many beautiful pictures of different kinds of tress from their country and other countries. Some of the trees may look very strange and wondrous to them. Ask them, "What are these? Where can you find these trees?" Take a globe or a map and point out where there are rainforests where these trees are found.
Connect to prior knowledge and experiences	**Think-Pair-Share (T-P-S)** Ask the students to **think** individually about all the ways in which we use trees: their value to us. Then share their ideas in a **pair** with one partner, filling out one of the tree graphic organizers. Then as a class, **share** their ideas and fill out a large tree organizer on the board. *Assessment: As the children work in pairs, circulate and observe how well they are doing, providing assistance to those who need it.*

Preview the cover of the storybook	Tell the class that you are going to read *The Great Kapok Tree* to them. Show them the cover picture and ask them if anyone has seen a kapok tree. Let them describe it and what they see on the cover. Point to the animals, the man with the ax, and all the flowers. Ask them where they think the story takes place and what they think the book is going to be about.
Pre-teach new vocabulary or expressions	Using picture cards of the individual animals, with their name on the card, teach the names of the animals. Introduce the rainforest, show them a map of the world where there are rainforests, and then point to the Amazon River and Brazil, where the story takes place. Have them name the animals. *Assessment: As the children name the animals, note pronunciation and later, if necessary, teach pronunciation by providing words with similar sound patterns.*
Give students a purpose for listening	Tell the students that as you read, you want them to listen specifically for the names of the animals and the value of the tree to that animal. They can take notes as you read.
Presentation	
Storytelling using the book	Break students into 10 pairs or groups, so each pair/group has one graphic organizer with WHO? WHAT? WHY? to use together. (Make sure that the students note the ways that animals communicate; for example, the boa constrictor hisses as he tells the man with the ax not to cut down the tree.) Assign each group an animal and tell them to write the name of the animal in the WHO box. WHO? *Boa constrictor* WHAT? *Hissed don't chop down the tree* WHY? *Ancestors lived there, tree of miracles* Pause with each page and review what happened with students. Cue each pair/group to take notes on their graphic organizer as you read. But also tell the students to listen to the information about other animals because they will need it later. *Assessment: Observe the pairs/groups as their turn comes to see if they are on task and able to do the work.*

Practice	
Retell part of the story	**Draw and Retell** Pairs or groups draw the scene about their animal and prepare to present "who," "what," and "why" based on the story. They take their notes from the graphic organizer and write the sentences they will present. Be sure each member of the group or pair presents an equal amount. Put all of the pictures on the board in the order of the story, then begin to retell the story, having each group present what they prepared. *Assessment: While the students are drawing their scenes, check the graphic organizers to be sure the information is accurate and to let students know if changes are needed.*
Controlled practice	Put up a large picture of the kapok tree. As you name an animal, ask students to explain the value of the kapok tree and point to the part of the tree that is valuable to that animal and say, _____ needs the tree for _____. *Assessment: Write the students' responses on the board (creating a number of sentences) and make needed changes in vocabulary, grammar, etc. Review these where needed.*
Application	
Independent activity: Personalize content	**Our Tree** Ask students to name the trees in their local context. "What trees do we have here?" Make a list. Then have students choose one, draw it, and write their own page modeled after what their animal said, using their own reasons for needing the tree. *Assessment: Collect these and briefly review each student's work. Provide praise.*
Assessment	
Assessment: Exit Ticket	As each student leaves class, ask them to name one of the animals and something that animal needs from the kapok tree. Or they can explain their own personal reason for needing trees.
Follow-up	
Homework	Ask the students to search for rainforests on the Internet and to see what other trees and animals live there. The next class will be about rainforests.

■ Teacher to Teacher

Teachers' Perspectives on Assessment

Countries and educational institutions have various policies and practices related to the use of traditional and alternative assessment, and the importance of appropriate assessment for young learners, as the following teachers from Oman and Croatia indicate.

> **"**As for assessment at the primary level in Oman which is from grades 1 to 4 (6–9 years old), there is a requirement of assessment, but they don't care that much about the traditional tests. They only assess by observation, different motivating activities, etc. However, I teach in an elementary school which has levels from 5 to 10 (9–15 years old) and here the assessment is necessary and we should follow the MOE assessment methods. In English, we have informal assessment which consists of continuous assessment and includes writing, reading, speaking, listening and vocabulary and grammar and informal records which are descriptive reports of each student's behavior, attitudes and progress and formal assessment which includes the short tests and the final tests from the MOE.**"**

> —*Asma Al Dhahab, Primary English Teacher, Oman*

> **"**I usually design my own assessment materials, taking into account the level and age of my learners, the aims I have set for them, and activities they feel comfortable and familiar with. I sometimes resort to the published tests I have if I find them appropriate to what I want to assess. I use published self-assessment materials. I practice both formative and summative assessment. I can't imagine proceeding to another unit or activity if I see that some students didn't understand what was to be done or if at least they didn't get the message right. I sometimes even change my lesson plan spot-on because of that. Summative assessment is somewhat obligatory, usually in a written form. I place summative assessments at the end of each unit. I used to have diagnostic tests and end-of-year tests but not anymore. I started using portfolios, i.e. my students carry notebooks where they write, draw, paste all given materials and their work. I try to check it regularly and write feedback to them and the parents. There is also an observation process, but the feedback is written to the school registry. The feedback from the observation process is usually orally presented to the parents by the class tutor, but sometimes I also write it in the portfolios.**"**

> —*Darija Sostaric-Zuckermann, Primary English Teacher, Croatia*

Portfolios are a particularly effective form of alternative assessment, providing information to students and their parents, as well as the teacher, as this teacher from Ukraine discusses.

"I also use portfolios for assessment. They have recently become an alternative to traditional assessment in Ukraine. The content is selected to show the growth of the students' achievement over time. My students and I select the work samples that go in portfolios. Such work engages students in self-assessment, showing them possibilities for reflection. Then in pairs or in groups students evaluate a sample they want to put in their portfolios. They discuss their strengths and weaknesses, thus improving their work. I usually involve students in meaningful activities that will be worth sharing with other students, teachers, parents. By the way, parents are great collaborators at home and at school.

[Recently, my students] were writing letters to their pen pals. I did not mark the mistakes in my students' portfolios; however, they were able to write some notes beforehand and ask me to check. Those letters were checked in the exercise-books; then the students worked individually and 'designed' their own letters, rewriting the content. There are some advantages in this process:

- students felt confident and secure;
- they practised their rewriting skills; and
- they could make some changes."

—*Nataliya Nayavko, Primary English Teacher, Ukraine*

Teachers also play an important role in preparing children for tests, as this teacher from Brazil discusses.

"I believe lots of things can influence a child's performance on a test, and definitely the teacher's methodology may be one of them. I wouldn't say it is the teacher's fault, but if most students in a class don't do well on a test, there is something wrong with the test or with the teaching. Before testing, we must be sure we have explored the topics thoroughly, providing every child with the opportunity to learn, which means exploring different intelligences. When testing children I think we have to bear in mind that they might not understand the instructions. Therefore, it's important to go through the test with them, explaining what they should do in each exercise. . . . Another important point is that teachers must know how their students are going to be tested so that they can prepare similar types of exercises to be done in class. It's different from preparing classes based on what students will be tested. It means our students will feel confident because they are familiar with that kind of activity; their anxiety will be under control. When teachers are not the ones who design the tests, it's essential to show them the test before students take it and listen to their opinions. Tests should reflect what we teach; there can´t be any surprises."

—*Ana Maria Scandiuzzi, EFL Instructor, Brazil*

Teachers also need to provide a variety of assessments. This teacher from Belarus talks about the range of assessments that she uses with her students.

"As for me, I use various types of assessment in my work. I want to share my experience of testing with you. Our books have thematic planning. At the end of the unit students write a test. It can be a vocabulary and grammar test. It includes five tasks, starting with less demanding word-level tasks and moving on to creative writing. I use speaking tests as well. . . . The first task encourages prepared speaking whereas the second task encourages children to speak spontaneously. My students like listening tests. Pictures, examples, lexical, grammar structures help young learners to cope with tests. I make sure that children understand instructions before they start doing the test. As we develop all-round communicative competence it's better to use oral tasks. Project work gives children an opportunity to use the language more freely and to communicate a message of their own. Projects involve creativity, drawing skills, develop basic presentation skills."

—*Irina Melikhava, Primary English Teacher, Belarus*

This teacher trainer has found a number of ways to assess students' speaking.

"If assessment implies a cycle of progress where teachers and learners reflect upon how to improve certain performance, speaking should be a progressive gathering of while-speaking information. . . . Collecting speaking evidence can be done through recordings. I remember my first collections of spoken evidence about 14 years ago were notes on students' performance and their written or oral reaction after having done a speaking activity such as an interview or a thematic presentation. Later, I started to take notes on checklists and rubrics so that students could have immediate feedback after some selected spoken interaction. They used to keep that sheet where we had written down comments on their performance and they decided by the end of the course if it had been helpful or not."

—*Luis Manuel Gonzalez Garcia, Teacher Trainer, Mexico*

■ Chapter Summary

To Conclude

Considerations for assessing young learners There are a number of issues that make the assessment of young language learners complex. These include (1) their age and overall development; (2) the degree of focus on oral skills in the classroom; (3) the types of activities used in teaching and learning; (4) the goals of the program; and (5) the approach to teaching and learning.

Understanding the broad topic of assessment involves becoming familiar with a number of basic terms and concepts Some of the important basic assessment terms and concepts include (1) assessment, testing, and evaluation; (2) informal and formal assessment; (3) formative and summative assessment; (4) criterion- and norm-referenced tests; and (5) integrative and discrete point tests.

Fundamental criteria to guide the development of language assessments In developing or selecting language assessments, it is important to determine their reliability, validity, practicality, authenticity, and washback.

Guidelines for effective assessment of young learners In addition to meeting the five fundamental criteria discussed above, assessments for young learners should: mirror learning, contribute to learning, motivate learners and build learner confidence, include a variety of techniques for learners' different intelligences and learning styles, allow all learners to experience success, be contextualized and reflect relevant tasks and language for young learners, and take place over time.

Purposes and types of formal tests The purposes and types of formal tests include diagnosing student learning difficulties or areas in need of further instruction (diagnostic tests); initially placing students at the proper language level (placement tests); measuring and reporting student progress in learning the curriculum (achievement tests); and providing an overall picture of a student's language development (proficiency).

Purposes and types of alternative assessments These alternatives to traditional assessment for young learners include: observations, conferences and oral interviews, writing samples, story retellings, projects, portfolios, other performances, and self- or peer-assessments.

Rating alternative assessments Differences in the type of assessment also result in differences in the ways in which these assessments are scored. Some ways of scoring or rating alternative assessments include: brief feedback, checklists, and rubrics.

Assessing oral language The major focus of assessment for young learners is on oral language development. Even after children have developed some literacy in English, assessment of oral language will continue to be important, since much of children's language learning will involve interacting with others orally. A number of activities are available to assess young learner listening and speaking skills.

Assessing written language Although oral language is the foundation for written and is more important for young learners, especially very young learners, standardized assessments ("high-stakes tests") usually involve reading and at least some basic writing, since written tests are much easier to administer and mark. Therefore, assessing reading and writing, with both alternative and traditional assessment, is important. A number of activities are available for assessing young learner reading and writing skills.

Assessing vocabulary and grammar The best way to assess proficiency in using vocabulary and grammar is within the context of assessing oral or written language skills, where students demonstrate their ability to understand or use English vocabulary and grammar in meaningful ways. However, because vocabulary and grammar are often tested separately in standardized tests, learners need to be prepared for these types of assessments in their classes.

■ Over to You

Discussion Questions

1. What are some types of alternative assessments you might use with young learners? What are the advantages and disadvantages of each? If you interviewed an EYL teacher, what did you learn about the types of assessments used in the class and the reasons for each. Were there any alternative or classroom-based assessment that the teacher uses?

2. Imagine you are an EYL teacher who is going to be evaluated on the basis of a teaching portfolio. What items would you want to include? What kinds of student work would you place in the portfolio and why?

3. What is the value of standardized assessments? What are their limitations? If possible, gather information about one of the commercial international English language tests for young learners—such as the Cambridge Young Learners English Test (YLE) or the Pearson Test of English Young Learners (PTE)—or a test given by a regional or national educational body (such as a Ministry of Education) and examine it in terms of the criteria for effective assessments for young learners discussed in this chapter. What language skills are assessed? How are they assessed? Are there any integrated tasks?

4. Think back to your experiences as a language learner. Which types of assessments were most useful to you? Which were least useful? Why?

<table>
<tr><td>**Lesson Planning**</td><td>Choose any lesson from your curriculum or from a teacher's edition of an EYL series and indicate the assessment techniques you would use. Focus especially on alternative assessments you can use while you are teaching the lesson. If there is no end-of-class or end-of-unit assessment, create one that integrates several of the four language skills (listening, speaking, reading, and writing).</td></tr>
<tr><td>**Write About It**</td><td>**Planning Assessments:** Now that you have had the chance to think about the special considerations we need to make when assessing young learners, what types of assessments do you plan to use with your young or very young learners? Write a plan of assessments that you wish to use and why. If you know of standardized tests that are used in your local schools (for placement, achievement, or proficiency), be sure to include these as well.</td></tr>
</table>

■ Resources and References

Print Publications

Alternative Assessment. (2001). Special issue. *Language Testing 18*(4).

Assessing Young Learners. (2000). Special issue. *Language Testing, 17*(2).

Brown, H. D., and Abeywickrama, P. (2010). *Language assessment: Principles and classroom practices,* 2nd ed. White Plains, NY: Pearson Longman.

McKay, P. (2006). *Assessing young language learners.* Cambridge, UK: Cambridge University Press.

O'Malley, J. M., & Pierce, L. V. (1996). *Authentic assessment for English language learners: Practical approaches for teachers.* Boston, MA: Addison-Wesley.

Useful Web Sites

Authentic Assessment Toolbox by J. Mueller: A practical approach for developing authentic assessment: http://jonathan.mueller.faculty.noctrl.edu/toolbox/index.htm

Common European Framework of Reference for Languages: Learning, Teaching, Assessment (CEFR): http://www.coe.int/t/dg4/linguistic/cadre_en.asp

Language Testing Videos with a focus on validity and reliability by G. Fulcher and R. Thrasher: http://languagetesting.info/video/main.html#list

Shaping the Way We Teach English: Alternative Assessment: http://oelp.uoregon.edu/shaping.html

Rubrics for Teachers: www.rubrics4teachers.com/

Understanding Assessment: A Tutorial on Assessment for Foreign Language Teachers: http://www.cal.org/flad/tutorial/

Can-Do Web Sites: The WIDA CAN-DO descriptors used in United States: http://www.wida.us/standards/CAN_DOs/

The Junior English Language Portfolio based on the Common European Framework of Reference for Languages: http://www.primarylanguages.org.uk/resources/assessment_and_recording/european_languages_portfolio.aspx

References

Bachman, L. (1990). *Fundamental considerations in language testing.* New York, NY: Oxford University Press.

Bachman, L., & Palmer, A. S. (1996). *Language testing in practice.* Oxford, UK: Oxford University Press.

Bachman, L., & Palmer, A. S. (2010). *Language assessment in practice: Developing language assessments and justifying their use in the real world.* Oxford, UK: Oxford University Press.

Bailey, K. (1998). *Learning about language assessment: Dilemmas, decisions, and directions.* Cambridge, MA: Heinle & Heinle.

Black, P., Harrison, C., Lee, C., Marshall, B., & William, D. (2004). Working inside the black box: Assessment for learning in the classroom. *Phi Delta Kappan, 86*(1), 8–21. Available at http://sasphhs.pennhillswiki.com/file/view/Article+BlackWrkBlBox.pdf/123146949/Article+BlackWrkBlBox.pdf

Black, P., & William, D. (1998). Assessment and classroom learning. *Assessment in Education, 5,* 7–74.

Black, P., & William, D. (2001). Inside the black box: Raising standards through classroom assessment. Available at http://weaeducation.typepad.co.uk/files/blackbox-1.pdf

Brewster, J., Ellis, G., & Girard, D. (2002). *The primary English teacher's guide.* London, UK: Penguin.

Brown, H. D., & Abeywickrama, P. (2010). *Language assessment: Principles and classroom practices,* 2nd ed. White Plains, NY: Pearson Education.

Butler, Y. G., & Lee, J. (2010). The effects of self-assessment among young learners of English. *Language Testing, 27*(1), 5–31.

Cameron, L. (2001). *Teaching languages to young learners.* Cambridge, UK: Cambridge University Press.

Clay, M. (2000). *Running records for classroom teachers.* Portsmouth, NH: Heinemann.

Crandall, J. A., & Grenblatt, L. (1999). Teaching beyond the middle: Meeting the needs of underschooled and high-achieving immigrant students. In M. R. Basterra (Ed.), *Excellence and equity in education for language minority students: Critical issues and promising practices* (pp. 43–80). Washington, DC: Mid-Atlantic Equity Center, The American University.

Dodge, J. (2009). *25 quick formative assessments for a differentiated classroom.* New York: Scholastic.

Ellis, G., & Morrow, K. (2004). *ELT Journal "Year of the Young Learner": Special collection.* Oxford, UK: Oxford University Press.

Fleurquin, F. (2003). Development of a standardized test for young EFL learners. *Spaan Fellow Working Papers in Second or Foreign Language Assessment, 1*(3), 1–23.

Gardner, H. (1983). *Frames of mind: The theory of multiple intelligences.* New York, NY: Basic Books.

Gardner, H. (1999). *Intelligence reframed: Multiple intelligences for the 21st century.* New York, NY: Basic Books.

Gattullo, F. (2000). Formative assessment in ELT primary (elementary) classrooms: An Italian case study. *Language Testing 17*(2), 278–288.

Gordon, T. (2007). *Teaching young children a second language.* Westport, CT: Praeger.

Hasselgren, A. (2000). The assessment of the English ability of young learners in Norwegian schools: An innovative approach. *Language Testing, 17*(2), 261–277.

Hasselgren, A. (2012). Assessing young learners. In G. Fulcher & F. Davidson (Eds.), *The Routledge handbook of language testing* (pp. 93–105). New York, NY: Routledge.

Hughes, A. (2003). *Testing for language teachers,* 2nd ed. Cambridge, UK: Cambridge University Press.

Hurley, S. R. & Blake, S. (2001). Assessment in the content areas for students acquiring English. In S. R. Hurley & J. V. Tinajero (Eds.) Literacy Assessment of Second Language (pp. 84–103). Needham Heights, MA: Allyn and Bacon.

Ioannou-Georgiou, S., & Pavlou, P. (2003). *Assessing young learners.* Oxford, UK: Oxford University Press.

Kirsch, C. (2008). *Teaching foreign languages in the primary school.* New York, NY: Continuum.

Lunn, R. L., & Gronlund, N. E. (2000). *Measurement and assessment in teaching,* 8th ed. Upper Saddle River, NJ: Merrill.

McKay, P. (2006). *Assessing young learners.* Cambridge, UK: Cambridge University Press.

McMillan. J. H. (2003). Understanding and improving teachers' classroom assessment decision-making: Implications for theory and practice. *Educational Measurement: Issues and Practices, 22,* 312–326.

McNamara, T. (2001). Rethinking alternative assessment. *Language Testing, 18*(4), 329–332.

Messick, S. (1989). Validity. In R. Linn (Ed.), *Educational measurement,* 3rd ed. (pp. 13–103). Washington, DC: American Council on Education/Macmillan.

Moon, J., & Nikolov, M. (2000). *Research into teaching English to young learners.* Pecs, HU: University Press Pecs.

O'Malley, J. M., & Pierce, L. V. (1996). *Authentic assessment for English language learners: Practical approaches for teachers.* Boston, MA: Addison-Wesley.

Paris, S. G., & Newman, R. S. (1990). Developmental aspects of self-regulated learning. *Educational Leadership, 25*(1), 87–102.

Paulson, F. L., Paulson, P. P., & Meyer, C. A. (1991). What makes a portfolio a portfolio? *Educational Leadership, 58*(5), 60–63.

Pierce, L. V., & O'Malley, J. M. (1992). *Performance and portfolio assessment for language minority students.* Washington, DC: National Clearinghouse for Bilingual Education. Available at http://www.ncela.gwu.edu/files/rcd/BE018651/PIG9.pdf

Pinter, A. (2006). *Teaching young English language learners.* Oxford, UK: Oxford University Press.

Puckett, M. E., & Black, J. K. (2000). *Authentic assessment of the young child.* Upper Saddle River, NJ: Prentice-Hall.

Rea-Dickins, P., & Gardner, S. (2000). Snares and silver bullets: Disentangling the construct of formative assessment. *Language Testing, 17*(2), 215–243.

Rea-Dickins, P., & Rixon, S. (1999). Assessment of young learners' English: Reasons and means. In S. Rixon (Ed.), *Young learners of English: Some research perspectives* (pp. 89-102). London: Longman.

Ross, S. (2005). The impact of assessment methods on foreign language proficiency growth. *Applied Linguistics, 26*(3), 317–342.

Saricoban, A., & Kuntas, E. (2010). Assessing young learners. In B. Haznedar & H. H. Uysal (Eds.), *Handbook for teaching foreign languages to young learners in primary school* (pp. 351–374). Ankara: Ana Yayincilik.

Shaaban, K. (2005). Assessment of young learners. *English Teaching Forum, 43*(4), 34–50.

Shohamy, E. (2001). *The power of tests: The impact of language tests in teaching and learning.* Harlow, UK: Longman.

Torrance, H., & Pryor, J. (1998). *Investigating formative assessment: Teaching, learning and assessment in the classroom.* Oxford, UK: Oxford University Press.

Wall, D., & Alderson, J. C. (1993). Examining washback: The Sri Lankan impact study. *Language Testing, 10*(1), 41–70.

Weigle, S. C. (2002). *Assessing writing.* Cambridge, UK: Cambridge University Press.

Weir, C. J. (1993). *Understanding and developing language tests.* London, UK: Prentice-Hall.

8

Classroom Management

■ Getting Started

Think About It

This chapter explores the teacher as manager from different perspectives. It outlines different aspects of managing the classroom that will help teachers reconsider their current approach and develop new strategies to cope with the challenges of teaching young learners. In addition, it encourages teachers to incorporate English into classroom management routines that will create an English-speaking environment.

Who was your favorite teacher in primary school? Why was s/he your favorite teacher? Describe her or him in a paragraph using the words in the Word Bank below.

Justin Guariglia/Getty Images

WORD BANK	
Personality	Rules
Control	Manage
Time	Organized
Patience	Routine

Who was your least favorite teacher in primary school? Why was s/he your least favorite teacher? Describe her or him in a paragraph using the words in the Word Bank above.

What do you think the biggest challenges are in managing young learners in the EYL classroom? Make a list that you can refer to at the end of the chapter.

Brainstorming Web

Brainstorm all the different ways a teacher is a manager. Complete the sentence in the center of the web: "An effective teacher is a good manager of _____." Try to think of as many different words as possible. One example has been given: "An effective teacher is a good manager of time."

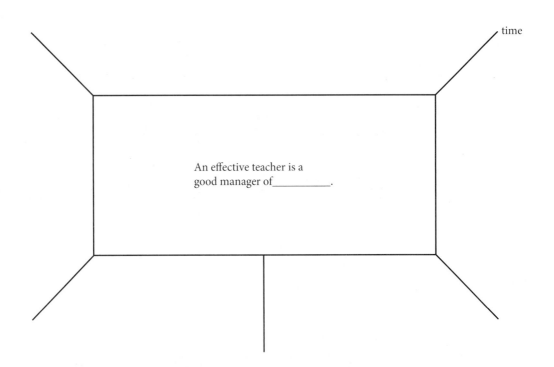

If possible, observe a fellow teacher who is considered a model primary school teacher. S/he does not have to be an English teacher. See what strategies and techniques s/he uses to manage young learners in her/his classroom. Write them down and decide which ones you could use to improve your classroom management skills.

■ Theory, Planning and Application

Why Teachers Need to Be Good Managers

Managing classrooms has always been a challenge for teachers. Whether the class has 15 students or 60 students at one time, or whether the class has students of the same age or many different ages, teachers everywhere find it challenging to keep YLs (Young Learners) engaged in the learning process without distraction. A well-known image from a Norman Rockwell painting depicts a common scene within a traditional American classroom where a boy is writing out his misconduct on the board as punishment for misbehaving. Although teachers today do not typically use this method of discipline any more, it shows the prevalence of managing learners through a system of punishment which still exists today, albeit in different forms.

Take a look at the rules established by an anonymous teacher. Think about whether this reflects how you approach your classroom.

Obviously this is a joke, one which is well known among teachers in the United States. You can find many stores that sell this on t-shirts, coffee mugs, and notepads because all teachers feel the common frustration of our young students being out of control in the classroom. This chapter will help you avoid feeling like the anonymous teacher who first wrote this comical classroom management joke.

Classroom management is an essential part of teaching young learners. The goals are "fostering student engagement and securing cooperation so that teaching and learning can occur" (Evertson & Emmer, 2013, p. 1). It is not enough to understand methods and approaches for teaching and learning a foreign language without paying attention to the basics of managing learners of a certain age. Unlike adults and even teenagers who can manage their own learning process and have the ability to understand why they are sitting in English class, children are ruled by their own immediate needs and desires, which usually do not include learning a foreign language. Therefore, English teachers of young learners need to develop a plan for managing their classroom that will keep learners engaged and on task and avoid giving them opportunities to misbehave and get out of control. After all, if your YLs are out of control, then they will not learn much English.

Managing a class full of YLs can be very difficult, particularly for new teachers or for experienced teachers who are teaching young learners for the first time. YLs have so much energy, are so easily distracted, and tend to be very egocentric. They can get rowdy fairly easily if you give them the chance. However, there are ways the teacher can keep control of the classroom while still giving students the chance to interact and be active in the learning process. The goal is to create a positive and productive atmosphere for learning to take place. In order to do this, teachers have to become good managers.

Teachers as Managers In the discovery activity, you brainstormed the different ways teachers are managers. Classroom management is often thought of as controlling the behavior of students, but there are so many aspects of teaching that can affect the behavior of students. This chapter will first explore different ways teachers are managers and give some practical tips for creating an effective environment for teaching.

Effective teachers need to be good managers of the following aspects of teaching:

- Time
- Activities
- Transitions
- Student behavior
- Conflict with and among students
- Atmosphere in the classroom
- Student feelings and emotions
- Teacher's own behavior
- Teacher's own feelings and emotions
- Students' use of L1 (native language)
- Teacher's use of L1

A skilled teacher consciously manages every aspect of the items above. Although every teacher must master them, a teacher of young learners has a greater challenge because, compared to adults, children have more difficulty managing their own behavior. In addition, a teacher of English as a foreign language has the added challenge of controlling the class in a language students may not respond to. In the following sections, the various items listed above will be grouped into the major aspects of classroom management that teachers need to explore:

1. Managing the pace of class
2. Managing behavior with routines
3. Managing behavior with rules
4. Managing the classroom climate
5. Managing the language used in class

1. Managing the pace of class Because young learners have short attention spans, teachers need to move quickly from activity to activity. Staying too long on one activity can make young learners bored and restless and cause some students to misbehave. In order to keep your students engaged, teachers need to master managing the following:

■ Time
■ Activities
■ Transitions

Managing time The teacher should keep the class moving from activity to activity and interject fun activities throughout the class period. If the class is engaging with never a dull moment, the time will fly and your YLs will not have long stretches of time to start misbehaving. Although the teacher has to maintain the pace of class, s/he should also remember to give enough "wait time" for students to answer. Wait time is the amount of time a teacher waits for a student to answer a question. For students learning a foreign language, it is necessary to give them enough time to formulate their answers in their heads before saying them out loud. The teacher can ask a question, provide sufficient wait time, at least 3–5 seconds, and then call on a student to respond. Although most teachers seem uncomfortable waiting more than 1 second for a response, waiting about 3–5 seconds can increase the quantity and quality of responses (Crooks & Chaudron, 2001; Nunan, 1991).

Managing activities Planning the materials and instructions for all activities ahead of time will help you keep the pace of your class. Fumbling around looking for materials or trying to think of ways to explain the activity directions on the spot can waste considerable time in the classroom and encourage your YLs to misbehave or become disengaged. If your activities need some supplies, like paper, markers, scissors, and glue, then you should organize the materials before the class and plan for some time to be spent passing out the supplies to each student. If the activity requires complicated instructions, then it will be important to prepare simplified instructions with a model to demonstrate. Particularly with group activities, teachers need to prepare carefully for every aspect of the activity.

Using transition activities Moving from one activity to the next takes planning and some creativity. For example, if you have students working in pairs on a dialog, you will need to get their attention before moving on to the next part of the activity. Use attention getters like whistles, bells, or even turning off the lights. Getting students' attention quickly and efficiently is important to keep the pace of the class. In addition, it is important to incorporate brain breaks. If you have a physical activity that requires students to move around, then you may want to transition to a quiet activity by using a brain break such as having YLs rest their heads in their arms on the desk. This will calm them down before you begin explaining the next activity. Later in this chapter you will find many suggestions for fun and snappy attention getters as well as effective brain breaks.

Experienced teachers seem to keep a good pace effortlessly, filling each moment of the classroom with engaging activities and smooth transitions. Undoubtedly these teachers have built-in purposeful routines that they have mastered after years of practice and experimentation. The next section will describe the kinds of routines that an EYL teacher can build.

2. **Managing behavior with routines** One of the main ways to manage a class full of young learners is to develop classroom routines. As Brewster, Ellis, and Girard (2002) explain: "Young children gradually become familiar with established routines that help them feel confident. Anxious or immature learners will tend to react negatively to changes in the normal classroom pattern, so it is a good idea to develop familiar patterns with young learners in their first year of schooling" (p. 219). For example, the teacher should establish daily routines such as:

- Starting the class with a greeting
- Designating classroom helpers ("helping hands")
- Taking attendance ("roll call")
- Establishing the date and day
- Establishing objective(s)

- Cleaning up the room
- Giving homework
- Ending the class

If a teacher establishes certain routines that YLs can expect, then students will have a sense of security every time they walk into the classroom. Some teachers put a routine map on the wall, so students have a visual cue of every part of the class period.

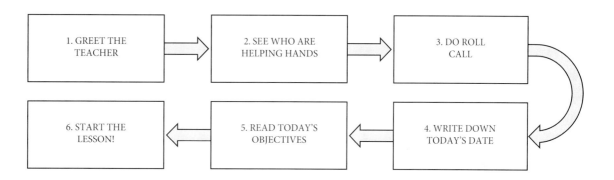

In addition, the teacher can designate certain parts of the board to communicate the day's objective(s) and the homework. In the example below, the teacher uses the abbreviation SWBAT, which stands for "Students will be able to" (see Chapter 3).

Monday, September 10, 2012
OBJECTIVES: SWBAT . . .

Identify different kinds of weather
Sing the weather song

HOMEWORK:

Draw your favorite weather

In this example, the teacher writes the date, objectives, and homework assignment on the left side of the board every day. Students know where to find the information every class. Or, if students are at a lower level, the teacher can build the same routine using visuals.

Later in this chapter, the section on Effective Classroom Management Activities will describe in detail lots of practical ideas for establishing classroom routines.

3.   **Managing behavior with rules**   Teachers of YLs always have rules. How you set up those rules and how you enforce them will determine your success as a teacher. Of course, appropriate rules depend on the school or classroom culture and could differ from country to country, region to region, or even school to school. We will look at the following aspects of using rules to manage your class effectively:

- Be sure you know the school rules and incorporate them into your classroom.
- Clearly communicate the rules and co-construct rules with students whenever possible.
- Be sure that the rules incorporate consequences for both positive and negative behavior.
- Enforce rules consistently and mediate conflict with and among students fairly.
- Involve parents or family members to help manage YLs' behavior.

Enforce school rules First, it is important for teachers to know what the school rules are and incorporate them into their classroom. For example, some schools have rules about students leaving the classroom to use the bathroom or to go to the school nurse. Many schools require students to carry a "hall pass" or some other object to indicate that they have permission to be out of the classroom. In addition, most primary schools have rules like no running in the hallway or no chewing gum in class. English teachers, like all teachers in a school, need to follow school rules and enforce them consistently.

Rules are clearly communicated and co-constructed Children actually like working within a framework of rules. The teacher should set up boundaries of acceptable and unacceptable behavior that are reasonable and consistent. YLs will feel more comfortable when rules and expectations for behavior are communicated clearly. This means establishing what these rules are at the very beginning of the school year. It could mean explaining the rules in students' native language and then establishing them in English. Teachers can even co-construct class contracts or class rules with older children, which helps them become more responsible for their own behavior (Brewster, Ellis, & Girard, 2004; Moon, 2000). When a list of rules is created as a class, and all students can participate in this process, teachers can more easily enforce the rules because students have a hand in making them. In fact, if the teacher and all students sign them like a contract, students will be more likely to abide by those rules. See the examples from Darija Sostaric Zuckermann in the Teacher to Teacher section of this chapter.

Consequences for positive and negative behavior When establishing the rules, teachers should communicate the expectations based on both positive behavior and negative behavior. Here are some basic rules that can be set by the teacher or co-constructed with the teacher's guidance:

Rules:
1. Do not talk when someone is talking.
2. Raise your hand if you want to say something.
3. Be kind to others.
4. Work hard.
5. Share.
6. Cooperate.

Once the rules are communicated, the teacher can establish consequences for certain actions. If there are no consequences, students won't follow the rules.

Many teachers like to hold students accountable to the group for their behavior. Teaching children that being disruptive affects the whole class is a good lesson in behavior. Here is an example in which students are not punished individually. Points are taken from a group rather than from each student individually. This is to encourage students to monitor each other and help the teacher enforce the rules. Then good behavior is rewarded for the groups of students who follow the rules. The teacher can keep track using points and smiley faces on the board or on a poster on the wall. Some teachers let students make up group names and keep points for their group. For example, each group could name itself after the members' favorite animal, video game character, or pop star. Then the group that has the least number of points for misbehaving at the end of the week gets their favorite song played for a 2-minute dance party, gets candy or stickers, or can line up first for recess. Depending on your country or school culture, you can decide on the appropriate reward. This could be a way to reward positive behavior instead of only punishing bad behavior.

In order to co-construct the consequences or to check comprehension of the rules, the teacher could create a presentation that highlights each situation one by one and elicits actions that are both positive and negative that will have the two different results. For example, the teacher could establish the rule:

Rule #1: Do not talk when someone else is talking.

The teacher can give a situation and then elicit the different behaviors students might exhibit.

SITUATION	☺ / ☹	ACTION	RESULT
The teacher is talking.	☺		Your group receives 1 point (or smiley face).
	☹		Your group loses 1 point.

Students might give the following behaviors:

SITUATION	☺ / ☹	ACTION	RESULT
The teacher is talking.	☺	*YOUR GROUP IS QUIET.* *YOUR GROUP IS LISTENING.* *YOUR GROUP IS PAYING ATTENTION.*	Your group receives 1 point (or smiley face).
	☹	*YOU ARE TALKING.* *YOU ARE LISTENING TO YOUR FRIEND.* *YOU ARE LOOKING OUT THE WINDOW.*	Your group loses 1 point.

This activity helps teachers establish the rules at the beginning of the class. If it is necessary to use L1 to help establish the rules, then the teacher should prepare for this and supplement the activity with visuals.

SITUATION	☺ / ☹	ACTION	RESULT
The teacher is talking.	☺		+1 point
	☹		−1 point

In addition, the teacher can create certificates for good behavior that students can earn over time. There are many free certificate maker Web sites that are made for teachers. You can type in students' names and text describing what the certificate is for. The certificates can be printed out and used as a reward for students to reinforce good behavior. Parents love to see their children receive certificates, and your YLs will feel proud of their achievement and most likely keep up their good behavior.

Enforce rules consistently and fairly It is very important to make sure you always enforce the rules consistently and fairly. This task will be easier if students have co-constructed the rules and consequences, because everything has been communicated openly and clearly. In addition, if students are given points in groups, they will also be "policing" their classmates to follow the rules and behave positively for the rewards. Sometimes teachers get tired of enforcing rules, so it may be necessary to establish a limit to the number of times rules can broken.

Involve parents in managing YLs' behavior It is possible to involve parents actively in managing YLs' behavior. One popular way teachers manage classroom behavior is with colored cards: green cards, yellow cards, and red cards. Everyone starts with a green card at the beginning of the day.

Students are told what each card represents:

Green card: You are doing well. Keep going!

Yellow card: You broke a rule and had to turn your card to yellow.

Red card: You broke the rules more than once and had to turn your card to red.

The teacher sets up cards on the wall—one set per student with their name on it. Students must turn their own card when they break a rule. This will make a YL more conscious of their responsibility for managing their own behavior.

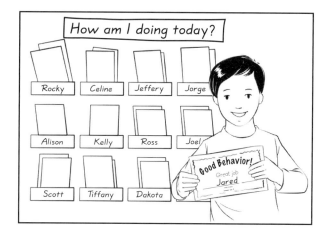

If a student reaches a red card, then the teacher can send home a notice to the parents. The teacher can create a form for parents like the one below to facilitate a discussion about classroom behavior between the child and his family. This letter will explain what rules the child broke and describe the behavior that is inappropriate. This could be for very extreme, unmanageable behavior like getting into fights, taking other students' belongings, or distracting other students by continuously talking to them during activities.

RED CARD LETTER

Date:

Class:

Dear _____ (parent's name):

_____ (child's name) had to turn her/his card to red. S/he broke the following class rules and exhibited inappropriate classroom behavior:

_____

_____

Please discuss appropriate classroom behavior with your child, check the box to confirm, and sign below.

❑ I have read this letter and discussed appropriate classroom behavior with my child.

Parent's signature: _____ Date: _____

Of course, this letter will need to be written in the parents' native language instead of English. With any communication from teacher to parents, the teacher should explain ahead of time what the system of discipline is and what the classroom rules are. The teacher could also develop a system of communication by e-mail and send the information directly to the parent instead of sending a letter home through the students.

4. Managing the classroom climate Managing the atmosphere in the classroom is one of the biggest challenges teachers face. In this section we will look at the physical environment as well as the emotional atmosphere of the classroom.

Physical environment The first aspect of the physical environment is the room and seating arrangement. For many teachers, the way the classroom is set up is completely out of their control. If you have the freedom to arrange the room, it is very important to create an arrangement that will have the following qualities:

- You can easily see all students from the front of the room.
- All students can see the front of the classroom including any presentation tools you may use, i.e., screen for projecting presentations, TV for videos, flip charts, white board.
- You can walk through the room with ease to check on students and monitor their progress during activities.
- The seats can be moved to be conducive to pair and group work.
- There is a designated area for supplies needed for various types of YL activities (markers, crayons, paper, scissors, glue).

However, if arranging the room is not possible because the seats are nailed to the floor or the room is too crowded to create enough space for walking around freely, then the teacher should consider planning activities that require lots of movement to be done outside or in the gym. Planning a class in a different location might be necessary to incorporate physical games or activities or even the use of technology like video or computers.

It is also important to make the space for YLs colorful and text-rich all around. If the teacher can use the wall space for brightly colored posters and pictures or samples of English language, it can help create an engaging environment for YLs. The class rules and classroom language could be made into posters and displayed on the walls. Another way to make the classroom a motivating place for YLs to learn is to display student work on the wall. This will give students a sense of accomplishment and also give you pictures and language to refer to while teaching. For information about how to utilize wall space, watch the videos called *If Walls Could Talk* (see link in Useful Web Sites at the end of the chapter).

Emotional atmosphere In addition to the physical environment, the teacher can manage the classroom climate by creating a positive emotional atmosphere, one that is comfortable for YLs to speak out in English. Ideally, the atmosphere should be engaging and motivating. The key is to build good relationships with students. Evertson and Emmer (2013) give these suggestions for teachers of YLs: ". . . while teachers need to work at building positive relationships with students, they need to be conscious of the tendency to favor those students who are most engaged. Teachers also need to manage 'boundaries' in the development of their relationships; teachers should be supportive adults, not buddies or pals" (p. 9). Although the ways in which teachers manage those "boundaries" is culturally based, the main idea is that the teacher is a supportive adult rather than a friend to students.

Another important aspect of the teacher's behavior is to manage student behavior by example. Treating all students equally and fairly is very important because we want to encourage all students to do their best, and we also want to be a model for YLs on how to be kind and respectful to all people. Weinstein, Romano, and Mignano (2011) explain, "Indeed, classroom management has two distinct purposes: It not only seeks to establish and sustain a caring, orderly environment in which students can engage in meaningful learning, it also aims to enhance students' social and emotional growth" (p. 5). All teachers of YLs are responsible for helping them grow into good, productive people and become good citizens in their country as well as the world. If the teacher has an approach that is consistent and treats all students equally and fairly and with kindness and understanding, then students will feel more secure and comfortable in class. Teachers should avoid having favorites and instead create a feeling of trust with all students.

Finally, teachers can create a good classroom atmosphere by catering to YLs' interests. This can be achieved by incorporating topics and activities that the students enjoy. Teachers can give students a survey at different times in the school year to find out what kinds of topics, projects, and materials they are interested in incorporating into the lessons. Even if you can only incorporate a few of their favorite songs in a semester or use clips from their favorite TV shows or cut-outs of their favorite cartoon characters every other unit, they will know that you are bringing in materials based on their requests, and this will help them stay engaged in class.

5. **Managing the language used in class** When teaching English to young learners, teachers also have to manage the language spoken in the classroom—both student and teacher use of L1 (native language). It is important for teachers to remember that their goal is to create an English-speaking environment. Of course,

sometimes use of L1 is unavoidable, but it is wise to use the native language as a resource only when necessary:

- To make a very difficult expression understood quickly
- To explain instructions for an activity

The important thing is to use L1 only when a particular expression cannot be easily shown through visuals or explained simply. For example, the beginning of every fairytale starts with "Once upon a time," which would be almost impossible to explain in English to beginner-level students. In this case it is better to translate the expression and then recast it. Then every time it is used at the beginning of a story, the students will recognize it and know that they are about to hear a fantastic fairytale (Shin, 2006).

When planning the use of the L1, teachers should carefully examine their language content and objectives for the day's lesson. If the instructions for a game are well beyond the current level of students' proficiency, then it would be better to use L1 to explain the activity. This will make the most of the limited time in class for students to practice using English at their level and achieve the language objectives set for that day.

Effective Classroom Management Activities

Most of classroom management is based on the characteristics of YLs and the fact that they are easily distracted and can't sit still. However, there is an added challenge for the EYL classroom because teachers are trying to conduct class in a language that is not the students' native language. Managing behavior while using a foreign language means that teachers have to teach classroom routines in English step by step. If students do not comprehend teachers' instructions and classroom routines in English, then the teacher won't be able to keep their attention. This section provides many ideas for managing your class successfully.

Add English to Classroom Routines and Procedures Here is a list of many different classroom routines and procedures. Add classroom language in English to them, and you will have a very rich English language environment. First, make a list to establish your classroom routines, then link them to certain expressions, and use them as much as possible. As mentioned in Chapter 4, it is very important to build classroom routines in English which are referred to as "social rituals" by Winn-Smith (2001, p. 22). These rituals can help YLs build real language in the classroom, especially if teachers take the time and effort to keep these routines consistent and train students in how to use English to accomplish these routines. Here are ten suggested routines:

1. Starting the class
2. Designating classroom helpers ("helping hands")
3. Taking attendance ("roll call")
4. Establishing the date and day
5. Establishing objectives
6. Preparing attention getters
7. Preparing brain breaks
8. Cleaning up the room
9. Giving homework (introducing the next class)
10. Ending the class

1. Starting the class The teacher greets students every day. The repetition of the greeting will help students use this real-life language with automaticity.

Teacher: *Good morning class!*

Class: *Good morning, Teacher!*

Teacher: *How are you today?*

Class: *Good. And you?*

Teacher: *I'm fine. Thank you!*

Then start the class with a cheer or a song to get them ready and excited for the lesson. For example, you can do an English Cheer. Each "X" stands for one clap.

ENGLISH CHEER
by Joan Kang Shin

English is fun! *(Move to the right)* X – X – XX – X

English is cool! *(Move to the left)* X – X – XX – X

I speak English! *(Point to yourself with your thumbs)* X – X – XX – X

And so do you! *(Point out to your class)* X – X – XX – X

Yaaaaaaay English! *(Bend down and shake your hands near the floor. Start softly, then get louder and jump in the air with your arms up cheering "English!" like waving pom-poms in the air.)*

Or perhaps students have a favorite song they just learned and want to practice. Just make sure you prepare some way for your students to start the day in a positive way.

2.   Designating classroom helpers Students can use classroom language while helping you manage the classroom. You can designate students for various roles or jobs for the class. It could be a job for a day or a week. Here are some jobs that YLs can do in the classroom:

- **Roll Caller:** Take attendance by calling out students' names and mark them present or absent after the student says, "Here!"
- **Paper Manager:** Pass out and collect papers, e.g., handouts, assignments, flashcards, picture cards.
- **Supplies Manager:** Pass out and collect supplies, e.g., colored paper, markers, crayons, scissors, glue.
- **Book Manager:** Pass out and collect books, e.g., textbooks, storybooks, readers.
- **Time Manager:** Keep track of time for a group activity or remind the teacher if it is a few minutes before the class is over. Students have to learn polite, respectful language to use, such as "Excuse me, Ms. Shin. We only have 1 minute."
- **Word Keeper:** Keep the class dictionary at her/his desk and look up a word when necessary.

Some teachers designate "Helping Hands" for each class. It goes with the expression to "lend a hand," or help someone out. In the picture below, the teacher posts the Helping Hands on the wall of the classroom.

Photo Courtesy of Terry Cook

Next to each hand is an envelope or pocket that has numbers corresponding to a numbered chair. So if #9 is the pocket for Supplies Manager, then the student sitting in chair #9 will help the teacher monitor the supplies that are used in class. For example, if the activity requires markers or crayons to draw a picture, the Supplies Manager in chair #9 will have to say "I'll lend a helping hand!" and then get up and pass out the supplies to each student. The teacher can require the Supplies Manager to use English, such as "Here you go" or "One for you, and one for you," or even count how many markers are being passed out and keep track of how many need to be collected at the end of the activity.

3. **Taking attendance ("roll call")** The teacher can designate one of the helping hands to be a roll caller. This person can call out students' names and mark them present or absent. The teacher can cue the roll caller and students to use English in different ways.

> Teacher: Roll Caller, please come here. Call each name nice and loud. Everyone, respond: "Yes, I'm here!"

Or the teacher could encourage a repetitive exchange.

> Roll Caller: Eugenia! Hello, how are you?
> Eugenia: Hello! I'm good. Thank you!

4. **Establishing the date and day** Before every class, it is important to establish the date. First, it will help with automaticity of the questions and answers for a commonly used communicative act. In addition, the teacher can model the correct way to write the date. After a while, the teacher can ask for volunteers to write the date on the board and lead that part of the class structure.

For beginner YLs it is important to distinguish the difference between the day and the date in English. Before saying the day, the students can sing the Days of the Week Song, which is fun and gets them ready to say what day it is.

DAYS OF THE WEEK SONG
(To the tune of The Addams Family)

There's Sunday and there's Monday.

There's Tuesday and there's Wednesday.

There's Thursday and there's Friday.

And then there's Saturday.

Days of the week *(snap snap)*

Days of the week *(snap snap)*

Days of the week

Days of the week

Days of the week *(snap snap)*

In addition, class will be more fun and interesting if there are special days that students can look forward to. Maybe Friday is always Storytelling Day. Or maybe Monday is Song Day. Students know it and can be excited about it.

5. **Establishing the day's objectives** It is important that teachers always go over the day's objectives. It will have the same form every day: SWBAT, and is a standard form of objective writing. Keep the objectives simple and write them on the board to refer to and assess progress during the class. It is a good habit for teachers to do this right before starting the lesson. Students will start to recognize the form "SWBAT" and will know what is expected of them during the class period. See Chapter 3 to review how to write objectives.

6. **Preparing attention getters** The teacher should prepare different strategies for getting students' attention during the lesson. Some teachers count down backwards "5–4–3–2–1!" and then punish students who did not quiet down. Some teachers clap rhythms and students repeat the rhythms. However, it is always more fun to get students to respond with their attention and say something in English. For example, teachers can use a Call and Response strategy. Here are a few popular ones:

1–2–3 EYES ON ME!

Teacher: *1–2–3 eyes on me!*

Students: *1–2 eyes on you!*

Then students should have their eyes on the teacher.

Whole Brain Teaching by Chris Biffle (2012) has numerous strategies for getting the attention of your class:

CLASS! YES!

Teacher: *Class!*

Students: *Yes!*

Students have to say "Yes" in whatever way the teacher says "Class." For example,

Teacher: *Class, class!*

Students: *Yes, yes!*

Or the teacher could try to make it funny by exaggerating the call and response.

Teacher: *Ooooooh class!*

Students: *Ooooooh yes!*

These suggestions and more from Chris Biffle can be found in his booklet called *Whole Brain Teaching: Lesson Design and Delivery* and on the following Web site: http://www .wholebrainteaching.com.

WHEN I SAY —, YOU SAY —!

Teacher: *When I say peanut, you say butter! Peanut!*

Students: *Butter!*

Teacher: *Peanut!*

Students: *Butter!*

The teacher can use new words to call and respond or let students decide the words at the beginning of class.

In addition to call-and-response strategies, teachers can use attention getters to signify the beginning of pair or group work. Here are two ways that are fun for YLs:

I LOVE ENGLISH!
by Joan Kang Shin
(To the tune of Frère Jacques)

I love English!

I love English!

Yes, I do!

Yes, I do!

Come and be my partner.

Come and be my partner.

Let's begin!

Let's begin!

READY? OK!

Students can look at each other and say, "Ready? OK!"

Teachers can come up with a whole range of attention getters that are fun and help signify the start of an activity, the end of an activity, or simply help the teacher redirect attention toward her/him in order to give some important information.

7.   Preparing brain breaks It is important to give young learners periodic brain breaks. You can put a break into a difficult activity to keep learners from getting frustrated or bored. You can give students a chance to stretch themselves out if they have been sitting for too long. For example, if students have been sitting and doing

Sometimes you want to call attention to something great a student has done, especially if it is something nice for the class. Maybe the child drew a picture of the class or brought in some cake for a special occasion. Maybe it is a student's birthday, and the teacher wants students to give some positive attention to her/him. The Appreciation Cheer can be used.

WHO DO WE APPRECIATE?

2–4–6–8

Who do we appreciate?

(Student name), (Student name)!

Yaaaaaaaay (Student name)!

a writing activity, the teacher can play a popular song and have students get up and dance next to their desk. Or you can give students a chance to rest if they have been up and active for a while. Maybe after students have been singing a song with lots of movement, they can relax and put their heads down on their desk for some quiet time, as discussed in Chapter 2, where students do Hand Shakes, after they have been writing and need to shake out the muscles in their hands. See the box for 20 different ideas for brain breaks.

8.   **Cleaning up the room** The teacher should always have a designated time to clean up the room before the class is done. Usually YL classes use manipulatives, markers, scissors, paper, handouts, and books, so there needs to be about 2–3 minutes designated for clean up. If the teacher has designated helping hands, such as a Paper Manager, Supplies Manager, and Book Manager, s/he can instruct them to be in charge of collecting any paper, supplies, and books that need to be collected or put away.

---

1. **Head Down:** Students put their heads down on their arms on their desks.

2. **Meditation:** Students close their eyes and breathe in and out on the teacher's cue.

3. **Head Roll:** Students roll their heads around clockwise a few times and then counterclockwise a few times on the teacher's cue.

4. **Hand Shakes:** Students shake their hands one at a time.

5. **Arm and Leg Stretch:** Students stretch their arms and legs standing up or sitting down. They can stretch their arms up, out to the side, out front clasping their hands, and out back clasping their hands.

6. **Back Stretch:** Students sit at their desks and turn around grabbing the back of their seat, and then turn the other way grabbing the back of their seat.

7. **Arm Circles:** Students stand up and swing their arms in circles going forward a few times and then backward a few times.

8. **Foot Circles:** Students stretch their legs and move their feet in circles, moving outward a few times and then inward a few times.

9. **Jumping Jacks:** Students stand up and do 10 jumping jacks (arms swing up to touch hands together with feet jumping apart, then jump back with feet together and arms at one's side).

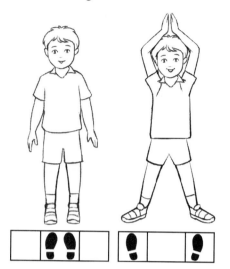

10. **Right Hand, Left Foot:** Students stand up and spread their legs about shoulder length apart. They bend down touching their right hand to their left foot. Then stand up and bend down touching their left hand to their right foot.

11. **Seat Running:** Students sit at their desks and run with their legs faster and faster at the teacher's cue.

12. **Seat Swimming:** Students sit at their desks and pretend they are swimming with their arms and upper bodies.

13. **Rhythm Repetition:** The teacher claps a rhythm and students repeat, over time, doing more and more complicated rhythms for students to follow.

14. **Wiggle It:** Students wiggle their whole body for 10 seconds. The teacher can mix it up and have them wiggle their bodies like a caterpillar or like a lion or like a fish.

15. **Yoga:** The teacher does yoga poses while describing them, such as lotus position, downward dog, cobra. Or the teacher and students can make up poses, such as shapes of letters, animal imitations, or any other pose that visualizes something students are interested in.

16. **Get Up and Sing:** The teacher leads students in one of their favorite songs, especially ones that use physical movement like Head, Shoulders, Knees, and Toes.

17. **Simon Says:** See Chapter 2 for instructions for Simon Says.

18. **Dance Party:** The teacher plays dance music in English that is popular with students and have them sing and dance for the length of the song as a break.

19. **Freeze Frame:** Play music and let students stand by their desk and dance. When you stop the music students have to freeze.

20. **I Spy:** Pick an object in the room. Say, "I spy with my little eye," and then give some description of the object, such as "I spy with my little eye something red" or "something small" or "something round." Then students have to guess what the object is. The person who guesses it correctly can pick the next object for others to guess and say, "I spy with my little eye. . . ."

9. **Giving homework (introducing the next class)** Before ending the class, the teacher might assign homework to students and tell students what to expect next class. If teachers use thematic unit planning, then the next class is likely to be connected topically to the class students just had. For YLs, homework should be kept very simple. For example, it could be to encourage students to bring their favorite toy to class for Show and Tell or to use in the next lesson. Or it could be to bring a picture of their family to the next class to learn the words for family members. For VYLs, it might be helpful to send a note home to their parents to make sure the homework is completed. See below for an example:

Date:
Class:

ENGLISH HOMEWORK

Next class (date): _____

Homework: _____

_____

_____

☐ I have read this paper and helped my child complete the homework assignment.

Parent's signature: _____ Date: _____

Note: This should be translated into parents' native language.

10. **Ending the class** Mark the end of the class time with a routine. In the example, the teacher has established a routine of using a chant for the end of the day:

END OF THE DAY CHANT

by Joan Kang Shin

You were awesome!

Hip hip hooray!

See you next class!

And have a great day!

This marks the end of the class, sends a positive message about students' performance in class, and gives them authentic language that they can use when saying good-bye in real life.

Designing a Classroom Management Plan

Here is a sample class structure plan that can help any teacher with classroom management. This can help you become a master at managing the structure and pace of your class and plan the routines you will establish.

CLASS STRUCTURE PLAN

1. START CLASS		
2. HELPING HANDS		
3. ROLL CALL		
4. DATE/DAY		
5. OBJECTIVES		
THE LESSON	6. ATTENTION GETTER	
	7. BRAIN BREAK	
8. CLEAN UP		
9. HOMEWORK		
10. END CLASS		

In this class structure plan, "THE LESSON" is your lesson plan. It could be the lesson in the required textbook for your school or a lesson plan you created yourself based on your school's curriculum. Regardless of the lesson you have planned for the day, you should also have a plan for the class structure that you follow routinely from day to day. This helps students know what to expect and helps them to follow the flow of class. The following example shows how to use a plan like this to help manage the pace of your class. After examining the example below, read the explanation for all seven parts of the class structure plan.

EXAMPLE CLASS STRUCTURE PLAN

1. START CLASS	TEACHER: Hello, Class! CLASS: Hello, Teacher! TEACHER: How are you today? CLASS: Great! How are you? TEACHER: Let's start class with a cheer! **ENGLISH CHEER**
2. HELPING HANDS	TEACHER: OK class. Before telling stories . . . please look at the wall. See who are my Helping Hands today. *(Say them each out loud. When you need the Supplies and Paper Managers, tell them to pass out supplies and students have to tell them "Thank you!")*
3. ROLL CALL	TEACHER: Roll Caller, please come here. Call each name nice and loud. Everyone, respond: "Yes, I'm here!"
4. DATE/DAY	TEACHER: What is today's date? CLASS: Today is September 3rd, Two thousand twelve. TEACHER: *(Write "September 3, 2012" on the board as students say the date correctly.)* **DAYS OF THE WEEK SONG** TEACHER: What day is it today? CLASS: It's Monday. TEACHER: And . . . what is Monday? *(with excitement)* CLASS: Monday is Storytelling Day! TEACHER: What do we do on Storytelling Day? CLASS: We tell stories!
5. OBJECTIVES	TEACHER: Class, let's read the objectives for today. "SWBAT. . . ." CLASS: SWBAT . . . Identify different sea animals. And tell a story called *The Rainbow Fish*.

THE LESSON	6. ATTENTION GETTER TEACHER: When I say rainbow, you say fish.
	7. BRAIN BREAK The Hand Shakes *(after working on mini-book)*

8. CLEAN UP	TEACHER: Supplies Manager, please collect the markers and glue. Say "Thank you" to each student. Paper Manager, please collect everyone's mini-book. Say "Thank you" to each student. Students, please respond, "You're welcome!"
9. HOMEWORK	TEACHER: Class! CLASS: Yes! TEACHER: Next class: Bring your favorite toy. It's Show and Tell! Here is your Homework Slip. (Give students the homework slip for their parents to check and sign.)
10. END CLASS	**END OF THE DAY CHANT** TEACHER: Good-bye, class! CLASS: Good-bye, Teacher!

In the example, the teacher decided to use the title of the story being told in the lesson for the Call and Respond: "When I say rainbow, you say fish" in order to give students practice with those words.

During the lesson, the students were given an assignment to create a mini-book (see Chapter 6), which required them to sit for a while and draw and write. The Hand Shakes got students to shake their hands out. The teacher leads them: "Shake your right hand 1–2–3. Switch! Shake your left hand 1–2–3." The teacher repeated this five times, so students could move a little and shake out their hands, which had probably been working hard, making their muscles tense.

Finally, remember to change your songs, chants, and attention getters periodically. You have to keep your class fresh and fun, and you will be teaching your students more English. It is important to build real language into the classroom. The repetition of these routines in English will help your young learners improve their ability to use English while keeping the pace of class.

■ Teacher to Teacher

Classroom Management for Young Learners

Classroom management is tricky because the approaches teachers use can depend on their country and culture. Here are some ways different teachers around the world find solutions to managing YLs in the classroom. First is a teacher from Turkey who takes into account YLs' characteristics to engage them successfully in the EYL classroom.

"I teach 3rd, 4th, and 5th grades which are really active not only linguistically but also physically so it demands hard work for me to settle them down and direct their whole interests to English lessons. One of the ways that I use for managing young learners' classes is to bring real-life objects into the classroom because it takes their attention immediately and I keep it hidden until the lesson reaches its peak. As an example of this, I was going to teach my third grade students vegetables and fruits in two lessons but they were very noisy and uninterested in the first lesson during which the only thing I was able to do was to keep them silent. I brought a basket of fruits into classroom after the break-time for the second lesson and I kept it aside and after I presented them their names and I gave them all fruits and said to them 'If you can say their names and form a sentence with that fruit in your hand, you can eat it' and they went crazy to name the fruits and form a sentence. That is to say, bringing the real world in class is one efficient way of both managing your class for positive atmosphere for learning and teaching English to young learners."

—*Ümit Cebeci, Primary English Teacher, Turkey*

An expert teacher from Brazil gives a comprehensive explanation of the main concerns for classroom management for an EYL teacher.

"I feel classroom management is one of the hardest parts of our jobs, and it is the most important aspect to be considered if we want to succeed. Whenever something goes wrong in relation to classroom management, chances are everything will go wrong in that particular class. Classroom management involves much more than just misbehavior. Eliciting some rules and the consequences for not following those rules from our students enables us to share the responsibility with them. Establishing the rules which we think are really important and explaining why these rules are important demonstrates the teacher is an authority in class and someone they can count on. However, what I feel is that children need to be constantly reminded of the rules established at the beginning of the year, which requires lots of persistence and patience. This can be done at the beginning of every class. One idea is to say a rule to students and they have to mime it. Later when they are familiar with the language of the rules, the teacher can mime and they come up with the rule.

Another important aspect when talking about classroom management is being consistent. A teacher who establishes the rule of raising hands before speaking, but who responds to a student's demands even though s/he has not raised his/her hand is showing that the rule is not to be followed. A teacher who says that only students who do their homework will get a happy face or a sticker and rewards someone who has forgotten the homework because s/he is a 'favorite' student is showing that the consequences depend on who breaks the rules. Finally, the consequences we establish need to be in accordance with the school policy, and once established they need to be followed.

Finding the balance between being nice and friendly and being firm and consistent is one of the secrets for succeeding in classroom management.**"**

—*Ana Maria Scanduzzi, EFL Instructor, Brazil*

Many of the teachers find it effective to co-construct a set of classroom rules for students to follow. One teacher describes co-constructing rules with students and putting them on a poster in the room for easy reference.

"I usually start the first class by making a poster-sized list of classroom rules. I always discuss rules my Ss think are reasonable regarding classroom behavior & consequences for breaking these rules. When my Ss agree on certain rules & consequences after voting, we hang up the final copy of classroom rules. I try to avoid using 'don't' or any word that implies a negative meaning when writing rules. Once the rules are set, they should be enforced consistently. I mean we should keep our words & do as we say. Sticking to rules & being consistent are paramount to being successful in managing the class and earning our Ss' respect. Once we lose our Ss' respect, we will consequently lose their attention.**"**

—*Oula Hamwieh, Primary English Teacher, Syria*

Instead of a set of classroom rules on a poster, some teachers prefer to use a class contract on paper. Here a teacher from Croatia describes contracts she makes for different grade levels that are co-constructed, signed by all students and teacher, and kept in students' notebooks for easy reference.

"Here are two examples of a class contract. The first one I use from grades 4 to 8; the second one I use in grades 1 and 2, and occasionally grade 3, depending how well they progress in reading.

I don't have my own classroom so displaying a list/poster of classroom rules is not really possible. But I make a classroom contract with the list of the things I find necessary to obtain a level of discipline and other responsibilities required from my students. They sign it and me too and they stick it into their notebooks. I do this on the first lesson of the course.

We go through the rules on the first lesson of the school year (sometimes students suggest some of the rules themselves, as was the case with the mobile phones or we rearrange the rule appropriately to a certain class). After discussion they and I sign it and date it. The contract goes (is pasted) to the first left blank page of the notebook and the right page is left blank for eventual comments on behavior, 'violation of contract' or praise on following the rules and contributions to the class. Also, if needed, the right page is used for eventual consequences when rules are broken or changes of the rules.**"**

—*Darija Sostaric-Zuckermann, Primary English Teacher, Croatia*

Darija's class contract for grades 4–8

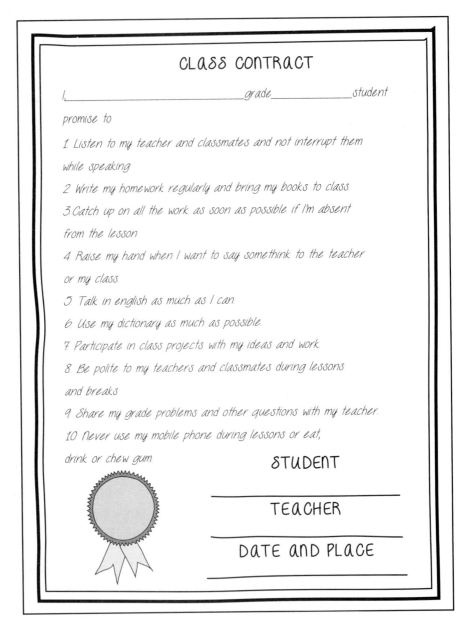

CLASS CONTRACT

I,_____grade_____student

promise to

1 Listen to my teacher and classmates and not interrupt them while speaking

2 Write my homework regularly and bring my books to class.

3 Catch up on all the work as soon as possible if I'm absent from the lesson

4 Raise my hand when I want to say somethink to the teacher or my class.

5 Talk in english as much as I can.

6 Use my dictionary as much as possible.

7 Participate in class projects with my ideas and work.

8 Be polite to my teachers and classmates during lessons and breaks

9 Share my grade problems and other questions with my teacher.

10 Never use my mobile phone during lessons or eat, drink or chew gum.

STUDENT
_____

TEACHER
_____

DATE AND PLACE
_____

Other teachers do not co-construct the rules, but enforce the class rules fairly and consistently.

"I don't discuss classroom rules with children, although as your posts show it may work. I just start using them with a new class and I am persistent about following the rules. For example, I'll never ask a student who doesn't have his hand up or chews a chewing gum. It doesn't take a lot of time—2–3 lessons are enough for students to remember and observe these regulations.

It's very difficult for me to write about punishments, as we actually don't have this practice in the centre. Punishment depends on an action committed by a student and may include an additional exercise to do. In any case I would be very careful about punishment and I'd prefer talking to a student separately about his/her behavior. I mentioned once Glasser's theory of basic psychological needs: freedom, belonging, safety, fun and success. Students' rebellious behavior may be caused by deprivation of any of these needs.

Darija's class contract for grades 1–3

Classroom management in its wider sense is a system of relationships between a teacher and students, and as any system based on human relationships it is to be ethical punishment. **"**

—Victoria Demidova, Primary English Teacher, Uzbekistan

Some teachers try to make students responsible for enforcing the class rules themselves. This teacher from Georgia encourages students to be responsible in small groups to help monitor student behavior.

"Classroom management is very challenging indeed. What I try in my classes is that my students create their rules how to behave and act during the lesson. They are responsible for their behavior as they create these rules themselves. It really works with students. One of the most effective techniques I use in my class is group responsibility. As students mostly sit individually but in rows, we have a competition called 'The Best Row.' The winner is the row which is the most of all organized and well behaved. During the lesson students try their best to be as attentive and mobilized as possible as they are not only responsible for their own behavior but the group as well.**"**

—Marika Galdava, Primary English Teacher, Georgia

Another innovative way to manage the classroom is to use different zones in the room for different types of communication. This creative teacher from Costa Rica explains how she uses different positions in the classroom to indicate different classroom actions.

"At the front of the class I use different spaces to specific purposes: at the right I give the instructions, at the middle I explain and at the left I call the attention. So, when students look at me at some of these spots, they become silent and pay attention to what I say.

I don't have a classroom, so I change the position in some classrooms depending on the furniture arrangement. I divided my space in front of the class into three spots indicated by the numbered stars.

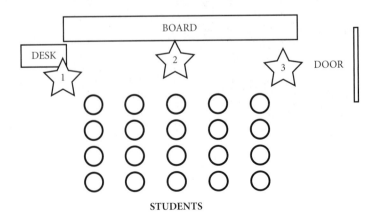

Position #1

The first is to check the attendance, check homework and review class work. This spot can vary in a classroom depending on the desk's position. It is located at the right of the classroom or near the desk.

Photo courtesy of Roxanne Vargas

Position #2

The second one is to do the Daily Routine, to do the Brain Gym, to sing and to explain the activities and to develop them. It is located at the middle or center of the front part of the class.

Photo courtesy of Roxanne Vargas

Position #3

The third one is to call their attention when I am going to explain something and they are doing something else, when I need to say something while they are doing an activity or when I need to stop an activity and when I need to call somebody's attention due to misbehavior. It is located at the left, near the door."

—Roxanne Vargas Lopez, Primary English Teacher, Costa Rica

Photo courtesy of Roxanne Vargas

Finally, since so much of the discussion among teachers regarding classroom management revolves around establishing classroom rules, whether it be teacher-determined or co-constructed with students, it seems fitting to end with the sentiments of one teacher in Sri Lanka.

"The word RULES should be replaced with a more meaningful and pleasant word like AGREEMENTS! Infact, we as good classroom managers have to adopt a strategy where the pupils are a part of the management. We must share responsibilities, however small our members are. How pupils understand their responsibilities solely depends on how much they are given the opportunity to be responsible. If a teacher gets the pupils' support when framing the agreements, the pupils are more aware of what is expected from them in return. They will feel responsible and confident about them. These agreements can be more clearly explained as Essential Agreements. The teacher and the pupils sit together and discuss with regards to the essential agreements before they are enforced. The pupils will get a comprehensive idea as to what is expected from them. The teacher, in return, will understand that the pupils are fully aware of the situation. As such, Essential Agreements will keep everyone alert and responsible. Such a classroom will be managed by its owners: the pupils and teachers alike!"

—Neelika Edirisinghe, Primary English Teacher, Sri Lanka

■ Chapter Summary

To Conclude

EYL teachers are managers in different ways Classroom management for young learners is challenging because of their natural characteristics. EYL teachers need to learn how to manage the pace of the class, YLs' behavior with routines and rules, the classroom atmosphere, and the language used in class to make an effective environment for learning English.

Establish classroom rules and be consistent YLs need rules to function in a classroom environment successfully. Teachers should clearly communicate these rules and be consistent in enforcing them with both rewards and punishments. If appropriate, teachers can co-construct the rules and consequences with students.

Create classroom routines YLs feel secure when they know what to expect during every stage of class. Build in classroom routines to help students know what is happening step by step. Even when your classroom routines are consistent, don't let your YLs get bored; introduce new songs, chants, or call and response within the class routines to keep students on their toes.

Integrate English into your routines Be sure to use classroom language in English and build routines that will help your students practice real English within the context of your classroom.

Prepare routines carefully with your lesson plans Be sure to prepare your class structure and routines as carefully as you plan your language lessons. Remember that YLs need a clear structure and routines that lead them from one step of your lesson to the next. In addition, the classroom routines can be integrated with the language in your lessons if you take the time to plan them together.

Classroom management is culturally based Remember that appropriate rules, routines, environment, and teacher–student relationships should be based in the culture of the local context.

■ Over to You

Discussion Questions

1. What are the characteristics of YLs that make classroom management more challenging than with adult and teenage learners?
2. What are some routines and rules that you will apply to ensure a well-managed EYL classroom?

3. If you cannot rearrange your classroom to facilitate pair and group work, what are some ways you can still do cooperative learning activities effectively?

4. What should be the role of a teacher? Authority? Friend? Parent? Something else? Based on your experience, culture, and new knowledge from this chapter, explain the appropriate role of a teacher in the EYL classroom.

5. Classroom cultures can be different from country to country as well as within a country. What strategies do you think would work well for your context? Explain what differences in culture or context would prevent certain strategies from working in your situation.

6. After reading the Teacher to Teacher section, do you think you could apply any of these classroom management strategies in your context? Which ones would make your classroom more effective for meaningful learning?

Lesson Planning

Choose any lesson for young learners from your curriculum or a textbook and use the class structure plan in order to prepare time for various classroom routines appropriate for your class. Fill in the class structure plan given in this chapter, and then think about how you might adjust it to create your own class structure relevant to your context.

Write About It

Teacher as Classroom Manager: Look at the list of challenges that you wrote before reading this chapter in the section called Think about It. As you read the chapter, did you identify some additional challenges that you hadn't thought of? What are some ways of meeting those challenges based on what you read in this chapter? What are some strategies that you plan to apply to your own classroom and why? How will implementing those strategies help you overcome the challenges of managing a class of YLs?

■ Resources and References

Print Publications

Biffle, C. (2012). Whole brain teaching: Lesson design and delivery. Retrieved from http://www.wholebrainteaching.com/downloads.html

Green, T. (2010). *How to be successful in your first year of teaching elementary school: Everything you need to know that they don't teach you in school.* Ocala, FL: Atlantic Publishing Group.

Evertson, C. M., & Emmer, E. T. (2013). *Classroom management for elementary teachers.* Boston: Pearson.

Weinstein, C. S., Romano, M. E., & Mignano, A. J. (2011). *Elementary classroom management: Lessons from research and practice.* New York: McGraw-Hill.

Useful Web Sites

123 Certificates: www.123certificates.com

Certificate Maker: www.certificatemaker.com

If Walls Could Talk videos: https://sites.google.com/site/shinjinshil/resources

Education World: www.educationworld.com

(click on the subheadings under School Climate for classroom management tips)

National Education Association, Classroom Management: www.nea.org/tools/ClassroomManagement.html

Teaching Channel: https://www.teachingchannel.org (click on the section called Behavior for classroom management tips)

Whole Brain Teaching: www.wholebrainteaching.com

References

Biffle, C. (2012). Whole brain teaching: Lesson design and delivery. Retrieved from http://www.wholebrainteaching.com/downloads.html

Brewster, J., Ellis, G., & Girard, D. (2004). *The primary English teacher's guide*. London, UK: Penguin.

Crandall, J. A. (2001). Rethinking classroom management: Creating an effective learning community. *ESL Magazine, 4*(3), 10-13.

Crooks, G., & Chaudron, C. (2001). Guidelines for language classroom instruction. In M. Celce-Murcia (Ed.), *Teaching English as a second or foreign language* (pp. 29–42). Boston, MA: Heinle & Heinle.

Evertson, C. M., & Emmer, E. T. (2013). *Classroom management for elementary teachers*. Boston, MA: Pearson.

Moon, J. (2000). *Children learning English*. Oxford, UK: MacMillan Heinemann.

Nunan, D. (1991). *Language teaching methodology. A handbook for teachers*. New York, NY: Prentice Hall.

Shin, J. K. (2006). Ten helpful ideas for teaching English to young learners. *English Teaching Forum, 44*(2), 2–7, 13.

Weinstein, C. S., Romano, M. E., & Mignano, A. J. (2011). *Elementary classroom management: Lessons from research and practice*. New York, NY: McGraw-Hill.

Winn-Smith, B. (2001). Classroom language. *English Teaching Professional, 18,* 12–14.

9 21st Century Skills in TEYL

■ Getting Started

The twenty-first century is not just different in number from the previous centuries. We are facing a new world in almost every area—education, technology, population, environment, politics, economics, etc. It is an interconnected world, in which education will play a major role in providing the skills needed for success. Teaching those skills is a requirement for all educators, including English language teachers. This chapter introduces the basic concepts of teaching twenty-first-century skills in the EYL classroom. It emphasizes the connection between teaching English as an international language and the skills YLs need to be successful global citizens who are prepared for our rapidly changing world. Without building skills for the new century, such as global citizenship and values, communication skills, active learning skills, and technology skills, our young learners will not be adequately prepared to use English in the modern world, which is becoming more interconnected each day.

Steve Bloom/Getty Images

Before reading this chapter, think about the skills that you believe are the most important for young learners in your country. What skills are needed for them to become successful people and citizens in your country? What skills are needed to become successful people and citizens in our world? Which of these skills have become more important since the turn of the century? Why? Which of these skills will be even more important 20 years from now? Why?

Discovery Activity

Twenty-First-Century Skills Chart

Make a chart that lists five important twenty-first-century skills that you believe are necessary for the education of our children. Be as specific as possible (see example given). Then put a check in the next column to show which ones you think you can integrate into your EYL class. Then check off the ones that you are currently integrating into your EYL class.

Twenty-First-Century Skills	Can Integrate into My EYL Class	Already integrating into My EYL Class
Example: Using Internet search engines (e.g., Google)	√	√
1.		
2.		
3.		
4.		
5.		

■ Theory, Planning and Application

Integrating Twenty-First-Century Skills into TEYL

The illiterate of the 21st century will not be those who cannot read and write, but those who cannot learn, unlearn, and relearn.

—Alvin Toffler

The world we live in is changing rapidly. The twenty-first century requires a new set of skills to keep up with our fast-paced, technology-driven world. Our children are growing up in a time of globalization in which our world is growing increasingly interconnected every day. Trilling and Fadel (2009) describe the shift we perceive in the following way: "This monumental shift from Industrial Age production to that of the Knowledge Age economy—information-driven, globally networked—is as world-changing and life-altering as the shift from the Agrarian to the Industrial Age three hundred and fifty years ago" (p. 3). This shift requires our young learners to prepare themselves to be more connected with people and products from around the world and skilled at searching and processing new information independently. Children growing up in the "Knowledge Age" will not be successful unless they learn how to process all the information that they will be inundated with throughout their lives. McCain and Jukes (2001) noted, "In the past, when information had a much longer shelf life, learning was something that was done once in your youth. Then you were done with learning for life. In the good old days, what you learned in your youth prepared you for your single career. Today, learning has become a lifelong process. Given the rapidly changing nature of our world, people of all ages must constantly learn and relearn what they need to know. What they learned yesterday may no longer be valid in tomorrow's world. Tomorrow, they will have to learn again because today's information will already be out of date" (p. 89). As Toffler noted in the quote at the beginning of this section, our students will need to be able to learn, unlearn, and relearn.

As described in Chapter 1, one twenty-first-century skill that has been identified by many countries as imperative for their young learners is proficiency in English. As we learned in Chapters 2 and 3, when teaching English as an international language, it is important to contextualize language instruction and incorporate real-life situations into the classroom that are relevant to children. This is impossible without addressing various twenty-first-century skills which are necessary for life in our modern world.

Sanjay Deva/Shutterstock.com

Dawn Shearer-Simonetti/Shutterstock.com

What are Twenty-First-Century Skills? First, twenty-first-century skills require taking a global perspective and integrating real-life skills when approaching all subjects in the educational curriculum. The Partnership for 21st Century Skills (2011), a U.S. educational organization that created a framework for twenty-first-century learning, believes that schools have to incorporate certain themes into the core subjects (i.e., English, world languages, arts, mathematics, economics, science, geography, history, and government/civics). These themes are:

- Global awareness
- Financial, economic, business, and entrepreneurial literacy
- Civic literacy
- Health literacy
- Environmental literacy

Furthermore, the Partnership for 21st Century Skills or "P21" (2011) outlined skills that are essential to incorporate into the curriculum for students in the United States to prepare them for life in this century. These skills are categorized into three main sets of skills: learning and innovation skills, digital literacy skills, and career and life skills.

21st Century Skills	
Learning and innovation skills	Critical thinking and problem solving
	Communication and collaboration
	Creativity and innovation
Digital literacy skills	Information literacy
	Media literacy
	Information and communication technologies (ICT) literacy
Career and life skills	Flexibility and adaptability
	Initiative and self-direction
	Social and cross-cultural interaction
	Productivity and accountability
	Leadership and responsibility

In *21st Century Skills: Learning for Life in Our Times,* Trilling and Fadel (2009) created a list referred to as the "7 Cs Skills" (p. 176):

- Critical thinking and problem solving
- Creativity and innovation
- Collaboration, teamwork, and leadership
- Cross-cultural understanding
- Communications, information, and media literacy
- Computing and ICT literacy
- Career and learning self-reliance

In *Assessment and Teaching of 21st Century Skills,* Binkley et al. (2012), based in Australia, also outlined the high-priority twenty-first-century skills, which are similar to P21's but conceptualized in a different way, breaking down the skills into four categories: ways of thinking, ways of working, tools for working, and living in the world.

Ways of Thinking

1. Creativity and innovation
2. Critical thinking, problem solving, decision making
3. Learning to learn, metacognition

Ways of Working

4. Communication
5. Collaboration (teamwork)

Tools for Working

6. Information literacy
7. ICT literacy

Living in the World

8. Citizenship—local and global
9. Life and career
10. Personal and social responsibility—including cultural awareness and competence (pp. 18–19)

These ten high-priority skills are organized in a way that can be helpful for teachers when integrating twenty-first-century skills into their curriculum.

Heidi Hayes Jacobs (2010), author of *Curriculum 21: Essential Education for a Changing World*, believes that to prepare our students for the twenty-first century, "we need to overhaul, update, and inject life into our curriculum and dramatically alter the format of what schools look like to match the times in which we live. Our responsibility is to prepare the learners in our care for their world and their future" (p. 2). Therefore, Jacobs recommends reviewing the content of curriculum in all areas for the following:

- A global perspective is developed and presented in the content area, where natural and viable.
- A personal and local perspective is cultivated so that each student can create relevant links to the content.
- The whole child's academic, emotional, physical, and mental development is thoughtfully considered in content choices.
- The possibilities for future career and work options are developed with an eye to creative and imaginative directions.
- The disciplines are viewed dynamically and rigorously as growing and integrating in real-world practice.
- Technology and media are used to expand possible sources of content so that active as well as static materials are included.
- The complexity of the content is developmentally matched to the age and stage of the learner. (p. 31)

No doubt it is essential for all schools around the world to prepare their YLs for life in our modern world. These main tenets from Curriculum 21 are a very helpful guide when applying twenty-first-century skills to the EYL classroom. In the next section, we will consider the content and skills that are developmentally appropriate for YLs and integrate well into the English language classroom.

How to Integrate Twenty-First-Century Skills into TEYL

When teaching children how to use English as an international language, it is important to integrate twenty-first-century skills that are associated with their use of English. For example, our young global citizens will grow up using English to communicate with people around the world, often through use of e-mail and social networking. They will use English to search for information and study different subjects such as science, medicine, and technology. Many will use English to do business with people around the world. Others will be involved in global problem solving with people from different countries. Young learners are not yet at the stage of life where they are considering their future careers. However, EYL teachers should focus on twenty-first-century skills that can be applied to young learners' real lives, and they should build skills at the young learners' developmental level that will be needed as they grow older. As our young global citizens grow in a world that is increasingly digitized and ever changing, it is important to prepare them to use English by applying the following considerations to your EYL curriculum:

1. Global perspective: global citizenship and values
2. Communication skills: communication and collaboration across cultures
3. Active learning skills: critical thinking and lifelong learning strategies
4. Technology skills: computer, information, and digital literacy

These considerations are all interconnected and overlapping. It would be impossible to discuss building communication skills without considering a global or intercultural perspective. Likewise, it is impossible to build skills in information literacy without discussing the need for critical thinking skills to interpret the infinite amount of information that can be found on the Internet. These considerations will be introduced one by one, but clearly they are interrelated, and teachers will find themselves infusing more than one in activities that they develop to build twenty-first-century skills.

1. **Global perspective** Globalization has made the world more interconnected, and English has become the world's main language for communication. When teaching English as an international language, it is important to help your students recognize that using English in real life means interacting with people from many other countries. First, they should be taught that they are not just learning English to communicate with Americans, Britons, Australians, or people of other Inner Circle countries. They may be using English as a lingua franca to communicate with people from all other countries and cultures. Therefore, a twenty-first-century skill associated with learning English is to become more interculturally aware and sensitive. EYL teachers have to take every opportunity to include information about other countries and cultures. This means using target culture materials from Inner Circle countries and international target culture materials from all other countries around the world in the Outer and Expanding Circles (see Chapter 1). Students need content and instruction that takes a global perspective, teaches about all cultures, and promotes positive attitudes toward people from all countries and walks of life.

In addition, it is important for teachers to help students become aware of their role as global citizens. Our children will grow up using English to contact others for various purposes, such as tourism, study, research, business, or diplomacy. Therefore, it is essential to instill good values and intercultural understanding so that young global citizens can be good, productive members of the global community in which they will be active participants. This includes building their respect not just for other people, but also for animals and the environment, recognizing that we are an integral part of a global ecosystem. This includes values such as caring about, respecting, and protecting our world. Below are some examples from a primary school English language series called *Our World* that integrates values such as respecting animals and protecting the oceans.

NATIONAL GEOGRAPHIC
Our World
Respect animals.

19 Look and read.

It is important to respect animals. Be kind and gentle.

Jane Goodall with chimpanzees

20 Read. Talk and write.

How can we respect animals?

We can _____ .

help
play with

We can be _____ .

gentle
kind

121

NATIONAL GEOGRAPHIC

Mission
Protect the oceans.

- Why must we protect the oceans? Discuss.

- Work in a small group. What can you do to help? Talk about your ideas and write the best ones in the box.

"With every drop of water you drink, every breath you take, you're connected to the ocean. No matter where on Earth you live. Taking care of the ocean means taking care of us."

Sylvia Earle, Oceanographer
Explorer-in-Residence

- Get together with another group. Share your ideas. Are they the same or different? Which idea does everyone like best?

Sylvia Earle

101

Provided by National Geographic Learning

2. **Communication skills** Communication and collaboration skills are important for all students. Teachers in all subject areas should be helping YLs develop their ability to work together in teams and communicate effectively. This is important in terms of YLs' general education, not just for the EYL classroom. However, when taking a global perspective, EYL instruction has to build effective communication and collaboration skills across cultures. One of the best ways teachers can equip students with good intercultural communication skills is to teach

them how to express their own culture in English. It is an extension of encouraging students to personalize what they are learning. In addition to connecting new language and content to themselves, students can also connect new content to their culture. Teachers can take target culture material and rewrite it with students to reflect their home culture. For example, a popular song to teach young learners in English is the Peanut Butter and Jelly Song.

Peanut Butter and Jelly Song

Refrain:

Peanut, peanut butter—and jelly!

Peanut, peanut butter—and jelly!

First, you take the peanuts and you crunch 'em, you crunch 'em. *(Repeat. Refrain.)*

Then you take the grapes and you squish 'em, you squish 'em. *(Repeat. Refrain.)*

Then you take the bread and you spread it, you spread it. *(Repeat. Refrain.)*

Then you take the sandwich and you eat it, you eat it. *(Repeat.)*

Mm mm mm mm mm mm—mm mm mm!

Mm mm mm mm mm mm—mm mm mm!

See https://sites.google.com/site/shinjinshil/resources to watch a video of the song.

This particular sandwich is very popular in the United States and is an example of introducing students to target culture materials. Students love singing this song because it is very funny at the end when they have to sing pretending their mouth is full of the peanut butter and jelly sandwich. It's a great lesson to teach about a particular food that is popular with American kids; however, it is also important to connect this lesson to students' real lives. Peanut butter is not commonly found in many countries, so students may need some realia, if teachers can find it. In addition, teachers can either create a new song or encourage students to write a new song with food from their own culture using the same fun tune and chant. Here are two new versions of the song from a teacher in Cape Verde:

Chicken Burger Song

Refrain

Chicken, chicken burger—and salad!

Chicken, chicken burger—and salad!

First you take the chicken and cook it, cook it! *(Repeat. Refrain.)*

Then you take the salad and prepare it, prepare it! *(Repeat. Refrain.)*

Then you take the bread and you fill it, fill it! *(Repeat. Refrain.)*

Then you take the burger and you eat it, eat it! *(Repeat. Refrain.)*

Orange Juice and Cake Song

Refrain

Orange, orange juice—and cake!

Orange, orange juice—and cake!

First you take the orange, and you cut it, cut it! *(Repeat. Refrain.)*

Then you take the sugar and add it, add it! *(Repeat. Refrain.)*

Then you take the cake and divide it, divide it! *(Repeat. Refrain.)*

Then you take the juice and drink it, drink it! *(Repeat. Refrain.)*

Then you take the cake and you eat it, eat it! *(Repeat. Refrain.)*

Created by students of Elsa Furtado from Cape Verde.

Teaching students how to express their own culture and preferences in English is a good start to help them communicate with others. After all, the first step closer to someone from another culture is to be able to express the wonderful things about your own culture in English. This is a beginning step toward effective intercultural communication.

Another important aspect of building good communication skills is to teach young learners how to work in groups and teams successfully. Collaboration skills are an extremely important twenty-first-century skill because children will grow up in our globally interconnected world. They will inevitably be working collaboratively in their future jobs, so any way that we can encourage teamwork among students is a great idea. However, this does not just mean putting them in groups and saying, "Go!" Teachers need to provide students the language skills and models needed for students to participate in group work successfully. See "TEYL Tips—Success with Cooperative Learning" in Chapter 4 for good suggestions, including:

- Planning groups in which the teacher can select students with different strengths
- Giving groups fun names so students can feel a sense of belonging to the group

■ Assigning roles in the group like reader, recorder, time keeper, and presenter

■ Providing a clear end product so students know what they are working toward

These are some ways teachers can help students build skills for collaborating effectively with one another. In addition to these helpful tips, it is important to teach and model courteous language and behavior. Below are examples of behavior and language you might model and encourage from students.

> If you ask for something, say "Please."
>
> If you receive something, say "Thank you."
>
> If someone needs help, ask "May I help you?" "Do you need help?"
>
> If someone helps you, say "Thanks for your help!"
>
> If you do something that hurts someone, say "I'm sorry."
>
> If you need the teacher's attention, say "Excuse me, Mr./Ms. _____."
>
> If you want to do something, like go to the bathroom, ask "May I use the bathroom?"
>
> If someone does a good job, say "Good job!" "Great work!"
>
> If someone has a good idea, say "Good/great/excellent idea!" "Good thinking!"

Even if the native language must be used first to explain the scenarios and the language, it is important for teachers to establish courteous behavior and language that will help young learners communicate politely in English.

3. **Active learning skills** As the quotation from Alvin Toffler at the beginning of the chapter suggested, literacy in the twenty-first century means having the ability to learn, unlearn, and relearn. Our ever-changing world that has become so technology and knowledge driven makes it possible for us to access so much information and communicate with people from all over the world. As Curtis Bonk (2009) said in *The World Is Open*, "Anyone can now learn anything from anyone at any time" (p. 7). However, this means that children need critical thinking skills to sift through all the information that they will find through all the new information sources. In addition, they will need to learn how to learn because the information of today will likely change tomorrow. With young learners who are still developing cognitively, it is still possible to develop them into active learners by teaching them how to ask and answer questions about information at different levels. See the box for examples of question words for each level of questioning based on Bloom's taxonomy.

Categories of questions and typical classroom question words based on Bloom's (1956) taxonomy (Brown, 2007). These are listed by level of critical thinking from lowest to highest.

1. **Knowledge questions:** Eliciting factual answers, testing recall and recognition of information
   Common questions words: define, tell, list, identify, describe, select, name, point out, label, reproduce. Who? What? Where? When? Answer "yes" or "no."

2. **Comprehension questions:** Interpreting, extrapolating
   Common question words: state in your own words, explain, define, locate, select, indicate, summarize, outline, match.

3. **Application questions:** Applying information heard or read to new situations
   Common question words: demonstrate how, use the data to solve, illustrate how, show how, apply, construct, explain. What is ___ used for? What would result? What would happen?

4. **Inference questions:** Forming conclusions that are not directly stated in instructional materials
   Common question words: How? Why? What did ___ mean by? What does ___ believe? What conclusions can you draw from . . . ?

5. **Analysis questions:** Breaking down into parts, relating parts to the whole
   Common question words: distinguish, diagram, chart, plan, deduce, arrange, separate, outline, classify, contrast, compare, differentiate, categorize. What is the relationship between? What is the function of? What motive? What conclusions? What is the main idea?

6. **Synthesis questions:** Combining elements into a new pattern
   Common question words: compose, combine, estimate, invent, choose, hypothesize, build, solve, design, develop. What if? How would you test . . . ? What would you have done in this situation? What would happen if . . . ? How can you improve . . . ? How else would you . . . ?

7. **Evaluation questions:** Making a judgment of good or bad, right or wrong, according to some set of criteria, and stating why
   Common question words: evaluate, rate, defend, dispute, decide which, select, judge, grade, verify, choose why. Which is best? Which is more important? Which do you think is more appropriate? (Brown, 2007, p. 220)

Very young learners may not be able to reach higher levels of critical thinking because they are not at a cognitive stage that can handle logical reasoning. However, young learners from 7 to 12 years old are developing their reasoning abilities, and teachers should use all levels of questioning as appropriate to encourage students' critical thinking skills. Remember, it is important to ask young learners both closed and open-ended questions. Open-ended questions won't have one right answer and can encourage students to think critically. For example, when checking both knowledge and comprehension of a story like Cinderella, a teacher could ask the following questions:

> Does Cinderella have a mother?
> Does Cinderella have a father?
> What is a stepmother?
> Is the stepmother kind to Cinderella?

There is just one correct answer for all these questions, so they are closed questions and are only based on recalling information from the text. They are considered at the knowledge and comprehension levels and are the lowest levels in terms of Bloom's taxonomy. Of course, these are important questions for checking comprehension. However, the teacher could also ask the following questions:

> Does the stepmother love Cinderella? Why do you think so?
> Is Cinderella happy? Why do you think so?
> Why is the stepmother mean to Cinderella?

These are open-ended questions that create opportunities for children to think critically about the situation. Students have to infer from the text and show a higher level of thinking to come up with answers. These questions may also get them to apply Cinderella's situation to their own life or analyze other information in the story. Using only closed questions based on recalling information from the text won't help children build critical thinking skills.

Eventually YLs should learn how to ask themselves questions in order to help them become more independent learners. If they will need to unlearn and relearn knowledge and skills, then they need practice at questioning and building strategies for learning. Teachers can use the "think-aloud" strategy to help model the kinds of questions students might ask themselves as they accomplish tasks in English. A think-aloud is a popular strategy for improving students' reading comprehension where teachers verbalize their thinking process as they gain comprehension from text (Davey, 1983; Wilhelm, 2001). The teacher asks questions about the text or information out loud and then verbalizes her/his thinking process and answers. S/he may still continue to have unanswered questions about the text and information and should verbalize those throughout the process. This will show students how to approach a text or activity with a critical mind and see the process of learning and gaining comprehension from text.

After the teacher does a think-aloud, students practice it by thinking aloud following the teacher's model. "As they think aloud, students respond to the text, identify big ideas, ask self-questions, make connections, figure out how to solve problems that arise, and reflect on their use of strategies" (Tompkins, 2010, pp. 473–474). Teachers can use this strategy to model any kind of task to help scaffold students' ability to be active learners who can function independently. Teachers have to plan think-alouds carefully, including the language they will use to demonstrate their thinking and learning strategies. Below are some questions and sentence starters a teacher might use and say out loud, so students can see a good model to help them become more independent readers and learners.

- What is the title?
- This makes me think of. . . .
- What does it mean?
- What does this word mean?
- I think it means. . . .
- What does this remind me of?
- This is just like/similar to. . . .
- What do I know about . . . ?
- This author also wrote. . . .
- Why did the author write . . . ?
- I think the story (text, activity) will be about. . . .
- I think the big idea is. . . .
- I am not sure about. . . .
- I am confused by. . . .
- I re-read this part because. . . .
- I wonder if. . . .
- I don't understand. . . .

- Why did this happen?
- This is different from what I expected.
- What will happen next?
- I feel . . . about this story (text, activity) because. . . .
- I still don't understand. . . .
- Some questions I still have are. . . .

Teachers can use Post-It or sticky notes and attach them to the text to remind themselves of the language they will use for the think-aloud. If students need some parts of the think-aloud in their native language because of their proficiency level, teachers should use it sparingly in order to build students' strategies for learning. The importance of this technique is to demonstrate critical thinking and learning strategies, so strategies modeled in the native language to build comprehension in English do model real life and should be incorporated by teachers as appropriate.

4. Technology skills English in the twenty-first century includes computer-mediated communication. Learning how to communicate using new technology, such as Web 2.0 or user-generated content, social media or social networking tools, and online Internet searching, goes hand-in-hand with learning English, since the language most often used in Web sites worldwide is English. According to a survey conducted by World Wide Web Technology Surveys (W3Techs; http://w3techs.com) in September 2012, 55.1 percent of Web sites are in English. The next highest is German, with only 6.4 percent. See below for a list of the other most used languages in terms of Web content.

English	55.1%
German	6.4%
Russian	5.1%
Japanese	4.9%
Chinese	4.7%
Spanish	4.7%
French	4.3%
Portuguese	2.2%
Italian	2.0%
Polish	1.5%

Turkish	1.2%
Dutch/Flemish	1.1%
Arabic	1.1%
Others	Under 1%

The most popular sites using English, according to W3Techs are: Google, Facebook, YouTube, Yahoo, Wikipedia, Live, Twitter, Amazon, LinkedIn, and Google.co.in. Since English is still the dominant language on the Internet, when students are researching information or communicating with people through various social networking sites, the predominant language being used is English.

This also means that it is important for teachers to help students improve their information and digital literacy, which entails using Internet search engines and basic skills for navigating Web sites effectively. Improving their ability to sift through so much information and make good decisions about which Web sites have good, reliable information and which ones may have certain biases, students need to apply critical thinking skills as described above. Teachers can use think-alouds when showing Web sites or teaching students how to conduct good Internet searches and use the same strategies for helping students learn how to learn.

Teachers should bring the real world into the language classroom and encourage students to participate in social networking, Web content creation, and sharing through wikis and blogs in English as appropriate for their YLs. To prepare students for this century in the EYL classroom, teachers should take the responsibility to improve their own knowledge and skills using the Internet and Web 2.0 tools and incorporate computer-mediated communication into English language instruction. However, Prensky (2011) warns that teachers should not get too caught up in technology tools as the key to improving students' twenty-first-century skills. He uses a helpful "verbs vs. nouns" metaphor (p. 7).

> . . . the "verbs" are the unchanging skills of education, such as thinking critically, communicating effectively, presenting logically, and calculating correctly. The "nouns" are the tools of education—the technologies that students use to learn and practice the skills. In the 21st century, nouns change with increasing rapidity. For example, for learning the underlying skills (verbs) of presenting, communication, and getting information, nouns (tools) currently used include PowerPoint, email, and Wikipedia. But while the verbs will not change over the course of a student's education, the nouns certainly will. Our pedagogy needs to focus on the underlying verbs, while providing students with, and employing, the best, most up-to-date nouns (tools) to do so. (p. 7)

Therefore, EYL teachers should incorporate the up-to-date technology tools students need for communication in English without forgetting that these tools constantly change; in fact instruction should focus on the skills and functions they are using the tools for. Some describe these skills as "new literacies" which are essential to teach young learners for success in this century. Tompkins (2010) outlines four Internet reading strategies:

- **Navigating:** Students navigate the Internet to search for and locate information

- **Coauthoring:** Students coauthor online texts as they impose an organization on the information they are reading

- **Evaluating:** Students evaluate the accuracy, relevance, and quality of information on Web pages

- **Synthesizing:** Students synthesize information from multiple texts (p. 7)

Fisher and Frey (2010) created a useful list of the "verbs" (or skills) students in the twenty-first century need to build with the "nouns" or tools that are currently being used for those functions. The list on pg. 341 mirrors Fisher and Frey's list; however, it includes updates based on the tools that are most commonly used at the time of this publication. This list also makes a distinction between tools that are computer-based versus Web-based tools. It is clear that the tools for accomplishing various functions are becoming more Web based and are easily accessible through the Internet. Hopefully this list will be helpful for EYL teachers in recognizing which tools can be used for various skills and applying them to their English language classroom.

Teachers can develop projects with young learners that include some of the tools listed above. For very young learners around 5–6 years old, you may Skype with a class in another country and have students say hello to each other or sing songs together. You could also take a video of your students singing a song in English and post it on YouTube with the lyrics. Then the teacher can send the link to parents and have them practice the song with their child at home for extra practice or even exchange links with another class (possibly in another country) and learn each other's songs.

For young learners around 7–8 years old, you could encourage them to do Internet research on another country by typing in "food in Thailand" or "clothes

Functions/Skills	Computer-Based	Web-Based
Storing	MP3 players, servers, flash drives	Dropbox, iCloud, Box
Listening	Podcasts, iTunes	Streaming media
Presenting	PowerPoint, Keynote	Prezi
Producing	GarageBand, iMovie, Final Cut, Jing, CamStudio	Wordle, Storybird, ToonDoo, ArtisanCam, Animoto
Communicating		E-mailing, text messaging, Skype, ooVoo
Sharing		YouTube, Pinterest, Flickr, blogs, vlogs, Scoop.it
Collaborating		Google docs and sites, Google calendar, Doodle, wikis, Delicious, VoiceThread
Networking		Facebook, Ning, MySpace, Twitter, Digg, Reddit, Google+
Searching		Google, Yahoo, Bing, StumbleUpon

in Peru" into Google Images and have them describe the pictures that come up. Or you could have students write a poem and teach them how to post it on a class wiki or blog. This is a product that you can show parents and share with your school community.

For your older young learners who are 9–11 years old, you could encourage them to make digital stories to post on YouTube by using images combined with PowerPoint, with their narration recorded using a screencast such as Jing. Or they could create a simple class slide show using PowerPoint, in which each student is responsible for one slide that includes an image (photo, drawing, clip art, etc.) and text (description, poem, quote, etc.). The theme for the digital stories or slide show can be connected to whatever the content of your class is. For example, it could be food from around the world, wildlife in different regions of the world, or just a personal expression of themselves after a unit on writing acrostic poems.

Teachers should explore the kinds of tools that are available and appropriate for their learners and begin incorporating technology tools as a part of the EYL curriculum in order to build real use of English in the twenty-first century, which is increasingly digitized and networked.

Designing a Technology-Based Thematic Unit

The following unit plan is based on an ongoing project using a class wiki to encourage students to use English for real communication. See below for the home page of a sample wiki for an English class in grade 4. This wiki was made using www.wikispaces.com.

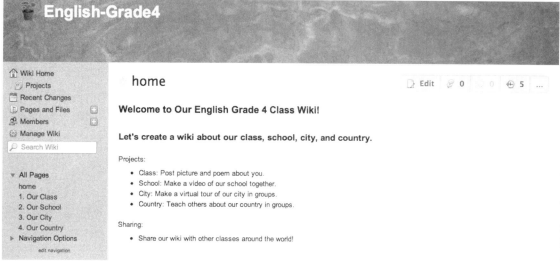

Provided by Jodi Crandall and Joan Shin

Use of Wikispaces is free, and teachers can create a new wiki for each new class. This wiki has four pages representing four different class projects:

- **Our Class:** This page will include a picture of each student and a personal poem written by each student. This project will be the culmination of a unit that introduces different types of poems.

Example of Our Class page:

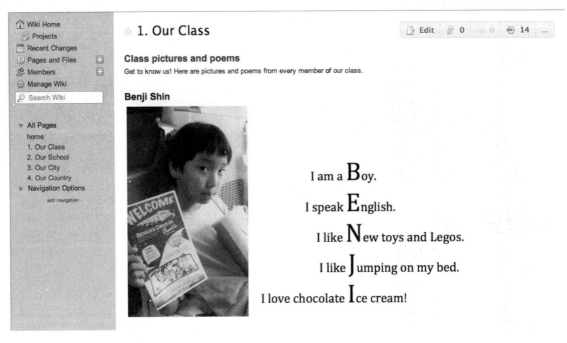

- **Our School:** This page will put up basic information about the school and a video tour of the school. The teacher will facilitate the process of making a video of the school and classroom. This project will be the culmination of group and whole-class discussions on who, what, when, where, and how to videotape a 5-minute introduction to your school.

Example of Our School page:

- **Our City:** This page will be a virtual tour of the city in which students live. Students will work in groups and decide what their city is famous for. Then they will take pictures with a camera, mobile device, or smart phone of places in the city that are considered landmarks, famous food or produce, typical architecture, typical clothes or crafts, sport teams, etc. Then they will, as a class, decide which pictures to put on the page and work in groups to write sentences about each. In addition, they will search the Internet for hyperlinks to other pages with pictures and information about their city and landmarks.

Example of Our City page:

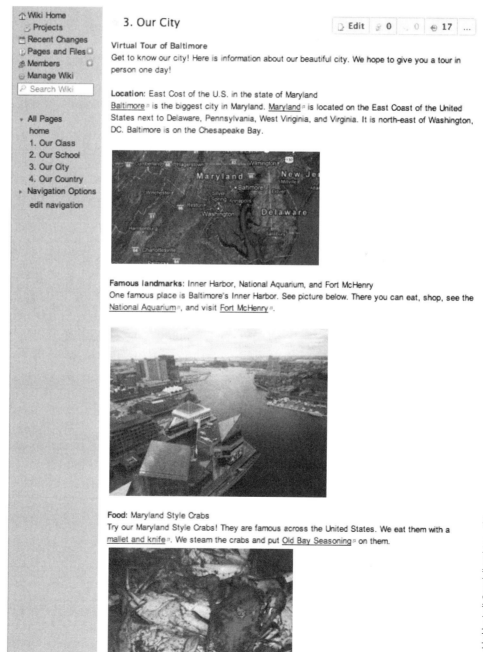

Provided by Jodi Crandall and Joan Shin

- **Our Country:** This page will show their country's Top Ten List. Students will work in groups and decide the top ten things to do in their country. For example, in the United States, the Top Ten List could include: Go to the top of the Empire State Building in New York City; visit the Smithsonian museums in Washington, D.C.; hike through the Grand Canyon in Arizona; eat a Philly cheesesteak in Philadelphia, etc. In addition, students have to create at least one hyperlink to an official Web site on that landmark or about that particular activity. All groups will post their top ten lists with hyperlinks on the wiki. In addition, the teacher can show students how to use Google Maps to put markers in the exact locations for each of the top ten things to do.

Example of Our Country page:

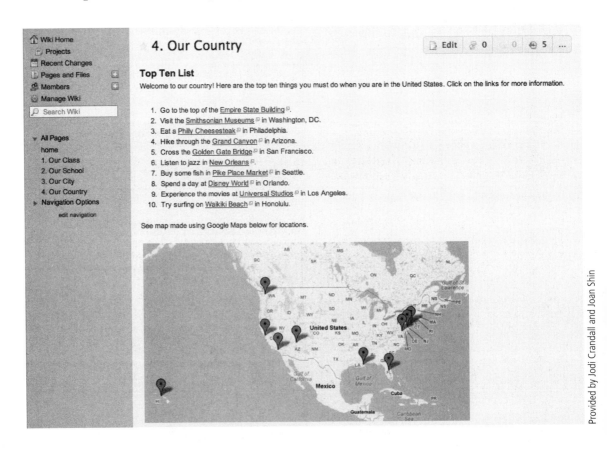

Provided by Jodi Crandall and Joan Shin

Once the wiki is completed, the teacher will exchange wikis with another 4th grade class from another country. Students will do a series of reading activities with the other class's wiki. If teachers want to look for other classes and other projects to get involved in, ePals (www.epals.com) is a good resource.

Sample Lesson

Class Wiki: Our City

Below is a lesson for the third project called Our City.

Class Wiki: Our City	
Student profile	Grade 4 or 5, high-beginner level of English language proficiency
Skills to be emphasized	Listening, speaking, reading, writing
Language	Vocabulary: city, virtual, tour, landmarks, museum, statue, market, harbor, food, famous, link, hyperlink Grammar: prepositions (in, on, at, across) *(New vocabulary will depend on the source of your Web page.)*
Objectives	By the end of this lesson, students will be able to: • Explain and show the location of their city • Describe famous landmarks in their city • Describe famous things (e.g., food, locations) from their city • Read about another city on another class wiki
Materials	**Computer with Internet** Wikispace class page at wikispaces.com (or use another wiki online) Picture of another class in another country (contact a teacher in advance to set up this class-to-class project) Handout with the text from the example Our City page. Whiteboard or flipchart
Warm-up **Before-reading Activities**	
Capture their attention	Show a picture of another class in another country. Ask students, "What is in this picture? Who are these people?" Tell them it is a picture from another 4th grade class from another country. "This is another 4th grade class. Can you guess where it is?" Tell them what country the class is from. "After we make Our City page, we will share our wiki with them!"
Connect to prior knowledge and experiences	"Let's look at our class wiki. What did we already do on our wiki?" Elicit the following answers from students: • Made pictures and poems about us • Made a video of our school and classroom • Sang a song on the video • Posted pictures on wiki • Posted video on wiki See wiki home page for ongoing project information.

Introduce lesson	"Today we are going to make another wiki page. It will be about Our City. It will be a virtual tour of our city."
Review vocabulary	Review the meaning of "tour" and prepare students for instruction on the word "virtual." "Do you know what a tour is?" Show picture of people on a tour in your country at a famous landmark. Elicit responses to these questions until students can verbalize that the people in the picture are on a tour. "What are these people doing? They are visiting from. . . . They are looking at. . . . They are on a tour." Next, review the video as a tour of the school. "What did we do on our wiki last time? Right, we made a video of our school and classroom. That was a tour of our school and classroom." Now try to elicit what "virtual" means. "But is the tour in person like this picture? No, it was 'virtual'; that means not real. It is not in person. It is 'virtual' because it is through the Internet and through video."

Presentation During-reading Activities	
Present text and check comprehension	Show students an example of a class wiki made by a class in Baltimore. See the Our City example page. Have students read the page and fill in a graphic organizer to check their comprehension of the following text (without the pictures). If there is only one computer in the room, project the wiki page on the screen or wall. If it is not readable, prepare a handout with the text for students to read at their desks. --- **WIKI PAGE TEXT** **Virtual Tour of Baltimore** Get to know our city! Here is information about our beautiful city. We hope to give you a tour in person one day! **Location:** East Coast of the U.S. in the state of Maryland Baltimore is the biggest city in Maryland. Maryland is located on the East Coast of the United States next to Delaware, Pennsylvania, West Virginia, and Virginia. It is northeast of Washington, D.C. Baltimore is on the Chesapeake Bay. *[Picture of map of Maryland]* **Famous landmarks:** Inner Harbor, National Aquarium, and Fort McHenry One famous place is Baltimore's Inner Harbor. See picture below. There you can eat, shop, see the National Aquarium, and visit Fort McHenry. *[Picture of Inner Harbor]*

	Food: Maryland-Style Crabs Try our Maryland-Style crabs! They are famous across the United States. We eat them with a mallet and knife. We steam the crabs and put Old Bay Seasoning on them. *[Picture of crabs]* **Sports teams:** Orioles Baseball Team and Ravens Football Team Here is a picture of the Oriole Park at Camden Yards. Nearby is the Ravens Football Stadium. People from Baltimore love their sports teams. The names of their teams are both names of birds: the oriole and the raven. *[Picture of Camden Yards]* **Famous Baltimore people:** Francis Scott Key and Edgar Allan Poe
	Francis Scott Key is a famous American. He wrote our national anthem, called the "Star Spangled Banner." He wrote the words during the War of 1812. Here is a video of the national anthem at Camden Yards before an Orioles baseball game. Edgar Allan Poe is another famous American. He was a writer and poet. He wrote many scary stories and a famous poem called "The Raven." Because of Poe's poem, the Baltimore football team is named the Ravens.

Graphic Organizer

Read the Our City page about Baltimore.
Write the key words in the chart about Baltimore.

	1. Baltimore	**2. _____**
a. Location		
b. Landmarks		
c. Food		
d. Sports teams		
e. Famous people		
f. _____		

Teach wiki page form and unknown words	Go over answers to the graphic organizer above. While explaining unknown words and phrases, such as Old Bay Seasoning, mallet, oriole, raven, etc., familiarize students with the hyperlinks on the page. Show them how to get more information by clicking on the words that are underlined.
Practice **After-Reading Activities (Speaking and Writing)**	
Controlled practice	**Whole-Class Brainstorm** The teacher has a brainstorming session on WHAT MAKES OUR CITY SPECIAL? Make a list of about five or six ideas and spell them out correctly on the board or on flipchart paper. This will help prepare them for the next activity.
Guided practice	**Pair Work** Students fill out the third column in the graphic organizer. Ask them to write their city name at the top in blank #2 (next to Baltimore). Then have students work in pairs to fill out one piece of information per row. Students can also think of another category and write it in blank #f (below e. Famous people). Your city may have a special kind of clothing, architecture, river, etc. The teacher will collect answers and make a big list for each category on the board or flipchart.
Independent activity	**Group Work** The teacher will break the students into six groups, one for each category: location, landmark, food, sports teams, famous people, and other. Then each group must write down four sentences about their category.
Application	
Create wiki	**Group Work** In groups, students take turns typing information into the class wiki page called Our City. They will follow the format: **Category:** Subheading Title **Four Sentences:** Xxxxxxxxxxxxxxxx. Xxxxxxxxxxxxxxxxxxx. Xxxxxxxxxxxxxxxxxxxxxxxxxxx. Xxxxxxxxxxxxxxxxxxxxxxx. *Example* **Food:** Maryland-Style Crabs Try our Maryland-Style Crabs! They are famous across the United States. We eat them with a mallet and knife. We steam the crabs and put Old Bay Seasoning on them.

Assessment	
Monitoring activities	The teacher must assess during all parts of the practice and application stages. Students will need immediate feedback on their choice of information and help constructing sentences that are comprehensible and accurate.
Assess for accuracy and give feedback	**Option #1:** The teacher can highlight in yellow the parts of the wiki text that have errors or mistakes. The class as a group can make corrections with the wiki page projected on the screen or wall. The teacher can make corrections on the wiki as students figure out the correct way to write the text (with the teacher's help). **Option #2:** The teacher can make corrections on the wiki. If students are too sensitive to correct each other's sentences, then the teacher may do the corrections outside of class, and then have students read through the correct version.
Follow-up	
Homework	Students will have one week to take the pictures they need to go with their text. The pictures will be uploaded to the wiki in one week.
Next class	In one week, the next project lesson will be on how to create hyperlinks. Students will do Internet research to find hyperlinks to other pages with pictures and information about their city and landmarks. Then they will create their hyperlinks in their text.

■ Teacher to Teacher

Twenty-First-Century Skills for Young Learners

Most teachers would agree that addressing twenty-first-century skills for young learners is a must in education. However, not all teachers find it easy to incorporate these skills in the EYL classroom. The following teachers explain their point of view related to incorporating these skills. First is a teacher from Belarus who describes the integration of social responsibility and problem solving into the curriculum.

"I strongly believe that 21st century skills are important for our students, and in our school we try to include them in the curriculum. For this we have a special lesson—a class hour where we discuss and solve different social problems, train children's personal skills and simply talk friendly solving their own problems. We have Self-Ruling days, when kids can train themselves in our roles, developing their leadership qualities. And we have a very good psychologist who is always there to help. She holds lessons and does tests to help us learn more about the kids."

—*Julia Khokhlova, Primary and Secondary English Teacher, Belarus*

A teacher from India describes how twenty-first-century skills are already integrated into the primary school curriculum.

"Today to survive in this digital era critical thinking, problem solving ICT application, team work and innovation are the skills we need. Our curriculum should include the above skills as they are the skills the employers need and they are the skills necessary for our learners' future. To keep at par with the need of the age, our curriculum should give importance to projects, individualized instruction, collaborative learning, Web Based learning and Lifelong learning. Our school curriculum gives importance to all the 21st century skills. ICT application and web based teaching are included in the school curriculum itself. To develop the critical thinking skills of learners project based teaching is followed. Importance is given to enquiry based learning. Asking questions, defining a problem, analyzing, peer learning, cooperative learning are promoted through the curriculum.

Most of the lessons have quizzes, projects and assignment to build team work among the students. To teach the lesson Animals on the Track a field trip is arranged to encourage enquiry based learning. After the field trip learners are asked to submit a project as a group work."

—*Joycilin Shermila Azariah, English Teacher Trainer, India*

One teacher describes how he integrates twenty-first-century skills into the EFL classroom by using project-based learning.

"The 21st century skills that English Teachers should develop in YLs are;
- IT skills
- Problem Solving
- Critical Thinking
- Creativity
- Identifying own self
- Communicating skills
- Listening skills
- Living in Peace
- Co-operation

These skills can be developed through activity based learning where students get involved themselves willingly. Using technology in teaching and promoting high standards of student involvement in the lesson and creating opportunities for the learner to widen their horizon in the area of topics that they learn is one step. Creating experiment based learning is another way of awakening their thinking power.

When planning the lessons, the teacher can make use of *3Hs*,
- *Head (Cognitive)*,
- *Hand (Psycho-motor) and*
- *Heart (Affective/Feelings)*

and the specific objectives of the lesson can be divided under these 3 sections where the student gets all the necessary abilities at the end of the lesson to become a knowledgeable, capable and worthy citizen for the country."

—Vidarshani Lalanthika Wijesinghe, Primary English Teacher, Teacher Trainer, and Lecturer in English, Sri Lanka

Some teachers may find it challenging to find support for building twenty-first-century skills, but as one teacher from Brazil describes, the English language classroom can be an ideal place to hone certain twenty-first-century skills.

"Although all 21st century skills are important for children's development, I believe that English teachers are very close to communication skills and global languages. As the world has become smaller, due to technology, it's essential to be able to communicate clearly these days, and the use of English as an international language gives this opportunity to many people around the world.

It's also important to teach children that nowadays we are all citizens of the world. We are all inserted in this cultural melting pot, in which countries and nationalities seem to lose their boundaries, in order to create a society that is connected worldwide through a range of communication tools in a very large scale.

Collaboration is also important, as it is known that we are all interdependent, in a world where economic policies are not isolated issues of a certain country or region, but affects all others in a chain of events, sometimes unpredictable.

As English teachers we can offer children a passport into this globalized world, using a language that, presently, can open doors to different cultures, not only to English speaking countries, but a whole society that speaks English around the globe."

—Carina Alice De Oliveira, English Teacher, Brazil

◼ Chapter Summary

To Conclude

Our rapidly changing world requires certain skills The world is changing quickly into a knowledge-based, information-driven global society. This requires an educational foundation that builds skills for our rapidly changing world.

Proficiency in English is one twenty-first-century skill Given the worldwide push to teach English at the primary school level, being able to use English as an international language for communication is clearly one twenty-first-century skill being emphasized in primary school curricula across the globe.

Global citizenship and values Ultimately the world will need citizens who care about its future and can work together to resolve global issues. Learning how to care for one another and the environment will help YLs be positive and productive citizens of our world.

Communication and collaboration across cultures YLs need to learn how to communicate effectively across cultures. One important way to help them communicate interculturally is to teach them how to express their own culture in English. In addition, teachers need to provide plenty of opportunities for group and team work to promote good collaboration skills.

Critical thinking and lifelong learning strategies Because the information of today will likely change tomorrow, YLs need critical thinking skills and must learn how to learn independently to help them cope with our rapidly changing world.

Computer, information, and digital literacy YLs will need computer, information, and digital literacy skills in English for their future studies and careers. Because of the quantity of information exchanged online, it is necessary for YLs to learn how to apply critical thinking skills.

■ Over to You

Discussion Questions

1. Why are people in the world more interconnected in the twenty-first century than ever before?
2. The Partnership for 21st Century Skills lists ten skills that students need to have. What are they?
3. Which three of the ten skills do you think are the most essential for YLs in your context? Why?
4. Why must taking a global perspective be an integral part of the EYL curriculum?
5. If English language proficiency is an important twenty-first-century skill, why do you think it was not included in the twenty-first-century skill frameworks presented in this chapter? Are there other languages that your students should learn?
6. For very young learners who are not highly developed cognitively, what are ways you can apply twenty-first-century skills in the curriculum for each category?
   a. Global perspective
   b. Communication skills
   c. Active learning skills
   d. Technology skills

Checklist for Curriculum Development

On pg. 390 there is a worksheet that has been made to help you assess how well your EYL curriculum infuses twenty-first-century skills. This can be used for the curriculum as a whole, one unit of instruction, or a lesson plan.

Twenty-First-Century Skills and English: What is the link between teaching English as an international language and twenty-first-century skills? Write about the connection between the use of English in global contexts and the skills needed to become a successful and productive citizen of our world. Give one or two examples of how you would address twenty-first-century skills in your EYL class on a regular basis in relation to your main points.

■ Resources and References

Print Publications

Beers, S. Z. (2011). *Teaching 21st century skills: An ASCD action tool.* Alexandria, VA: ASCD.

Bellanca, J., & Brandt, R. (Eds). (2010). *21st century skills: Rethinking how students learn.* Bloomington, IN: Solution Tree Press.

Collins, M. (2008). *Global citizenship for young children.* London: Sage Publications.

Jacobs, H. H. (2010). *Curriculum 21: Essential education for a changing world.* Alexandria, VA: ASCD.

Partnership for 21st Century Skills. (2009). *P21 framework definitions.* Washington, DC: Author. Accessed at www.p21.org/documents/P21_Framework_Definitions.pdf on August 18, 2012.

Useful Web Sites

Assessment and Teaching of 21st Century Skills: http://atc21s.org

The Critical Thinking Community: www.criticalthinking.org

Curriculum 21: www.curriculum21.com

Partnership for 21st Century Skills: www.p21.org

References

Binkley, M., Erstad, O., Herman, J., Raizen, S., Ripley, M., Miller-Ricci, M., & Rumble, M. (2012). Defining 21st century skills. In P. Griffin, B. McGaw, & E. Care (Eds.), *Assessment and teaching of 21st century skills* (pp. 17–66). Dordrecht: Springer.

Bloom, B. S., & David, R. K. (1956). *Taxonomy of educational objectives: The classification of education goals, by a committee of college and university examiners. Handbook 1: Cognitive domain.* New York, NY: Longman, Green.

Bonk, C. J. (2009). *The world is open: How Web technology is revolutionizing education.* San Francisco: Jossey-Bass.

Brown, H. D. (2007). Teaching by principles: An interactive approach to language pedagogy. White Plains, NY: Longman.

Davey, B. (1983). Think-aloud: Modeling the cognitive processes of reading comprehension. *Journal of Reading, 27*(1), 44–47.

Fisher, D., & Frey, N. (2010). Preparing students for mastery of 21st century skills. In J. Bellanca & R. Brandt (Eds), *21st century skills: Rethinking how students learn* (pp. 221–240). Bloomington, IN: Solution Tree Press.

Jacobs, H. H. (2010). *Curriculum 21: Essential education for a changing world.* Alexandria, VA: ASCD.

Marzano, R. J., & Heflebower, T. (2012). *Teaching and assessing 21st century skills.* Bloomington, IN: Marzano Research Laboratory.

McCain, T., & Jukes, I. (2001). *Windows on the future: Education in the age of technology.* Thousand Oaks, CA: Corwin Press.

Partnership for 21st Century Skills. (2011). *Framework for 21st century learning.* Washington, DC: Author.

Prensky, M. (2011, January 24). The reformers are leaving our schools in the 20th century: Why most U.S. school reformers are on the wrong track, and how to get our kids' education right for the future. *Strategic News Service Newsletter, 14*(4). Retrieved at http://marcprensky.com/writing/+Prensky-The_Reformers_Are_Leaving_Our_Schools_in_the_20th_Century-please_distribute_freely.pdf

Shin, J. K. & Crandall, J. A. (Eds.) (2013). Our world. Boston, MA: National Geographic Learning/Cengage Learning.

Tompkins, G. E. (2010). *Literacy for the 21st century: A balanced approach.* Boston, MA: Allyn & Bacon/Pearson Education.

Trilling, B., & Fadel, C. (2009). *21st century skills: Learning for life in our times.* San Francisco, CA: Jossey-Bass.

Wilhelm, J. D. (2001). *Improving comprehension with think-aloud strategies.* New York, NY: Scholastic Inc.

10 Professional Development

■ Getting Started

Teaching is "the learning profession" (Darling-Hammond & Sykes, 1999). As teachers, we naturally develop over time as we gain experience, especially if we enjoy teaching (Foord, 2009). In the beginning, you may find that just becoming comfortable as an EYL teacher takes most of your time and energy. But over time, you will want to take advantage of available professional development activities or even to set up a short-term or long-term action plan for your own development.

As an EYL teacher, you may also find that your role changes over time: You may become the chair of your department; you may be asked to coordinate testing or professional development for your program or a number of schools; you may even decide to pursue a graduate degree and become a university EYL teacher educator. Each of these roles offers an opportunity for gradual, continuous professional development and for participation in new professional development activities. The same is true if you remain an EYL teacher. You may be asked to participate in teacher training programs offered by your school, but you will also want to identify professional development activities you choose to participate in, sometimes in cooperation with colleagues at your institution or in settings around the world (Crandall, 1998; Edge, 1992, 2002). This chapter introduces a number of these options.

Think About It

As you finish this book (and possibly a course in Teaching English for Young Learners), think about what you have learned about teaching young learners. What questions do you still have? What challenges do you think you will face? Briefly fill out the following chart and share your ideas with another student or colleague.

WHAT I HAVE LEARNED	QUESTIONS	POSSIBLE CHALLENGES

Discovery Activity

Brainstorming Web

Now look at the questions and challenges you listed. How will you answer these questions? Where can you turn to get help with the challenges? What are some types of professional development that might be available? Who might be able to help you?

Brainstorm the people you can turn to and the kinds of professional development (PD) activities that you might be able to participate in. Be sure to consider activities available through technology. If possible, you may also want to interview an EYL teacher to find out what challenges s/he has faced and the resources (people and activities) s/he has found to help her/him in meeting those challenges.

Theory, Planning and Application

Why Professional Development Is Important

Teaching is lifelong learning. One of the joys of teaching is the opportunity to explore new ideas and new ways of teaching as we try to meet the needs of an ever-changing group of learners. If you have never taught young learners, then you will be learning a great deal during your first years about how to plan, manage, teach, and assess young learners. Some you will learn from experience. Some you may learn by talking with or observing more experienced colleagues. You may also continue to grow as a teacher of young learners by participating in professional development activities sponsored by your school or by a professional association, some of it face-to-face and some of it through online sources. If you are an experienced teacher, you may find that working with colleagues on curriculum or lessons or participating in a conference will enable you to share your experiences, develop a larger network of colleagues, and provide some new ideas or activities for your classroom (Crandall, 2001; Egbert, 2003).

The field of TEYL is constantly changing and growing, and you will want to find appropriate ways to keep current. Being an effective EYL teacher requires "the knowledge, skills, and sensitivities of a teacher of children" and "of a teacher of language," and the ability to balance these effectively in teaching (Brewster, Ellis, & Girard, 2010, p. 269). You may want to create a professional development action plan for your first year of teaching to enhance your "knowledge, skills, and sensitivities," and then refer to it throughout the year to see how you are progressing. In that action plan, you may want to set goals that focus on techniques of teaching as well as goals focused on English language development and the use of the first language. Even English-speaking teachers may need to reflect on their use of the first language and of English in their classrooms (Brewster, Ellis, & Girard, 2010).

Approaches to Professional Development

When thinking about some possible people and activities that could help you develop as a teacher, they likely could be grouped under one of the following three approaches to professional development, as identified by Wallace (1991):

- Theory-to-practice approach
- Coaching or mentoring approach
- Reflective approach

Theory-to-Practice Approach A theory-to-practice approach (or teaching as science) is one in which teachers learn from experts by reading about their theories or listening to them speak at major conferences or in online webinars or podcasts, and then apply what they have learned in their teaching. This is likely the major way that you learned in a teacher education program. And though current approaches to professional development (as well as teaching) are more focused on experience, and less on the transmission of ideas, one still can learn a lot from this approach by taking graduate classes, participating in workshops or seminars, or engaging in online discussion groups where experts and colleagues engage in discussion.

White Packert/Getty Images

Coaching or Mentoring Approach A coaching or mentoring approach (or teaching as craft) is one in which less experienced teachers (or those with less experience in a particular skill or activity, such as using technology resources) learn from those with more experience and then apply that to their own teaching. Sometimes this involves collaborative coaching or even team teaching (Joyce & Showers, 1995; Knight, 2009).

Jack Hollingsworth/Getty Images

Reflective Approach A reflective approach (or teaching as critical thinking) is one in which teachers critically analyze or research, reflect upon, and adapt their own practice (Farrell, 2007, 2012; Richards & Lockhart, 1994; Wallace, 1996).

Tara Moore/Getty Images

Key to all three approaches is reflection. As Wallace (1991, 1996) and others (Crandall & Finn Miller, 2014; Freeman, 1998; Murray, 2010) have indicated, critical reflection is an important component of any approach to professional learning, including the approaches that consider teaching as a science or an art. Taking a graduate course, participating in an online discussion board, or being part of a study circle at your school or with colleagues from a number of schools all require critical analysis and reflection about what one has read or discussed. Likewise, participating in a coaching or mentoring relationship involves not only observing and discussing teaching and learning with a colleague, but also reflecting upon what has been observed or discussed. Technology has made it possible to engage in many more professional development activities and to network with other EYL teachers around the world. In the end, of course, you will construct your own conception of effective teaching and learning through multiple avenues, and you will want to share that with other teachers through the range of professional development activities discussed below.

Effective Professional Development

If you have been teaching for some time, you probably have been involved in professional development activities that are organized by your program or school. While your attendance at these was likely to be required, you may not have had any input into determining the topic or the types of activities that were involved. If you are a new teacher, you may still find that you will be expected to attend workshops that are planned by administrators, but you may also have the opportunity to help plan your own professional development activities. In fact, creating a professional development action plan with your own short-term and long-term objectives and some of the ways you plan to achieve these objectives is an excellent idea, even if your institution does not request it. "The most effective professional development begins with your concerns and your classroom. Just as effective language lessons address the needs of learners, professional development for language teachers should be relevant to your particular needs" (Crandall & Finn Miller, 2014). Each teacher has unique strengths and needs. If you are an experienced teacher, you are likely to want and need different opportunities for professional development than those of a beginning teacher.

In general, effective professional development:

- Takes place over time; it does not consist of isolated, unrelated workshops
- Emphasizes concrete activities, not abstract theory
- Involves teachers in the planning
- Provides teachers with opportunities to share their knowledge and experiences
- Focuses on the classroom and student learning
  (Darling-Hammond et al., 2009; Desimone, 2011; Guskey & Yoon, 2009; Timperley et al., 2007)

Effective professional development also requires key attitudes on the part of the teacher, such as being open to new ideas, taking responsibility for one's learning, and reflecting on professional development experiences (Foord, 2009).

Professional Development Activities

One way of thinking about opportunities for professional development is through the five categories identified by Foord (2009, p. 14), which he describes as concentric circles, with "You" at the center and "You and your profession" on the outside:

- You: reading alone or reflecting upon your own classes
- You and your students: getting feedback or new ideas from students
- You and your colleagues: learning or getting support from other teachers through mentoring, peer observation, or team teaching
- You and your school: carrying out projects and interacting with administrators
- You and your profession: participating in professional associations or learning communities and writing for publication

These are not necessarily the order in which you will engage in effective professional development. Nor are they necessarily in the order that will be most effective. Nor are they mutually exclusive. You may be engaged in learning from your colleagues and then reflecting upon what you have learned in a teaching journal. Or you may work collaboratively on a curriculum development project with other teachers and then present that curriculum at a meeting of a national or international professional association. But they are one way of thinking about the teacher development resources available to you, and in time you will want to explore all of these possible directions. Some of the ways of developing yourself as a teacher include:

- Engaging in reflective teaching and practice—including keeping a teaching journal, participating in a reflective teaching group, or developing a teaching portfolio
- Coaching and mentoring—including team teaching
- Observing classes—including collaborative peer observation and self-observation
- Engaging in teacher research—including action and collaborative action research
- Participating in continued formal and informal learning—including participating in workshops, podcasts, seminars, webinars, online discussion lists, graduate classes, and learning communities
- Participating in professional associations and conferences
- Networking through social media and blogs
- Learning from your students
- Developing instructional materials and curricula
- Writing for publication

Engaging in Reflective Teaching or Practice

According to Farrell (2012), "There is growing recognition within the field of language education that individual teachers must constantly reshape their knowledge of teaching and learning throughout their careers," and "There is also a need to reflect on our knowledge about language teaching throughout our careers in order to stay fresh and avoid burnout. Thus, language teachers must take on the role of reflective practitioners in order to continue to develop professionally" (p. 23).

Reflection helps us to learn from our experiences, to become more conscious of what we do and why we are doing it, and to analyze the results through systematic collection and analysis of information (Richards & Lockhart, 1994; Zeichner & Liston, 1996).

There are three main types of reflective practice:

- **Reflection-in-action:** thinking about what we are doing while we are doing it, in the classroom

- **Reflection-on-action:** thinking about the class after it is over

- **Reflection-for-action:** using what we have learned from our reflections to plan for future classes
  (Schon, 1983, 1987)

The last, of course, is the ultimate goal of reflection: to help us plan for and implement more effective teaching and learning in our classes. Our reflections can be captured in a teaching journal or teaching portfolio, or in discussions with our peers (for example, in a reflective teaching group).

Keeping a teaching diary or journal As you complete a class, you may want to make some notes about what went well or what you might want to change next time. You could do this on your lesson plan, but you may also want to engage in a bit more analysis and reflection. Keeping a teaching diary or journal encourages active reflection and provides a place where you can record these reflections (Appel, 1995; Bailey, Curtis, & Nunan, 2001; Richards & Farrell, 2005). It will also allow you to go back through a year (or more) and see what progress you have

Maya Choi/Getty Images

made—what new insights you have about your teaching, your students, and their learning. It will also help you in making instructional decisions (Bailey, 1990; Moon, 2000; Pinter, 2006).

One way of organizing the information is to develop a set of questions to answer, such as:

- What is one thing about the class that pleased me? Why?
- What is one thing that did not go well? Why?
- What might I do differently next time to address the problem?

You might also want to make a list of aspects of teaching and learning to consider, such as:

- Planning the lesson
- Beginning the lesson
- Giving directions
- Making yourself understood in English
- Managing the class
- Encouraging participation by all learners
- Providing feedback
- Helping learners to develop listening, speaking, reading, or writing skills
- Introducing and practicing vocabulary
- Reducing teacher talk and increasing student talk
- Other goals that you have

It is best to write down your thoughts as soon after the class as possible, at least during the same day.

At first, it might be best to record your impressions of only one class or perhaps to compare two classes in which you taught the "same" lesson. Over time, you may only want to record insights on classes that were particularly meaningful, either because they went so well or because something that you had thought would be successful turned

Nada Kujundžić, a primary English teacher and Ph.D. student from Croatia, reflects on her lesson at the end of the day, noting on the lesson plan what was successful, whether she has achieved her objectives, and how she might improve it:

"Prior to this learning program, I perceived lesson plans as no more than lists of activities, and reminders of which materials I need to bring with me to the classroom. I would usually glance at them before the beginning of the lesson, and rarely referred to them during the lesson itself. Reading the texts and my colleagues' posts, as well as preparing the thematic unit plan, helped alter my perspective for the better. I am beginning to take lesson planning much more seriously. Furthermore, I now use lesson plans as a means of self-evaluation and self-monitoring. At the end of the day, I go through each lesson plan and try to assess (as objectively as possible) how successful each activity was and whether or not I managed to achieve all the teaching objectives; I also try to determine the strong and weak point of the lesson, and come up with ways to improve it."

out not to have worked. One advantage of a teaching diary is its privacy: You can record your concerns, criticism, and praise without fear of anyone else reading it. If you want, however, you can also share some of what you have recorded with your colleagues as they go through similar phases in their careers.

Participating in a reflective teaching group You may want to start meeting with a group of colleagues to discuss problems or issues you are having with your teaching and, with your colleagues' help, think through ways of addressing these. In a reflective teaching group, at each meeting one teacher talks about a concern, then answers questions from other colleagues, thinks about some possible directions, asks colleagues for other options, and then decides on a course of action, tries it out in subsequent classes, and reports back to the group at their next meeting. The group should be small, and it's best to have a facilitator to guide the discussion. It's important that colleagues not provide advice until the teacher has both completed the discussion of the problem and offered some ideas that s/he has to address it. Teachers who have participated in these groups find not only that they change some of their teaching practices, but that they also change their thinking about teaching, so that they become more inspired and feel greater connection with their colleagues.

Developing a teaching portfolio If you were in a teacher education program or applied for teacher certification, you undoubtedly had to keep a teaching portfolio—a collection of documents, with written reflective commentary, that helps you to better understand your own teaching and provides others with an opportunity to review it as well. According to Brown and Wolfe-Quintero (1997), portfolios are "a purposeful collection of any aspect of a teacher's work that tells the story of a teacher's efforts, skills, abilities, achievements, and contribution to her/his colleagues, institution, academic discipline or community" (p. 28). Portfolios are often used for evaluation, but they can also be powerful ways to understand and document your professional growth (Porter & Cleland, 1995; Tanner, 2003). Your portfolio should contain examples of both your own work (for example, lesson plans, materials you have created, and proposals you have written for conference presentations) and your students' work, with commentaries about each. The comments you write about each document are entered in your portfolio, and a look back through previous documents can provide concrete evidence of your own growth. Over time, you can add and remove documents. You may also want to scan these and make yours an e-portfolio for easier maintenance.

Coaching and Mentoring
If this is the first time you have taught EYL or you are in a new school, you may want to see if you can find a more experienced

teacher who can help you get oriented to both the EYL program and the school. This teacher may also be someone you can turn to when you have questions or are facing challenges in your teaching. You will also want to meet with this teacher on a regular basis to discuss what you have observed and any concerns you might have (Crandall & Finn Miller, 2013; Holcomb & Green, 1998; Malderez, 2009).

As you become more experienced, you will want to offer to help other new teachers. You will find that in doing so, you will also learn a great deal about your own views of teaching and learning (Richards & Farrell, 2005). Even early in your career you may find yourself in a mentoring or coaching role. For example, you may find that you have much more experience and knowledge about how to integrate technology into your teaching than many of the other EYL or content teachers; offer to share that expertise with other teachers, perhaps through informal mentoring or longer-term coaching as they try to implement some of your suggestions.

Coaching and mentoring are particularly effective because they provide ongoing professional development that is teacher-directed, collaborative, and focused on immediate concerns and contexts. It has been shown to increase the use of new teaching strategies, improve student achievement, and provide teachers with an increased sense of confidence in their teaching (Joyce & Showers, 1995; Knight, 2009; Teemant, Wink, & Tyra, 2011).

Team teaching You may also want to engage in co-teaching as a means of both mentoring others and receiving mentoring (Bailey, Curtis, & Nunan, 2001; Crandall, 1998). This can be especially productive when each of you has something special to share and to learn. You could collaborate with another EYL teacher or with a mainstream or content area teacher who shares your students. If the other is another EYL teacher, you can work together to prepare a lesson and collaborate in teaching it, learning from each other the various types of activities, feedback, classroom management, and other strategies that you use. You may even want to divide the instruction to showcase each of your strengths.

If you co-teach with a mainstream or content area teacher who shares your students, you may want to focus your attention on the students who are having difficulty in your English class—those who are shy, who seem bored, who present classroom management problems. Notice how this other teacher works with these students. In the process of teaming, you can also learn more about the knowledge and skills that your students are learning in their other classes, as well as some classroom activities that other teachers use. In turn, you can provide the other teacher with knowledge about how languages are learned and taught, and even give some English language equivalents of the vocabulary and topics that are being taught (Crandall, 1998).

Observing Classes   Observations are usually a part of a mentoring or coaching relationship. They can also be engaged in as a means of self-reflection. Unfortunately, observation has often been thought of only as a means of teacher supervision or evaluation. However, it can also be a meaningful way of expanding your knowledge of teaching and learning (Bailey, Curtis, & Nunan, 2001; Malderez, 2009). As you observe other teachers' classes, see how they introduce new topics, recycle vocabulary or grammar, engage in formative assessment, motivate shy students to participate, manage different grouping patterns, deal with disruptive students, or almost anything about which you have questions. You may want to look at the number of suggestions provided by Wajnryb (1992) for classroom observation tasks and ways to analyze these.

Sometimes "master" or experienced teachers will have an open-door policy or set aside particular times when they welcome observers. If you are in a mentoring relationship with one of these teachers, you may want to talk with the teacher before observing the class, to understand the teacher's objectives as well as decisions concerning activities, types of grouping, or other factors in the lesson plan. You may want to set a time to meet after the class to discuss your observations and to ask any questions you might have. In your discussions, the teacher you observed will also have an opportunity to reflect and to learn from the experience (Richards & Lockhart, 1994).

spe/Shutterstock.com

sheff/Shutterstock.com

Collaborative peer observation You may also want to set up paired observations with other teachers in the school. In the case of a regular classroom teacher or a teacher of another subject (such as math, science, or social studies), you can observe your students in that teacher's classes, noting how they respond to different activities that may be conducted in their first language. If they are in English-medium subject-matter classes, you can note the difficulties students are having with those content classes and plan to integrate more of that content (specialized vocabulary, types of written texts, tests) into your classes. That content teacher can also observe your classes and note the various ways that you make new vocabulary and topics understandable through use of visuals, gestures, role plays, and the like (Crandall, 1998). If the teacher is another EYL teacher, you may want to focus on an area of your own teaching that you have questions about, such as how to provide effective feedback or how to differentiate instruction to accommodate all students, including those who are having difficulty as well as those for whom the lessons are easy (Crandall & Greenblatt, 1999; Gebhard & Oprandy, 1999; Richards & Farrell, 2005).

Self-observation With access to video or audio recording equipment, you can also record your own classes, then analyze and reflect upon how you used the time, how your lesson progressed, whether you interacted with all the children, or how much time you spent talking and how much time you had the children engaged in talking or writing. You may want to draw a seating chart of your classroom and then note each time that each child spoke when the students were engaged in whole-class activities. You could even see which ones volunteered and which ones you called upon. If you want to get into even more detail, you can note whether the children asked or answered questions by placing a Q or A next to each student's name. You can even note whether a student raised her/his hand by putting a V (for Volunteering) next to the Q or A. With a video, you can also look at individual students to see how many times they talked in pairs or in small group work. (Thanks to colleague Ron Schwartz for this system.)

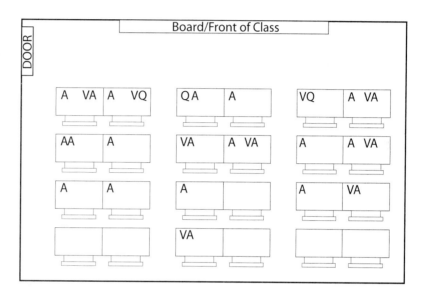

You may also want to look closely at several 5-minute segments to see how much time you were talking and how much time the children were using English (in both speaking and writing). Making a number of recordings over the span of a term or a school year and analyzing and reflecting on them will help you to see how much you have grown as a teacher during the year.

Another way to learn from videos of your teaching is to organize your analysis by your lesson plan. This might involve answering questions such as:

- Did I anticipate the problems my students had?
- Did I achieve my lesson objectives?
- Did the students understand my directions?
- Were all students engaged?
- How much time did I talk?
- How much time did my students talk?
- Did I provide feedback to my students?
- Was the learning environment supportive?

(Adapted from Foord, 2009, p. 32)

You might want to award yourself points or evaluate yourself on each category, and from that, identify an area in which you might want to improve.

Engaging in Teacher Research As you teach, you will naturally begin reflecting on your classes and learners and think about things you might want to consider adding or changing. For example, based on the results of your self-observations or your reflections in your teacher journal, you may want to see if there are ways in which you can encourage more children to interact using English. Or you may want to try out a new activity or a new way to informally assess your learners and see the results. Teacher research can range from this informal look at and adaptation of your own teaching to more formal action research. By engaging in teacher research, you will become a more reflective teacher, evaluating your teaching and seeking ways of improving it and growing professionally (Allwright & Hanks, 2009; Burns, 2011; Freeman, 1998; Johnson & Golembek, 2011).

Action research Action research focuses on understanding the causes of a problem or asking a question to answer and then, as the name implies, taking action to address the problem or to answer the question. It may be undertaken by an individual teacher who wants to find a way of improving instruction, or by a group of teachers with a common problem, or even by an entire school (often in response to testing results). Action research provides a concrete focus, often on a particular type of classroom activity. It usually involves a cycle that begins with identifying a problem or question, collecting information, planning ways to address it, trying it out, collecting data, and then reflecting upon its success and identifying ways it might be improved even further, which can often lead to another cycle of planning and implementation (Wallace, 1991).

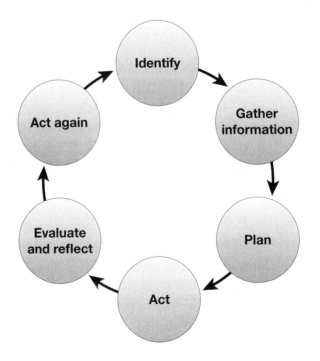

An action research project might involve taking the results of the self-observation, discussed on p. 392, and then identifying ways of decreasing the amount of teacher talk and increasing the amount of student–student interaction in English, perhaps by talking with other teachers or reading about how other teachers have attempted to increase the amount of student participation. The following are some other possible questions for action research in early language programs:

- What themes or content topics are most interesting to children at particular grade levels?
- What differences exist between successful and less successful language learners in these area(s)? Select one or two only:
  a. Attitudes toward the target language and culture
  b. Access to/use of L2 outside of school (e.g., parents, community, television)
  c. Use of appropriate language learning strategies
  d. Level of achievement in L1 language arts
  e. Transfer of knowledge, skills, or strategies from L1
  f. Level of self-confidence in own language learning ability

- What are students' reactions to/acceptance of particular instructional techniques (e.g., cooperative learning, information gap activities, instruction in learning strategies, grammar explanation and practice, Total Physical Response, teaching to different learning styles)?
- What types of assessment measures (e.g., oral interviews, role plays, multiple choice, cloze exercises, writing samples, portfolios) are best suited for assessing children's language proficiency in a particular area or in general?
  (Chamot, 1994, p. 6, cited in Curtain & Dahlberg, 2010, p. 508)

Action research can lead not only to improved teaching and learning, but also to greater self-confidence as a teacher and often, as the results are shared with others, to more recognition of you as a teacher.

Collaborative action research Action research can also be undertaken by a group of teachers who discover a common problem. The introduction of a new curriculum, textbook, or assessment or a change in procedures may require changes in teaching, but to determine what these should be requires research, discussion, reflection, and then implementation of a new approach. The results of collaborative action research are not only improved teaching and learning, but also the development or strengthening of a community of practice (Ferrance, 2000). Pairing new teachers with more experienced teachers in collaborative action research can benefit both: New teachers learn from their more experienced colleagues, and more experienced teachers benefit from both the enthusiasm of new teachers and new theories or practices (Burns, 2011; Samaras, 2010).

Participating in Continued Formal and Informal Learning

Today there are almost too many ways to continue to learn as a teacher. As mentioned above, it is possible to participate in local, regional, national, or international workshops and seminars, some of which are available as podcasts or webinars (virtual seminars). With current technology, it is also possible to take online graduate courses or even get an advanced degree fully online or in hybrid programs, with some online and some face-to-face courses. These courses may not only increase your knowledge about teaching and learning, but may also provide you with concrete activities for your classes or ideas to research in your own classes. They also link you with a network of professional colleagues whose experiences and teaching contexts may enrich your own perspectives on teaching and learning. You may begin primarily as a learner, but over time, you may find that you are leading one of these yourself. In some cases, participating in these (especially graduate classes) can lead to new employment opportunities (Crandall & Finn Miller, 2014).

Becoming part of a learning community With the incredible range of resources available through the Internet, it is possible to read current articles or to explore an area of interest that you were not able to do previously. You can do this independently, but dialoging with other colleagues may make the experience much richer. (See Sato, 2003, for a discussion of how her participation in a teacher study group as a high school teacher in Japan led her to develop an informal group when she moved to university teaching.) You may even be able to do this with colleagues in other countries, sharing your ideas with them as well as learning from them.

Joining an e-mail discussion group You might want to become part of an online discussion group focused on an area in which you are particularly interested (for example, integrating technology into language teaching or language assessment). In these groups, teachers and other educators post questions or concerns that are then discussed by whoever is interested. Usually there is a moderator who may initiate the discussion or even invite a recognized expert who has thought about an issue to answer questions and suggest readings for further learning. This is also a good place to receive quick advice when you are facing a challenge. You can find dozens of discussion lists through Dave's ESL Café. Simply scroll down to "Teacher Forums" and you will find several lists of interest for TEYL.

You can also attend workshops or register for podcasts or other online professional development opportunities that are often available without cost. Short-term online professional development courses or certificate programs offered by universities, the TESOL International Association, or the U.S. Department of State can also be good opportunities to learn more about best practices in TEYL while also building a community of practice with other teachers who face the same or similar challenges. Studies have shown that these online learning environments can be very effective in building professional connections and finding solutions to teaching challenges through the social interaction that occurs in the discussion forums in online courses (Shin & Bickel, 2008, 2012). One obvious example of this is the Teacher to Teacher section in each chapter of this book. The source for all of the ideas and examples shared by teachers around the world were taken from the discussion board posts and assignments from online professional development courses on TEYL.

Participating in Professional Associations and Conferences

One of the best ways to keep up to date as an EYL teacher is to participate in professional associations or organizations. Two international associations that are focused directly on English language teaching are Teachers of English to Speakers of Other Languages (TESOL) and the International Association of Teachers of

English as a Foreign Language (IATEFL) (their Web sites are provided at the end of the chapter). Both have special interest groups on teaching English to primary or elementary school children. Besides an annual conference, they also provide publications, extensive online teaching resources, and other professional development opportunities such as symposia, workshops, podcasts, or webinars. There is also a professional association focused specifically on teaching young learners: the National Network for Early Language Learning (NNELL). Although its membership is principally foreign language teachers in the United States, their issues and concerns are likely to be relevant to TEYL as well. There may also be local, regional, or national English language teaching associations that you can participate in; because you may share similar contexts, students, and curricula, you may find that these are more helpful, especially in your first years of teaching. They can help you keep in touch with other EYL teachers (which will be especially important if you are the only EYL teacher in your school) and to learn from others and share your teaching insights both informally and more formally through conference presentations.

Photo Courtesy of Terry Cook

After you have attended a conference and become familiar with the participants and their experiences, you should also consider making conference presentations. You might want to begin by giving a workshop or a poster session, perhaps with another teacher, on some instructional materials or curricula that you have developed. You may want to share the ways in which you manage difficult activities (such as Readers' Theater) or encourage students to write. Over time, you may also want to get more active in association activities and leadership—serving on committees, volunteering during conferences, working on a publication, or developing teaching standards.

Networking Through Social Media Such as Facebook and Blogs

Another way to share ideas with colleagues is through social media sites such as Facebook. Often these are created as a result of conferences or online courses, so teachers can continue to discuss TEYL topics, share helpful teaching ideas or resources (such as Web sites), and provide information about upcoming professional development events, or announcing their own PD events and publications.

TEYL Facebook Group An example is the TEYL Facebook group, which has approximately 1300 members and growing. It was created in 2005 in conjunction with an online TEYL professional development course at the University of Maryland Baltimore County, but the group is open and anyone can join. There is an assignment in the last course unit for teachers to join the group and post a message. The members of this group are very active, posting questions and classroom ideas about TEYL. They also post announcements and photos about conference presentations they do and PD events they participate in.

Blogs also provide an amazing resource for teachers to find and share information with others and to become members of virtual communities of practice with colleagues from around the world. Blogs not only provide useful resources (such as articles, lesson plans, videos, and podcasts); they also provide a place where you can talk with colleagues and contribute to an online community. Bloggers also list the blogs they follow on their web sites, so you can easily locate other blogs of interest (Crandall & Finn Miller, 2014).

Learning from Your Students

Students are our most important source of information about our success as a teacher, but with young learners, getting direct feedback may be difficult. However, there are a number of ways in which we can get informal feedback. For example, all teachers have "bad days" in which whatever we try with our students doesn't seem to work. We can follow that class with one in which we begin by asking students to rank a series of activities from those they like best to those they like least. Or you can talk with a small group of students (turning the interview into a small group discussion, where children can respond to each other's ideas) while others are engaged in other activities about things they like or don't like about learning English (for example, their textbook or activities) or the ways that they best learn (for example, asking them how they remember vocabulary) (Pinter, 2006). Interviews with very young learners (and perhaps with all young learners) will require the use of the first language. Questionnaires may also need to be provided in the first language, though Pinter (2006, p. 148) suggests that children can be asked to evaluate activities by circling their answers ("I like listening to stories" or

"I can count to 100 in English") or placing a checkmark next to things they would like to do again (such as "Sing a song?" or "Make a puppet and talk about it?")

		YES 😊	NO ☹
	Making puppets		
	Singing a song		
	Drawing pictures		
	Reading stories		

The more you can learn about each of your students, the more likely you will be able to provide a range of activities to appeal to all of your students' learning style preferences (or multiple intelligences). At a minimum, learning about their likes and dislikes, their hobbies and interests, and some of their reasons for learning English will help create a more learner-centered, inclusive EYL classroom (Foord, 2009).

You can also invite your students to teach you or the class something. This might involve sharing a game or activity that they do at home. In settings with children from several different cultures, you could also invite parents to share with the class. While this may involve using a language other than English, you could follow up with key words in English and frames by which to remember what they have seen and heard:

__(Name)_____ shared a __(game, song, etc.)_____ with us.

__(Name)_____ likes _____.

If your students all speak another language or languages, and you do not, you can also learn some of their language(s), perhaps even creating a chart of vocabulary in one or more languages spoken by your students.

Finally, you can alter aspects of your teaching, the classroom environment, the organization of your lesson, or the materials, and get students' responses, while remembering that young learners like and feel more confident with routines. Still, a small adjustment might increase learner engagement and also help you to fine-tune your own teaching (Fanselow, 1987).

Developing Instructional Materials and Curricula

Although you will probably be assigned a curriculum or a textbook that you are expected to use in your teaching, you will likely find that as you get to know your learners, you will have some good ideas for different or additional activities that your learners will find interesting and motivating. Some of these may have been tried in class, or they may be activities other teachers told you about. Adapting these and creating materials helps to keep teaching fresh. Developing these with colleagues will enable you to share your ideas and learn from your colleagues about classes, students, and activities that have been identified as successful. You may want to post these materials to a local EYL blog or share them with a larger audience, through a discussion list or blog. You may also want to work with other teachers in identifying technology resources and adapting these for use in your classes.

Writing for Publication

As you become more confident of yourself as a teacher, you may want to consider not only presenting your ideas at professional conferences, but also writing about these ideas for publication. You may want to begin by writing for a newsletter or teacher magazine (or even starting a newsletter for your institution, if one has not been published). You could also coedit or coauthor a publication with someone who has previously published or as a way of dividing up the task. Even experienced and expert teachers and teacher educators often choose to collaborate on articles or books, since the conversations that emerge in planning and writing for publication often result in more and better ideas. Offering to write a review of a textbook or other TEYL publication may provide you with your first publication, and usually a complimentary copy of the book.

Conclusion

You are a member of what may be the most demanding profession of all. We often hear about how difficult it is to be a doctor, a lawyer, or an engineer. But teachers need to make hundreds of decisions during the day, as they decide on what needs to be reviewed, what needs to be repeated, what kinds of feedback to provide, how to encourage a student who is having difficulty, how to prevent another student from taking too much class time, and the like. Being a professional means continuing to learn to maintain or even improve your knowledge and skills as a teacher. You can learn so much from others—from reading or listening to experts, talking to or observing other teachers, listening to your students and, most of all, from reflecting on your own experiences. Over time, as you continue in your career in English language teaching, you may find that you begin to take on more administrative or leadership tasks such as managing a program, serving on a textbook selection committee, or helping to write TEYL standards. Take advantage of these opportunities to become a teacher leader, as you will continue to learn and grow and remain an active member of the teaching profession. If you are an experienced teacher of adults, there is still much to learn about teaching young learners.

Aleksandra Popovski Golubovikj, a school director and active member of her professional association in Macedonia, says:

"Every teacher learns something new from every class he/she teaches every single day, from every article that is read, every workshop or conference that is attended. Teachers are life-time learners who never grow too old to teach someone younger than them."

A colleague, Ron Schwartz, often begins his workshops and talks with the following warning (adapted from Buddha):

Don't believe a word I say.

Don't believe a word you hear.

Don't believe anything that you read,

Until you think about it, personalize it, and try it out.

If it works, use it.

We would add: Talk about it with others, make presentations about it at conferences, write about it for publication, and, most of all, continue to experiment and learn from your teaching.

■ Teacher to Teacher

Continuing to Learn as an EYL Teacher and Applying That Learning to EYL Classes

As teachers completed their online TEYL courses provided by the University of Maryland, Baltimore County (UMBC), they were asked to reflect on the experience and how they were going to apply what they had learned from the readings and the online discussions with teachers from many other countries. Here are some of their responses:

Many teachers learned ways to change the curriculum and instruction to motivate young learners better and provide for a range of learning styles, as this teacher educator from Japan discussed.

> "Creating a positive and meaningful learning environment is imperative for many Japanese schools. Thus, I would like to redesign and strengthen the curriculum to provide a solid foundation, practical techniques, and various activities (games, songs, chants, storytelling, etc.) that I learned in this course. Children are full of physical energy and physically active.... Many target children are visual and kinesthetic learners, so using realia and physically active activities addresses the needs of many target children.... Learning by doing is imperative for teacher education, too.... As a teacher educator, I would like to prepare quality teachers who are confident in conducting English activities and can create a positive and meaningful learning environment for all children through a well-designed curriculum providing a solid foundation and practical experiences."

> —*Chie Ohtani, Teacher Educator, Japan*

This next teacher, from Ecuador, entitled her reflection "A Really Young Learner English Teacher," summarizing much of what she has learned. Note her emphasis on the relationship between the teacher and the students, as well as the importance of understanding the characteristics of young learners, the classroom environment, the focus on meaningful content, and the kinds of activities to use. Training to become a foreign language teacher of adults is not enough.

"If we really want to be an English teacher of young learners we must learn lots of things, like how to do a class plan, YL characteristics, the environment they are in, theories, methods and strategies, and overall how to strengthen the relationship between the teacher and the YL. . . . We are working with kids, we could be qualified teachers, with new techniques, but we learn in our universities the procedures for teaching adults, and if we work with YLs we must prepare ourselves to become a YLs teacher. Teachers when planning have to know that is easier for YLs to learn when they have the new knowledge in context, when it's meaningful for them, with realia, with stories, with movements of their bodies, with gestures and recycling in different ways everything they learn. Younger learners in general are active, very receptive, creative, social. They like to play, they learn by doing and their attention span is very short. They need clear rules and routines to develop their confidence. Teachers must create an environment for communication, so students communicate in English because everything has meaning for them, and it could be in a natural form. . . . We can work all the four skills, integrating the skills around a theme to make the students enjoy the learning process. It could be through drawing, playing, doing plays or drama, singing, cooking, or doing any thing that has meaning for them. [We can use] thematic units according to their real life situations, instead of teaching grammar or vocabulary in isolation."

—*Monica Carrera S., Primary and University English Teacher, Ecuador*

This school director from Macedonia reflects on what she has learned and how she is going to use that information to change her school. She also plans to share that information with colleagues in her professional association, ELTAM (English Language Teachers Association of Macedonia) through workshops and newsletter articles, and she plans to submit proposals not only to the next ELTAM conference, but also to the TESOL and IATEFL conferences.

"Being a school director, an active member and General Secretary of ELTAM—English Language Teachers' Association of the Republic of Macedonia—will enable me to spread the message and share the knowledge about young learners I have gained during this course. Teaching English to young learners is the least talked about topic in Macedonia although it is of the utmost importance because of the lowering of the compulsory age for English language learning. Teachers are not familiar with the theories and methods of teaching English to learners at a young age. That is why I have already made plans for the first cycle of workshops on classroom management around the country and that will only be the beginning. Other workshops will deal with other aspects of teaching young learners.

Also, my article for ELTAM Newsletter will allow me to explain to the readers how beneficial courses such as this can be for them and their professional development regardless of the number of years they have been teaching. Since I am the newsletter editor as well, the Practical Tips section will be devoted to tips on teaching this specific group of students. In order to reach a greater, more international audience, I plan to submit a proposal on teaching young learners for the next TESOL and IATEFL conferences, and of course, the ELTAM international conference. I would like to show my colleagues that there is nothing to be afraid of.**"**

—Aleksandra Popovski Golubovikj, School Director and General Secretary, English Language Teachers Association of Macedonia

Another teacher and teacher educator from Azerbaijan also plans to share what she has learned with all of her language teaching colleagues, from primary through secondary grades. She has already told them some of what she was learning by taking an online graduate course with participants from around the world. Now she plans to share that knowledge more broadly with other teachers at the AzETA (Azerbiajan English Teachers Association) conference.

"All the experience gained at the UMBC course I am planning to apply into my teaching and teacher-training program for Azerbaijani teachers. . . . I can share gained experience with my school colleagues. [Already] at one of the school meetings I've made a speech about UMBC units and their importance not only for English teachers but also for all subject teachers as it teaches all about different strategies of pedagogy, instruction, and curriculum development. The students of primary, secondary and high schools don't study at separate buildings in Azerbaijan. They study at the same school building and therefore all subject teachers can participate at school meetings. I've been teaching at a school which is in the biggest district of Baku. I'll give presentations in some of meetings there and at other district schools and education departments. I am member of the Azerbaijan English Teachers' Association. I'll participate in AzETA workshops, seminars, conferences, methodology meetings, and round table tasks and share my gained course experience there. I am intending to visit regions together with other AzETA members, giving presentations at regional schools so they could benefit from this and use it in their teaching . . . [in] the areas perceived as in most need for teachers of Azerbaijan schools.**"**

—Gamar Rustamova, Primary and Secondary English Teacher and Teacher Trainer, Azerbaijan

Even if one has completed an English language teacher education program and had some opportunity to observe and do some practice teaching, there is still so much more to learn. Continuing professional development has been important to this teacher from Croatia, and she, like several others above, plans to share what she has learned with others and to continue her "self-development" by reading, attending workshops and seminars, and giving presentations and workshops on what she has learned.

"In Croatia, teacher training is part of the methodology course, which is obligatory for all students in their third year of studying English. In the first semester, students go to elementary schools, and in the second semester, to private or public high schools. Each semester one has to sit in for ten lessons, and then teach one lesson him/herself. Somehow, this does not seem to be enough. . . . Having successfully completed my training, did I feel competent and eager to shape young minds? Sadly, no. I soon got a job at a foreign language schools and had to learn (from more experienced colleagues, but mostly from my own mistakes) as I went along. But all the time I felt the need to somehow expand and improve my knowledge and training. It was with this aim in mind that I applied for the UMBC course.

The online teaching program exceeded all my expectations. Not only did I accomplish my primary goal (i.e. learn about different teaching techniques and activities appropriate for young learners), I gained so much more, both in terms of professional and personal development. I rarely get a chance to converse with other teachers; staff meetings at my school are few and far between, and most of my college friends moved back to their hometowns after graduation, so we do not communicate very often. Therefore, I relished the opportunity to discuss various aspects of teaching and share ideas and experience with colleagues from around the world. Not only did I meet exciting new people, but also became a part of a community of professionals with whom I hope to continue communicating in the future as well. The interesting and stimulating discussions we had helped relieve much of my professional anxiety, as I came to realize that I was not alone in having these feelings, and that others faced similar problems and dilemmas as well. My colleagues have taught me so much, and their supportive and positive responses and comments helped increase my confidence. . . . Developing a more profound understanding of the rationale for lowering the age for compulsory foreign language instruction, and the nuances of teaching English to young learners made me reconsider my role as a teacher.

Considering what a positive experience this form of professional development has been, I am keen on participating in similar programs, workshops and seminars. Prior to this course, I was never in the habit of reading journals or other types of publications concerned with foreign language instruction, but now I intend to keep myself more informed and up to date.

Having learned the importance of creating a dialogue with my professional community (both in my own country and abroad), I wish to give something back to that same community by talking about my experience with the course, and encouraging others to apply as well. I have already discussed this with the head teacher at my school, and she has agreed to let me give a short lecture on the program after the next school meeting. In case my colleagues should be interested, I would also like to give additional lectures and/or workshops on the characteristics of young learners, effective activities for developing the four language skills, and assessment for young learners. I am especially keen on this last topic, as I believe that, by getting my colleagues familiar with and (ideally) enthusiastic about alternative methods of assessment, I may be able to bring about positive changes in this respect. Finally, looking back on my experience of the teacher-training program that I described at the beginning of the essay, I would like to address teacher trainees at the Faculty of Humanities and Social Sciences, and talk about the challenges of working with young learners. Finally, I would do my best to encourage them to continue working on their professional self-development after they graduate.**"**

—*Nada Kujundžić, Primary English Teacher and Ph.D. student, Croatia*

▪ Chapter Summary

To Conclude

The importance of continuing professional development Teaching is lifelong learning. The field of TEYL is constantly changing. It is important to find ways of keeping current, learning new theories and techniques to meet the needs of an ever-changing group of young learners.

Three approaches to professional development Although there are many approaches to professional development, most of them can be grouped under one of three approaches: theory-to-practice, coaching and mentoring, or reflection. Teacher reflection may consist of independent activities, but it is also a part of the other two approaches.

Characteristics of effective professional development In general, effective professional development takes place over time; it does not consist of isolated, unrelated workshops. It should be planned by teachers and focus on the classroom and student learning. It should also provide teachers with opportunities to share their knowledge and experience. If it involves theory, it should emphasize how to apply that theory.

Effective professional development activities There are countless ways to continue to grow as an EYL professional. These include: (1) reflection in the form of teaching journals and portfolios and participating in a reflective teaching group, or developing a teaching portfolio; (2) coaching and mentoring; (3) observing classes, including your own; (4) engaging in teacher research; (5) participating in continued formal and informal learning through online and face-to-face workshops, podcasts, seminars, webinars, online discussion lists, and graduate classes; (6) participating in professional associations and conferences; (7) networking through social media and blogs; (8) learning from your students; (9) developing instructional materials and curricula; and (10) writing for publication.

■ Over to You

Discussion Questions

1. What are some reasons for engaging in professional development activities? If you were to select one professional development activity from this chapter, what would it be? Why do you think it would be helpful to you?

2. What are some challenges you face in participating in professional development (limited time away from teaching, limited access to the Internet, etc.)? What are some alternative ways you can meet your professional development needs?

3. If you are currently teaching, what are some principles or activities from this book that you have tried with your young learners? What was effective? What were the problems? Reflect on those experiences and discuss what you learned from the experience. If you have not taught, what have you learned from this book that you think will be important when you begin teaching?

4. If you have attended a professional conference or participated in a professional organization, what were the benefits? What have you learned from the experience? What would you tell another EYL teacher who is thinking about attending a professional conference? What might s/he learn?

5. If you have observed an experienced EYL teacher, what did you learn from the observation? If not, what would you like to focus on if you were to observe an EYL teacher?

6. Have you conducted any classroom research? If so, what did you learn? If not, what might be some aspects of teaching and learning that you would like to research?

7. If you were to make an action plan for your professional development, what would be some short-term goals? What would be some long-term goals?

Lesson Planning

Think about an activity that you have used either in your teaching or in a teacher education class. If you wanted to share this with other colleagues, how might you do so? Write a brief plan for a workshop that you could give to other teachers, perhaps at your school or at a local conference. In the workshop provide the following:

- The audience for the workshop and what they probably know about TEYL
- What you will be adding to their knowledge
- The students who will participate in the activity (age and level of English)
- A description of the activity
- How you would prepare students for the activity (especially the vocabulary)
- The kinds of informal assessment you might use with the activity

Write About It

Challenges: A number of teachers and teacher educators have attempted to list the major challenges facing teachers. Here are some that they have identified:

1. Managing classes
2. Motivating students
3. Assessing student work
4. Organizing work
5. Meeting the needs of different students
6. Obtaining needed resources

Compare these with the challenges you listed at the beginning of the chapter and select one from either or both lists to discuss. Why do you think this would be most challenging for you? Based on the range of professional development possibilities discussed in this chapter, how might you extend your knowledge about and your skills in dealing with this challenge?

■ Resources and References

Print Publications

Bailey, K. M., Curtis, A. & Nunan, D, (2001). *Pursuing professional development.* Boston, MA: Heinle Cengage.

Burns, A. (2011). *Doing action research in English language teaching: A guide for practitioners.* New York, NY: Routledge.

Egbert, J. (Ed.). (2003). *Becoming contributing professionals.* Alexandria, VA: TESOL.

Farrell, T. S. C. (2004). *Reflective practice in action: 80 reflective breaks for busy teachers.* Thousand Oaks, CA: Corwin Press.

Foord, D. (2009). *The developing teacher: Practical activities for professional development.* Surrey, UK: Delta ELT Publishing.

Richards, J. C., & Farrell, T. S. C. (2005). *Professional development for language teachers.* Cambridge, UK: Cambridge University Press.

Wajnryb, R. (1992). *Classroom observation tasks: A resource book for language teachers and trainers.* Cambridge, UK: Cambridge University Press.

Useful Web Sites

http://busyteacher.org/12058-tips-for-staying-fresh-as-a-teacher.html

http://iteslj.org/links/

http://languageteachingtips.wordpress.com/2012/06/20/keeping-a-reflective-teaching-diary/

http://wiki.literacytent.org/index.php/PDMethodsMatrix

http://www.teachertrainingvideos.com/

http://www.yltsig.org/

http://www.tesol.org/

http://www.iatefl.org/

http://nnell.org/

http://www.eslcafe.com/

References

Allwright, D. & Hanks, J. (2009). *The developing language learner: An introduction.* Basingstoke, UK: Palgrave Macmillan.

Appel, J. (1995). *Diary of a language teacher.* Oxford, UK: Heinemann.

Bailey, K. M. (1990). The use of diary studies in teacher education programs. In J. C. Richards & D. Nunan (Eds.), *Second language teacher education* (pp. 215–226). New York, NY: Cambridge University Press.

Bailey, K. M., Curtis, A., & Nunan, D. (2001). *Pursuing professional development: The self as source.* Boston, MA: Heinle Cengage.

Bailey, K. M., Dale, T., & Squire, B. (1992). Some reflections on collaborative language teaching. In D. Nunan (Ed.), *Collaborative language teaching and learning* (pp. 162–178). Cambridge, UK: Cambridge University Press.

Brewster, J., Ellis, G., & Girard, D. (2010). *The primary English teacher's guide.* Essex, UK: Pearson.

Brown, J. D., & Wolfe-Quintero, K. (1997). Teacher portfolios for evaluation: A great idea or a waste of time? *Language Teacher 21*(1), 28–30.

Burns, A. (2009). Action research in second language teacher education: Research and practice. In A. Burns & J. C. Richards (Eds.), *The Cambridge guide to second language teacher education* (pp. 289–297). New York, NY: Cambridge.

Burns, A. (2011). *Doing action research in English language teaching: A guide for practitioners.* New York, NY: Routledge.

Burton, J. (2009). Reflective practice. In A. Burns & J. C. Richards (Eds.), *The Cambridge guide to second language teacher education* (pp. 298–307). New York, NY: Cambridge University Press.

Chamot, A. U. (1994). CALLA: An instructional model for linguistically diverse students. *English Quarterly, 26*(3), 12–16.

Cornett, J., & Knight, J. (2009). Research on coaching. In J. Knight (Ed.), *Coaching: Approaches and perspectives* (pp. 192–216). Thousand Oaks, CA: Corwin Press.

Crandall, J. A. (1998). Collaborate and cooperate: Teacher education for integrating language and content instruction. *English Teaching Forum, 36*(1), 2–9.

Crandall, J. A. (2000). Language teacher education. *Annual Review of Applied Linguistics, 20,* 34–55.

Crandall, J. A. (2001). Keeping up to date as an ESL or EFL professional. In M. Celce-Murcia (Ed.), *Teaching English as a second or foreign language,* 3rd ed. (pp. 535–552). Boston, MA: Heinle & Heinle.

Crandall, J. A. & Finn Miller, S. (2014). Effective professional development for English as a second/foreign language teachers. In M. Celce-Murcia, D. Brinton, & M. A. Snow (Eds.), *Teaching English as a second or foreign language,* 4th ed. Boston, MA: National Geographic Learning/Cengage Learning.

Crandall, J.A. & Greenblatt, L. (1999). Teaching beyond the middle: Meeting the needs of underschooled and high-achieving immigrant students. In M.R. Basterra (Ed.) *Excellence and equity in education for language minority students: Critical issues and promising practices* (pp. 43-80). Washington, DC: Mid-Atlantic Equity Center, The American University.

Curtain, H., & Dahlberg, C. A. (2010). *Languages and children: Making the match,* 4th ed. Boston: Pearson.

Darling-Hammond, L., & Sykes, G. (1999). *Teaching as the learning profession: Handbook of policy and practice.* San Francisco, CA: Jossey-Bass.

Darling-Hammond, L., Wei, R. C., Andree, A., Richardson, N., & Orphanos, S. (2009). *Professional learning in the learning profession: A status report on teacher development in the United States and abroad.* Dallas, TX: National Staff Development Council.

Deacon, B. (2003). Priceless peer-mentor observation. In J. Egbert (Ed.), *Becoming contributing professionals* (pp. 81–88). Alexandria, VA: TESOL.

Desimone, L. M. (2011). A primer on effective professional development. *Kappan Magazine, 92*(6), 68–71.

Edge, J. (1992). Co-operative development. *ELT Journal, 46*(1), 62–70.

Edge, J. (Ed.). (2002). *Continuing professional development: Some of our perspectives.* Canterbury, UK: IATEFL Publications.

Egbert, J. (Ed.). (2003). *Becoming contributing professionals.* Alexandria, VA: TESOL.

Fanselow, J. (1987). *Breaking rules.* White Plains, NY: Pearson.

Farrell, T. S. C. (2007). *Reflective language teaching: From research to practice.* London, UK: Continuum Press.

Farrell, T. S. C. (2012). Reflective practice as professional development. In C. Coombe, L. England, & J. Schmidt (Eds.), *Reigniting, retooling and retiring in English language teaching* (pp. 23–32). Ann Arbor, MI: University of Michigan Press.

Ferrance, E. (2000). Themes in education: Action research. *Educational Alliance,* 1-34. Available at: http://www.lab.brown.edu/pubs/themes_ed/act_research.pdf

Foord, D. (2009). *The developing teacher: Practical activities for professional development.* Surrey, UK: Delta Publishing.

Freeman, D. (1998). *Doing teacher research: From inquiry to understanding.* Boston, MA: Heinle.

Gebhard, J., & Oprandy, R. (1999). *Language teaching awareness: A guide to exploring beliefs and practices.* New York, NY: Cambridge University Press.

Guskey, T. R., & Yoon, K. S. (2009). What works in professional development? *Phi Delta Kappan, 9* (7), 495–500.

Holcomb, S., & Green, M. (Eds.). (1998). *Peer support: Teachers mentoring teachers.* Washington, DC: National Education Association Professional Library.

Johnson, K. E., & Golembek, P. (2011). *Research on second language teacher education: A sociocultural perspective on professional development.* New York, NY: Routledge.

Joyce, B., & Showers, B. (1995). *Student achievement through staff development.* White Plains, NY: Longman.

Knight, J. (2009). *Coaching: Approaches and perspectives.* Thousand Oaks, CA: Corwin Press.

Malderez, A. (2009). Mentoring. In A. Burns & J. C. Richards (Eds.), *The Cambridge guide to second language teacher education* (pp. 259–268). New York, NY: Cambridge.

Moon, J. (2000). Why did I do it like this? Planning for children's language learning. *Children learning English.* Oxford, UK: Macmillan.

Murray, A. (2010). Empowering teachers through professional development. *English Teaching Forum, 1,* 2–11.

Numrich, C. (1996). On becoming a language teacher: Insights from diary studies. *TESOL Quarterly, 30*(1), 131–151.

Pinter, A. (2006). *Teaching young language learners.* Oxford, UK: Oxford University Press.

Porter, C., & Cleland, J. (1995). *The portfolio as a learning strategy.* Portsmouth, NH: Boynton/Cook.

Richards, J. C., & Farrell, T. S. C. (2005). *Professional development of language teachers: Strategies for teacher training.* Cambridge, UK: Cambridge University Press.

Richards, J. C., & C. Lockhart. (1994). *Reflective teaching in second language classrooms.* New York, NY: Cambridge University Press.

Samaras, A. P. (2010). *Self-study teacher research: Improving your practice through collaborative inquiry.* Thousand Oaks, CA: Sage.

Sato, K. (2003). Stating a local teacher study group. In T. Murphy (Ed.), *Extending professional contributions* (pp. 97–104). Alexandria, VA: TESOL.

Schon, D. A. (1983). *The reflective practitioner: How professionals think in action.* New York, NY: Basic Books.

Schon, D. A. (1987). *Educating the reflective practitioner: Towards a new design for teaching and learning in the profession.* New York, NY: Basic Books.

Shin, J. K. (2006). Ten helpful ideas for teaching English to young learners. *English Teaching Forum, 44*(2), 2–7, 13. Available at http://exchanges.state.gov/englishteaching/forum/archives/docs/06-44-2-b.pdf

Shin, J. K., & Bickel, B. (2008). Distributing teaching presence: Engaging teachers of English to young learners in an international virtual community of inquiry. In C. Kimble, P. Hildreth, & I. Bourdon (Eds.), *Communities of practice: Creating learning environments for educators* (pp. 149–178). Charlotte, NC: Information Age Publishing.

Shin, J. K., & Bickel, B. (2012). Building an online community of inquiry with participant-moderated discussions. In L. England (Ed.), *Online language teacher education: TESOL perspectives.* New York, NY: Routledge (Taylor Francis).

Tanner, R. (2003). Outside in, inside out: Creating a teaching portfolio. In J. P. Byrd & G. Nelson (Eds.), *Sustaining professionalism* (pp. 19–25). Alexandria, VA: TESOL.

Teemant, A., Wink, J., & Tyra, S. (2011). Effects of coaching on teacher use of sociocultural instructional practices. *Teaching and Teacher Education, 27,* 683–693.

Timperley, H., Wilson, A., Barrar, H., & Fung, I. (2007). *Teacher professional learning and development: Best evidence synthesis iteration.* Wellington, NZ: Ministry of Education.

Wajnryb, R. (1992). *Classroom observation tasks: A resource book for language teachers and trainers.* Cambridge, UK: Cambridge University Press.

Wallace, M. J. (1991). *Training foreign language teachers.* Cambridge, UK: Cambridge University Press.

Wallace, M. J. (1996). Structured reflection: The role of the professional project in training ESL teachers. In D. Freeman & J. C. Richards (Eds.), *Teacher learning in language teaching* (pp. 281–294). New York, NY: Cambridge University Press.

Wallace, M. (1998). *Action research for language teachers.* Cambridge, UK: Cambridge University Press.

Zeichner, K. M., & Liston, D. P. (1996). *Reflective teaching: An introduction.* Mahwah, NJ: Lawrence Erlbaum.

Worksheets

English Education Profile

Use this worksheet to help you write your own English Education Profile for your country or region.

English language policy (for country/region) *What are the major features of that policy?*	
Is there an official English/language policy? If so, who developed it (the Ministry of Education?) and when?	
At what age is English introduced in public schools?	
How many years of English are required?	
What are the objectives of teaching English to young learners?	
What type(s) of English programs are required or permitted?	
Is there a national curriculum? Please describe it briefly.	
Are there required textbooks? If so, what kinds of activities are included in the EYL books?	

English requirements and environment at your school *Describe the English class environment and your opinion on its effectiveness.*	
Describe your classroom environment.	
Describe your students (age, gender, level of English proficiency).	
How many hours per day is English taught?	
How many days per week do children receive English instruction?	
Does this differ/increase in later grades?	
What kinds of materials and resources are available to you?	
Is there Internet access?	
What opportunities do your students have to use English outside the classroom?	
What do you feel is most effective about the language policy and the environment in your school?	
What do you think is most challenging?	
What changes would you make?	

Class Observation

I. Describe the profile of the class.
Before you observe the class, meet with the teacher and establish the class profile.

1. Grade/age(s) and proficiency level of class

2. Number of students in class (male and female students)

3. Content and objectives of the lesson being observed and how it relates to previous lessons or following lessons (Is it part of a thematic unit?)

II. Describe the physical environment.
Before the lesson begins, notice how the room is set up.

4. Does the teacher have her/his own classroom? Or does s/he share the room with other teachers?

5. How are the chairs, desks, and other furniture arranged?

6. What do you see on the walls?

7. What other materials and objects are in the room?

III. Describe the lesson.
As you observe the class, take notes on what you see.

8. Do students have a required textbook? What textbook is being used and what level is used for the class you observed?

9. What are the lesson objectives? Do the objectives relate to language, content, or both? Were they predetermined by the required school or state curriculum?

10. How does the teacher begin the lesson?

11. How is new vocabulary introduced?

12. How are new language structures presented?

13. How do students practice new language?

14. Do students have the opportunity to listen/speak/read/write?

15. What techniques does the teacher use to make input comprehensible?

16. Do students interact with the teacher? With other students?

17. How often do students participate? In what ways do they participate? Are all students actively involved in the class?

18. How does the teacher assess student progress? How does the teacher assess achievement of objectives?

19. How does the teacher give students feedback? How does the teacher correct errors?

20. How does the teacher end the lesson?

21. Does the teacher assign homework or give other follow-up activities?

Twenty-First-Century Skills Integration

Use this worksheet to analyze your EYL curriculum for twenty-first-century skills.

1. Write YES or NO for each item.
2. If you marked YES, briefly describe which part of your curriculum reflects that item.
3. If you marked NO, try to incorporate that item into your curriculum and describe it.

Does Your EYL Curriculum . . .	YES/NO	Describe Your Curriculum
1. Global perspective: global citizenship and values		
a. Take a global perspective and present content about different international cultures?		
b. Promote intercultural sensitivity and positive attitudes toward people from other cultures and all walks of life?		
c. Help students to be good global citizens who value, respect, care for, and protect our world and environment?		
2. Communication skills: communication and collaboration across cultures		
a. Improve students' intercultural communication skills?		
b. Give students the opportunity to express aspects of their own local culture in English?		
c. Provide chances for students to work in groups or teams to practice their collaboration skills?		
d. Give students practice using courteous language and behavior?		
3. Active learning: critical thinking and lifelong learning strategies		
a. Develop students' critical thinking skills to interpret information in texts and media?		
b. Use different levels of questioning appropriately to encourage higher levels of critical thinking (i.e., knowledge, comprehension, application, inference, analysis, synthesis, evaluation)?		
c. Model using think-alouds to teach learners how to think and learn independently?		
4. Technology skills: computer, information, and digital literacy		
a. Incorporate different technology tools to help build students' skills in computer-mediated communication (both computer-based and Web-based applications)?		
b. Encourage students to create projects using Web tools (for storing, listening, presenting, producing, communicating, sharing, collaborating, networking, and searching)?		

Index

B

Bachman, L., 247, 251, 267
Bahous, R., 192
Bahti, M., 211
Bailey, K., 257, 265
Bailey, K. M., 363, 364, 366, 367
Bamford, J., 174
Barone, D., 164
Bauman, James, 170
Bazo, P., 116
Beck, I. L., 166
before-storytelling activities, 216–219
    capturing attention, 217
    connecting to prior knowledge
        and experiences, 217
    giving students a purpose for listening, 219
    prediction about story, 219
    pre-teaching new vocabulary or
        expressions, 218
    reviewing language, 218
behavior(s)
    courteous, 335
    with routines, managing, 292–294
    with rules, managing, 294–300
Bialystok, E., 7
Bickel, B., 373
Biffle, C., 307
bilingualism, 7
    additive, 10
    cognitive advantages of, 7
    global awareness and, 6
    intercultural competence and, 6
    mental flexibility and, 7
    value of, 7
Binkley, M., 328
Black, J. K., 257, 259
Black, P., 249, 252
Blake, S., 256
blogs, 375
Bloom, B. S., 336
Bloom's taxonomy, 335–337
bodily-kinesthetic (body smart) intelligence, 38
Bonk, C. J., 335
book manager, 304
bottom-up listening, 110–112
Boyle, O. F., 169
brain breaks
    preparing, 307–308
    young learners, 30
brainstorming (Writing Workshop), 192–193
Brewster, J., 39, 68, 113, 117, 124, 161, 165,
        181, 214, 255, 256, 261, 263, 265, 275,
        292, 295, 358
Brown, D. H., 123
Brown, H. D., 247, 248, 251, 256, 257, 336

Brown, J. D., 365
Bruner, J., 34
Burns, A., 3, 4, 11, 370, 372
Butler, Y. G., 13, 261

C

Cabrera, M. P., 116
Calkins, L. M., 192
Cameron, L., 12, 34, 41, 42, 94, 117, 123,
        126, 161, 166, 245, 247, 252, 253, 254
career and life skills, 327
caregiver speech, defined, 40
Carrell, P. L., 169
Carroll, J. B., 6
The Cat in the Hat (Dr. Seuss), 212
Chamot, A. U., 371
Chance, K. S., 212
Chaudron, C., 291
Chicken Burger Song, 333–334
choral reading, 173
Chung, Alton, 214
Cinderella stories, 211
classroom cleaning, 308
classroom climate, managing, 300–301.
        See also classroom management
    emotional atmosphere, 301
    physical environment, 300
classroom environment
    English-speaking, 40, 41, 58
    for L1 and L2 acquisition, 39–40
classroom helpers, 304–305
classroom interaction
    giving examples, 129
    paraphrasing, 129
    personalizing, 129
    question and answer (Q&A), 128–129
    repetition, 128
classroom language, 113, 114
classroom management, 287–323
    activities, 302–311
    behavior with routines, managing,
        292–294
    behavior with rules, managing, 294–300
    classroom climate, managing, 300–301
    effective activities, 302–311
    language used in class, managing,
        301–302
    pace of class, managing, 291
        activities, 291–292
        time, 291
        using transition activities, 292
    plan, 311–313
    purpose of, 301
    teacher to teacher, 313–320

during-reading activities, 181–182
during-storytelling activities, 220–221
   creating own ending, 221
   questions, use of, during, 220
   repetition, 220
   TPR (Total Physical Response), 221

E

early-exit bilingual programs. *See* transitional bilingual
   programs
early language learning
   benefits of, 4–7
   optimal conditions for, 5
   reasons for, 5–7
*An Early Start: Young Learners and Modern Languages in
   Europe and Beyond* (Nikolov and Curtain), 13
echo reading, 171
Edge, J., 356
editing (Writing Workshop), 193
editing checklist, 194
education, value of English language for, 3–4
effective assessment, 253–256
   activities, 266–275
   build learner confidence, 254–255
   contextualized, 255–256
   contribution to learning, 254
   learners to experience success, 255
   mirror learning, 253
   motivate learners, 254–255
   take place over time, 256
   variety of techniques
      for learners intelligences, 255
      for learners learning styles, 255
e-friends. *See* e-pals
Egbert, J., 358
Ellis, G., 39, 68, 113, 117, 124, 161, 165, 181, 214, 245, 255,
   256, 261, 263, 265, 275, 292, 295, 358
Emmer, E. T., 290, 301
emotional atmosphere, 301
employment, value of English language for, 3–4
ending class, 311
Enever, J., 3, 13
English as a foreign language (EFL), 3
English as an international language (EIL), 3
English as a second language (ESL), 3
English cheer, 303
English language
   benefits of early language learning, 4–7
   as classroom language, 302–311
   value for education and employment, 3–4
English vocabulary, 115
e-pals, 197–198, 346
Erstad, O., 328
European Commission, 5
evaluation, 247. *See also* assessment

evaluation questions, 336
Evertson, C. M., 290, 301
"Expanding Circle" countries, 3, 4
Explorer magazine, 176
extensive reading. *See* independent reading
EYL curriculum, 330
EYL program models, 7–11
   dual-language programs, 10
   effective, 7–11
   FLES programs, 8–9
   FLEX programs, 8
   language immersion programs, 9–10
   transitional and maintenance bilingual programs, 10–11
EYL programs
   characteristics of, 13
   common features of, 13
   effective models, 7–11
   factors affecting success of, 7–12
   pitfalls to avoid in, 12–13
   planning for success in, 7–13
EYL teachers, appropriately trained, 11

F

Facebook, 375
Fadel, C., 326, 328
Fanselow, J., 377
Farrell, T. S. C., 360, 362, 363, 366, 368
Faulkner-Bond, M., 9, 10, 11
Federer A., 192
Ferrance, E., 371
Feunteun, A., 93
Finn Miller, S., 360, 361, 366, 372, 375
Fisher, D., 341
FLES (foreign language in the elementary school) programs, 8–9
   content-based, 9
   content-enriched, 9
   goal of, 8–9
Fleurquin, F., 265
FLEX (foreign language exploratory or experience) programs, 8
fluency *vs.* accuracy, 123–124
Foord, D., 356, 361, 369, 377
formal assessment, 248. *See also* assessment
formal learning, 372–373. *See also* learning
   e-mail discussion group, joining, 373
   learning community, becoming part of, 373
   participating in, 372–373
formal tests
   achievement tests, 258
   diagnostic tests, 257–258
   placement tests, 258
   proficiency tests, 258
   purposes and types of, 257–258
formative assessment, 248–249. *See also* informal assessment
formulaic language, 124
Fountas, I. C., 195